India and the Islamic Heartlands

Based on the chance survival of a remarkable cache of documents, *India and the Islamic Heartlands* recaptures a vanished and forgotten world from the eighteenth century spanning much of today's Middle East and South Asia. Gagan Sood focuses on ordinary people – traders, pilgrims, bankers, clerics, brokers, scribes, among others – who were engaged in activities marked by large distances and long silences. By elucidating their everyday lives in a range of settings, from the family household to the polity at large, Sood pieces together the connective tissue of a world that lay beyond the sovereign purview. Recapturing this obscured and neglected world helps us better understand the region during a pivotal moment in its history, and offers new answers to old questions concerning early modern Eurasia and its transition to colonialism.

Gagan D. S. Sood is Assistant Professor in Early Modern International History in the Department of International History at the London School of Economics.

India and the Islamic Heartlands

An Eighteenth-Century World of Circulation and Exchange

Gagan D. S. Sood

CAMBRIDGE
UNIVERSITY PRESS

CAMBRIDGE
UNIVERSITY PRESS

University Printing House, Cambridge CB2 8BS, United Kingdom

Cambridge University Press is part of the University of Cambridge.

It furthers the University's mission by disseminating knowledge in the pursuit of education, learning and research at the highest international levels of excellence.

www.cambridge.org
Information on this title: www.cambridge.org/9781107121270

First published 2016

Printed in the United Kingdom by Clays, St Ives plc

A catalogue record for this publication is available from the British Library

Library of Congress Cataloguing in Publication data
Sood, Gagan D. S., 1976–
India and the Islamic heartlands : an eighteenth-century world of circulation and exchange / Gagan D. S. Sood (London School of Economics and Political Science).
Cambridge, United Kingdom : Cambridge University Press, 2016. |
Includes bibliographical references and index.
LCCN 2015041998| ISBN 9781107121270 (hardback) |
ISBN 9781107551725 (paperback)
LCSH: India – Relations – Islamic countries. | Islamic countries – Relations – India. | India – Social life and customs – 18th century. | Islamic countries – Social life and customs – 18th century. | Merchants – India – History – 18th century. | Pilgrims and pilgrimages – India – History – 18th century. | Educational exchanges – India – History – 18th century. | Intercultural communication – India – History – 18th century. | India – Commerce – Islamic countries. | Islamic countries – Commerce – India.
LCC DS35.74.I56 S66 2016 | DDC 303.48/2540176709033–dc23
LC record available at http://lccn.loc.gov/2015041998

ISBN 978-1-107-12127-0 Hardback
ISBN 978-1-107-55172-5 Paperback

آگاه دلا اُمید گاهها

Contents

Figures

Maps

Tables

Preface and acknowledgements

This book seeks to recapture a world that spanned much of India and the Islamic heartlands in the eighteenth century. That, of course, is easier said than done. Long vanished and largely forgotten by posterity, this world *can* be recaptured. But to do so requires an unorthodox approach. The unorthodoxy of this approach lies in the need to bracket high politics and warfare, as well as the great religious traditions, sciences and belles-lettres. These are matters that have been at the centre of empire and civilisation as traditionally construed. Bracketing them has the invaluable benefit of allowing more mundane parallels and linkages to come into view. These in turn allow us to reconstruct the connective tissue of an obscured and neglected world that was not just significant in its own time and place, but in others too. That significance ultimately derived from the types of individuals who inhabited it and the activities in which they were involved. These individuals formed a sub-elite class that cut across religions, ethnicities and polities. They were collectively mobile and literate, and purposefully engaged in activities marked by large distances and long silences. Prominent among their activities were trade, finance, pilgrimage, study, news-gathering, translation, brokerage and transport, all of which were undertaken for a variety of motives, not least livelihood, piety, status, curiosity and adventure.

The impulse to recapture the world of such individuals has its origins in two magnificent works of historical analysis. One is Kirti N. Chaudhuri's *Asia before Europe*. The other is Marshall Hodgson's *The Venture of Islam*. In different ways, these works have stirred my imagination and moved my spirit. Together, they have led me towards the present book. They also gesture towards the main scholarly traditions to which this book cleaves. Through Chaudhuri, it is joined to the Annales School, even as I forswear any attempt at total history as an unattainable ideal. Through Hodgson, it is joined to the burgeoning field of global history, which has posthumously embraced him as a global historian avant la letter.

Of course, to say this is merely to avow a lineage. That my book is in keeping with that lineage stems from the empirical source at its core.

Details about this source's nature and provenance are given in the pages to follow. But because of its centrality, a few prefatory words may be in order. The source around which this book is built may be envisaged as a postbag of documents. They consist mainly of letters, receipts, certificates and depositions in Arabic, Persian and Ottoman Turkish that were composed in the 1740s by, and for, an assortment of remarkably unremarkable individuals. It is their very ordinariness that makes them stand out and draws our attention. What is more, while home for these individuals was confined to specific areas of India or the Islamic heartlands, many of their interests were regional in scope. This is amply documented in their correspondence. As January 1748 approached, they entrusted their freshly written correspondence to the care of relatives, friends, colleagues, employees and servants who were taking passage on a ship about to sail from Basra, at the head of the Persian Gulf. The ship's final destination was Bengal, with plans to drop anchor en route at Cochin and Nagapattinam. But owing to an act of piracy on the high seas, those entrusted with this correspondence were never to make their deliveries.

Yet this act of piracy allowed their correspondence to survive down to the present. By studying it carefully in a manner which bears comparison with Emmanuel Le Roy Ladurie's *Montaillou*, we are thus able to recapture a regional-scale arena of activities that was populated by a kaleidoscope of inconspicuous, footloose types. This was a vernacular world of broader historical significance which was soon to vanish and be forgotten. It lay mostly beyond the sovereign purview, spanning much of India and the Islamic heartlands. To the extent I succeed in recapturing it, I hope this book will facilitate a better understanding of the region in the middle of the eighteenth century. This was a pivotal moment in the region's history, characterised by an absence of great hegemons and a plethora of 'successor' regimes. It was a fraught moment, a moment of unscripted possibilities. Through this better understanding, I hope this book will also encourage further work that moves us closer to answering several of the big, outstanding questions. Some of these concern India and the Islamic heartlands in the context of early modern times; others concern the impact on the region of later European dominance and imperialism.

The responsibility for any shortcomings in this book lie with me. Its achievements, however, are another matter. Big or small, they would have been inconceivable without the many kinds of help I have received over the years that this book has been in the making.

Technically, the greatest challenge was posed by the languages in which the sources were written and their cultural milieux. Scholars with a masterful command of their subject deepened my understanding of these issues, steering me away from untold mistakes and misinterpretations. Ensconced in his Pearson sanctum, Adel Allouche patiently revealed to me the mysteries of Middle Arabic, brought to life and rendered meaningful through his stories of the Tunisia in which he had grown up. Abbas Amanat generously shared hours of his time with me as together we pored over Persian documents in *shikastah*, imparting the sensibility required to discern their message and their poetics. My thanks to Muzaffar Alam – Alam sahib – know no bounds for showing me that the Persian of Mughal India has not been totally lost to us, and for his gentle encouragement, suggestions and criticisms, all deriving from his incomparable learning. Hadi Jorati was kind enough to put his encyclopaedic knowledge of Classical Persian at my disposal so as to resolve a number of knotty linguistic conundrums.

The research that I have carried out for this book was only possible because of the goodwill and the resources funnelled my way by myriad institutions and by the individuals who run them. With Suzanne Roberts leading the charge, the staff of Sterling Memorial Library were unstinting in their support of my project, responding to all my needs as and when they arose. The late, much-loved Florence Thomas, who knew everyone and everything, from her office at the pulsating heart of Yale's History Department, kept all of us in order and moving in the right direction, with an abundance of warmth, humour, grace, intelligence and unerring good sense. Fr Delio Mendonça, SJ, opened up for me the Xavier Centre of Historical Research in Alto Porvorim, Goa, making it a home away from home. At the Maharashtra State Archives in Mumbai, Shri Karade was firm but fair in the face of my insistent questioning, granting me special permission to enter the chamber housing the documents and to check its contents for myself. My unorthodox demands received a sympathetic hearing from the wise, elegant and trusting Smt. Malathy, whose authorisation allowed me access to the hidden treasures under her charge at the Tamil Nadu State Archives in Chennai.

For facilitating my research, I am also grateful to the staff of the Asia and Africa Reading Room of the British Library (London); the Caird Library in the National Maritime Museum (London); the Map and Large Document Reading Room of the National Archives (Kew); the Manuscripts Department of the Bibliothèque nationale de France, site Richelieu (Paris); the Archives nationales d'outre-mer (Aix-en-Provence); the Archives de la Chambre de commerce et d'industrie de Marseille; the National Records and Archives Authority of Oman (Masqat); the Oriental Records Division of the National Archives of India (New Delhi); the Asiatic Society (Kolkata); the Historical Archives of Goa (Panjim); and the Government Oriental Manuscripts

Library (Chennai). The research undertaken in these institutions was predicated on the material support, for which I am extremely thankful, provided by the Master and Fellows of Clare College (Cambridge); the Paul Mellon Fellowship Programme; International Security Studies (Yale University); the Master and Fellows of Davenport College (New Haven); the Yale Center for International and Area Studies; the John Perry Miller Fund (Yale University); the John F. Enders Fund (Yale University); the Fox International Fellowship Program (Yale University); the Hugh Fulton Byas Memorial Fund (New Haven); the Beinecke Library Fellowship Program (Yale University); the Economic History Society (UK); the Institute for Historical Research (London); the Master and Fellows of Wolfson College (Cambridge); the Vasco da Gama Chair at the European University Institute (Florence); and the Brady-Johnson Program (Yale University).

By good fortune en route to this book, my life became entwined with the lives of individuals from a range of backgrounds, whose experience has been formative for my scholarship. Hospitable and loyal, with the sharpest and most capacious of minds, John Lewis Gaddis early on took an interest in me, and remained a steadfast supporter, adopting at times the role of a veritable deus ex machina. For some of my key concepts and the way in which I relate to historical scholarship, I am beholden to the insights, pointers and above all the inspirational example of the great Chris Bayly, who is sadly no longer with us, but whose exceptional legacy will endure and thrive. Andrew Preston gave me a much needed and sympathetic outsider's perspective at a crucial moment when my overall argument was in flux. A series of focused discussions with Adeel Khan, centring on recent developments in the anthropology of religion, were instrumental for leading me to the mature version of my book's conceptual framework. Mushegh Asatryan cheerfully answered my barrage of questions about Islam, Sufism and Armenian culture. My introduction to Sanskritic India, the history of religion and the marvels of Italian philology had to await the inimitable Federico Squarcini, who gave me at the same time the first hint of what a truly non-centric, non-hegemonic, non-teleological history might actually look like in practice. With the lightest of touches, Stephen Smith was resolute in reminding me about the realities of academic life, in prodding me to reframe my approach and language so as to make my scholarship more visible and appealing, and, though always primed to debate the metaphysical, in never letting me forget the importance of rigour and the nuts-and-bolts of the historian's craft. The force of nature that is the iconoclastic Anthony 'Tony' Hopkins spirited away any doubts I might have had about my larger agenda, convincing me that there are verities which are eternal, that reality need not crowd out one's ideals. I thank Richard Drayton for his comradeship, honesty and advice, and for our many intellectually zestful exchanges. Toni Dorfman, Cynthia Farrer and Eva Wrightson have my everlasting gratitude for their companionship, understanding and kindness, memories of which I hold very dear.

I have been blessed by the presence of guides within (and without) academia, who have stayed the course with me, through all the ups and downs. It starts with PK – Paul M. Kennedy – who told me to follow my star, and gave me the wherewithal to do that through his patronage, his conviviality, his humanity, his countryside walks, his story-telling, his love of literature, and his earthy, warm, Anglo-Saxon prose. Keith Wrightson's profound sensitivity for his subject, dedication to his field and quiet authority taught me about the stuff of life, the art of recapturing vernacular worlds lost in the mists of time, the power of simplicity and a perfectly weighted judgement. I find it impossible to imagine a finer tutor and interlocutor than Scott A. Boorman, whose beautiful mind, polymathic learning, generosity towards students and colleagues alike, and commitment to his vocation are the embodiment of a scholarly vision that is a marvel to behold. Patrick K. O'Brien is a phenomenon, a leader par excellence, a fount of wisdom, a guru of divine-like proportions, who, possessed of a steely determination, is resolved through history to make our world a better place, and who has transformed my lot in our here-and-now. I shall forever remain indebted to William Gervase Clarence-Smith for championing my cause and for his indefatigable critical engagement, buttressed by a peerless command of historical detail, a voracious intellectual appetite and a knowledge of what is happening in today's academic history that is second to none.

Finally, there are those who have intimately lived this book with me, and with me experienced its pains and joys, offering succour and giving meaning to a life in the humanities. My *amico-fratello* Brooks Prouty is a fellow wayfarer, philosophically and aesthetically, forgiving, compassionate and elevating, teasing out the best in those who are drawn into his universe. With Raphaël Taylor, I have journeyed far and wide, coming to appreciate, and cherish, his musical and artistic sensibilities, from which I have gained so much. My loving, big-hearted family – my father, my mother and my two brothers – have always been there for me, through thick and thin, an unbreakable, constant bedrock amidst the vagaries of fate. And then there is the one who intuitively comprehends those populating the pages to come, who gave their world visible form by painting the wheel-map which adorns the cover, who truly knows what it is I am doing and why: my wife, Natasha, to whom I dedicate this book.

Note on spelling and transliteration

Given the differences between the languages of the sources on which this book is based – Arabic, Persian, French and Portuguese, among others – there is no single or obvious approach to their spelling and transliteration. The approach crafted for this book thus represents a pragmatic compromise between the ideals of accuracy, consistency and readability. Originally foreign words that have been absorbed into today's English lexicon are given in their standard English spelling (so Sufi not *Ṣūfī*, rupee not *rūpayā*). This extends to names of places that are familiar to us in English (so Aleppo not Ḥalab, Karbala not Karbalāʾ, Bengal not Bangālah or Bangla). Otherwise, directly quoted words from the sources are written in one of the established transliteration systems for the language most closely associated with them. Specialists interested in such matters will be able to identify these systems without difficulty. The complicating factor is that many of the words in question were present in multiple languages (e.g., *davlat, ṭāʾifa, vakīl*). Fortunately, they tended to figure more prominently in one language compared with the others found in the sources. That is ultimately what determines the choice of the transliteration system for such words in this book.

Abbreviations

ADM	Admiralty Records
ANOM	Archives nationales d'outre-mer
BL	British Library
BnF	Bibliothèque nationale de France
CdI	Fonds Ancien ou de la Compagnie des Indes
EI2	Encyclopaedia of Islam, 2nd edn
FC	Fonds ministériels, Premier empire colonial
HAG	Historical Archives of Goa
HCA	High Court of Admiralty and Colonial Vice-Admiralty Courts
HCR	High Court Records
IOL	India Office Library
IOR	India Office Records
MHR	Mhamai House Records
Misc	Miscellaneous Records
MRC	Mayor's Court and Recorder's Court
MSA	Maharashtra State Archives
Mss Eur	India Office Private Papers
MssOcc	Collections du département des manuscrits, Division occidentale
NA	National Archives
NAF	Nouvelles acquisitions françaises
TNSA	Tamil Nadu State Archives
XCHR	Xavier Centre of Historical Research

Prologue

'How wonderful it is when shahs caress the beggar!' In this pronouncement, we can sense gratitude and joy. But there is relief here too. Though the beggar did eventually receive a shah's caress, it had been a long time coming, and its realisation was anything but straightforward.

To begin with, however, all had gone to plan. In the middle of the eighteenth century, the nawab of Bengal, ʿAlī Vardī Khān, and some of his nobles decided to donate a sum of money to their Sufi brethren – the *ahl-i ḥāl* – in the shrine city of Najaf. A thousand rupees were gathered for this act of piety. But how to get the money there safe and sound? That was the task which fell to the nawab's chief steward, Muḥammad ʿAlī Khān. He approached a certain Minas who, so he had been informed, was about to leave Bengal on a commercial venture to Basra. Minas, an Armenian Christian and a headman of the local association of merchants, agreed to undertake the commission. And so the charity money in the form of newly minted silver Muḥammad Shāhī sikka rupees was handed to him for delivery in Basra. The award of this commission seems to have raised Minas's profile among Bengal's nobility. It certainly brought him to the attention of Mīr Muḥammad ʿAlī Majhalibandarī and Mīr Muḥammad Kāẓim. Motivated by more worldly concerns than the nawab, the mīrs wanted to send a miscellany of items to Najaf, which included packages of 'Gujarati' and 'Patna' paper, bundles of cloth, 'Hindi' hookah pipes and apple-flavoured tobacco. Minas was prevailed upon to take these under his charge as well.

The voyage lasted more than half a year. In July 1747, when news reached Najaf by letter of the arrival in Basra of Minas – and the donation – it 'washed away despair and ignorance from the ear'. The news had been long anticipated and its arrival was treated as little short of deliverance. The 'marvellous favour' of the charity – allowing its Sufi beneficiaries in Najaf to 'touch the hem of the good fortune of the great ones' – was a cause for joy. It meant that they would no longer have to take out further loans of which there had been talk of late. It meant that they could pay off their debts. But as their despair and ignorance were washed away, a fresh set of challenges emerged.

News of the donation's arrival in Basra had travelled to Najaf well in advance of the donation. Eager to collect it as soon as possible, the Najaf Sufis drew up a document that granted power of attorney and issued it in the name of Sayyid ʿĪsā. This authorised and instructed him to collect from Minas the charity money, together with the other items from Bengal, and to send them on to Najaf by courier with the necessary licence. For that to happen, however, Sayyid ʿĪsā had to be in Basra himself. But his presence could not be vouchsafed; it was rumoured that he might be on his way to Baghdad. To deal with that eventuality, the document had an addendum stating that, in the agent's absence, the same power of attorney was to be given to Ḥājī ʿAbd al-Hādī.

The document was entrusted to a courier for delivery in Basra. This was the very courier who had first brought news from Basra of the donation's arrival there. He was now in a tremendous hurry to get back to the port. As the season was fast drawing to a close, the ships at Basra would shortly be leaving for India and he needed to catch them before they departed. The Sufis, however, needed no encouragement; they too wanted their letters to find passage on these ships so that their gratitude might reach their Bengali benefactors at the earliest. To this end, and avowing much regret, they kept their news unusually brief, only enclosing the most essential receipts. The rest they left up to God, praying that he allow their letters to 'arrive the same season'. But their prayers were in vain. When the courier arrived in Basra, he found to his dismay that the ships scheduled to leave had already raised anchor and put to sea. The correspondence of the Najaf Sufis would now have to wait another season before being able to continue its journey to Bengal.

While the ships might have left, Minas had not; he still had unfinished business in Basra. As he had been the one to bring the correspondence from Bengal for the Najaf Sufis, it was only natural for him to carry their responses back to Bengal. Minas agreed to do so. But his involvement with the Najaf Sufis did not stop there. Though the goods noted in the power of attorney had been handed over to their agent in Basra without a hitch, not so the charity money.

The charity money had originally been given to Minas in rupees for him to deliver in Basra, having converted it into a local currency. This seemed a perfectly reasonable proposition because Minas had the reputation, experience and contacts, and Basra was the area's main commercial hub. It was decided that the delivery would be made in tomans, which enjoyed widespread acceptance. But when the Najaf Sufis were told the rate at which Minas had converted their money, they were shocked. To their mind, the rate for one thousand newly minted silver Muḥammad Shāhī sikka rupees should have been seventy-five tomans. Indeed, that had been the going rate for rupees of this kind in Basra's recent past. But Minas was offering not seventy-five, nor seventy (which was already very dear) nor sixty-five (which the Sufis would have been able to stomach), nor even sixty. No, his best offer was a derisory fifty tomans, meaning a loss of twenty-five tomans. In the Sufis candid opinion, 'not being given a grain more than fifty tomans was a novel extortion'. The blame for this they placed squarely on Minas. They accused him of acting in bad faith.

Nevertheless, 'given the time and the state of affairs and their distress and indebtedness', the Najaf Sufis consented to this rate for the sake of receiving something – anything – sooner rather than later. It was rendered palatable, however, by the thought of compensation from Minas through a court in Bengal. Letters were written to their distant patrons describing their unhappy situation and suggesting ways of proceeding against Minas. These too were given to Minas, blissfully unaware of their contents, to carry back to Bengal the following season. But it was not to be. Fate had something very different in store for the letters of the Najaf Sufis.[1]

The foregoing account of the charitable donation has been pieced together from the source lying at the core of this book. This source, essentially a collection of documents in Persian, Arabic and Ottoman Turkish, is today housed in the British Library in London. I came across it unexpectedly towards the end of 2002 while leafing through a heavy, well-thumbed catalogue. The entry noted the presence of 'a volume of 84 foll., containing miscellaneous Oriental letters of various sizes ... [which] relate to private matters and business transactions. They are mostly written ... in the town of Basra and on the Malabar coast to correspondents in Bengal. Their dates range about AH 1180 (AD 1747).'[2]

A spare description, but enticing. If nothing else, it is exceedingly rare for such material to survive down to the present. Excited by the possibilities, I called up the volume. On opening it, I saw that the 'Oriental letters' were pasted on to its folios giving it the appearance of an album. As I began trying to make sense of them over the months that followed, a mystifying pattern started to emerge. On the reverse side of many of the so-called letters, I noticed brief statements composed at a later date and in a different hand from the ones responsible for the original text. They were, moreover, written in Spanish. Sometimes they averred that 'this document is a receipt in Persian', at other times 'this letter does not concern the Santa Catharina'. Even stranger, these statements were

[1] Citations to the source on which this account of the charitable donation is based are given in the discussion of intermediation in Chapter 7 on everyday practices.

[2] Charles Rieu, *Catalogue of the Persian Manuscripts in the British Museum* (London, 1879–95), i, 407.

signed off by two individuals, a Jacob Treve, in Latin script, and a Stephan Khodchidchan, in Armenian script. Why this mixture of Spanish and Armenian? I asked myself. What (or who) was the Santa Catharina? Why this interest in letters that do *not* concern the Santa Catharina? And how did this most un-English potpourri of documents find its way into one of the most establishmentarian of British institutions? Baffled but curious, I began looking for answers. That is what led me to the story of the *Santa Catharina*'s final voyage[3] – and to the writing of this book.

The *Santa Catharina* was a ship of 220 tons burden that could carry twelve carriage guns and about seventy men. It was built in the mid-1730s in Bago, in present-day Burma. Originally christened the *Marie Joseph* by its French owners from Bengal, it was renamed the *Santa Catharina* following its purchase at auction in September 1746 by the Portuguese subjects João de Faria Leitão and Antonio Caetano de Campos. Soon thereafter, a 'company' of Armenians in Calcutta hired the ship for a freight voyage to Basra and back. The very same Minas who had agreed to ensure the safe passage of the nawab's charity money was appointed to travel on the ship as the company's supercargo. Granted full powers to act on his principals' behalf, he had formal authority to decide where to drop anchor during the voyage, and for how long. He also had responsibility for executing the instructions regarding the merchandise and other items placed in his care.

In January 1747, the *Santa Catharina* set sail from Chandannagar, with Leitão as its supposed captain. It carried iron and lead as ballast. It also carried two passports – one Portuguese, the other Armenian – as a precautionary measure. The ship's progress down the Hugli River was punctuated by halts to pick up bales of silk and other manufactured cloth, mainly from Dhaka, as well as rice, which was poured in among the bales so as to keep it on an even keel. Over the next six months, the *Santa Catharina* travelled down the Bay of Bengal, stopped for water and wood in Cochin on the Malabar coast, crossed the Arabian Sea and entered Persian Gulf, before finally reaching Basra, where the cargo was delivered up. Preparations for the homeward voyage were made between October 1747 and January 1748. During this time, the ship was laded with chests of silver (in the form of zolota coins), with coral, Venetian necklaces, glass, pearls and other gems, and with dates, almonds, pistachio nuts, walnuts, wine, rose water and an assortment of dried fruits. Early in February, the *Santa Catharina* left Basra, now with several Frenchmen

[3] The details of this story are taken from NA/HCA/42/25 (St Catharina), NA/HCA/42/26 (St Catharina) and NA/ADM/51/615 (Medways Prize).

among its passengers. It arrived safely in Cochin the following month, and there the ship remained, flying Armenian colours, until the middle of April. Misfortune did not strike until the next leg of its voyage. On the morning of Saturday 11 May, at a distance of some five leagues southward of Nagapattinam on the Coromandel coast, the *Santa Catharina* encountered the *Medway's Prize* and was ordered to halt. The sails were dropped without demur; no one was prepared to disobey a British man-of-war on patrol for enemy targets.

Before long, an officer from the man-of-war was seen in a boat making his way to the *Santa Catharina*. While en route, he noticed a boy throw a sheaf of papers into the sea from the master's cabin. His suspicions were aroused. He made a quick detour and was able to save many of the papers before they vanished into the deep. On reaching the deck, the officer asked for the captain to present himself. He then proceeded to interrogate him about the *Santa Catharina*'s cargo, its passport, and the last port-of-call and its final destination. As Leitão was fielding these questions, one of the men in the officer's retinue went on to the poop to check for himself the ship's colours. With a lamp, he signalled his findings to the *Medway's Prize*. The officer had learnt in the meantime of the Frenchmen on board. Suspecting the presence of French goods too, the captain was informed that the *Santa Catharina* would have to be taken to the commodore of the British squadron, based at nearby Fort St David. This was not good news. Britain was still at war with France over the matter of the Austrian Succession; all French vessels and cargos were liable to seizure and condemnation as enemy property.

The seizure of the *Santa Catharina* set in motion a chain of events that would end with the papers it was carrying – which included the letters of the Najaf Sufis – being exiled by their captors to London. That these papers have come down to us is a quirk of history. It is only because they were unwittingly ensnared in hostilities between European powers that they survive at all. This, of course, was unfortunate for their would-be recipients. They had no choice but to continue waiting for word from their correspondents far away to the west. Their loss, however, is our gain. Their letters allow us to reconstruct the knitted, entangled dealings which lay beyond the ambit of sovereign rule; they allow us to recapture a world of circulation and exchange that spanned much of India and the Islamic heartlands in the eighteenth century.

Introduction

Stories like those found in the prologue – of the charitable donation wending its way to Najaf, of the homeward journey of the *Santa Catharina* – fill the pages of this book. They are stories about people, knowledge and objects, about their movements over large distances and the long silences that followed in their wake, about the individuals whose livelihoods ushered them towards their eventual fates. The telling of such stories reveals a myriad of everyday concerns. These concerns reveal in turn a world – an arena of activities – which in the eighteenth century straddled both of what we today call South Asia and the Middle East. The activities that are at issue here were of a specific kind, pivoting on types of circulation and exchange which helped sustain the ambient polities of the time. In this book, I attempt to recapture the arena resulting from these activities in the period before its unravelling under the press of Europe's modern global empires.

Betwixt and between

That this arena and its world were soon to change out of all recognition is undeniable. But to say that is to view them in retrospect. In the middle of the eighteenth century, one might just as reasonably say that they, and India and the Islamic heartlands more generally, brimmed with unscripted possibilities. After all, the Safavid empire was no more after its sudden collapse, albeit survived for a time by a dynasty still imbued with a potent aura;[1] the Mughal empire had been hollowed out, the emperor a figurehead in a decaying capital, reduced to sanctifying the rule of others;[2] the Ottoman empire was a fragmented congeries of autonomous districts and provinces, their governing households tending to put their own interests before those of

[1] Rudolph P. Matthee, *Persia in Crisis: Safavid Decline and the Fall of Isfahan* (London, 2012); Laurence Lockhart, *The Fall of the Safavid Dynasty and the Afghan Occupation of Persia* (Cambridge, 1958).

[2] William Irvine, *Later Mughals*, vol. I: *1707–1720*, vol. II: *1719–1739* (Calcutta, 1922); Jadunath Sarkar, *Fall of the Mughal Empire*, 4 vols. (Calcutta, 1932–50).

the ruling dynasty.[3] Thus, ever since the great conquests of the Mongol warlord Timur more than three centuries before, the region was *bereft* of rulers who sought, and could plausibly aspire towards, universal dominion. If we also bear in mind that European imperialism had yet to be intimated by contemporaries, then the middle of the eighteenth century reveals itself as a special moment in the region's history, a moment offering a remarkably wide array of prospective futures. Perhaps the clearest testament to this is the new regimes that thronged the territories of its once great Islamicate empires. (See Map 1.)

These successor regimes provide the backdrop to this book. But in describing them, it is all too easy to get lost in their details. For the purposes of this book, I simplify the matter by marshalling them into four groups distinguished by how their rulers related to their subjects and to the old imperial centres.[4] One group is formed by the regimes that emerged in Awadh and Bengal, together with those based in Hyderabad, Arcot and Baghdad. For each of these regimes, the founders of what would become the ruling families or households in the eighteenth century were products of the old imperial centres. They were high-level officials in the mould either of Murshid Qulī Khān in Bengal – nobles intimate with the court in Delhi – or of Ḥasan Pasha in central and southern Iraq – slave (*mamlūk*) graduates of the palace schools in Istanbul. Appointed by the emperor as governors of their respective provinces early in the century, they were there as the representatives of the imperial elites of Delhi or Istanbul into which they had been fully assimilated. As the years passed, however, they transformed themselves into effectively independent rulers. They amalgamated fiscal, military and judicial powers that had previously been kept separate, and took over direction of the revenue system within their provinces. Even so, they continued to acknowledge the emperor as their suzerain, claiming to govern in his name and more often than not remitting tribute to him. The tribute aside, those who succeeded the regimes' founders maintained their predecessors' general policy towards the old imperial centre. It was maintained even though what now counted in their succession was lineal descent from the founder or membership of the household established by him. They were no longer appointees of Delhi or Istanbul, and their decisions took little or no heed of the emperor.

[3] Bruce McGowan, 'The age of the ayans, 1699–1812', in Halil Inalcık and Donald Quataert (eds.), *An Economic and Social History of the Ottoman Empire, 1300–1914* (Cambridge, 1994), 637–758; Donald Quataert, *The Ottoman Empire, 1700–1922* (2nd edn, Cambridge, 2005).

[4] What is presented here is in effect a typology of sovereign regimes. Though I consider it best suited to the subject of this book, others are conceivable. For a different typology, see Christopher A. Bayly's in *Imperial Meridian: The British Empire and the World, 1780–1830* (London, 1989), 16–61.

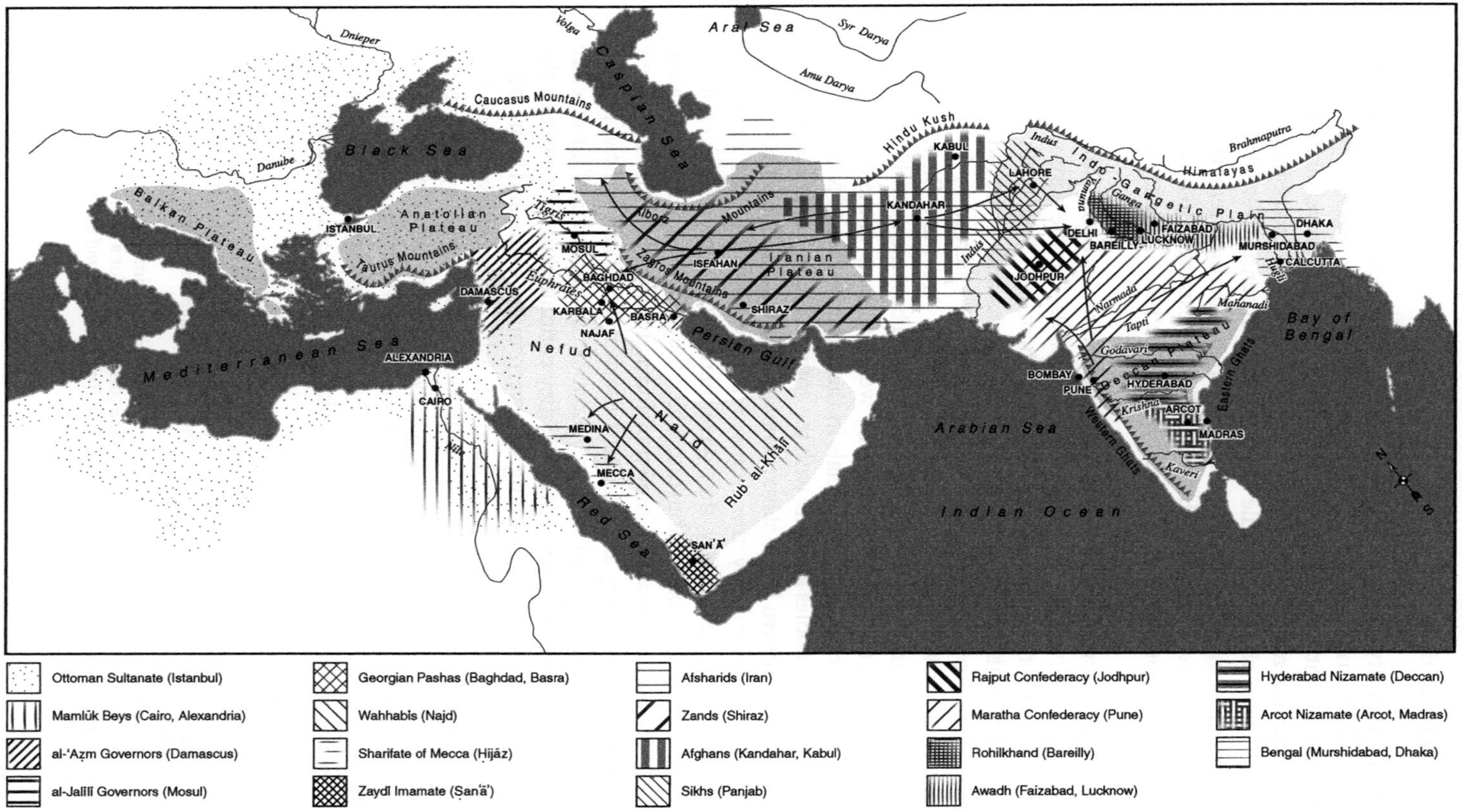

Map 1. The polities of the region, *c.* 1750.

However, they continued to seek his stamp of approval, not least because it conferred legitimacy on their rule.[5]

Rulers who claimed to govern in the emperor's name also presided over a second group of regimes. But these differed in that their rulers were *not* products of the old imperial centres. In the middle of the eighteenth century, those who governed Egypt, Gujarat and Rohilkhand (in northern India) were all outsiders to the households, courts and bureaucracies of Istanbul and Delhi. They had unilaterally wrested control of their regimes, and they switched between bouts of consolidation and campaigns of military adventure or warlordism. These rulers were outsiders in another sense too. By background, they were, respectively, Circassians (or Georgians), Marathas and Rohilla Afghans. So their ethnic roots lay outside the particular regime over which they exercised dominion; in some cases, those roots lay outside even the outer reaches of the Ottoman and Mughal empires at their most expansive in earlier times.[6]

In contrast, the rulers of a third group of regimes had deep roots within their regimes that long preceded their accession. They form a long list, and include: the Maratha Peshwas in western and central India; the Rajput chieftains in northern India; the Sikh khalsa in Panjab and northwestern India; the Zaydī imams in highland Yemen; the

[5] Bernard S. Cohn, 'Political systems in eighteenth century India: the Banaras region', *Journal of the American Oriental Society* 82:3 (1962), 312–20; Richard B. Barnett, *North India between Empires: Awadh, the Mughals and the British, 1720–1801* (Berkeley, CA, 1980); Michael H. Fisher, *A Clash of Culture: Awadh, the British, and the Mughals* (New Delhi, 1987); Muzaffar Alam, *The Crisis of Empire in Mughal North India: Awadh and the Punjab, 1707–48* (Delhi, 1986); John R. McLane, *Land and Local Kingship in Eighteenth-Century Bengal* (Cambridge, 1993); Sushil Chaudhury, *From Prosperity to Decline: Eighteenth Century Bengal* (New Delhi, 1995); Kumkum Chatterjee, *Merchants, Politics and Society in Early Modern India: Bihar, 1733–1820* (Leiden, 1996); Karen Leonard, 'The Hyderabad political system and its participants', *Journal of Asian Studies* 30:3 (1971), 569–82; Muzaffar Alam and Sanjay Subrahmanyam, 'Exploring the hinterland: trade and politics in the Arcot Nizamate (1700–1732)', in Rudrangshu Mukherjee and Lakshmi Subramanian (eds.), *Politics and Trade in the Indian Ocean World: Esssays in Honor of Ashin Das Gupta* (Delhi, 1998), 113–64; ʿAbd al-Raḥmān ibn ʿAbd Allāh al-Suwaydī, *Tārīkh ḥawādith Baghdād wa-al-Baṣra min 1186 ilā 1192 h./1772–1778 m.* (Baghdad: Wizārat al-thaqāfa wa-al-fanūn, 1978); Tom Nieuwenhuis, *Politics and Society in Early Modern Iraq: Mamluk Pashas, Tribal Shaykhs and Local Rule between 1802 and 1831* (The Hague, 1982); Thabit A. J. Abdullah, *Merchants, Mamluks, and Murder: The Political Economy of Trade in Eighteenth-Century Basra* (Albany, NY, 2001).

[6] Kenneth M. Cuno, *The Pasha's Peasants: Land, Society and Economy in Lower Egypt, 1740–1858* (Cambridge, 1992); Michael Winter, *Egyptian Society under Ottoman Rule, 1517–1798* (London, 1992); Jane Hathaway, *The Politics of Households in Ottoman Egypt: The Rise of the Qazdaglis* (Cambridge, 1997); Jane Hathaway, *A Tale of Two Factions: Myth, Memory and Identity in Ottoman Egypt and Yemen* (Albany, NY, 2003); Ghulam A. Nadri, *Eighteenth-Century Gujarat: the Dynamics of its Political Economy, 1750–1800* (Leiden and Boston, 2009); Stewart Gordon, *Marathas, Marauders and State Formation in Eighteenth-Century India* (Delhi, 1994); Iqbal Husain, *The Ruhela Chieftaincies: the Rise and Fall of Ruhela Power in India in the Eighteenth Century* (Delhi, 1994).

Hashemite Sharīfs in the Holy Cities of Mecca and Medina; the al-Jalīlī family in northern Iraq; and the al-ʿAẓm family in Syria. All these rulers shared ethnic ties with many, if not most, of their subjects. They also belonged to lineages or communities with a tradition of leadership that often extended to landowning. Some, like the leading figures of the al-ʿAẓm family, were elevated into the imperial nobility and treated as members of the elites in the capital (while never letting go of their provincial roots). Others, like the Marathas, gained fame and notoriety for their wars of conquest and plunder, frequently at the expense of the capital. Though ruling independently in practice, if not in theory, most of these rulers were careful to pay at least lip service to the incumbent Ottoman sultan or Mughal padshah.[7]

A fourth group of regimes may be labelled tribal confederacies. They hailed mostly from the frontier areas of the Islamicate empires into whose administrative systems they had never been properly incorporated. The relationship of the rulers to their subjects was complicated. They were often multiply connected through a variety of kinship ties. With the regimes led by the Afsharids and the Zands, Iran hosted two of the region's most prominent tribal confederacies in the middle of the eighteenth century. Following Nādir Shāh's assassination in 1747, the Afghan Abdālī contingent of his army returned to its home territories in what would later became Afghanistan. This contingent formed the kernel of the Durrānī regime that dominated the area for the remainder of the

[7] Frank Perlin, 'Of white whale and countrymen in the eighteenth-century Maratha Deccan: extended class relations, rights and the problem of rural autonomy under the Ancien Regime', *Journal of Peasant Studies* 5:2 (1978), 172–237; André Wink, *Land and Sovereignty in India: Agrarian Society and Politics under the Eighteenth Century Maratha Swarajya* (London, 1986); Dilbagh Singh, *The State, Landlords and Peasants: Eastern Rajasthan in the 18th Century* (Delhi, 1990); Nandita Prasad Sahai, *Politics of Patronage and Protest: the State, Society, and Artisans in Early Modern Rajasthan* (New York, 2006); J. S. Grewal, *The Sikhs of the Punjab* (Cambridge, 1990); Purnima Dhavan, *When Sparrows Became Hawks: the Making of the Sikh Warrior Tradition, 1699–1799* (New York, 2011); Ḥusayn ʿAbd Allāh ʿAmrī, *Miʾat ʿām min tārikh al-Yaman al-ḥadīth, 1161–1264 H/1748–1784 M* (Damascus, 1984); Ḥusayn ʿAbd Allāh ʿAmrī, *The Yemen in the 18th and 19th Centuries: a Political and Intellectual History* (London, 1985); Ismail Hakkı Uzunçarşılı, *Mekke-i mükerreme emirleri* (Ankara, 1972); John L. Meloy, *Imperial Power and Maritime Trade: Mecca and Cairo in the Later Middle Ages* (Chicago, 2010); Dina R. Khoury, *State and Provincial Society in the Ottoman Empire: Mosul, 1540–1834* (Cambridge, 1997); Abdul-Karim Rafeq, *The Province of Damascus 1723–1783* (Beirut, 1966); Karl K. Barbir, *Ottoman Rule in Damascus, 1708–1758* (Princeton, NJ, 1980); Abdul-Rahim Abu-Husayn, *Provincial Leaderships in Syria, 1575–1650* (Beirut, 1985); Linda Schilcher, *Families in Politics: Damascene Factions and Estates of the Eighteenth and Nineteenth Centuries* (Stuttgart, 1985); Herbert Bodman, *Political Factions in Aleppo, 1760–1826* (Chapel Hill, NC, 1963); Bruce A. Masters, *Origins of Western Economic Dominance in the Middle East: Mercantilism and the Islamic Economy in Aleppo, 1600–1750* (New York, 1988); Abraham Marcus, *Middle East on the Eve of Modernity: Aleppo in the Eighteenth Century* (New York, 1989).

century. Though the Safavid empire had vanished, the Durrānī rulers tended to avow respect for surviving members of the dynasty, which still had prestige and enjoyed popular veneration. In contrast, the movement known as the Wahhābīya, which by the middle of the century had established a regime in central Arabia based on tribal solidarity and religious fervour, was aggressively opposed to the Ottoman empire and its dynasty. Such differences notwithstanding, all these regimes were capable of fielding conquest armies that were highly effective in looting settled areas and hauling back vast quantities of plunder from distant places. With varying degrees of success, they also tried to secure regular tribute from the lands that they managed to conquer. The most successful of their campaigns were led by the Afsharid Nādir Shāh and Aḥmad Shāh Durrānī, warlords and military adventurers par excellence.[8]

If nothing else, the foregoing discussion shows that sovereignty over the territories of the Ottoman, Safavid and Mughal empires in 1700 had, half a century later, devolved to an assortment of successor regimes. Accounts of many subjects central to these regimes have found their place in modern scholarship. But not given their due, or simply absent from these accounts, are activities to do with specifically regional-scale circulation and exchange. As a result, the factors accorded an *active* historical role in this scholarship are interpreted either as internal to the region's individual empires or regimes, or as operating on trans-regional or global scales, and so emanating from outside India and the Islamic heartlands. Now, it is widely accepted that the polities of India and the Islamic heartlands experienced developments in the eighteenth century that were remarkably similar in nature. Without doubt, major elements of this story are to be found within the polities of the region and in the relationship of these polities to trans-regional and global concerns. But there were also parallels and linkages on *regional* scales that were of fateful significance for India and the Islamic heartlands in the eighteenth century. There is general consensus in the scholarly literature that much of this region was in an exceptionally disturbed condition in the middle of the century. And yet transactions marked by large distances and long

[8] Michael Axworthy, *The Sword of Persia: Nader Shah, from Tribal Warrior to Conquering Despot* (London, 2006); Ernest S. Tucker, *Nadir Shah's Quest for Legitimacy in Post-Safavid Iran* (Gainesville, FL, 2006); John R. Perry, *Karim Khan Zand: a History of Iran, 1747–1779* (Chicago, 1979); Jos J. L. Gommans, *The Rise of the Indo-Afghan Empire, c. 1710–1780* (Leiden, 1995); Ḥusayn Khalaf al-Shaykh Khazʿal, *Tārīkh al-Jazīra al-ʿArabīya fī ʿaṣr al-Shaykh Muḥammad ʿAbd al-Wahhāb* (Beirut: Maṭbaʿa dār al-kutub, 1972); ʿAzīz al-ʿAẓma, *Muḥammad ibn ʿAbd al-Wahhāb* (Beirut: Riyād al-Rayyis lil-kutub wa-al-nashr, 2000).

silences continued to take place. How is that possible? How can these two facts be reconciled?

I argue that the kernel of the answer is to be found in a coherent, self-regulating arena of activities which spanned much of India and the Islamic heartlands in the period, and which existed mostly, if not entirely, beyond the sovereign purview. By reconstructing the connective tissue of this arena, and thereby recapturing its world, the present book will hopefully serve to rebalance prevailing interpretations of the region at a pivotal moment in its history. This was a moment that brimmed with unscripted possibilities, a moment that in retrospect bridged multiple transitions – between different kinds of imperial governance, between mercantile and industrial capitalism, between older and newer forms of globalisation. By extension, this book is intended as a contribution to the reassessment currently taking place of our general understanding of India and the Islamic heartlands in the period before European dominance.

Framing modern scholarship

The historiographical reassessment presently under way of early modern South Asia and the Middle East is being propelled by work that transcends the bounds of any one polity or regime. Especially salient in this regard is research over the past two decades on religious and scholarly networks, and the diffusion and mixing of ideas from afar; diaspora communities and communal identities; trade, goods and money; languages, communication and intelligence; and travel, exploration, pilgrimage and migration.[9] In contrast, the interests of earlier generations of scholars working on the period seldom transcended individual polities or regimes, despite notable efforts that sought to draw attention to this lacuna and the importance of filling it.[10] The broadening of interests evidenced by more recent work might suggest that the state of research in the pertinent fields is robust. Relative to the situation in analogous

[9] Citations to this recent work are found throughout the substantive chapters of this book.

[10] Of particular note were the efforts by Marshall G. S. Hodgson, Joseph F. Fletcher and Frank Perlin. See Edmund Burke III, 'Marshall G. S. Hodgson and the hemispheric interregional approach to world history', *Journal of World History* 6:2 (1995), 237–50; Joseph F. Fletcher, 'Integrative history: parallels and interconnections in the early modern period, 1500–1800', *Journal of Turkish Studies* 9 (1985), 37–57; Frank Perlin, *Invisible City: Monetary, Administrative and Popular Infrastructures in Asia and Europe, 1500–1900* (Aldershot, 1993). For a recent statement from the perspective of an Ottomanist, see Suraiya N. Faroqhi, *The Ottoman Empire and the World around It* (London, 2004).

fields dealing with Europe's or China's past, however, this would be an optimistic view.

These are without doubt exciting times for historians working on India and the Islamic heartlands in precolonial times. On one level, this may be put down to a convergence of perspectives. Never before have so many parts of the globe been studied within the shared framework of the early modern world. This approach, long cultivated by scholars working on European expansion overseas, has since the 1990s been adopted by a growing number of Sinologists, South Asianists, Persianists and Ottomanists. Their contributions, often innovative, certainly challenging, have forced historians to look anew at the world in this period and reconsider the grand narratives that bind it to modern times. The sense of excitement is reinforced by the emergence of 'global history' over the past generation.[11] More so than ever before, scholars are aware that regional-scale studies need to be inserted into the consciousness – and publications – of historians and social scientists who are currently engaged in attempts to construct global histories.[12] This awareness is buttressed by the realisation that we have yet to grasp adequately the historical significance of activities which cannot be shoehorned into categories such as state, empire and civilisation.[13]

But if we tune out the aspirational rhetoric and consider the substance of the received scholarly literature on premodern India and the Islamic heartlands, we find that on subjects of unimpeachable importance – subjects like childhood, literacy, peasant life or the environment – there are glaring, even surprising, weaknesses and gaps. This underlies the pioneering nature of the recent work noted above. Hopefully, when we look back upon it in years to come, we will be able to say that it was seminal. But much more progress needs to be made before we reach that point and the challenges in the meantime are manifold. Above all, owing to the small number of specialists currently active in the pertinent fields and the magnitude of the tasks confronting them, the intensity of

[11] Landmark studies in this still developing field include Marshall G. S. Hodgson, *Rethinking World History: Essays on Europe, Islam, and World History* (Cambridge, 1993); Kenneth Pomeranz, *Great Divergence: Europe, China and the Making of the Modern World Economy* (Princeton, NJ, 2000); Victor Lieberman, *Strange Parallels: Southeast Asia in Global Context, c. 800–1830,* vol. I: *Integration on the Mainland* (Cambridge, 2003), vol. II: *Mainland Mirrors: Europe, Japan, China, South Asia, and the Islands* (Cambridge, 2009); Geoffrey Parker, *Global Crisis: War, Climate Change and Catastrophe in the Seventeenth Century* (New Haven, CT, 2013).

[12] Exemplary in this regard are John Darwin, *After Tamerlane: the Global History of Empire since 1405* (London, 2007) and Bartolomé Yun-Casalilla and Patrick K. O'Brien (eds.), *The Rise of Fiscal States: a Global History, 1500–1914* (Cambridge, 2012).

[13] The point is well made in Tirthankar Roy's recent article, 'Where is Bengal? Situating an Indian region in the early modern world economy', *Past and Present* 213 (2011), 115–46.

scholarly engagement is often low. This makes it difficult to foster a joint commitment to the broader debates or engender the necessary collective will to answer the bigger questions. As a result, the most relevant works on the same theme are often at great remove in space and time from one another.

Research on the part of the world addressed in this book therefore continues to be fragmented or narrowly conceived. This is exemplified by the absence to date of sustained deliberation of the geographical and temporal framings within which such research is articulated. Specialists on the whole still work in channels framed primarily by religious and state- or Europe-centred perspectives. This poses a major difficulty because such perspectives are not well suited for making sense of the pioneering scholarship of recent years on individuals, commodities, organisations and livelihoods that embraced multiple polities and regimes. No matter how much empirically grounded research is carried out, if the prior framing is at odds with their provenance, the findings cannot be situated in the context appropriate to them and thus discerning their proper historical significance is rendered impossible. That is perhaps the most persuasive argument in favour of a systematic discussion of our prior framings.

Even though such discussion has yet to occur, scholars over the last half-century have employed a wide range of geographical notions in trying to get to grips with the part of the world over which the Ottoman, Safavid and Mughal empires, and their successor regimes, are commonly said to have exerted some form of dominion.[14] Some of these have been particularly influential for our understanding of periods before the start of the consolidation of Europe's global empires in the nineteenth century. The best known are entities such as Egypt, Iran, Syria, Turkey and India, which are primarily modern and political in character. These have been used alongside more capacious notions within which such states are often subsumed, and over the boundaries or definitions of which, in the case of, say, the Middle East or Asia, there is no consensus. Cross-cutting both these types of entities are civilisational or ethno-cultural complexes to which numerous labels – the Turco-Mongol world, Indo-Persia, Persianate, the Muslim Mediterranean, to name but four – have been attached. Finally, there are clusters of interrelated notions defined by

[14] The scholarly literature on the topic is surveyed in David Ludden, 'Presidential address: maps in the mind and the mobility of Asia', *Journal of Asian Studies* 62:4 (2003), 1057–78. This may be usefully supplemented by Martin W. Lewis and Kären E. Wigen, *Myth of Continents: a Critique of Metageography* (Berkeley, CA, 1997) and Michael E. Bonine, Abbas Amanat and Michael E. Gasper (eds.), *Is There a Middle East? The Evolution of a Geopolitical Concept* (Stanford, CA, 2012).

either political economy (the trading world of maritime Asia being a well-known example) or formal sovereignty (such as the *ṣūbah* of Bengal or the Ottoman *eyalet* of Baghdad). That such geographical notions are useful is evidenced by the work which they have facilitated, be it as research perspectives on the region or as concepts in narrating its past. They are, however, accompanied by analytical limitations. Specifically, they direct attention towards the concerns of the region's sovereigns and their officials, or of the Europeans in their diverse guises; or they privilege the region's conspicuous elites who monopolised the realms of high politics, warfare, government bureaucracy, art, the belles-lettres and formal learning.

These analytical limitations also extend to the periodisations in support of which the geographical notions above have often been deployed. For scholars of earlier generations, stories of the region's past drew on dynasties and civilisations for their sustenance. While their imprint can still be seen in today's formulations, the thresholds of their grand historical transitions or ruptures are essentially a function of how power was structured: the start or end of a period invariably coincides with the imminent unravelling or disintegration of the pre-existing order, or with the formation or consolidation of a new one. For histories covering the Islamic world in its entirety or large portions of it, this principle ensures the primacy of politics and religion.[15] These in turn ensure the centrality of the literate and urban conspicuous elites. Where the main focus is on activities that were not the sole preserve of such elites, some of these are made to conform to the elite's architecture of power, while others are placed beyond its ken by asserting the absence of major changes before the onset of modern times. The limitations of privileging conspicuous power to such a degree are especially acute for those modes of life and work that – like small-scale artisanal manufacturing or arbitration within kinship groups – were frequently autonomous of elite politics and culture, or which – like pilgrimage, trade, finance, education and transport – crossed and re-crossed political and cultural frontiers as a matter of course. Such modes have witnessed many changes over time, and these

[15] This principle may be seen at work in the histories published over the past three decades: Gerhard Endress, *An Introduction to Islam*, trans. Carole Hillenbrand (New York, 1988); Albert H. Hourani, *A History of the Arab Peoples* (London, 1991); Jean-Claude Garcin *et al.*, *États, sociétés et cultures du monde musulman médiéval: Xe–XVe siècle*, 3 vols. (Paris, 1995); Bernard Lewis, *The Middle East: 2000 Years of History from the Rise of Christianity to the Present Day* (London, 1995); Francis Robinson (ed.), *Cambridge Illustrated History of the Islamic World* (Cambridge, 1996); John L. Esposito (ed.), *The Oxford History of Islam* (Oxford, 2000); Ira M. Lapidus, *A History of Islamic Societies* (2nd edn, Cambridge, 2002); Stephen F. Dale, *The Muslim Empires of the Ottomans, Safavids, and Mughals* (Cambridge, 2010).

cannot always or readily be made to cohere with the narrative arcs suitable for telling the histories of the region's conspicuous elites.

Given these established geographical and temporal framings, significant features of the region treated in this book are at present closed off to us for the period before the nineteenth century. The cultural-civilisational and imperial-political perspectives largely responsible for this state of affairs are, moreover, reinforced by two other characteristics of the inherited scholarly literature. One is a longstanding tendency to generalise from the margins, particularly 'maritime Asia', based mainly on research into the records of the European East India companies and the papers of European private traders and merchant-officials.[16] The second is the widespread use of categories, such as 'state', 'market, 'society', that are anachronistic or derive from historical experiences foreign to India and the Islamic heartlands.[17] In the book's conclusion, I address this cluster of issues by considering, within the framework outlined below, the history of the region in the context of the early modern world and of its differentiated transitions into modern times. I argue that the time is now ripe for a thorough re-examination of the standard accounts which currently prevail of this part of the world immediately prior to European dominance.

The arena of circulation and exchange

In order to avoid or surmount the limitations of the existing scholarship, the framework adopted in this book differs from those found in the received literature. This framework cannot be understood politically or culturally or ecologically, in terms of, say, empires or religious traditions or physical geography. Rather, it is built around an analytical imagery envisaged as a coherent and self-regulating arena of activities that was regional in scope.[18]

[16] For valuable guides to the historical scholarship on maritime Asia (or, as it is increasingly being called, the Indian Ocean rim) since the arrival of the Portuguese, see Sinnappah Arasaratnam, 'Recent trends in the historiography of the Indian Ocean, 1500 to 1800', *Journal of World History* 1:2 (1990), 225–48; John E. Wills, 'Maritime Asia, 1500–1800: the interactive emergence of European domination', *American Historical Review* 98:1 (1993), 83–105; Marcus P. M. Vink, 'Indian Ocean studies and the "new thalassology"', *Journal of Global History* 2:1 (2007), 41–62.

[17] Jos J. L. Gommans makes a similar point in his introduction to the special issue on 'Empires and emporia: the orient in world historical space and time', *Journal of the Economic and Social History of the Orient* 53:1–2 (2010), 3–18. Earlier generations too were well aware of this matter. To take just two examples, see the comments by Abraham Udovitch and Anouar Abdel-Malek in their contributions to Michael A. Cook (ed.), *Studies in the Economic History of the Middle East from the Rise of Islam to the Present Day* (Oxford, 1970).

[18] The introductory chapter by Igor Kopytoff in Igor Kopytoff (ed.), *The African Frontier: the Reproduction of African Traditional Societies* (Bloomington, IN, 1987) presents a very useful discussion of coherent, large-scale social entities that have existed without an observable centre. This requires the informal enforcement of norms, which is the subject

From a functional viewpoint, this arena was responsible for the circulation and exchange of valued items, especially goods, tokens, ideas and information. These items could travel long and short distances, and readily crossed political and cultural boundaries. Their flow was organised and managed by individuals who, as a class and relative to their surrounding polities, were inconspicuous, literate, worldly and mobile (or had interests that were mobile). They operated under the auspices of a broad spectrum of associations – family households, spiritual fraternities, ethnic communities, trading diasporas, contractual partnerships – and exhibited a diverse array of linguistic, occupational and religious commitments. Their overarching arena of circulation and exchange was decentralised and in practice regulated by themselves alone. It was also essential for the well-being of the region's polities. Even so, the region's more conspicuous elites, notably its governing officials, tended to keep their distance from the arena's inner workings. The arena's active participants in turn seldom enjoyed de jure access to sovereign authority. In schematic outline, then, these are the basic characteristics of the individuals and of their arena of activities that this book aims to recover.

For heuristic purposes, I approach this arena of circulation and exchange as one composed of structures of several different kinds. These structures – which I define loosely as patterned social behaviour that endured and was meaningful to contemporaries – were held together by a variety of flows and interactions. (See Map 2.) And it is these structures which, *as a collective*, were unique to the arena, and, by extension, to the region as a whole. This is a critical point worth reiterating: my claim for what was unique about the arena of circulation and exchange relates not to its structures in isolation, which may or may not have been true of social life in other parts of the world; the uniqueness applies rather to its collective of structures. It should also be borne in mind that, while these structures (and the arena within which they were subsumed) were deeply entwined with the region's states, empires, societies and ecumenes, they are *not* reducible to any of the latter.[19]

The effort expended in crafting this analytical framework is ultimately justified by its usefulness. I note here briefly three of the ways in which it has proved valuable to me. The first is that it does not prejudge the nature

of Robert C. Ellickson's stimulating book *Order without Law: How Neighbors Settle Disputes* (Cambridge, MA, 1991).

19 There are strong resonances between my approach to the arena and the approach framing Emmanuel Le Roy Ladurie's *Montaillou: village occitan de 1294 à 1324* (Paris, 1975). Also of relevance is the notion of 'institutional arrangements' discussed in John Middleton, 'Merchants: an essay in historical ethnography', *Journal of the Royal Anthropological Institute* 9:3 (2003), 509–26.

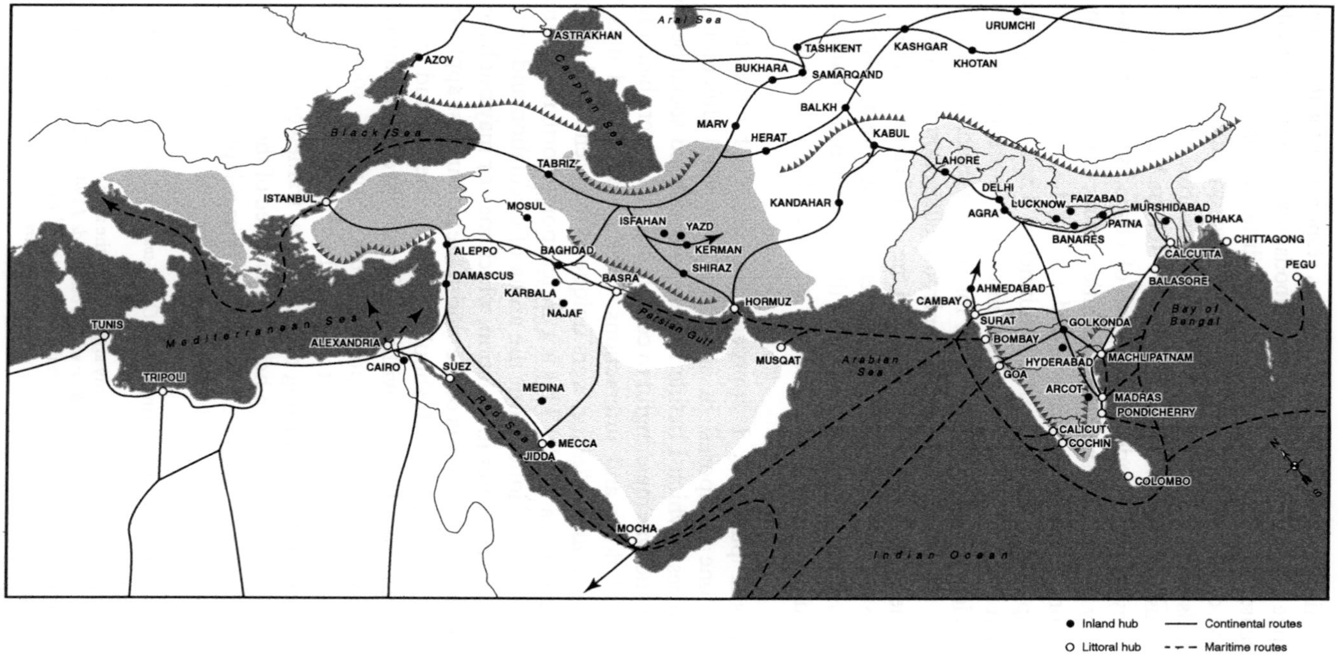

Map 2. Continental and maritime routes, *c.* 1750.

of the activities which were regional in scope. Their resulting arena cannot be interpreted solely or even mainly from the standpoint of trade or culture or diaspora, despite these being crucial to it. Similarly, it must not be viewed through the lens of the Islamic religious traditions alone, or of the affairs of their adherents, notwithstanding their centrality. I have therefore sought to inject this book's framework with sufficient flexibility to allow for emic description and analysis.[20] This makes it possible to minimise recourse to terms, typologies and taxonomies that were anachronistic or foreign to India and the Islamic heartlands before modern times. If we wish to make fullest sense of their past in our here-and-now, I maintain that it is essential we take into account the conceptual repertoire which was familiar to locally resident contemporaries.[21]

A second benefit of the framework stems from apprehending the region through the optic of circulation and exchange. By doing so, it becomes easier to bypass or transcend several contrasting polarities that have left a deep – and, I would argue, questionable – imprint on received scholarship. The most pertinent of these are the South Asia/Middle East, Asia/Europe, maritime/continental, indigenous/foreign and cognitive/material oppositions. And then there is a third way in which the framework is useful. Because of the prior agnosticism with regard to size, form and limits, it supports the discovery of parallels and linkages at dimensions that were appropriate to the specific activities historically associated with the arena.

Defining the region: an Islamicate Eurasia

That very agnosticism gestures to the importance of particular kinds of sites and spaces for this book's analytical framework.[22] Because my concern is with activities vested in circulation and exchange, settlements – towns, ports, oases – constituted fixed points at which

20 On emic – and its corollary etic – modes of analysis, see Thomas N. Headland, Kenneth L. Pike and Marvin Harris (eds.), *Emics and Etics: the Insider/Outsider Debate* (Newbury Park, CA, 1990).

21 Even works of recent decades that argue against unwarranted Eurocentrism and modernist teleologies have failed to take proper heed of this point and thus fall short of their self-proclaimed goals. Of those written on the grandest scales, telling examples include Janet L. Abu-Lughod, *Before European Hegemony: the World System AD 1250–1350* (Oxford, 1989); Kirti N. Chaudhuri, *Asia before Europe: Economy and Civilisation of the Indian Ocean from the Rise of Islam to 1750* (Cambridge, 1990); Jerry H. Bentley, *Old World Encounters: Cross-Cultural Contacts and Exchanges in Pre-modern Times* (New York, 1993); Christopher A. Bayly, *The Birth of the Modern World, 1780–1914: Global Connections and Comparisons* (Oxford, 2004).

22 For a stimulating discussion of space as an analytical notion, see David Harvey, *Spaces of Global Capitalism: a Theory of Uneven Geographical Development* (London, 2006).

transactions were initiated or completed. But as ordinary dealings within the arena were at the same time characterised by large distances and long silences, this means that its space was not confined to any one settlement or, indeed, polity. It is in this specific sense that the concerns of individuals whose livelihoods were made through the arena were regional in scope. Awareness of this helps us distinguish these individuals from their surrounding populations and identify what aspects of their everyday lives need to be examined. It also gives us a handle on the dimensions of the pertinent space. As is generally accepted now, prior to industrialisation and the consolidation of Europe's modern global empires, there were several kinds of activities that operated mostly on regional scales. I maintain that this was true of a certain subset of activities to do with the circulation and exchange of people, knowledge and objects. Of course, this begs the question: what was the regional entity appropriate to circulation and exchange, and how should it be labelled?

It has long been presumed that there existed a regional entity which embraced much of today's South Asia and the Middle East in premodern times. With Marshall Hodgson at the forefront,[23] scholars over several generations have invoked this entity in a variety of ways. They include historical geographers,[24] orientalists and area studies specialists,[25] historical sociologists and students of comparative politics,[26] world historians,[27] and those working in the Annales, dependista and world systems traditions.[28] Of course, these scholars did not need to be convinced of the usefulness of the region as a unit of analysis.[29] At the same time, the specific manner in which they marshalled this regional

[23] His magnum opus being *Venture of Islam: Conscience and History in a World Civilization*, 3 vols. (Chicago, 1974).

[24] From an earlier generation, they are exemplified by Owen Lattimore, *Studies in Frontier History: Collected Papers 1928–1958* (London, 1962). In the vein of global history, the most stimulating recent contributions that take geography seriously, without indulging in environmental determinism, are Lieberman, *Strange Parallels* and Parker, *Global Crisis*.

[25] Among the many examples that could be given, see Lapidus, *A History of Islamic Societies*; Sheila Blair and Jonathan Bloom, *The Art and Architecture of Islam, 1250–1800* (New Haven, CT, 1994).

[26] The early classics include Arnold J. Toynbee, *A Study of History*, 12 vols. (London, 1934–61) and Shmuel N. Eisenstadt, *Political Systems of Empires* (New York, 1963).

[27] The seminal work was, of course, William H. McNeill's *The Rise of the West: a History of the Human Community* (Chicago, 1963).

[28] Applied to the Islamic world, see John O. Voll, 'Islam as a special world-system', *Journal of World History* 5:2 (1994), 213–26.

[29] The case in favour of regions as units of analysis is presented forcefully in Roy Bin Wong, 'Entre monde et nation: les régions braudéliennes en Asie', *Annales* 56:1 (2001), 5–41. This may be profitably juxtaposed with Anthony G. Hopkins, 'The historiography of globalization and the globalization of regionalism', *Journal of the Economic and Social History of the Orient* 53:1 (2010), 19–36.

entity is not suited to comprehending circulation and exchange in past contexts.

In light of these predecessors, the approach taken in this book to the region as an arena of activities is a novel perspective.[30] Its nature and value may be understood in two ways. For one, it offers a new analytical orientation that clarifies or helps resolve a number of outstanding historiographical issues. Those entwined with the fate of the continental routes across Eurasia in the period, the relationship of sovereign regimes to their ambient polities in early modern times, the 'general crisis' of the eighteenth century, and the changes wrought by European colonisation are discussed in the concluding chapter. But for me to do that with credibility, the regional entity discerned through this novel perspective needs to be empirically and historically substantiated. That is the second way in which its nature and value may be grasped. It can be thought of as an organising category or, alternatively, a research paradigm which tries to make sense of certain recent findings derived from the extant record. And it does so, I suggest, in a manner that marks an advance on what has been attempted thus far.

One consequence of this book's approach is that the regional entity under examination does not conform to any geographical area which has currency today. Nevertheless, there are continental areas – like India (*al-Hind* or *Hindustān*), the Islamic heartlands (or the central Islamic lands), Arabia (*Jazīra al-ʿArab*), the *Mashriq*[31] – and maritime areas – like the Red Sea, Persian Gulf, the Arabian Sea – which coincide with it in significant ways. Because of their familiarity to many readers, I often draw upon these terms in my reasoning to make it more accessible. But wherever they are deployed, it is always in a qualified sense. They capture or express at best a portion of the regional entity that is the actual subject of my book. This is because, in the final reckoning, these areas are to be understood as nested within, or subsumed by, an 'Islamicate Eurasia'. And what invests this regional entity with meaning is the arena of circulation and exchange; it is the arena that constitutes its historical substance and gives it concrete form.[32]

30 Though developed independently, there is a familial resemblance between my notion of the arena and 'Zomia' or 'High Asia'. Some historians have recently expressed interest in the latter. For an introduction, see Jean Michaud, 'Editorial – Zomia and beyond', *Journal of Global History* 5:2 (2010), 187–214.

31 Details on these terms may be found in John B. Harley and David Woodward (eds.), *The History of Cartography*, vol. II, bk 1: *Cartography in the Traditional Islamic and South Asian Societies* (Chicago, 1992).

32 Though such an approach does not produce a clear delineation of frontiers and boundaries, the inner and outer limits of the arena (and thus of the region) may in principle be located where there occurred, compared with its interior, a significant weakening in the patterning of the arena's structures and a major reduction in the density of their interconnections.

In adopting this label – Islamicate Eurasia – 'Eurasia' is invoked in a narrow, literal sense. The qualifying word 'Islamicate', however, is sufficiently uncommon that I state here my rationale for using it. It was originally coined by Marshall Hodgson in the 1960s.[33] He justified the neologism on the grounds that the default term 'Islamic' is so closely associated with the religious traditions of Islam and with the doings of Muslims that it cannot be readily extended to other aspects of the more capacious polities of which they were part. Islamicate, in contrast, is relatively free of such associations. This makes it appropriate for emphasising the everyday social and cultural complexes typically found in premodern polities that were under some form of Islamic dominion. Such was Hodgson's rationale and, as the situation has not changed much in the interim, his is my rationale too. For my purposes, the chief analytical value of Islamicate is that, while acknowledging the significance of Islam and of Muslims, it also permits (i) meaningful involvement in the life of the region's polities of non-Muslim individuals, organisations and groups, and (ii) for polities to be interpreted as Islamicate without themselves being under direct Islamic rule. This flexibility is essential if we are to take full account of the empirical findings to follow.

The sources and everyday life

The link between this book's framework and the sources at its empirical core is a methodology that has two main strands. The first is an emic mode of reasoning which stresses philology, or close-grained textual analysis, of the sources. This is in part a consequence of the availability and accessibility of the evidence. Travel accounts aside, the kinds of evidence used to support this book's argument are hard to come by. Where sources containing such evidence are amenable to study, they tend to be extremely patchy in coverage. What this means in practice is that the most fruitful approach to interpreting this material is a philologically informed reading.[34] Its necessity, however, is rendered palatable by the advantages which accompany such a mode of reasoning. Above all, it allows the traces left in the sources by the vernacular behaviour of

[33] For his definition of Islamicate, together with a discussion of the surrounding terminological issues, see Hodgson, *The Venture of Islam*, I, 56–60.

[34] Master practitioners of this methodology from a previous generation include Shelomo D. Goitein and Franz Rosenthal. As examples, see Shelomo D. Goitein, *A Mediterranean Society: the Jewish Communities of the Arab World as Portrayed in the Documents of the Cairo Geniza*, 6 vols. (Berkeley, 1967–93); Franz Rosenthal, *Gambling in Islam* (Leiden, 1970); Franz Rosenthal, *'Sweeter than Hope': Complaint and Hope in Medieval Islam* (Leiden, 1983); Shelomo D. Goitein and Mordechai A. Friedman, *India Traders of the Middle Ages: Documents from the Cairo Geniza 'India Book'* (Leiden, 2008).

contemporaries to motivate and guide the terms, typologies and taxonomies used in this book. By thus being mindful of these contemporaries' own sensitivity towards their immediate surroundings and broader environment, I hope to recapture the world that they themselves experienced and knew.[35] This is most apparent in the choice and configuration of topics discussed in the book's individual chapters. I have striven throughout to ensure that their discussion is in harmony with the emic behaviour – the everyday feelings, thoughts and actions – of those who figure in the pages to come.

The second strand of the methodology is provided by documentary sources. In an ideal scenario, the textual sources for recapturing the arena of circulation and exchange would be the writings composed by and for the region's inhabitants who themselves actively participated in this arena in the course of their daily lives. Unfortunately for us, those involved were rarely, if at all, encouraged to cultivate avowedly self-reflective genres of writing. The most prized sources in their absence are personal and business correspondence, the working papers of established organisations and groups, and depositions in arbitrated or mediated disputes. Compared with these, the other major types of sources which have traditionally been mined for this part of the world before the nineteenth century – court annals, dynastic chronicles, travel accounts, scholarly treatises, the official records of the European East India companies – are pitched at several removes from its quotidian reality. Such a separation is to be expected if only because their authors or their audience tended not to be permanent and active fixtures in the arena at issue here. At best, this fact vitiates their utility as sources for discerning the arena as it really was; at worst, it creates barriers that are insuperable. I have therefore decided to bracket literary and official sources in favour of documentary and non-official sources.

So this book is based on evidence that provides us with the most unfiltered access to the vernacular actions, thoughts and feelings of the arena's people. The evidence mainly derives from a source which is akin to the miscellany found in an ordinary postbag. This postbag furnishes the story which opens the prologue. In 1748, it was being conveyed by a ship, the *Santa Catharina*, which was en route from Basra on the return leg of a freight voyage. As recounted in the prologue, the ship was captured off India's Coromandel coast by a squadron ordered by the British Crown to attack French settlements and vessels in the 'East'.

[35] In different ways, this hope is inspired and nurtured by three celebrated works in, respectively, the Annales, microstoria and postcolonial traditions: Le Roy Ladurie's *Montaillou*; Carlo Ginzburg, *Il formaggio e i vermi: il cosmo di un mugnaio del '500* (Turin, 1976); Amitav Ghosh, *In an Antique Land* (London, 1992).

The present character and disposition of this source results from subsequent efforts made by the British – first in Fort St David, later in Europe – to prove in English courts of law that the *Santa Catharina* was a French vessel. As the War of the Austrian Succession was still in progress at the time, to do so would have made it a legitimate prize. This entailed the confiscation, transfer to England and archiving in London of all writings discovered on board at the moment of its capture.[36] These writings are to a large extent in non-European languages and non-Latin scripts. Many of them deal with the management of the ship and its cargo. But a significant fraction had been entrusted to its passengers by individuals at Basra and by those at other places where the ship had dropped anchor on its homeward journey from Basra for recipients or intermediaries at ports lying on the ship's expected itinerary.

Taken as a whole, the material seized from the *Santa Catharina* is thus similar in character to what one might find in a postbag – with all the possibilities and challenges that a postbag poses for a historian. Composed almost entirely in Arabic, Persian and Ottoman Turkish, the material consists of about a hundred personal, business and official letters, notarised documents, accounts, petitions, contracts, receipts and formal certificates of appointment. These were composed between 1745 and 1748, and exhibit a wide range of rhetorical conventions and styles that invoke the local idiom, the spoken argot and the classical forms of the relevant languages in varying combinations. Their authors and recipients include men, women, fathers, sons, wives, mothers, uncles, brothers, sisters, nephews, scholars, teachers, students, partners and employees.[37]

By any reasonable yardstick, these individuals embody a representative sample of those who resided in the administrative, commercial, educational and spiritual centres of Islamicate Eurasia at the time, *and* who actively participated in its arena of circulation and exchange. The

[36] The writings that have survived and that I have been able to locate thus far are today preserved in the British Library, London (BL/Lansdowne/1046) and in the National Archives, Kew (NA/HCA/30/682, NA/HCA 32/1833, NA/HCA/42/25 (St Catharina)). This material's nature, provenance and fate is discussed at length in my unpublished paper 'The many identities of the *Santa Catharina*: sovereignty and conflict of laws in mid-eighteenth-century England', presented at the Northeast Conference on British Studies, Montreal, Canada, 2004. The paper is available on request.

[37] A qualitative distinction needs to be made between the male and female 'authors' of these documents. In most instances of a letter purportedly written by a woman, its scribe (*kātib*), who was invariably a man and usually kindred, is named towards its end, appending his own greetings to the addressee. See, for example, BL/Lansdowne/1046, docs. 12, 69, 70. This is not observed in letters written by men. At a minimum, the difference suggests that few, if any, women in this arena had writing literacy. The extent of their reading literacy remains an open issue.

principal value of their writings lies in the abundance of details to do with their ongoing daily lives. They give us a keen sense of their vernacular concerns, and in several instances provide us with multiple perspectives on affairs that formed part and parcel of the messy stuff of life. Like the Cairo Geniza collection, albeit on a far more modest scale, the source offers us a window on to everyday realities for individuals in a period before modern times who did *not* belong to the conspicuous elites.[38] It gives us, as a result, a myriad of insights into previously obscured or neglected aspects of the daily lives of those who were active in the region's arena of circulation and exchange. And even for subjects where the information is fragmentary, the material serves to enhance our analytical imagination.

Notwithstanding these advantages, the *Santa Catharina* postbag has obvious challenges as a source. In particular, its coverage of important topics is often non-existent or elusive. Where this is not the case, we are still constrained by the fact that the coverage is situated within highly restricted time horizons. A great deal is also taken for granted for the simple reason that the writings had to be salient to present concerns and were intended for immediate consumption; their contents are not reflective in any general sense, and were certainly not composed for wide dissemination or for posterity. In order to temper these biases and limitations, I make use of material from several other documentary collections,[39] and of depositions submitted by plaintiffs and defendants in disputes heard before Bombay Mayor's Court.[40] More detailed information on these sources is given in the parts of the book where they are used most extensively. In addition, I draw on a number of travel accounts by authors known either to have been conversant with the relevant local or regional languages, or to have had long personal experience of what they discuss.[41]

A map for the reader

There is more than one way of charting a course through this book. The individual chapters can be viewed as self-contained. They have

38 On the nature of the Cairo Geniza collection and its interest for scholars, see Shelomo D. Goitein, 'The documents of the Cairo Geniza as a source for Mediterranean social history', *Journal of the American Oriental Society* 80:2 (1960), 91–100.

39 Historical Archives of Goa, Panjim (Persian Documents); Bibliothèque nationale de France, Paris (MssOcc/NAF/8992–9114); Xavier Centre of Historical Research, Alto Porvorim, Goa (Mhamai House Records).

40 Maharashtra State Archives, Mumbai (Misc/HCR/MRC).

41 Of greatest importance are the travel accounts of Abraham-Hyacinthe Anquetil-Duperron and Carsten Niebuhr.

value in their own right for their empirically grounded analysis of significant historical topics, many of which have yet to be adequately studied by scholars. But the book's chapters also cohere in relation to one another if taken as presented. They form successive phases in a broad progression, albeit with pauses and detours, from the intangible to the palpable. This progression is similar to how Emmanuel Le Roy Ladurie recaptured the world of a medieval village in his classic *Montaillou*. But the movement here occurs in the opposite direction to his because of the qualitative differences between the world of Le Roy Ladurie's village and the world that this book is seeking to recapture. A third way of reading this book is to treat the final two chapters as a discussion of the arena in the full regional and historical setting proper to it. From this vantage, the detailed examination of its major aspects in the preceding chapters provides the necessary background. So there is no single or correct way of reading this book. In order to help readers chart the best course for themselves, there follows an outline of its reasoning.

In Chapter 1, an account is given of the cognitive patterns available to the arena's people. It is through these that they accessed and made sense of their mundane surroundings. The patterns took the form of concepts and images that were usually, though not always, verbalised.

The next five chapters examine the manner in which individuals with livelihoods vested in circulation and exchange actually confronted their world as they knew it. By detailing both the fundamental realities that imbued their everyday lives and their associated behavioural tendencies, I aim to elucidate the arena's ontology. Chapters 2 and 3 on the cosmic order and the familial order are about features of life in the arena that were viewed as universal, immutable and timeless. Whereas Chapter 2 centres on this-world and the world-to-come, on the divine figures that populated them, and on piety, fate and death, Chapter 3 centres on the most intimate of relationships – between a father and a son, a wife and a husband – and the visceral emotions and foundational duties with which they were infused. In contrast, the following three chapters – on the relational order, the communications order and the political order – deal with features of the arena that were viewed as manmade and temporal, features that had to be suffered in order to survive, and to be embraced in order to survive well. These three chapters discuss in turn the significance of plurality, and the kinds of relationships that prevailed among intimates and among strangers; the character and function of language, writing and couriers; and the ways in which the arena and the polities it intersected were reconciled to one another through the articulation of power.

From a focus on matters of being, Chapter 7 on practices shifts the attention to the ordinary skills and techniques necessary for circulation and exchange on regional scales. It describes how letters were composed and comprehended, intermediation by agents and brokers, the art of negotiation, and the practicalities of settling transactions deferred in time.

Chapter 8 apprehends the dynamics of the arena through its flows and interactions as revealed in four case studies. Two of them are of the trajectories fashioned by the relationships between individuals who made a living as brokers, agents, merchants and bankers; the other two are of family households that had regional interests which derived from their involvement in the arena.

The book closes with a chapter in which I consider how standard interpretations of the Middle East and South Asia prior to European dominance fare in light of the findings presented here and in other recent publications. I conclude with a reflection on the most promising lines of historical enquiry opened up by these findings (and by the approach framing this book).

1 Cognitive patterns: approaching the world

> For three years now, we have not seen from you a letter . . . And in these three years, I have written nearly a hundred letters. And some of them I have sent to Basra, and some of them to Egypt . . . Some I wrote to the heights of the Malabar and some I wrote to Cochin. I am at a loss in the matter of where to write, O my son, because I don't know where you are.[1]

So went a father's lament, entrusted to a letter in January 1748 and sent in hope eastward from Basra. His incessant worrying had tired him out. All his efforts so far had been in vain. Three years on, having journeyed every avenue known to him, he was on the verge of giving up, of finally resigning himself to his son's loss. Whether he did so or not, we cannot say. But his quest – unhappy, long and increasingly desperate – would have been impossible were it not for a basic human drive, a drive to experience, represent, interpret and explain one's surroundings.

That drive is the insight framing the present chapter's enquiry into what I call 'cognitive patterns'. Within the setting of the arena familiar to this father from his younger days, cognitive patterns performed a dual function. Whether as concepts or images, it was through such patterns that individuals accessed their temporal world beyond themselves, and made sense of it to their own satisfaction. At the same time, the very act curtailed how the world might be accessed, and what kinds of senses be made of it. The patterns responsible for this were not any single individual's construction. Rather, they were transmitted from generation to generation through natural language, gestures or other forms of non-verbal communication.[2] This passage over time was, of course,

[1] BL/Lansdowne/1046, doc. 68.

[2] In arriving at this understanding of communication via non-verbal means, I have found the classic works of Erving Goffman of particular help, especially his *The Presentation of Self in Everyday Life* (New York, 1959) and *Interaction Rituals: Essays on Face-to-Face Behaviour* (New York, 1967). For a useful collection of essays about the ways in which the past may be approached through the lens of gesture, see Michael J. Braddick (ed.), *The Politics of Gesture: Historical Perspectives* (Oxford, 2009).

never perfect, nor was it simple; it was inflected through an amalgam of experiences – inherited, personal and collective – that sustained and transfigured the patterns, and occasionally generated new ones. So their genealogies are complicated. Furthermore, the patterns were always 'out there' as a shared social resource, openly available to all individuals who participated in the arena.[3] The fact of their historical prevalence does not, however, make the task of recovering them any the easier. This is because, while all such patterns could in principle be verbalised by contemporaries using conventional words or phrases – and, indeed, many were expressed in this fashion – others in practice tended to be expressed corporeally or visually, and were *not* associated with standardised terms. The latter is especially true of those vernacular concepts and images that were seldom, if ever, subject to formal deliberation.

Without having awareness of, and the capacity to tap, the widely dispersed reservoir of concepts and images, the arena's people would have been unable to contemplate, let alone undertake, the ordinary stuff of life. Cognitive patterns in this sense were necessarily prior to their everyday actions, thoughts and feelings. This underscores their historical importance, and ought to be reason enough for scholars to examine them systematically and in depth. But the fact is this has yet to happen for those inhabitants of India and the Islamic heartlands who did *not* belong to the conspicuous elites. As a result, we remain ignorant of the concepts and images that were formative for the great majority of the region's population. This chapter, by virtue of its focus on the cognitive patterns vested in the arena of circulation and exchange, thus contributes towards filling a historiographical lacuna.

The description and analysis presented in the pages to follow are organised around the spheres of social communication that were embraced by the arena's participants themselves in relation to their temporal environment. These spheres differ markedly from their modern Western analogues – the social, the economic, the cultural and the political, above all. Moreover, it was rare for the spheres to be explicitly avowed; to a far greater extent than today, they were embedded in, and articulated through, vernacular behaviour.[4] By means of a close-grained analysis of the personal correspondence that was written, circulated and

[3] A similar presumption underpins the attempt to reconstruct the semantic history of the 'culture-concept' in its European setting in Andrew Sartori, 'The resonance of "culture": framing a problem in global concept-history', *Comparative Studies in Society and History* 47:4 (2005), 676–99.

[4] For highly stimulating reflections on the subject of spheres of social communication, especially in relation to modernity, see Niklas Luhmann, *Essays on Self-Reference* (New York, 1990) and Bruno Latour, *Nous n'avons jamais été modernes: essai d'anthropologie symétrique* (Paris, 1991).

read within the arena in the middle of the eighteenth century, I set out to recover these spheres. This is possible because they were innate to the very grammar, lexicon and idiom of the three main regional languages of the period, Persian, Arabic and Ottoman Turkish.[5] It is also worth noting that the labels under which the spheres are elaborated in this chapter – 'identity and belonging', 'measurement and transactions', 'sovereignty and power', 'locality and space' – are my constructs, and imposed from without. Nevertheless, I have striven to ensure that these labels are in keeping with their empirical substance. In the final reckoning, however, each sphere is determined not by its label but by its manifestation as specific concepts and images in relation to one another.

Identity and belonging

It was in encounters outside the intimate community that the arena of circulation and exchange was at its most visceral, with each and every interaction reaffirming its existence. Because such interactions were an unavoidable and basic feature of daily life, I begin my investigation of the prevailing cognitive patterns with those marshalled for comprehending and communicating the presence of outsiders, particularly strangers.[6] The language of the documents suggests that this normally occurred in two ways: through markers of identity attached to the person of an individual and through the collectives to which he belonged. Stated thus, the ways in which people were represented and interpreted in the arena have similarities to how we do such things today (quite possibly they are true of all premodern literate polities imbued with specialisation). But that is not to gainsay significant differences. These differences are revealed in the details of the markers of personal identity and the collectives actually invoked.

Personal identity was conceived primarily along cultural, relational and social lines. First, let us consider cultural markers of identity. As their distribution in Table 1 shows, there existed a rich lexicon for specifying one's ethnicity (or subjecthood).[7] This probably reflects the everyday

[5] As many of the linguistic elements relevant to cognitive patterns were held in common by these three languages in the eighteenth century, I do not identify the original language of the texts in which the words and expressions discussed in this chapter are noted. To do so would serve little purpose, and even be misleading. For a description of the cornucopia of languages that marked India and the Islamic heartlands in the period, see Chapter 5 on the communications order.

[6] The notion of the stranger, and the related notions of intimates and the intimate community, are discussed in Chapter 4 on the relational order.

[7] My understanding of ethnicity is informed by Fredrik Barth, who defines an ethnic group in terms of 'self-ascription': the members of the group select and use a handful of cultural

Table 1. *Cultural markers of identity.*

Ethnicity (or subjecthood)	Religion
Abyssinian (*ḥabashī*)	Christian (*masīḥī, naṣārā*)
Afghan (*afghān*)	Muslim (*muslim, muwaḥḥid, mu'min*)
Angria (*angrīyah*)	
Arab (*'arab*)	
Armenian (*armanī, julfānī*)	
Bengali (*bangālī*)	
Dutch (*falmankī, walandīz*)	
English (*ankrīzī, inklīz*)	
European (*farangī*)	
French (*farāsīs, faransāwīya*)	
Indian (*hindī*)	
Kurd (*kurd*)	
Qizilbash (*ghizilbāsh*)	
Persian (*'ajam*)	
Portuguese (*putakīsh, purtukish*)	

Source: BL/Lansdowne/1046.

utility of attributes such as 'Abyssinian' and 'Dutch'. In contrast, relatively few religious attributes were deployed. Those deployed were in practice confined to 'Muslim' and 'Christian'. Intriguingly, while adherents of the Hindu and Jewish traditions were resident in most of the region's settlements in recognised and established communities, the documents that I have examined do not contain a single explicit reference to their religious traditions. When such individuals do crop up – and they do so regularly – they were invariably denoted by their given names or by the occupations typically associated with them.[8] Even for Muslims and Christians, their religion was usually left unstated. This is despite it being

attributes, such as dress, language, general style of life or house-form, as 'overt signals or signs' of their distinctiveness. Fredrik Barth (ed.), *Ethnic Groups and Boundaries: the Social Organization of Culture Difference* (Boston, 1969), 14. As for my understanding of subjecthood, it is informed by two formal documents in Ottoman Turkish that use the word *tawābi'* ('subjects') within the expression في الاصل هندستان توابعلرندن ('[he] originally being from among the subjects of Hindustan'). BL/Lansdowne/1046, docs. 82, 83. Drawing on this usage, I take subjecthood to refer either to exclusive allegiance to a given sovereign or to attachment to the land of a recognised sovereign regime. In the linguistic practice of the period, it was generally not possible to draw a clear distinction between ethnicity and subjecthood. That is why I treat them together in this section.

8 Compare that with the end of the eighteenth century and after when the label 'Hindki' appears to enter common usage. On this development in the context of Afghanistan and the transition to colonialism, see Shah Mahmoud Hanafi, *Connecting Histories in Afghanistan: Market Relations and State Formation on a Colonial Frontier* (Stanford, CA, 2008), 8–10, 23–30.

a central element of their persona in public. Religion, it seems, then, played second fiddle to ethnicity (or subjecthood) as a marker of belonging within the arena. One way of making sense of this situation is that, in a context where a given religious tradition often had a multitude of ethnicities affiliated to it, religion per se was frequently too coarse-grained an attribute for conveying sufficiently useful information about an individual.[9] Thus, the Basra-based Armenian Masʿūd was described by his Shīʿī associate only twice as 'the Christian'. In every other instance, he was identified by his ethnicity.[10]

The second category of identifiers invoked to distinguish individuals were relational markers. Some examples are listed in Table 2. As the terms *anīs al-ghurabāʾ* ('close friend of strangers'), *khvājah* ('gentleman merchant'), *jān* ('spirit') and *nūrchashm* ('the light of [my] eye', 'darling') show, they were chiefly complimentary or affective in nature. In this register, they echoed or asserted what the ties meant to those involved, and were of particular value for signalling their – factual, imagined or desired – relationship or degree of proximity. By means of, say, *mushfiq* ('compassionate', 'kind') and *qiblah-i qadrdān* ('pivot of the just esteemer'), these ties could be expressed directly, with the focus on the recipient. It was just as common, however, to gesture towards ties in a self-referential manner. This could be through ritualised activities, which in the cases of *dāʿī* ('one who prays') and *davlatkhvāh* ('well-wisher') indicate devotion to the addressee. It could also be through ritualised deference, which often shaded into self-abasement with the use of expressions such as *jārīya* ('[female] slave' or 'slave-girl') for wife or '[we being] among the humblest of the servants of [your] salt-nourishing servants'.[11]

Cultural and relational markers were complemented by markers of social identity. These latter in effect designated an individual's formal status and role in the prevailing political order, and may be seen in Table 3, where they are grouped by title, occupation and rank or office. Some of the titles, like *janāb*, were honorific, denoting high respect. Others, like *muqaddasī*, gestured to an accomplishment or, like *sharīf*, were an accident of birth. The markers make it clear that many of the

[9] This is especially true of the designator Muslim. In fact, other than in documents that were expressly religious or legal in character, it was rare to describe individuals overtly as Muslim. For details on the genealogy of, and scholarly debate on, the terms 'Muslim', 'Hindu' and their cognates, see Wilfred Cantwell Smith, *On Understanding Islam: Selected Studies* (The Hague, 1981), 41–77; David N. Lorenzen, 'Who invented Hinduism?', *Comparative Studies in Society and History* 41:4 (1999), 630–59; David N. Lorenzen, 'Hindu sects and Hindu religion: precolonial and colonial concepts', in Cynthia Talbot (ed.), *Knowing India: Colonial and Modern Constructions of the Past* (New Delhi, 2011), 251–78.

[10] BL/Lansdowne/1046, docs. 6, 26.

[11] BL/Lansdowne/1046, doc. 8.

Table 2. *Relational markers of identity.*

Direct		Indirect	
Complimentary	Affective	Devotional	Deferential
anīs al-ghurabā' ('close friend of strangers')	*'azīz* ('dear')	*'ābid* ('worshipper', 'adorer')	*'abd, bandah, ghulām, khādim, khidmatkār* ('slave', 'servant')
āqā ('sir')	*akh, barādar* ('brother')	*dā'ī, du'āgū* ('one who prays')	*aḥqar, ḥaqīr, kamtarīn, khākpā, khāksār* ('humble', 'vulgar')
efendi, ṣāḥib ('lord', 'gentleman')	*bābā* (for referring to juniors)	*davlatkhvāh* ('well-wisher')	*'ājiz* ('weak', 'impotent')
fayḍbakhsh, fayḍrisānah ('bestower of bounty')	*barkhurdār* ('successful', 'prosperous', refers to juniors)	*mukhliṣ* ('devoted')	*'āṣī, muqassir* ('sinner')
khātūn ('lady')	*dūst, ṣadīq, yār* ('friend')		*bandah-yi fidavī* ('devoted servant')
khvājah ('gentleman', man of distinction)	*ghālī* ('precious')		*faqīr* ('pauper', 'dervish')
mawlā, khudāvand, sayyid ('master', 'lord')	*ḥabīb, muḥabb* ('loved', 'darling')		*faqīr-i dūr uftādah* ('uncomprehending pauper')
mihrbān, mushfiq ('compassionate', 'kind')	*jān* ('vitality', 'spirit', 'energy')		*kanīz, jārīya* ('[female] slave', 'slave-girl')
mūsā ('monsieur', mister)	*jār* ('neighbour')		*rūsiyāh* ('black-faced')
mushfiq al-fuqarā' ('kind towards the paupers')	*mukarram, akram* ('most generous', 'venerated')		
qiblah-yi qadrdān ('pivot of the just esteemer')	*nūrchashm* ('light of the eye', 'darling')		
qiblah-yi dū jahān ('pivot of the two worlds')	*rūḥ* ('breath of life', 'soul', 'spirit', 'essence')		

Source: BL/Lansdowne/1046.

Table 3. *Social markers of identity.*

Titles	Occupations	Ranks/offices
honorific *bahādur* ('valiant') *ḥaḍra* ('presence') *janāb* ('honour') **for accomplishments** *fakhr al-tujjār* ('the pride of the merchants') *ḥājj, ḥājī* (one who has performed the pilgrimage to Mecca) *kahf al-ḥājj wa-al-mu'tabarīn* *muqaddasī* ('holy') *'umdat al-tujjār* ('the chief of the merchants') **by birth** *khānṣāḥib* (nobleman) *miyān* (nobleman) *mīr, mīrzā* (prince, lord, son of a lord) *sayyid* (descendent of the Prophet Muhammad) *sharīf* (honourable)	**trade and finance** *baqqāl* ('grocer') *dallāl* ('broker') *gumāshtah* ('agent') *khidmatkār, ajīr* ('servant', 'employee') *mahājan* ('moneylender') *nāẓir* ('supervisor') *ṣāḥib-i ikhtiyār* ('endowed with authority') *tājir, savdāgar* ('merchant') *vakīl* ('agent') *waṣīy* ('executor') **shipping and maritime** *gūlah-andāz* ('gunner') *mu'allim* ('pilot', 'sailing-master', 'mate') *nākhudā* ('skipper', 'master') *qabṭān* ('captain') *sārang, sarhang* ('boatswain', 'chief of lascar crew') *tandīl* ('head of a body of men', 'boatswain') **writing and bookkeeping** *ḥāfiẓ al-kitāb, kātib, kātib al-aḥruf* ('scribe', 'secretary') *kirānī, karānī* ('clerk', 'accountant') *munshī* ('clerk', 'scribe') *nivīsandah, sāhūkār* ('writer') **communication** *chāpār, qāṣid, sā'in* ('messenger', 'courier', 'runner') *turjumān* ('interpreter) **religion and education** *akhvānd, murabbī* ('tutor', 'preacher') *'ālim* ('scholar') *kāhin* ('diviner', 'priest') *mullā* ('theologian', 'cleric') *pīr* ('guide', 'saint')	**Ottoman empire** *bāshā, ḥākim* ('governor', 'ruler') *kāhiya* (chief officer of a district or province) *mutassalim* (provincial governor) *nā'ib* ('deputy', 'viceroy', 'representative') *qāḍī* ('judge') *ṣāḥib al-muhr* ('keeper of the seal') *wazīr* (vazir) **Iran** *kadkhudā* ('village headman') *muḥassil* ('tax collector') *pādishāh* ('shah', 'ruler') *vāli* ('governor') *sarkār-i divān* (a high official at court) **India** *khānsāmān* ('chief steward') *nawwāb* ('governor') *qāḍī* ('judge') *rājā* ('king') **Eastern Christianity** *qadīs* ('saint') *qissīs* ('priest') *shammās* ('deacon') **Islamic traditions** *'ālim* ('scholar') *darbān-i 'Alī Mūsā Riḍā* ('gatekeeper of the shrine of 'Alī Mūsā Riḍā') *imām* *khalīfa* ('successor') *mullā* ('theologian', 'cleric') *murīd* (Ṣūfī novice or disciple) *shaykh* **maritime Asia** *daraktūr* (the VOC's governor on the Malabar, based in Cochin) *gūrnar ganral* (the British governor-general in Calcutta) *qanṣul* (the Compagnie des Indes' consul in Basra)

Source: BL/Lansdowne/1046.

recognised occupations in the arena were rooted in trade, finance, transport, writing and book-keeping.[12] But they also flag the significance of couriers, interpreters, tutors, scholars, teachers and spiritual guides. As for the ranks and offices contained in the correspondence, they were generally conferred or sanctioned from above, especially by sovereign regimes, religious organisations and the European East India companies.

Just as foundational as the markers noted above were terms denoting collectives. See Table 4 for some of the most common examples. The collectives to which these terms refer were normally bounded in number and self-aware as coherent groupings. They were verbalised by means of lexicon and rhetorical techniques that, notwithstanding their spare character, were flexible enough to capture the salient features of their diverse environment. This coheres with a paucity of specialised terminology in everyday parlance for designating particular organisations or groups, such as the family firm or neighbourhood associations, even though these were vital – and known as such – for sustaining life in the arena. One of the rare exceptions is the *mahājanī*. Associations of this type would lend money, say, to Shīʿī families living in Bengal who found themselves unexpectedly in financial need while their menfolk were abroad.[13]

But such direct, technical language is hardly ever seen in the correspondence. This is because several alternatives performed essentially the same function, and did so well enough. The simplest of these tapped a small number of generic nouns in order to signify a wide spectrum of collectives, the specific one intended being defined by the relevant context. Take *ṭāʾifa* as an example. Its base meaning is 'people'. But other rankings are associated with it too. In appropriate circumstances, *ṭāʾifa* could stand in for 'clan', 'tribe', 'extended family', 'intimate community',[14] 'religious minority' or 'nation'.[15] The term *ahl* is synonymous with *ṭāʾifa* when used in the sense of 'people'. But in other scenarios, *ahl*

[12] Cf. the discussion of merchants and their employees in Shelomo D. Goitein, *A Mediterranean Society: the Jewish Communities of the Arab World as Portrayed in the Documents of the Cairo Geniza*, vol. I (Berkeley, CA, 1967), 149–64.

[13] BL/Lansdowne/1046, doc. 11. Not much is known about the actual nature and role of *mahājans* in northern India before the nineteenth century. For valuable insights, see Dilbagh Singh, 'The role of mahajans in the rural economy in eastern Rajasthan during the 18th century', *Social Scientist* 2:10 (1974), 20–31. The present state of the scholarship on *mahājans*, in the context of business history, is discussed in the early chapters of Dwijendra Tripathi, *Oxford History of Indian Business* (New Delhi, 2004).

[14] BL/Lansdowne/1046, doc. 68, in which a father informed his son that all 'the children of our *ṭāʾifa*' send him their greetings.

[15] BL/Lansdowne/1046, docs. 67, 70, in which there is reference to the Dutch and French *ṭāʾifas*.

Table 4. *Collective markers of identity.*

Specialised terminology	Generic nouns	Nominal phrases
dhimma	*ahl*	'all the relatives'
ḥalqa	*bayt*	'group of the kindred and loved ones'
mahājanī	*ḥavīlī*	'people [or inhabitants] of the house'
takīya	*khānah*	'all the darlings'
	ru'āyā	'group of the acquaintances and the brothers and the friends'
	ṭā'ifa	
		'group of the small and the big'
		'all the merchants'
		'group of the men [or people] of the ship'
		'community of the Dutch'
		'group of the Afghans'
		'group of the Kurds'
		'gathering of the unitarians'
		'people of prayer'
		'group of the Muslims'
		'people of ecstasy'
		'people of the paths and the truths'
		'group of the village'
		'residents of Basra'
		'people of [or from] Shirāz'
		'people of the world'

Source: BL/Lansdowne/1046.

could mean 'followers' or 'inhabitants',[16] or, more commonly, 'kin', 'relatives' or 'intimate community'.[17] Similar remarks apply to *bayt, khānah* and *ḥavīlī*. They were frequently invoked when speaking of the home, the household or the family,[18] the social constellations that exerted by far the greatest influence on the daily lives of the region's inhabitants. These were the senses in which they were most often understood. Their other established meanings were brought to the fore by the specifics of the context.[19]

While generic nouns such as *ṭā'ifa* and *ahl* were certainly not ignored, it was much more common to deploy nominal phrases when referring to the region's collectives. These nominal phrases were constructed by attaching to one of several words that mean 'inhabitants', 'group', 'people', 'gathering', 'troop' or 'all' the operative quality shared by each of its members. That quality could be residence, occupation, degree of intimacy or religious

16 BL/Lansdowne/1046, docs. 82, 83. 17 BL/Lansdowne/1046, docs. 67, 68, 73.
18 BL/Lansdowne/1046, docs. 3, 7, 9, 13, 23, 28, 35, 48, 49, 65.
19 See, for example, BL/Lansdowne/1046, docs. 6, 7, 9, 13, 14, 17, 21, 38.

affiliation. Having done so, the resulting phrase then functioned as a noun. In southern Iraq, one might talk about the extended family as 'all the relatives' (*jamīʿ al-ahl, jamīʿ al-aqribāʾ, jamīʿ al-aqārib*).[20] It was more frequent, however, to convey the idea of the family, or family household, through the phrase 'the people [or inhabitants] of the house' (*ahl al-bayt*).[21] When describing individuals belonging to a particular confessional tradition or hailing from a certain place, *ahl* reappears but now in the form 'the people of ecstasy' (*ahl-i ḥāl*, i.e., a Sufi group)[22] or 'the people of [or from] Shiraz' (*ahl-i Shirāz*).[23] Similarly, 'all the Julfan merchants' (*jumlah-yi tujjār-i julfānī*)[24] denoted the body of recognised Christian traders who resided in the Isfahan area, whereas on board a ship the officers and passengers – though not, it must be stressed, the ordinary crewmen – were designated by phrases such as 'the group of the people of the ship' (*jamāʿah-yi ahl-i jahāz*)[25] or 'the men of the ship' (*mardumān-i jahāz*).[26] There were exceptions such as 'the young and the great, 'the old and the young', 'the friends and the loved ones', 'the gentlemen and the friends' (*khurd o kalān*,[27] *kibār wa ṣighār*,[28] *al-aṣdiqāʾ wa-al-muḥibbīn*,[29] *ṣāḥibān u dūstān*[30]). Here, the collective entity is implicit; it was the context that determined whether the entity being referred to was the family household, the extended family, the local neighbourhood or the intimate community at home. So there were clear differences between the types of nominal phrases found in the arena. But notwithstanding the differences, these nominal phrases all bear witness to the fact that their ambient social collectives were composed of individuals with stable and widely understood attributes.

Taken as a whole, the everyday lexicon analysed in this section shows that the individuals populating the arena were identified by what were often publicly visible personal attributes and by the collectives to which they belonged. The first took the form of cultural, relational and social markers; the second made explicit the pertinent biographical features which they all shared. The lexicon's great advantage was its blend of precision and flexibility. It enabled the region's inhabitants to specify

[20] BL/Lansdowne/1046, docs. 67, 68, 71.
[21] BL/Lansdowne/1046, docs. 12, 65, 69, 70, 71, 73, 74, 76.
[22] BL/Lansdowne/1046, doc. 27. [23] BL/Lansdowne/1046, doc. 14.
[24] BL/Lansdowne/1046, doc. 14. [25] BL/Lansdowne/1046, docs. 4, 5.
[26] BL/Lansdowne/1046, doc. 5.
[27] BL/Lansdowne/1046, doc. 49. Elsewhere, the standard pattern reasserts itself: 'all of the young and the great gentlemen' (*jamīʿah-yi khwurd o kalān-i ṣāḥibān, hamah-yi khwurd o kalān, jamīʿah-yi khwurd o kalān*). BL/Lansdowne/1046, docs. 13, 23.
[28] BL/Lansdowne/1046, doc. 68. In other documents, this phrase is prefaced by a general collective: 'people of the house, young and old' (*ahl bayt ṣighār wa kibār*). BL/Lansdowne/1046, doc. 73.
[29] BL/Lansdowne/1046, doc. 72. [30] BL/Lansdowne/1046, doc. 49.

and communicate effectively their arena's many varied associations. At the same time, it acknowledged the great diversity in the backgrounds of the individual participants. As I argue later in this chapter, much the same approach prevailed in making sense of the activities on which their livelihoods depended.

Measurement and transactions

A large proportion of the livelihoods made in the arena of circulation and exchange depended on transactions that at some point entailed measurement. So how measurement and transactions were conceived is key to any examination of the arena's cognitive patterns. The documents show that these patterns exhibited two distinct orientations: one towards the environment within which transactions were undertaken, the other towards the specifics of the items transacted. But before considering them in detail, a prior question needs to be answered: how did contemporaries express the general notion of a transaction?

The language used for discussing transactions was normally very simple and clear. Sayyid Muṣṭafā wrote from Cochin in 1748 that, on reaching Basra, he would send home detailed news of 'buying and selling' (*kharīd o farakht*).[31] A few years later, an official of a small Arabian Sea port used the term 'buying-selling' (*bīʿ shira*) in a letter soliciting foreign shippers and traders to his port.[32] In 1777, a broker informed his principal on the Malabar coast about the efforts he was making on his behalf 'for buying and for selling' (*lil-bīʿ wa-lil-shirā*) in Mocha.[33] Occasionally, there is a term found in the correspondence – *kār*[34] or *matjar*[35] or *muʿāmalah*[36] – that may be taken to refer to transactions as an abstract notion. More frequently, however, we see agglutinative verbal nouns like 'buying and selling', 'buying-selling'. These were understood to be synonymous either with commerce in general or with local business opportunities at the time. Rhetorically, these verbal nouns were telescoped into and envisaged as a specific type of dealing among individuals. Such dealings were certainly central to many transactions. But the language rooted in them was not intended just to be treated literally. Terms such as 'buying-selling', while conveying a tangible sense of the mundane

[31] BL/Lansdowne/1046, doc. 49.
[32] HAG/Persian Documents, doc. 27. It is worth noting that formally Arabic, unlike, say, German or Persian, is not an agglutinative language. So by the rules of classical grammar, it is not permissible to fuse words in order to construct a new one. In vernacular usage, however, such rules were often relaxed or even ignored. *Bīʿ shira* is an instance of this.
[33] MssOcc/NAF/9005: 2–9. [34] BL/Lansdowne/1046, docs. 49, 73.
[35] BL/Lansdowne/1046, docs. 73, 74. [36] BL/Lansdowne/1046, docs. 27, 31.

relationships and activities that constituted their social fabric, also expressed a much larger and more complex reality.

In considering the immediate context of these relationships and activities, a first – and quite natural – impulse would be to look for an entity akin to our present-day 'market'. And were we to do so, we would find the term *bāzār*. This certainly evokes aspects of what we today ordinarily understand by the market, say, the physical location where goods are brought and sold,[37] or where prices are negotiated and disseminated.[38] But the use of such terms in the mid-eighteenth century was the exception. It was more common to discuss the proximate environment of the 'buying-selling' under the rubric of the 'situation, circumstances' (*aḥwāl*,[39] *kayfiyat*[40]), or the 'news' (*akhbār*,[41] *ḥaqāʾiq*[42]), or the 'events' (*ḥawādith*,[43] *ḥikāyat*[44]). So let us put to one side the issue of the market and enquire instead into the kinds of information communicated under the rubric of such terms. This perspective offers greater promise for discerning the cognitive patterns germane to the status, trajectory and possible outcome of a transaction.

Perhaps the most noteworthy aspects of the information communicated are its qualitative nature, its breadth of coverage and its internal knittedness. The documents show that, while quantitative details were far from absent, they were also far from sufficient. I begin with prices.[45] Several terms were available to contemporaries for denoting them. Among the most common in the period were *nirkh*, *qīmat* and *thaman*. Subject to unexpected fluctuations both within and between seasons, these were rarely, if at all, known beforehand with any precision. The prices at which to buy and sell at some future date were thus frequently not quantified. The partner, agent or broker was asked instead to use his judgement and transact at the best 'current price' available at the time.[46] Occasionally, a correspondent would try to convey a sense of the overall state of prices at his settlement. This typically necessitated recourse to broad and rather vague sentiments like 'good' (*malīḥ*),[47] 'expensive' (*ghalāʾ*)[48] or 'sweet' (*ḥulw*).[49]

37 BL/Lansdowne/1046, docs. 26, 31, 73. 38 BL/Lansdowne/1046, doc. 73.
39 BL/Lansdowne/1046, docs. 3, 7, 9, 12, 16, 18, 21, 22, 25, 28, 30, 31, 33, 34, 35, 40, 49, 50, 55, 56, 60, 66, 69, 70, 71, 72, 73, 74, 75, 76.
40 BL/Lansdowne/1046, docs. 7, 21, 33, 49.
41 MssOcc/NAF/9005: 2–9; BL/Lansdowne/1046, docs. 3, 7, 16, 18, 21, 27, 35, 65, 66, 70, 72, 74, 75.
42 BL/Lansdowne/1046, docs. 39, 49, 54, 55. 43 BL/Lansdowne/1046, doc. 7.
44 BL/Lansdowne/1046, doc. 3.
45 Cf. the discussion of market price in Goitein, *A Mediterranean Society*, I, 218–20.
46 NA/HCA/42/25 (St Catharina).
47 MssOcc/NAF/8992: 87, 88–9; BL/Lansdowne/1046, docs. 73, 74.
48 BL/Lansdowne/1046, docs. 66, 74. 49 BL/Lansdowne/1046, doc. 73.

More often, however, information regarding prices was communicated through proxies. The most popular of these was the level of supply and demand, or, what essentially amounted to the same thing, the presence of buyers and sellers. These details were valued for their direct and immediate correlation with price. They could be relayed in simple, idiomatic language, frequently tinged by naturalistic imagery: 'there are no goods (*māl*) nor buyers';[50] '[concerning] our *māl*, [we] are incapable of [selling it]';[51] 'there is no *bāzār*';[52] 'the broadcloth is not moving (*mā yamshī*)'.[53] At other times, the descriptions were more fulsome. The French were informed by their brokers in Mocha in the 1770s that 'the demanded Pondicherry cloth is absent (*ma ʿdūm*) [here]. When you write a letter to Pondicherry, inform [them that] whoever comes [here] at the start of the season will gain an advantage (*khayr*).'[54] Ḥājī ʿInāyat Allāh deposed in 1747 that he had been unable to find a buyer for his principal's goods in Basra, as a result of which nothing was sold 'except a little'.[55] At about the same time, ʿAbd al-ʿAṭī in Iraq wrote to his brother-in-law telling him that 'the Indian muslin (*shīshān*) are not welcome in Aleppo and no one is wearing them because they are heavy (*thiqāl*)'.[56] 'With regard to the situation (*aḥwāl*) in Aleppo this year,' he continued, 'it is better than the previous year. [Things are] a bit cheaper (*shuwayya rakhṣ*) there and it is less oppressive.'[57]

Obviously related to local supply and demand was the number of ships and caravans that arrived and departed each season. The intimate link between this and prices was occasionally made explicit. Gujarati brokers working in Mocha in 1776 noted, for example, that the local price of the 'goods' (*māl*) had fallen soon after the arrival of more ships.[58] Details about their movement were provided in their correspondence, though this occurred far less often than we might expect. When such information was forthcoming, it could be accompanied by remarks on the cargo being carried, and its origin or destination. But this is uncommon.[59] More common were remarks that sought to capture the vitality of 'buying and selling' at the settlement. Similar to their descriptions of the general price level, writers often tapped naturalistic imagery in order to communicate the prevailing conditions. Occasionally simple words, such as 'stagnant' (*kasād*), would suffice.[60] At other times, greater detail was provided. In

[50] BL/Lansdowne/1046, doc. 66. [51] BL/Lansdowne/1046, doc. 73.
[52] BL/Lansdowne/1046, doc. 73. [53] MssOcc/NAF/9011: 36–7.
[54] MssOcc/NAF/9005: 64–7. [55] BL/Lansdowne/1046, doc. 6.
[56] BL/Lansdowne/1046, doc. 71. [57] BL/Lansdowne/1046, doc. 71.
[58] MssOcc/NAF/8992: 87, 88–9.
[59] Among the exceptions are HAG/Persian Documents, doc. 27, MssOcc/NAF/8992: 87, 88–9, MssOcc/NAF/9005: 64–7, MssOcc/NAF/9011: 36–7.
[60] BL/Lansdowne/1046, doc. 66.

one unusually expressive instance from 1748, Ismāʿīl Qāsim Ṭarabzāwī in Surat was told by his father, 'the *bāzār* in Basra is weak (*fātir*), there is no *bāzār* and business (*ashghāl*) is suspended, and business (*al-kār*) is inactive'.[61] Attempts were also made to describe the season as a whole (*mawsim*), whose start- and end-points were determined by fairly predictable changes in the weather.[62] To do so pithily was acceptable; a whole season could be summed up as 'good' (*malīḥ*).[63]

These accounts – accounts of prices, supply and demand, of the movement of ships and caravans, of the prevailing state of affairs – were threaded through by information on a range of other topics no less salient for apprehending mundane transactions. Correspondents would often update one another about who else was actually or potentially involved in the transactions to which they were party. Markers of identity played a prominent role here. So in discussing caravans or ships, it is quite normal for the ethnicity or subjecthood of the individuals in charge to be noted.[64] These details, even in isolation, gave the recipient a fair idea of their origins and the cargo they had imported, and of their subsequent itinerary and the items they were likely to carry away with them. The information also brought to mind received opinion on how individuals of that kind might be expected to behave in the course of a transaction, which, as discussed in Chapter 6 on the political order, had a bearing on reputation and creditworthiness. This probably lay behind the Parsi Dunjishaw's demand in 1777 that any final agreement be in writing – the usual oral understanding would not suffice – before he would even consider purchasing a ship belonging to a *British* private trader.[65] But there was nothing hard and fast about such received opinions; by themselves, they rarely determined behaviour. They went into the mix alongside highly personalised remarks. A telling instance of this may be found in a letter by Jīvan and Krishan sent from Mocha in 1776. They informed their would-be employer that the *baniyā* broker (*dallāl*) recently arrived from Surat 'is not good. He is disgraceful, a great failure . . . a thief [in] whom we have no [trust].'[66]

Though government officials and the ruling elites seldom engaged with the arena as *active* participants, a wary eye was kept on them by those who did actively participate. Doing so was only prudent because of their ability

61 BL/Lansdowne/1046, doc. 73.
62 Cf. the discussion of *mawsim* in Goitein, *A Mediterranean Society*, I, 276–7.
63 MssOcc/NAF/8992: 87, 88–9.
64 For example, HAG/Persian Documents, doc. 27, MssOcc/NAF/8992: 87, 88–9, MssOcc/NAF/9005: 64–7, MssOcc/NAF/9011: 36–7, BL/Lansdowne/1046, docs. 2, 4, 5, 13, 14, 45.
65 MSA/Misc/HCR/MRC/42: 628–727.
66 MssOcc/NAF/8992: 87, 88–9.

to facilitate or hamper many of the livelihoods involving circulation and exchange on regional scales. They formed part of the arena's political order. Kūdarjī and Guyal, Gujaratis based in Mocha, knew this only too well. That is why they were quick to inform their principal on the Malabar coast in 1778 that 'at our place, the governor Faqīh ʿAlī is very agreeable (*malīḥ*)'. And this was not mere rhetoric because 'he worked with the gentleman (*ṣāḥib*) from Mauritius considerately (*murāʿāt*) and honourably (*nāʾmūs*) to the extent possible'.[67]

Such interest in conspicuous sovereignty merged into concern for security of person and property. This was among the most basic of concerns in the arena and its discussion is certainly not neglected in the correspondence. In 1747, a Shīʿī at Basra instructed his son in Surat not to send any goods or money the coming season partly because 'the roads are not settled (*mustaʿdal*)'.[68] Similarly, Antonio de Quental, a Luso-Indian based in Calicut, told his employer in the 1770s that the uncertain political environment had made the normal route along the southwest coast of India unsafe for transporting money.[69] This kind of news jostled with remarks on one's personal state of mind and body. Such information was of obvious – and not simply utilitarian – interest to all parties in a relationship, especially when separated by large distances and long silences. As Chapter 5 on the communications order shows, details were frequently demanded, and often furnished.

The preceding analysis has highlighted the types of information commonly exchanged among correspondents active in the arena. All these types were viewed as significant facets of a transaction's salient 'circumstances' or 'news'.[70] They give us useful insights into what constituted the notional transaction's setting and, more pertinently, how this setting was experienced, represented, interpreted and explained. At the same time, what we have elaborated is a composite. Such a composite will always lack the immediacy of a case study or a sustained illustration. In order to provide that immediacy, the example which follows reveals the deeply entwined nature of the different types of information discussed above, and the value accorded them by contemporaries.

In 1747, ʿInāyat Allāh, a Shīʿī from Najaf, wrote from Basra to several of his associates in Bengal. The proximate reason for doing so was a recent

[67] MssOcc/NAF/9011: 36–7. The reading of the names of the Gujarati authors of this letter is uncertain.
[68] BL/Lansdowne/1046, doc. 73. [69] MssOcc/NAF/8998: 13.
[70] Of course, as detailed in later chapters, the information relayed was seldom confined to transactions, especially in correspondence between intimates. There are intriguing resonances between my analysis here of the information found in the correspondence and Shelomo D. Goitein's analysis of the same facet of the Cairo Geniza material in his *A Mediterranean Society*, I, 195, 200–4, 302–4.

letter from his principal in Bengal, ʿAbd al-Karīm. In this letter, ʿInāyat Allāh was accused of being insufficiently attentive to his principal's interests and of unacceptably poor results in recent dealings on his behalf. ʿInāyat Allāh was ordered to transfer all of ʿAbd al-Karīm's assets to his brother, then in Basra, and to remit to Bengal any proceeds from the goods he had been able to sell. In effect, ʿInāyat Allāh had been fired.

Evidently worried about the harmful consequences that this might have for his reputation in Bengal, let alone the injustice of it all, ʿInāyat Allāh responded in robust fashion. He dispatched straightaway a long and detailed letter in which he strenuously refuted ʿAbd al-Karīm's accusations. Accompanying it were letters to his other associates in Bengal, describing, justifying and defending his role in the affair. He wrote about his circumstances and activities over the past few years, the state of the country in and around southern Iraq, and the commercial venture at issue. All these matters were relevant, as ʿInāyat Allāh saw it, to his dealings on behalf of ʿAbd al-Karīm and by extension the transactions on which his livelihood depended. Throughout, he placed great stress on the difficulties under which he had been labouring of late. 'For five years, I have experienced troubles and losses ... By *khudā*! others would not put up with more than what I suffer.'[71] Switching rhetorical tack, he told his correspondent about his 'troubles and embarrassment' over the past few years, during which 'I have suffered material (*mālī*) and profound (*jānī*) losses'.[72] Soliciting their sympathy for his situation, he wrote to his far-off friends and colleagues that, if anyone wants 'an account (*aḥwāl*) of these parts, tell [him] that the place of all [of them] in the noble shrines (*amākin-i musharrafah*) is very, very empty'.[73]

ʿInāyat Allāh's lament appears not to have been without cause. For several months, he had been very ill in Basra, which had left him 'bed-ridden' (*ṣāḥib-i firāsh*) and unable to work.[74] Pouring misfortune upon misfortune, he also had to contend with the continuing warfare, arbitrary impositions from on high, and an unsettled province. The late siege of Basra had only recently been lifted;[75] Iran's new would-be padshah (following the death of Nādir Shāh) was refusing to honour the debt owed to the 'people' by his predecessor;[76] the fresh loans exacted from the same people had produced a general scarcity of specie in the area;[77] and, making an already bad situation even worse, 'the Arabs are in conflict with each

[71] BL/Lansdowne/1046, doc. 24. [72] BL/Lansdowne/1046, doc. 26.
[73] BL/Lansdowne/1046, doc. 29. [74] BL/Lansdowne/1046, docs. 6, 14, 17.
[75] BL/Lansdowne/1046, doc. 6, 17. [76] BL/Lansdowne/1046, doc. 14.
[77] A contemporary French resident of Isfahan noted that so much of the money previously in private hands had been confiscated by the new ruler that no one in his realm was willing or able to lend money. NA/HCA/30/682 (1 December 1747).

other and there is a lot of insecurity'.[78] To a correspondent familiar with the place in happier times, he wrote, 'At present, you will not recognise this country.'[79] Still, it was not all gloom and doom. ʿInāyat Allāh had rejoiced when he learnt of Nādir Shāh's death. He held on to the hope that, now the 'accursed one (*gūr bih gūr*) has gone to hell',[80] he could look forward to a future in which 'the affairs of everyone progress well'.[81]

These developments on the personal, local and geopolitical levels had, in ʿInāyat Allāh's approach to the world, ramifications for conduct in everyday life. One of the ways in which 'the oppression and harm' of Nādir Shāh's reign had made dealings in the arena more challenging was extended journey times. It was better, for example, to travel to Najaf via the longer, but safer, route that passed through Karbala.[82] As for the specific reasons that ʿInāyat Allāh gave for his failure to sell, he highlighted his illness, the Ottoman–Iranian conflict, the siege of Basra and the disturbed state of the country. Very few were thus willing or even able to buy at the prices that ʿAbd al-Karīm had specified in his original instructions, and no one in Basra had been prepared to take responsibility for their sale when ʿInāyat Allāh was unwell or away.[83] In his letters, then, ʿInāyat Allāh describes a complex and interconnected reality in which many factors were in play. In trying to convey the what, the how and the why of a single venture, he ranged back and forth across the boundaries of the political, social, economic, private and public spheres familiar to us today. This is because ʿInāyat Allāh did not subscribe to these spheres and the boundaries between them. His understanding was different to ours. His was symptomatic of a more general, and widely dispersed, behavioural tendency towards the world, to which I return in Chapter 5.

The focus up to this point has been on the cognitive patterns framing the notional transaction and the context deemed proper to it. One might say that these concerned the transaction's external aspects. The articulation of its internal nature, however, required a different – though complementary – set of concepts and images. And these primarily operated at the scale of the individual transaction. Two modes of articulation dominated here: specification in stable, objective terms, and specification in terms of an often monetised exchange value. To keep the analysis of these two modes manageable, the discussion below is restricted to transactions in physical items.[84]

[78] BL/Lansdowne/1046, doc. 26. [79] Ibid. [80] BL/Lansdowne/1046, doc. 14.
[81] BL/Lansdowne/1046, doc. 29. [82] Ibid.
[83] BL/Lansdowne/1046, docs. 6, 14, 17, 26, 29.
[84] This discussion is obviously relevant to accounting, recordkeeping, documentation and, more generally, the calculus underpinning transactions. I defer explicit treatment of these issues to chapters 4 and 7 on the relational order and on everyday practices.

In the first mode, goods were commonly described on two distinct levels, each characterised by a particular lexicon.[85] The more general level was populated by words such as *māl, davlat, māyah.* Agnostic in relation to the object's type, number or size, these words could refer equally to consumables or non-consumables. Their role was to signal the presence of physical, movable items that could be bought and sold. Used alongside them were words such as *jins* and *matā'* that were normally reserved for consumables, thus excluding items like precious metals and gems. In other respects, however, they were identical in meaning and usage. The details of the goods in question were given at the more specific level of description. Here, they were defined by their conventional name, and by the type and number of packages – the documents mention *bastah, ṭāqa, fard, buqja, kīsah, ṣurrah* – in which the goods were transported and stored. The sources offer little or no explicit information about the raw materiality of the goods per se, about, say, their quality, weight or physical dimensions. Such information must have been communicated by proxy through their conventional names. Similarly, the fact that the weight of the packaging was seldom given suggests each type of package (perhaps uniquely associated with particular goods) had fixed dimensions. In contrast, precious non-consumables, especially gold, silver and gems, usually had their weights noted. Their accompanying name relayed information about their composition and quality. And if the non-consumable item was coined metal, the number of coins was frequently stated, in addition to their conventional name and total weight.

In the second mode, the transacted item's value was established.[86] This could be done in terms of money units that had a physical presence and were locally accepted as a valid currency. It could also be done in terms of 'imaginary' money units, in tomans or sikka rupees, for example, which were widely used for accounting purposes. An alternative was to specify the value by weight of a commodity that doubled as a standard measure. This commodity was invariably a precious metal of known and constant purity and composition, to which labels such as 'Indian gold'[87] or 'Nadiri gold'[88] were applied. The weight could then be converted using tables of exchange and basic arithmetic into a local currency or into one of the more popular accounting units.

The foregoing, somewhat abstract, analysis may be rendered more tangible by considering the sum remitted from Basra by 'Ināyat Allāh,

[85] Cf. the concept, enumeration, packaging and storage of goods discussed in Goitein, *A Mediterranean Society*, I, 210–11, 332–9.
[86] Cf. the discussion of the nature of money in ibid., I, 229–40.
[87] BL/Lansdowne/1046, doc. 49. [88] BL/Lansdowne/1046, doc. 26.

with whose predicament we have just been acquainted.[89] As part of the agreement that settled his outstanding accounts with his principal in Bengal, he took 128 ashrafi coins from his principal's *māl* (minus charges and other expenses). He placed them in a small cloth bag (see Figure 1), variously termed a *kīsah* or *ṣurrah*.[90] The bag's fabric was woven from rough, thick yarn and, when full and sealed, it had the shape of an elongated cylinder, about eight inches in length and two inches in girth.[91] With the silver coins inside and bearing 'Ināyat Allāh's seal, it was handed in early 1748 to a courier in Basra for delivery in Bengal. Accompanying the bag were letters that contained further details. They described the money – the *vajh* – that was being remitted in several different ways. The value of the 128 ashrafis was stated in terms of a local currency (Basra *nirkh*), a standardised precious metal ('white gold' of Basra *ṣarf*) and general accounting units (tomans and dinars).[92] For added precision, 'Ināyat Allāh also noted the weight of the coins in Shirazi *mithqāl*s.[93]

As this example suggests, there was widespread, probably universal, familiarity with the notion of money in the arena (at least as a medium of exchange and as a unit of account). At the same time, the sources contain no single word or phrase that is solely and unambiguously a preserve of 'money' as an abstract concept.[94] Instead, money was expressed using language that was far from unique to it and which stressed one or more of its salient attributes. When referred to as *māl, naqd, zar* and *māyah*, the main attributes in play were its materiality and its fungibility, albeit as a special kind of commodity from which money was frequently coined. Terms such as *mablagh, qīmat, miqdār, vajh* and *thaman*, in contrast, evoked money's peculiar quality of possessing a general value that was both quantifiable and desirable, especially for receiving and making payments. And then, most explicitly and narrowly of all, money was denoted

[89] The logistics surrounding the remittance of this sum also provide telling insights into the techniques employed to ensure that a valuable package would actually reach the hands of its intended recipient, and into the nature and role of formal documentation and record-keeping. I draw on these insights in chapters 5 and 7 on the communications order and on everyday practices.

[90] BL/Lansdowne/1046, docs. 14, 17, 45. [91] NA/HCA/32/1833, doc. 27.

[92] BL/Lansdowne/1046, docs. 14, 17, 45. [93] BL/Lansdowne/1046, doc. 14.

[94] The absence offers indirect support for approaching monetary history in this period, not in terms of an abstract concept 'money', but in terms of disaggregated monies, or monetised substances. In this approach, the starting assumption is that each of the monies, crafted from, say, gold, silver, copper or cowrie shells, is associated with a distinctive value system. For the argument in favour of this approach, see Dennis O. Flynn and Arturo Giráldez. 'Introduction: monetary substances in global perspective', in Dennis O. Flynn and Arturo Giráldez (eds.), *Metals and Monies in an Emerging Global Economy* (Aldershot, 1997), xv–xl.

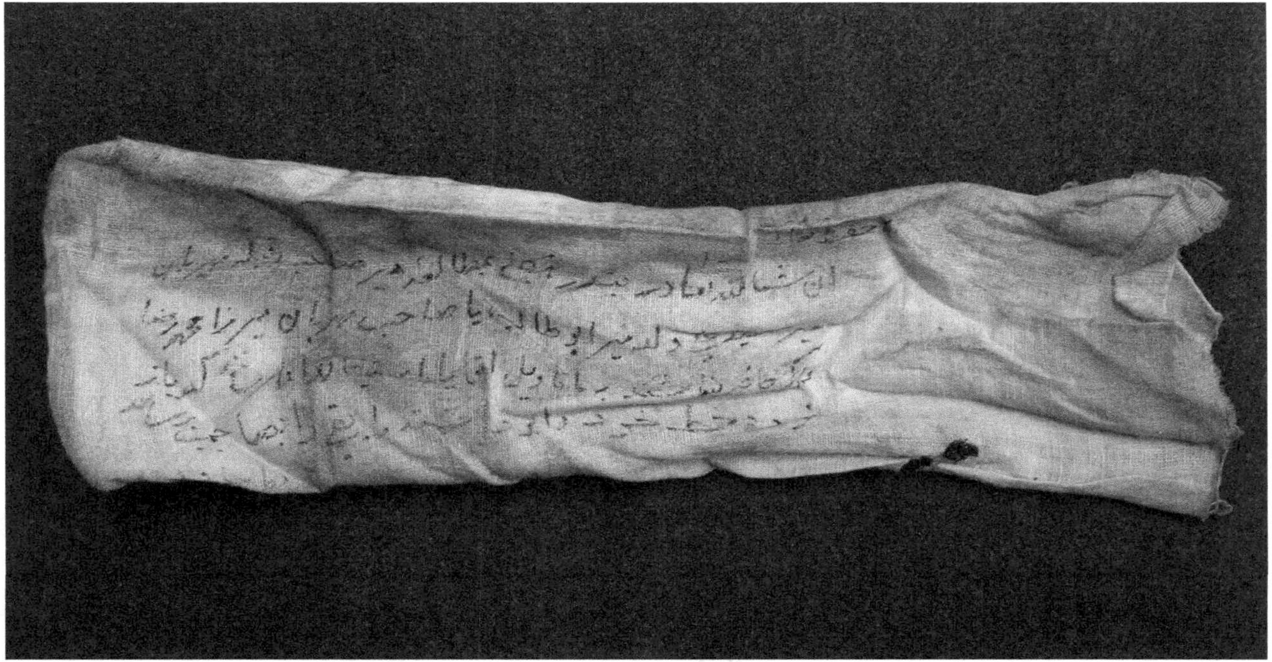

Figure 1. Cloth bag for precious coins.
Source: NA/HCA/32/1833.

by the names of generally known types of coins and currencies, such as dirham, para, kuruş, Arcot rupee and Tabrizi toman. The meaning in this usage might be restricted to that given type of coin or currency, or could be intended as a broader expression of monetary value.

Within the arena, money usually cropped up when discussing matters to do with livelihood. But money was not confined to them; the idea also seems to have had a meaningful presence in other spheres of everyday life. The following two examples gesture towards intriguing – if elusive – facets of this presence. Both are found in letters written in the late 1740s and addressed to a Shukr Allāh, at the time based in India. Among other news, the letters informed him about his mother back home in southern Iraq. In one, an uncle told him about her recent difficulties. But when she sought help from her birth family, nobody was willing to give her anything, not even 'a single *miṣrīya*'.[95] The *miṣrīya*, literally a coin of paltry denomination, was invoked in order to highlight the perceived failure to fulfil a basic duty of consanguine kindred towards another, at least within their intimate community at home. In another letter to Shukr Allāh, this time from his brother-in-law, he was told that if his mother 'sees a single para from [you] or from the hand of your most honourable father, it is known by me that it becomes for her by means of this a consolation which is better than if a thousand kuruş came to her from another source (*bāb*)'.[96] We see in these words a clear analogy between, on the one hand, her sentiments for the menfolk in her nuclear family compared with her sentiments for her more distant kindred, and, on the other hand, the difference in value between 'a single para', a coin of modest worth, and 'a thousand kuruş', a considerable sum of money.

If nothing else, these two examples show that the most intimate features of relationships within a family and between kindred could be interpreted through a money prism, being marshalled, say, to buttress condemnation of a perceived failing or to throw into sharp relief deeply held sentiments and expectations. At a minimum, these examples demonstrate that money was a source of images and concepts available to the arena's people to help them come to terms with their broader surroundings, and these extended far beyond livelihoods and into the sphere of familial and intimate relationships. Of course, this raises more questions than it answers: what was the nature of the value imputed to money? Where was money situated within the larger system of values? How did the various functions of money in this larger system relate to one another? Fascinating and important as these questions are, with the state of research being what it is, credible answers are still some way off. Nevertheless, I hope that such

[95] BL/Lansdowne/1046, doc. 67. [96] BL/Lansdowne/1046, doc. 71.

examples and the questions which they elicit show research on the subject is possible and warrants serious investigation.

The cognitive patterns vested in mundane transactions and measurements examined in this section reveal that the arena's participants tended to avoid abstract formulations, such as that the 'market' and 'money', preferring in their place terminology characterised by rootedness and specificity. We see this most clearly in the quantitative measurements – of size, weight and value – that formed the substantive core of individual transactions. Alongside this, we see a tendency among the arena's people towards a broad and heavily qualitative outlook on their lives and surroundings. As Chapter 5 shows, this tendency was related to the major constraints imposed on everyday life by large distances and long silences, and the uncertainties which stemmed from them. All this is reflected in the kinds of information typically relayed in their correspondence. A significant element of that information concerned the exercise of sovereignty and power within their polities. It is to this we now turn.

Sovereignty and power

Many of the transactions and encounters which characterised the arena of circulation and exchange took place in well-defined localities. In cases of settlements, both inland and on the coast, the arena's people had by necessity to contend with entities wielding sovereign power over their ambient polity. This section focuses on how the region's inhabitants represented and interpreted that authority.

In the middle of the eighteenth century, there existed claims to, and assertions of, sovereign power in every settled and cultivated part of Islamicate Eurasia. That is probably an uncontroversial statement. However, those engaged in circulation and exchange displayed a curious lack of interest in sovereign power, be it in their immediate surroundings or farther afield. This is not to say that the world of rulers, officials and administrators is absent in their correspondence. Rather, the world of these conspicuous elites tended to be approached through a narrow and highly selective filter. In the context of the eighteenth century especially, such a stance is noteworthy – and even surprising.

As described in the introduction, the scholarly literature views the region in this century as marked by political upheavals and military conflicts. These upheavals and conflicts were happening on multiple scales and produced major transformations in the fabric of its polities within the span of a lifetime. The situation in the mid-eighteenth century seems to have been particularly acute. In Iraq, for example, there were fresh, destabilising waves of raids and migration from the Najd following the rise of the Wahhābīs in the 1740s,[97] while relations between the Ottomans and Iranians remained mired in a state of war.[98] The assassination of Iran's ruler, Nādir Shāh, in 1747 and the death the same year of Iraq's effective ruler, the Ottoman governor Aḥmad Pasha, only added to the prevailing uncertainties.[99] In the meantime, though the situation in Bengal was on the whole stable under ʿAlī Vardi Khān (r. 1740–56), several destructive campaigns were waged against his regime by Maratha armies from central India.[100] The arena's participants had by any contemporary measure an unusually comprehensive experience of India and the Islamic heartlands. They also had the capacity to observe and articulate this experience. So the curious manner in which they tended to conceptualise sovereign power in their correspondence is notable, and needs explaining.

There were three main ways in which, from the arena's perspective, sovereignty and power were conceptualised. One was to reduce them to the legitimate ruler, his personally delegated representatives, and their interrelationships. The members of this most exclusive of clubs were imagined as embodying the polity over which they had formal jurisdiction. This image was manifested verbally through the virtual absence of direct references to the regimes over which they presided. Instead, we see in the sources recurrent and widespread use of regnal titles, like *sulṭān, bāshā, imām, pādishāh, nawwāb* and *rājā*, or metonymic expressions of their formal authority, like *darbār, dargāh-i ʿarsh* and *sarāy*. As for the titles bestowed upon – or more often in the eighteenth century wrested by – their representatives, they varied greatly from polity to polity.

Take the case of the Arab territories of the eastern reaches of the Ottoman empire in the 1740s. The documents note the presence of a *ḥākim* ('governor'), *mutasallim* (provincial governor), *nāʾib* ('deputy', 'representative', 'viceroy') and *kāhiya* (chief officer of a district or

[97] Ḥusayn Khalaf al-Shaykh Khazʿal, *Tārīkh al-Jazīra al-ʿArabīya fī ʿaṣr al-Shaykh Muḥammad ʿAbd al-Wahhāb* (Beirut: Maṭbaʿa dār al-kutub, 1972); ʿAzīz al-ʿAẓma, *Muḥammad ibn ʿAbd al-Wahhāb* (Beirut: Riyād al-Rayyis lil-kutub wa-al-nashr, 2000).

[98] ʿAbd al-Raḥmān ibn ʿAbd Allāh al-Suwaydī, *Tārīkh ḥawādith Baghdād wa-al-Baṣra min 1186 ilā 1192 h./1772–1778 m.* (Baghdad: Wizārat al-thaqāfa wa-al-funūn, 1978); Tom Nieuwenhuis, *Politics and Society in Early Modern Iraq: Mamluk Pashas, Tribal Shaykhs and Local Rule between 1802 and 1831* (The Hague, 1982); Thabit A. J. Abdullah, *Merchants, Mamluks, and Murder: the Political Economy of Trade in Eighteenth-Century Basra* (Albany, NY, 2001).

[99] Michael Axworthy, *The Sword of Persia: Nader Shah, from Tribal Warrior to Conquering Despot* (London, 2006); Ernest S. Tucker, *Nadir Shah's Quest for Legitimacy in Post-Safavid Iran* (Gainesville, FL, 2006); Jos J. L. Gommans, *The Rise of the Indo-Afghan Empire, c. 1710–1780* (Leiden, 1995).

[100] Jadunath Sarkar, *Fall of the Mughal Empire*, vol. I: *1739–1754* (Calcutta, 1932).

province). Accounts of what happened to these officials following the death in 1747 of Iraq's governor, Aḥmad Pasha, convey the impression of formal sovereignty as vested in the very person of such individuals. In the midst of the confusion surrounding the succession, a Shīʿī living in Basra wrote to his son in Surat saying that the *ṣāḥib al-muhr* ('master of the seal') from Diyarbakır had been put in charge of Baghdad, and that Basra was now under the control of the *mutasallim* Muḥammad Pasha Īlchī.[101] Aḥmad Pasha's death was obviously unexpected. It had created a power vacuum. The letters indicate the haste with which the Porte sanctioned new high-level appointments so as to fill the vacuum, and maintain at least a modicum of imperial order and rule. Among the terms used by our observed to describe the men appointed is *muṣāḥib al-sulṭān* ('the companion of the sultan').[102] This harmonises with the idea of a select group of leading officials as vital for the functioning of government, the extent of their authority being in direct proportion to the strength of their personal ties to the Ottoman sultan in distant Istanbul. In this conception, formal sovereignty over the polity is conflated with the sultan and his ruling companions, and is deemed to have no viable existence independently of them.

A second way in which sovereign power was perceived was through territorially demarcated units. These units could be primarily for the purposes of extracting revenue and for bureaucratic control, as exemplified by the *parganah* and *jāgīr* in India[103] and the *amlāk-i mulkī* in Iran.[104] They could also refer more generally to settled areas over which a ruler exercised his fullest authority, such as *mulk* ('rule', 'sovereignty', 'possession'),[105] *maḥrūsa* ('protected')[106] and *sarkār*.[107] What they all have in common is that they represented only a portion of the larger entities over which the supreme rulers claimed jurisdiction. At the same time, nowhere in the language used by the arena's people do these larger entities exist in

101 He also noted that Salaymān Kāhīya was given Adana.

102 BL/Lansdowne/1046, docs. 73, 74.

103 BL/Lansdowne/1046, docs. 8, 50. For a detailed account of these units from the sovereign's perspective, see Irfan Habib, *The Agrarian System of Mughal India, 1556–1707* (3rd edn, London, 2012).

104 BL/Lansdowne/1046, doc. 7. The standard work on the history of land revenue administration in Iran is Ann K. S. Lambton, *Landlord and Peasant in Persia: a Sudy of Land Tenure and Land Revenue Administration* (rev. edn, London, 1969).

105 BL/Lansdowne/1046, docs. 3, 10, 39, 40, 60. In the documents, the word is written as ملك. There are two possible readings of this: *mulk* and *milk*. The latter has a more specialised meaning than *mulk*. It is a legal concept in Islamic law that refers to ownership in the sense of 'the right to the complete and exclusive disposal of a thing', and is to be distinguished from 'possession' (*yad* or *mulk*). Joseph Schacht, *Introduction to Islamic Law* (Oxford, 1964), 136–9. Of course, both meanings, which overlap considerably, might have been intended in the documents.

106 BL/Lansdowne/1046, docs. 12, 67, 68, 82, 83.

107 NA/HCA/32/1833; BL/Lansdowne/1046, doc. 30.

abstraction, which, in today's parlance, we might call 'states' or 'empires'. If such entities did in fact exist as meaningful, integrated and self-perpetuating phenomena, then the closest that contemporaries came to recognising them was, as noted above, in terms of their constitutive units.

Territoriality per se is less prominent in the third way in which legitimate temporal authority was articulated. This was done by means of terms which may be described as imperial – *rūm*[108] – or folkloric – *'ajam*,[109] *angria*,[110] *'arab*[111] – or some combination of the two – *Īrān*.[112] These terms functioned as synecdoches: while by themselves they suggested large, ill-defined entities, contemporaries knew very well that the whole actually referred to that part of it invested with agency. The location of this agency, however, could differ greatly; it could be found in a people, a tribal confederacy or a dynastic legacy, each with its own distinct set of historical and cultural associations.

As should be clear by now, the sphere of conspicuous sovereignty and power could be, and often was, expressed in positive senses. But no less interesting are the lacunae with regard to this sphere. The most significant of these lacunae can be viewed as counterparts of the three modes of conceptualisation described above. Thus, the documents do not contain even the most cursory discussion of the political or bureaucratic institutions responsible for governance, and, by extension, of any changes or trends in them. Nor do we see any accounts of the quotidian machinations of the metropolitan ruling elites. While the arena's people discuss political and military events, there is no suggestion of a desire, let alone attempt, to place them in a broader context, or to interpret them for their possible ramifications for their own future prospects. All this is reflected in the vernacular lexicon's immediacy and functional tilt. So we find explicit references to territorial units whose rationale was to raise money for the sovereign and his officials, or to help maintain order around major settlements, especially the principal seats of government. What we do not find in the documents is language that might denote abstract sovereignty or power in this world, in the form of, say, a state or empire. Similarly, there is no obvious appreciation of the sphere of conspicuous sovereignty and power having a past, or indication that those who were active in the arena possessed a memory of this past. There is also no discussion of loyalty or allegiance to a given ruler, or, more generally, of subjecthood. If

108 BL/Lansdowne/1046, doc. 14; *rūm* refers to Anatolia and, by extension, to the Ottomans.
109 BL/Lansdowne/1046, doc. 14; *'ajam* refers to the Persians.
110 BL/Lansdowne/1046, docs. 2, 4, 5, 11, 13.
111 BL/Lansdowne/1046, 26.
112 BL/Lansdowne/1046, docs. 9, 14.

this quality was thought meaningful, one might expect it to be reflected in attitudes to identity and belonging. But, as noted earlier in this chapter, the sources are bereft of markers of sovereign identity that were indigenous to the region. Nobody, for example, was described as a Mughal or an Ottoman. In light of these lacunae, it is hardly surprising that the arena's people expressed no secular wish to intervene actively, systematically and purposively in the affairs of rulers and their officials.

The foregoing account of what is *not* expressed in the documents, coupled with the cognitive patterns marshalled for the various spheres of life embraced within the arena, helps us make better sense of what *was* expressed in them. One of the main findings of the earlier analysis of identity and belonging is that the arena's people chose to conceptualise those they encountered on a daily basis in terms of markers of personal identity and in terms of collectives. This dovetails with the practice highlighted in the present section of collapsing sovereign power into an elite group of individuals. However, the interests of those responsible for circulation and exchange did not extend to the everyday affairs of such conspicuous individuals. This was because the arena's people envisaged them as existing apart from the realities of their own lives.[113] If my supposition is correct, then ethnicity would have served to reinforce that orientation. We have already seen that ethnicity was a key marker of identity and a common attribute of collectives. It is thus quite understandable that the realm of sovereign power too would often be interpreted along such lines. As for the territorial units invoked by the arena's people, these can be rationalised from a pragmatic standpoint. The examination in the previous section of information deemed relevant to transactions showed that money and security were two fundamental concerns within the arena. Consequently, there was a keen awareness of entities crafted or delineated by governments for physical control and for taxation. Turning finally to imperial designations, these cleaved to the region's inherited mythologies, forming part and parcel of the repertoire of figures and values from which its inhabitants fashioned stories of themselves as indigenes. Thus to draw on this repertoire in order to describe the sphere of those directing affairs of state is only to be expected. Indeed, as the following section argues, the use of this repertoire was not just limited to sovereignty and power, but also extended to conceptions of place.

[113] I do not mean by this that conspicuous elites were irrelevant for life within the arena. On the contrary, conspicuous elites and the arena's participants were integral to the fabric of the region's polities as a result of their mutual need for one another. This mutual need, however, was inflected through the prevailing commitment to corporatism, hegemony and precedence, which institutionalised the distinction between the arena and the realm of sovereign power, and kept them apart. This facet of India and the Islamic heartlands is examined in Chapter 6 on the political order.

In view of all this, can we say anything about the types of situations which would reliably prompt the arena's people to remark upon the world of rulers, their officials and administrators? I limit myself to the two types especially prominent in the documents. One of them had no direct or immediate bearing on the interests of those active in the arena. The most common situations of this type were sudden transitions or crises. Correspondents generally noted the deaths of rulers[114] and the accession of new ones,[115] warfare between sovereign powers,[116] and the departure and arrival of high-ranking individuals.[117] The mere fact that such events were mentioned – even if briefly, from a distance and in a stylised manner – reveals awareness of some kind of deep relationship between the arena of the conspicuous elites and that of circulation and exchange.

In the other type of situations, the presence of the sphere of conspicuous sovereignty and power in their everyday affairs was so invasive that it simply could not be ignored. Some of these situations, which are considered at length in Chapter 6, were systemic and predictable. This was the case for, say, the assessment and payment of customs duties on the import or export of goods; the use of facilities, like warehouses and berths for ships, over which the local government exerted a monopoly;[118] the appointment of an official translator or broker within the polity;[119] travel over routes that the ruling elites were able to block unless formal authorisation (*dastūr*) was sought, given and purchased, often in the form of a *dastak* or passport.[120] Knowledge about such rent-seeking impositions was widely dispersed and invariably taken into account when planning for transactions vested in circulation and exchange.

However, other situations of this latter type could not be so easily foreseen. They were of grave concern if security of person and property was at issue. To state the obvious, such risks were greatest during unsettled times, like those which prevailed in Iran in the years leading up to Nādir Shāh's assassination, when plundering seems to have been rife, causing fear, migration, hunger and death.[121] Closely related to the matter of security was sovereign debt and the taxation policies of the ruler. Now it is possible that changes decreed by fiat could lessen the financial burdens on residents of the polity, as occurred earlier in Nādir Shāh's reign following an unexpectedly remunerative military campaign in northern India.[122] But this was rare. It is more usual to find in

[114] BL/Lansdowne/1046, docs. 14, 17, 26, 29, 73, 74.
[115] BL/Lansdowne/1046, docs. 73, 74; MssOcc/NAF/9011: 36–7.
[116] BL/Lansdowne/1046, docs. 6, 14, 17, 26.
[117] BL/Lansdowne/1046, docs. 73, 74; MssOcc/NAF/9011: 36–7.
[118] BL/Lansdowne/1046, doc. 2. [119] BL/Lansdowne/1046, docs. 67, 70, 71.
[120] ANOM/CdI/B/49; BL/Lansdowne/1046, docs. 17, 43.
[121] BL/Lansdowne/1046, docs. 3, 7, 9, 28.
[122] NA/HCA/30/682 (undated); BL/Lansdowne/1046, doc. 32.

the documents remarks on what contemporaries deemed arbitrary exactions. This was the view expressed by Yaʿqūb ʿAbd al-Karīm in 1747, when he wrote to a kinsman in Calcutta, 'If you ask about the Christians of Baghdad, none of them have anything in their possession because of the crimes (*al-jarāʾim*) of the governors (*ḥukkām*) towards the church.'[123]

Whatever the particulars of the situation prompting them, these accounts are all momentary, anecdotal and interrupted in nature; they contain little sense of a sustained, conscious and ongoing engagement with those who wielded sovereign power in the settlements where their authors and recipients made their homes and their livelihoods. Rather, their interaction with the ruling elites appears to have been fleeting, characterised by pragmatism and a readiness to take advantage of changing circumstances. Moreover, what interaction there was tended to be oriented towards the locus of centralised authority. One of the first acts in 1747 of the newly proclaimed padshah in Iran was to seize the property of his assassinated predecessor, Nādir Shāh. Sensing an opportunity to recover the sum of one lakh rupees (Rs 100,000) owed to the 'people' (*mardum*) by Nādir Shāh, a contemporary noted that 'the Europeans (*farangān*) and all the Julfan merchants presented many petitions and put on a great deal of pressure' on him to honour that debt. But they also took precautions in the event the new ruler proved no less rapacious than Nādir Shāh. And so '[large] sums [of money] were spent in order that the padshah would desist [from taking] the assets of the people'.[124] When we place this alongside other documents which touch on conspicuous sovereignty and power, we find an image of a supreme but vulnerable individual residing in his fortress capital. The capital is surrounded by territory that is under his sway nearby, but over which his authority wanes with increasing distance, until a kind of no-man's-land is reached, separating formally adjacent polities.

Locality and space

Given the nature of their experiences, those active in the arena of circulation and exchange undoubtedly had a keen spatial appreciation of their surroundings at large. Though this does not equate to our notions of cartographic mapping, the evidence shows that a significant portion of them were aware of numerous places with a definable presence spread across great areas.[125] And this accumulated knowledge imbued the fabric of their lives.

[123] BL/Lansdowne/1046, doc. 76. [124] BL/Lansdowne/1046, doc. 14.

[125] This awareness, and thus indigenous mapping traditions, existed despite the absence of words in the region's principal languages that unequivocably and uniquely meant 'map'. On these premodern Indian and Islamic mapping traditions, see Susan Gole, *Indian Maps and Plans: From Earliest Times to the Advent of European Surveys* (New Delhi, 1989);

Hannā b. ʿAbd al-Dāʾim, with whom this chapter begins, is a case in point. That knowledge had been his constant guide in an unfinished quest which was very close to his heart. 'For three years now,' he wrote in 1747 to his son from his home in southern Iraq:

> We have not seen from you a letter . . . And in these three years, I have written nearly a hundred letters. And some of them I have sent to Basra, and some of them to Egypt (*Miṣr*) . . . Some I wrote to the heights of the Malabar and some I wrote to Cochin. I am at a loss in the matter of where to write, O my son, because I don't know where you are. If I could, by the power of *allāh*, I would send you the letters with the birds.[126]

This lament reveals the intensity of feelings that fathers could have for their sons, a topic examined in Chapter 3 on the familial order. What is more pertinent here is the visceral sense it gives us of the vast expanse over which it was *unremarkable* for individuals such as Hannā b. ʿAbd al-Dāʾim to travel and maintain ties, and over which their mind's eye could sweep with practised ease. Evidently, this world of theirs encompassed territories as far apart as India, Egypt and Iraq. (See Map 3.)

It is reasonably well established that individuals engaged in circulation and exchange were able to conceive of – and operate on – grand scales, and that they were driven to do so for a multiplicity of reasons. What is much less understood are the limits beyond which they seldom ventured in mind or in person. On collating the places mentioned in the documents examined for this book, two features stand out. Several dozen places scattered over huge distances – which I term 'settlements' and 'countries' – are mentioned by name, some of them frequently. At the same time, the outer boundaries of this domain never extend beyond continental Eurasia and the Mediterranean basin to include parts of the world that were incommensurate with *Islamicate* polities.[127] So not a single place – be it a region, province, district, city, port, town, village or oasis – is referenced in, say, sub-Saharan Africa, Christian Europe, Southeast Asia or East Asia.[128] In other words, the polities within which these

John B. Harley and David Woodward (eds.), *The History of Cartography,* vol. II, bk 1: *Cartography in the Traditional Islamic and South Asian Societies* (Chicago, 1992).

126 BL/Lansdowne/1046, doc. 68.

127 On the meaning of 'Islamicate' and its genealogy, see the Introduction.

128 This fact suggests that exceedingly few of those indigenous to the region ever ventured beyond its frontiers by choice. Suraiya Faroqhi makes the same observation in her *The Ottoman Empire and the World around It* (London, 2004), 129. For the rare exceptions to this rule, see Cemal Kafadar, 'A death in Venice (1575): Anatolian Muslim merchants trading in the Serenissima', *Journal of Turkish Studies* 10 (1986), 191–218; Gilles Veinstein, 'Marchands ottomans en Pologne-Lituanie et en Moscovie sous le règne de Soliman de Magnifique', *Cahiers du monde russe* 35:4 (1994), 713–38; Molly Greene, *Christians and Muslims in the Early Modern Mediterranean* (Princeton, NJ, 2000); Gad G. Gilbar, 'Muslim *tujjār* of the Middle East and their commercial networks in the long nineteenth century', *Studia Islamica* 100/101 (2005), 183–202.

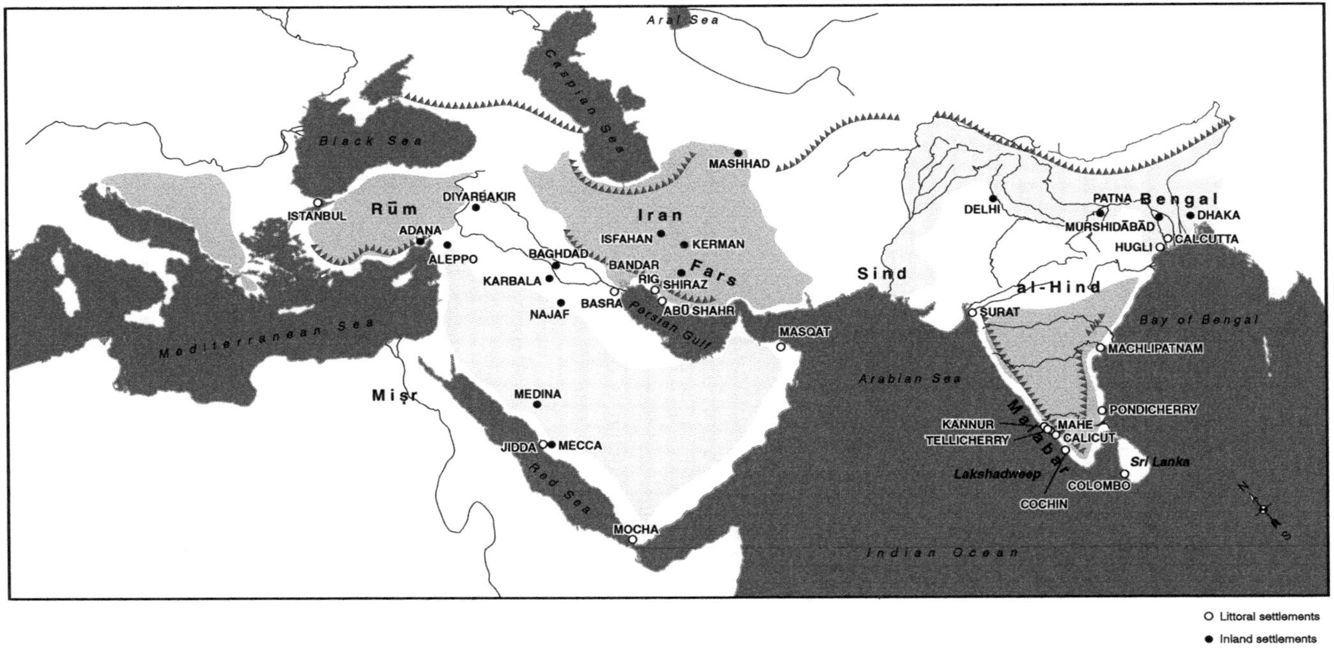

Map 3. Islamicate Eurasia, *c.* 1750.

individuals lived and travelled were always profoundly familiar to them. This reality underpins the claim that the personal, collective and inherited experiences of the physical environment of such individuals were in practice confined to what was essentially an 'Islamicate Eurasia'.[129]

Within this region, then, how did its inhabitants conceive of settlements? This is nicely illustrated in a series of letters written by Sayyid Muṣṭafā. He was a Shīʿī en route to Basra who found himself stranded in Cochin in 1748 on an unscheduled stop. To reassure his correspondents at home in Bengal, who seemingly knew little if anything about Cochin, several facts were invoked to help them picture his current predicament. The settlement was described using several terms (*maqām, jā, makān*)[130] that indicate a definable 'place'. Its name was often prefaced with the word for 'port' (*bandar*).[131] Sayyid Muṣṭafā further noted that it was a 'Dutch possession'[132] and found 'half-way to Basra'.[133] Taken together, this suggests that places such as Cochin were not thought of in terms of their longitude and latitude, or in some other technical manner which fixed their absolute location. Rather, they were specified in terms of their surrounding area, in this case the Malabar region; the basic features of their ambient polity, here a port under Dutch control; and their position relative to other places with which there was greater familiarity, Cochin as situated between Bengal and Basra.

As seen in Table 5, Cochin is one of more than a dozen settlements explicitly identified in the documents that adjoined or had easy access to the high seas. Alongside them were mentioned a similar number of inland settlements. In some cases, such as Aleppo,[134] Diyarbakır[135] and ʿAẓīmābād (Patna),[136] the normal practice was to use the basic name on its own. But that was the exception; for most settlements, their toponyms were combined with an attribute that captured something meaningful about the place. Basra, for example, was occasionally preceded by the word 'port' (*bandar*) or 'town' (*madīna*), while Cochin tended to be accompanied by *bandar*.[137]

129 Similar points are made by Goitein in relation to the Mediterranean in his *A Mediterranean Society*, I, 42–3, 211.
130 BL/Lansdowne/1046, docs. 40, 56, 60.
131 BL/Lansdowne/1046, docs. 37, 38, 39, 49, 50, 54, 58.
132 BL/Lansdowne/1046, docs. 39, 40, 60. The original phrase used in the document that I have translated as 'Dutch possession' is ملک ولنديز. On the possible readings of ملک, particularly on the relationship between *mulk* and *milk*, see fn. 105 above.
133 BL/Lansdowne/1046, docs. 39, 40, 49, 50, 58.
134 BL/Lansdowne/1046, docs. 65, 66, 70, 71, 78.
135 BL/Lansdowne/1046, doc. 74.
136 BL/Lansdowne/1046, docs. 30, 33.
137 In the documents examined, Basra is mentioned 110 times. The frequency distribution of attributes used with the toponym, which on occasion is qualified by more than one simultaneously, is: no attribute, 90; *bandar* ('port'), 13; *madīna* ('town'), 4; *balda*

Table 5. *Littoral and inland settlements.*

Littoral	Inland
Abū Shahr (Bushehr)	Adana
Basra	ʿAẓīmābād (Patna)
Colombo	Baghdad
Hugli (Hooghly)	Diyarbakır
Istanbul	Ḥalab (Aleppo)
Jidda (Jeddah)	Isfahan
Kannur (Cannanore)	Jahāngīrnagar (Dhaka)
Kochi (Cochin)	Karbala
Kolkata (Calcutta)	Kerman
Kozhikode (Calicut)	Mashhad
Machlipatnam (Machlibandar)	Mecca
Mahe (Mahé)	Medina
al-Mukhā (Mocha)	Murshidābād
Puducherry (Pondicherry)	Najaf
Rīg (Bandar Rig)	Shāhjahānābād (Delhi)
Surat	Shiraz
Thalassery (Tellicherry)	

Source: BL/Lansdowne/1046.

More rarely, the settlement's name was denoted not by its unique toponym but by qualifying a larger entity, which was often the country in which it lay. So *bandar-i Kālī Saylān* ('the port of Sri Lanka')[138] was used in reference to Colombo, and major settlements in India were not uncommonly termed as *baldat Bangālah* ('the town of Bengal')[139] or *maḥrūsat al-Hind* ('the guarded city of India').[140]

Such attributes and qualifications were there not merely for adornment, or because of the dictates of prevailing etiquette or protocol; they also served useful purposes. They could highlight salient features of the settlement's heritage or history, like Baghdad *Dār al-salām* ('the House of Peace'),[141] Basra *mubārak* ('blessed'),[142] Shiraz *Dār al-ʿilm* ('the House of the Knowledge'),[143] Isfahan *Dār al-sulṭana* ('the House of the

('town'), 1; *mubārak* ('blessed'), 1; *maḥrūsa* ('protected'), 1. Cochin is mentioned 25 times, and the frequency distribution of attributes used is: no attribute, 7; *bandar*, 16; *maḥrūsa*, 1; *makān* ('place'), 1.

138 BL/Lansdowne/1046, doc. 8.

139 BL/Lansdowne/1046, doc. 75; NA/HCA/32/1833/9.

140 BL/Lansdowne/1046, docs. 67, 68. While the actual places referred to by such names might not be known to us today, identifying them would have posed no problems for contemporaries who would have been fully aware of the relevant context.

141 BL/Lansdowne/1046, doc. 63. 142 BL/Lansdowne/1046, doc. 2.

143 BL/Lansdowne/1046, doc. 14.

Table 6. *Continental and maritime countries.*

Continental	Maritime
Bengal	Lakshadweep
Fars	Sri Lanka
al-Hind, Hindustān (India)	Suvali
Iran	
Malabar	
Miṣr (lower Egypt)	
Rūm (Anatolia)	
Sind	

Source: BL/Lansdowne/1046.

Sultanate'),[144] Hugli *mubārak*[145] and Hugli *maftūḥ* ('open' or 'conquered').[146] Others gestured towards its spiritual importance. Shīʿīs, for example, invariably referred to their two greatest shrine cities in Iraq as *Najaf-i ashraf* ('Noble Najaf') and *Karbalāʾ-yi muʿallā* ('Exalted Karbala'); along with other Muslims, they referred to their holiest sites in the Ḥijāz as *Makka al-mukarrama* ('Revered Mecca') and *al-Madīna al-munawwara* ('Luminous Medina'). In such instances, the epithets were so closely associated with the place that they were essentially fused into the name. And then there were terms which flagged aspects of the settlement's major functions, or its administrative or political status. The most commonplace found in the documents are *bandar, maḥrūsa, balda, madīna* and *shahr* ('town' or 'city').

These littoral and inland settlements are to be contrasted with a group of larger entities that I call 'countries' for convenience.[147] They are listed in Table 6. As with settlements, two general types of countries may be discerned in the documents: those located on a continental landmass and those taking the form of an island or island cluster. Unlike settlements, the basic toponym normally sufficed on its own, whether referring to a significant portion of Iran or the Indian subcontinent, like Fars or Bengal, or to a big island, like Sri Lanka. While these names communicated a flavour of where the country lay and of its proportions, its boundaries or

[144] BL/Lansdowne/1046, docs. 7, 9, 15, 28.
[145] BL/Lansdowne/1046, doc. 43; NA/HCA/32/1833/41.
[146] BL/Lansdowne/1046, doc. 8; NA/HCA/32/1833/32.
[147] A justification for this is the presence of two words in the documents – *vilāya* and *bilād* – which may be translated as 'country' or 'this part of the world'. BL/Lansdowne/1046, docs. 3, 26, 28, 51, 65, 69.

frontiers were usually ill-defined and open to interpretation.[148] What is beyond doubt, however, is that these toponyms did *not* coincide with any contemporary state. Rather, they invoked one, or a combination, of the area's historical, cultural or topographical qualities.[149] And these were known, even if in a distorted or confused fashion, throughout the region, echoing a tradition that, in the Islamic world at least, goes back to 'human' and classical geographers of the ninth and tenth centuries.[150]

Whether speaking of countries or settlements, the documents reveal that relatively few descriptive attributes were in common use, and those that were bore no immediate relation to the current ruler exercising formal authority over the place. They point instead to its history or function or prestige. It would seem that, in keeping with the findings of earlier sections, the language deployed for specifying a place's location and character was determined chiefly by inherited, confessional or practical considerations, not submission to a sovereign entity. The mental map that this as a whole expresses is akin to a constellation of brightly shining and distinct ports, towns and cities embedded in a country, a kind of hazy nebula, in an otherwise dark background. In the minds of those who lived, worked and travelled within the region, these places were linked by a dense, criss-crossing network of land and sea routes, understood in relative, rather than absolute, terms.[151]

Such a map was essential for helping the arena's people to assimilate cognitively their experiences of India and the Islamic heartlands. Among its most noteworthy features was the tendency to shun or ignore territorial frontiers and boundaries of any kind. In our times, the most popular choices for demarcating such frontiers and boundaries are topographical features and political control. The region's literate, urban and mobile inhabitants undoubtedly had the experiential, conceptual and lexical wherewithal to imagine and verbalise basic attributes of their physical

[148] The partial exceptions to this were the outer bounds of islands and, more generally, of transitions between land and sea. These are sometimes noted explicitly. So a Shīʿī traveller mentioned that his ship on a recent voyage had reached the 'frontier' or 'outskirts' (*sarḥadd*) of Lakshadweep before being surrounded by Angria pirates (*rāhzan*). BL/Lansdowne/1046, doc. 11.

[149] For example, the fact that Lakshadweep embraces a cluster of islands in the Arabian Sea was occasionally hinted at by prefacing its name with the word *hār*, meaning 'string' or 'necklace' in Hindi and Persian. BL/Lansdowne/1046, doc. 13.

[150] On these genres, see M. J. L. Young, J. D. Latham and R. B. Serjeant (eds.), *Religion, Learning and Science in the ʿAbbasid Period* (Cambridge, 1990), 307–319 and the essays by Gerald R. Tibbets in Harley and Woodward (eds.), *The History of Cartography*.

[151] Thongchai Winichakul has attempted to recapture indigenous mental maps of premodern Thailand that are similar in kind to the one presented here. See his *Siam Mapped: a History of the Geo-Body of a Nation* (Honolulu, HI, 1994).

geography, such as the course of a river or the break between the foothills of a mountain range and the neighbouring flood-plain.[152] But their correspondence suggests that, with the partial exception of coastlines,[153] physical geography was not a primary filter through which they viewed their world. Similarly, the letters that they dispatched while on the move display no real awareness of passing between districts, crossing into a new province or traversing the marches of a kingdom. On this basis, we may hazard that most political markers of separation were fanciful abstractions conjured up by rulers and their courtly bureaucrats with little or no practical significance for those actually responsible for flows and transactions on regional scales.

[152] Understandings of physical geography in the region in premodern times are discussed in Michael D. Bonner, 'The naming of the frontier: ʿAwāṣim, thughūr, and the Arab geographers', *Bulletin of the School of Oriental and African Studies* 57:1 (1994), 17–24 and Ralph W. Brauer, *Boundaries and Frontiers in Medieval Muslim Geography* (Philadelphia, 1995). For a good, succinct treatment of Islamicate Eurasia's physical geography and its historical role, see André Wink, 'From the Mediterranean to the Indian Ocean: medieval history in geographic perspective', *Comparative Studies in Society and History* 44:3 (2002), 416–45.

[153] BL/Lansdowne/1046, docs. 8, 11, 70.

2 A cosmic order: the meaning and end of life

> Anyhow, what can one do since whatever is the wish of *khudā* the high, it happens thus. I am so completely bereft of fortune and impious that whatever I wanted did not happen. That which *khudā* wanted, it happened thus.[1]

Whether at home, in the temple or on board a ship, whether going about one's daily routines or reflecting upon eternity, life was imbued with certain realities. Contemporaries in the arena approached these realities as intrinsic and unalterable. The nephew who wrote the words above in Cochin in 1748 was no exception. These were the realities that motivated and guided an individual's mental, emotional and corporeal behaviour. It is they, together with the behavioural tendencies associated with them, that generated the arena's dominant values, habits and tastes. Their interest for us lies in the fact that the ontology expressed by them framed dealings vested in everyday circulation and exchange.[2] In this chapter and the next, two specific clusters, or 'orders', of these intertwined realities and behavioural tendencies are considered: in one – a cosmic order – my concern is with matters that tend to be the preserve of religion; in the other – a familial order – my concern is with relationships within the family household.

[1] BL/Lansdowne/1046, doc. 37.

[2] In arriving at this conception of ontology, I have found the following works useful: Donald E. Brown, *Human Universals* (New York, 1991); Rita Astuti, 'Are we all natural dualists? A cognitive developmental approach', *Journal of the Royal Anthropological Institute* 7:3 (2001), 429–47; Pascal Boyer, *Religion Explained: the Evolutionary Origins of Religious Thought* (New York, 2001); John Clammer, Sylvie Poirier and Eric Schwimmer, 'Introduction: the relevance of ontologies in anthropology – reflections on a new anthropological field', in John Clammer, Sylvie Poirier and Eric Schwimmer (eds.), *Figured Worlds: Ontological Obstacles in Intercultural Relations* (Toronto, 2004), 3–22; Philippe Descola, 'Beyond nature and culture', *Proceedings of the British Academy* 139 (2006), 137–55; Reinhart Koselleck, *Futures Past: On the Semantics of Historical Time*, trans. Keith Tribe (New York, 2004); Amiria Henare, Martin Holbraad and Sari Wastell, 'Introduction: thinking through things', in Amiria Henare, Martin Holbraad and Sari Wastell (eds.), *Thinking through Things: Theorising Artefacts Ethnographically* (London, 2007), 1–31.

It makes sense to discuss these two orders as a pair. This is because both were characterised by unquestioning acceptance of their perceived essences, arguably their signal attribute. Contemporaries may well have been aware of the realities at their core. Nevertheless, these realities were treated as part of how things are, have been and shall be.[3] Thus the attitude of the arena's people towards them was largely uncritical. Whatever questioning took place – and questioning there was – was pitched at other levels and oriented towards other ends. As a result, a major component of the cosmic and familial orders was situated within the arena's taken-for-granted foundations. This has a practical consequence. It means that the pertinent metaphysics is not immediately visible to us. But all is not lost; this metaphysics may still be reconstructed, albeit indirectly, through the patterns of behaviour with which it was entwined, and which it helped foster. That is what accounts for the attention paid here to these patterns.

The distinctive nature of the cosmic and familial orders as a pair is thrown into sharp relief by the cognitive patterns studied in the preceding chapter. There the focus was on the vernacular concepts and images dispersed throughout the arena and available to its participants. What should be noted is that these concepts and images were *not* embedded in specific individuals; they were conveyed instead through shared language, be it verbal or gestural. Furthermore, they were mainly invoked to access and make sense of the environment within which their daily affairs were situated. The cosmic and familial orders, in contrast, cannot be comprehended apart from individuals. Their realities ultimately inhered within identifiable individuals, and it was identifiable individuals who were their primary carriers and transmitters. This is not to suggest that their significance was confined to individuals in isolation; rather, their significance is to be found in the orientations towards certain patterns of acting, thinking and feeling that were *outwardly* directed. These behavioural tendencies ultimately enmeshed individuals with, and were consequential for, their environment. Hence, we are not talking about individuals per se in these two chapters; we are talking about individuals in active involvement with what existed beyond their persons.

The arena's prevailing orders are key to any understanding of the whys and the hows of participation in activities rooted in regional-scale circulation and exchange. While the historical scholarship has little to say about such matters, their importance cannot be overstated. Fortunately, the documents examined for this book open a window on to this aspect of the

[3] This is the key feature differentiating the cosmic and familial orders from the other three orders – the relational, the communications, the political – examined later in the book.

arena. Discussion of the familial order is deferred to the Chapter 3. In this chapter, I focus on the order most closely related to the religious traditions which characterised India and the Islamic heartlands in the eighteenth century. The realities that their adherents embraced – concerning this world and the next, concerning divinity, fate, death and the after-life – shaped their behaviour towards belief, piety, ritual, charity, livelihood and divine invocation. The task for this chapter is to study these realities and the patterns of behaviour associated with them.

The correspondence typically exchanged among the arena's people gives ample evidence that its authors and recipients took for granted a dimension which existed apart from them as individuals, and which was impervious to full comprehension by their physical senses. This dimension, which I shall call for convenience the 'cosmos', was, despite its material elusiveness, of manifest significance to them. The documents allow us to gain a purchase on it in two ways: through accounts of observable behaviour which expressed that cosmos and through accounts which were an expression of that cosmos in their own right.[4] (See Map 4.)

For complex, literate polities in premodern times, issues relating to the cosmos have usually been elaborated from the standpoint of a specific religious tradition[5] or through the comparative study of religions.[6] Though the subject of religion is clearly relevant to this chapter, it is not, however, at the centre of my enquiry. The subject is instead subsumed within a broader enquiry into the arena's cosmological ways of being. The main thrust here is chiefly towards vernacular understandings of the cosmos and mankind's relation to it, and how these intersected with daily life in the arena. To recover this facet of its ontology, I look not to theology or canonical texts but to ordinary personal correspondence.

The first attribute to note about the cosmos avowed by those involved in circulation and exchange was the host of entities that pervaded it. These entities, all personified to a large extent, were continuously evoked,

4 My method takes heart from Wilfred Cantwell Smith's *The Meaning and End of Religion: a New Approach to the Religious Traditions of Mankind* (New York, 1963), the influence of which is reflected in the subtitle of this chapter. For a useful critique, highlighting the possibilities and limitations of Cantwell Smith's method, see Talal Asad, 'Reading a modern classic: W. C. Smith's *The Meaning and End of Religion*', *History of Religions* 40:3 (2001), 205–22.

5 Among the classics written from this standpoint are Alessandro Bausani's *Persia Religiosa* (Milan, 1959) and Annemarie Schimmel's *Mystical Dimensions of Islam* (Chapel Hill, NC, 1975).

6 For an account of the state of the field, see Johann P. Arnason, S. N. Eisenstadt and Bjorn Wittrock (eds.), *Axial Civilizations and World History* (Leiden, 2005).

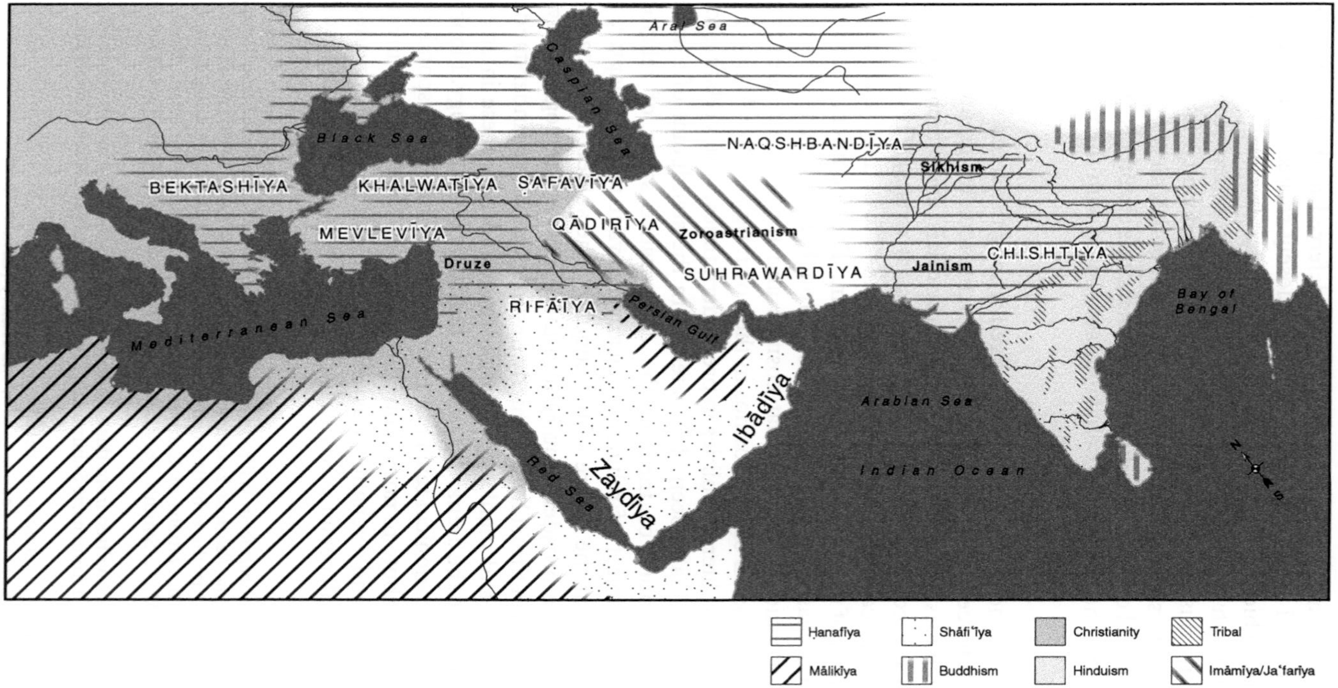

Map 4. The religious traditions of India and the Islamic heartlands.

imbuing everyday language within the arena. They possessed qualities which were not found in the mundane realms, nor among humans, qualities that were capable of transforming their present and future, and the worlds they inhabited. One entity among them stands out for being especially prominent, and for being uniquely privileged. This entity was universally embraced in the arena, transcending families, communities and religious traditions. In Arabic, *allāh* and *rabb* were the terms most commonly reserved for it; in Persian, they were *allāh*, *rabb*, *khudā* and *īzad*. These terms were in effect synonymous, and seem to have been treated as interchangeable within each language. That is why I shall use in their place the single word 'God'. Whenever this word is used, however, it should be borne in mind that the figure intended by it was not confined to any one of the arena's religious traditions. Rather, it was a characteristic of the arena as a whole.[7]

Generically male in gender,[8] God was frequently called upon, talked about and prayed to. This could be done through invoking him directly by name. Writing in Najaf in 1747, a Shīʿī known as Shāh Kawthar stated that 'everywhere I depend only on *khudā*. In the two worlds, in my solitude I have [just this] one companion.'[9] He was also invoked in ways that were less direct. Those familiar with the main Arabic-script languages of the time had available to them a rich trove of words and phrases associated with God. Drawing on this trove, the arena's people alluded to him either through his established qualities or through the modes by which he interacted with human beings and their affairs. Notwithstanding its formulaic character, this language gives us a sense of God's nature and capabilities within the cosmos. He was both friend and judge. He was all-knowing and all-powerful. He was the giver and taker of whatever he wished, at the time and manner of his choosing. He figured in the lives not just of those who embraced God; he was present in everyone's life within the arena and beyond, regardless of background or creed.

This was the God known by the author responsible for the words with which this chapter opens. It is certainly in keeping with his remark,

7 This shared characteristic was one of a set of shared fundamental categories and ordering principles – a metaphysics – which allows us to treat the arena as a unified, singular entity. It also allows us to range across religious traditions and ethnic communities, without needing to stop at the notional boundaries between them. Of course, collectives defined in those terms exhibited great plurality and this fact is of major historical significance. But their plurality and significance lie at levels other than the metaphysical. I deal with the issue of plurality in chapters 4 and 6 on the relational and political orders.

8 In the Arabic texts, when directly referred to in the third person, God was invariably in the singular and male in gender. In the texts in Persian, a language without gender, God was directly referred to in either the third person singular or plural. Until it is shown to the contrary, I shall assume that in Persian too God was gendered male.

9 BL/Lansdowne/1046, doc. 30.

'Whatever is the wish of *khudā* the high, it happens thus.'[10] That wish could be to alleviate hardship. Niʿmat Allāh wrote to a kinsman from Basra, 'Earlier we had told you about the events that happened to us and the difficulties that we suffered. Well, by the power of the creator, [they] are all over.'[11] It could be to hasten a return. Sayyid Muṣṭafā told his son from Cochin, 'Do not be anxious. If *allāh* the high wishes, by means of spiritual and temporal (*dīnī va dunyavī*) powers, [our] reunion will take place before long.'[12] Indeed, there seems to have been the general presumption that God always sought to make things better, for 'why should the master of the two worlds cause trouble'.[13] While much about God's nature and capabilities was revealed through his presence, what occured in his absence is also telling. In particular, godlessness rendered comprehensible the otherwise incomprehensible vicissitudes of weather, health and safety. This is why a Shīʿī in Najaf could put in his letter to a patron in Bengal that 'without the most sacred, divine essence, [I] do not have confidence these parts will be free of oppression'.[14]

God was certainly exceptional because of his unmatched knowledge and power. But he was not alone. There existed others in the cosmos who bore a familial resemblance to him. However, there was no consensus within the arena over who or what these figures were. Some, like Iskandar (or Alexander), were dispersed throughout India and the Islamic heartlands.[15] Others operated within more restricted bounds, which were often dictated by the avowed religious persuasion. It is also probable that they varied among communities and extended families which nominally cleaved to the same religious persuasion. In daily exchanges between the Armenians of Iran, Iraq, Gujarat and Bengal, for example, Jesus, the Virgin Mary and, to a lesser extent, the saints were the principal figures after God.[16] In contrast, the Shīʿīs of Bengal and Iraq venerated the lives and teachings of God's prophet Muḥammad and his family, as well as the Imāms, ʿAlī and Ḥusayn foremost among them.[17]

[10] BL/Lansdowne/1046, doc. 37. [11] BL/Lansdowne/1046, doc. 67.
[12] BL/Lansdowne/1046, doc. 49. [13] BL/Lansdowne/1046, doc. 33.
[14] BL/Lansdowne/1046, doc. 30. [15] BL/Lansdowne/1046, docs. 7, 37.
[16] BL/Lansdowne/1046, docs. 67, 68, 69, 70, 71, 76. On the Armenians, see *A Chronicle of the Carmelites in Persia and the Papal Mission of the XVIIth and XVIIIth Centuries*, 2 vols. (London, 1939); Aptin Khanbaghi, *The Fire, the Star and the Cross: Minority Religions in Medieval and Early Modern Iran* (London, 2006).
[17] BL/Lansdowne/1046, docs. 3, 37, 38, 39, 49, 56, 58, 82, 83. On the Shīʿīs, see Hamid Algar, 'Shiʿism and Iran in the eighteenth century', in Thomas Naff and Roger Owen (eds.), *Studies in Eighteenth Century Islamic History* (London, 1971), 288–302; Juan R. I. Cole, *Roots of North Indian Shīʿism in Iran and Iraq: Religion and State in Awadh, 1722–1859* (Berkeley, CA, 1988); Richard M. Eaton, *The Rise of Islam and the Bengal Frontier, 1204–1760* (Berkeley, CA, 1993).

These divine-like figures existed in two separate 'worlds' (*jahān, dār, ʿālam, dunyā*). However, it is not clear from the correspondence whether their presence in them was simultaneous or whether it was in one at a time. Be that as it may, the two worlds constituted the cosmos for the arena's people. There was 'this world' and there was 'the world-to-come', between which, for mortal man at least, no overlap was observable.[18] The differences between the worlds were stark, most of the essential characteristics of one being an inversion of the other. This world was where humans were born and lived out their earthly years, a world fully accessible to the physical senses. Again and again, it was stressed that for each individual alive right now this world is 'transitory',[19] 'ephemeral',[20] 'passing'.[21] How different, then, the hereafter, which was home to God's 'heavenly kingdom',[22] or to his 'paradise',[23] a 'refuge'[24] where one might look forward to a 'happy eternity'.[25] That was, of course, a much desired fate, captured in the commonplace sentiment: 'may you be successful in your worldly and other-worldly goals and needs'.[26] Interestingly, few dared utter the other possibility in the world to come – that of 'hell' (*jahannam*)[27] – despite knowing it was all too real a prospect.

Material well-being was of supreme concern, if not *the* supreme concern, to many in this world. But the arena's people also knew that, as 'life is transient'[28] and 'everything comes to an end [and] stops',[29] material riches mattered not a whit in the other world. Indeed, so went a popular refrain: 'nothing remains to anyone from this world [after death] except the good [things] that one does [now]'.[30] It was understood that the world of the hereafter is forever and intangible. But human beings, while alive and confined to this world, could have no personal experience of it. Such personal experience came only with death and migration from this world to the next. Hence the constant preoccupation with that passage, especially with its certitude and finality. A father took care to remind his son that 'when it finally becomes necessary for me to let go of this world, I will seek refuge with the rightful master'.[31] This was clearly intended as a template for his son to model himself on. 'Please understand and perceive', the father continued, 'the form of death is the same for

18 BL/Lansdowne/1046, docs. 16, 56, 76, 80. 19 BL/Lansdowne/1046, docs. 49, 69.
20 BL/Lansdowne/1046, doc. 71. 21 BL/Lansdowne/1046, doc. 82.
22 BL/Lansdowne/1046, docs. 76, 77. 23 BL/Lansdowne/1046, docs. 21, 54.
24 BL/Lansdowne/1046, doc. 21. 25 BL/Lansdowne/1046, doc. 71.
26 BL/Lansdowne/1046, doc. 33. 27 BL/Lansdowne/1046, doc. 14.
28 BL/Lansdowne/1046, doc. 41. 29 BL/Lansdowne/1046, doc. 71.
30 BL/Lansdowne/1046, doc. 76. 31 BL/Lansdowne/1046, doc. 56.

everyone.'[32] A brother-in-law was told that 'there is no escape from death', and this is the case 'whether we are rich or poor'.[33]

Left at that, however, this would have been death as biological fact, true yet trivial. But death did not just mark a conclusion; it was not merely a gateway between this world and the other world. Rather, it was in itself constitutive in light of what had preceded it, and of what was to follow. It was 'the Day of Calling',[34] 'the Day of Resurrection'.[35] So death and the passage into the after-life were not straightforward or simple affairs, of significance only for a person's physical being. It was also the one juncture at which God, who has 'in his hands this world and the next',[36] was sure to intervene. And this intervention took the form of judgement. At death, account was taken of all that an individual had done during his mortal life, and its evaluation determined his fate in the world to come. By means of this divine intervention, this world and the other world did not merely coexist; they were inextricably enmeshed. It was the moment when the recently deceased's temporal comportment would, through God's judgement, get its just reward.[37] So it mattered profoundly what one did while alive.

But it was not only consideration of the after-life that informed behaviour in the here-and-now. This is because God's intervention was not confined solely to death and the transition between the two worlds. It could also occur while one was very much alive. Hence the maxim that only 'if *allāh* the high wishes, will I obtain the desires of [this] world and the next'.[38] This-world interventions differed, however, in one key respect: their uncertainty. While death always entailed judgement of some kind, with consequences for the future in the world to come, such intervention during life in this world was far less predictable; it was not known when and how God might involve himself in human affairs, even though action of any kind was possible at any moment. Thus, if he so desired:

> [God] may provide for you and guard you and protect you and help you up and [ensure] no enemies rejoice at your misfortune and take care of you in straightened circumstances and grant [your wishes], [so that you are] restored in heart and mind. May he return you to us in safety.[39]

Despite the uncertainty, there was never any doubt over God's capacity to determine one's future in this world. It was therefore entirely reasonable to proclaim that, when all is said and done, 'work (*kār*) happens [solely] through *khudā*'.[40] Indeed, to have it any other way

[32] BL/Lansdowne/1046, doc. 58. [33] BL/Lansdowne/1046, doc. 71.
[34] يوم التناد. BL/Lansdowne/1046, doc. 21.
[35] يوم القيامة. BL/Lansdowne/1046, docs. 79, 80. [36] BL/Lansdowne/1046, doc. 56.
[37] BL/Lansdowne/1046, docs. 38, 71, 76. [38] BL/Lansdowne/1046, doc. 56.
[39] BL/Lansdowne/1046, doc. 77. [40] BL/Lansdowne/1046, doc. 49.

would be troubling; it might give rise to the spectre of irreligiosity, since, as a wife put it to her husband, 'what proceeds in accordance with [God] is what happens to created beings concerning the affairs of this world'.[41] As for God's divine companions, they too were known to have the power to shape the temporal affairs of men – and not always to a lesser extent. This knowledge sustained the Shīʿī dictum if 'you depend in every task on the honourable Imām Ḥusayn ... everything will be well', that 'through the grace of Imām Ḥusayn ... will the end result deliver comfort and cause you no doubts', that 'the possibility of gain ... comes through the bounty of the Imām, which would not be realised even by innumerable efforts'.[42]

Although it was in the hereafter that the benefits of a life lived in accordance with God's wishes would be most fully realised, it was possible for some of the benefits to be conferred in the present. In either case, a large degree of personal freedom or individual autonomy was permitted or, arguably, required. There was a strong presumption that only the pious – those who comported themselves in line with the 'revealed law' (*sharʿ*)[43] – stood any hope of having a successful and happy future, whether in this world or in the one to come. It was frequently said among Muslims that 'nothing will function except through love of the Prophet's family ... [So] it is necessary to live according to their commandment.'[44] As a result, the arena's people faced a clear choice: either follow God's will as expressed in his words or through the exemplary models provided by the biographies of the divine figures, or not and thus suffer the consequences in this life and in the after-life.

The foregoing appears to be in conflict, however, with another attitude that was no less pervasive within the arena. In the latter, the view was that this world, let alone the next, is wholly in God's hand; that it is he who dictates the lives of men and controls their future; and that it is he who permits – and sometimes ordains – whatever happens in the here-and-now. The presumption was that human beings do not, and cannot, determine their own fate. All they can do is call upon God and the other godly figures, and praise them and petition them. And if they choose to listen, the future might be tilted in the individual's favour, and those near and dear to him might be granted exemption from hardships and be allowed a life of goodness. This second attitude indicates extreme predestination or helpless fatalism, which held that the arena's people had little or no measurable latitude to chart their own course through life.

With the current state of research on the topic being what it is, these two attitudes cannot be easily reconciled – and perhaps in principle are *not*

[41] BL/Lansdowne/1046, doc. 69. [42] BL/Lansdowne/1046, doc. 49.
[43] BL/Lansdowne/1046, docs. 63, 77, 81, 82, 83. [44] BL/Lansdowne/1046, doc. 49.

reconcilable. All we can say for the moment is that both were widely adopted and, if taken as stated, give rise to a blatant contradiction, at least from the perspective of our modern sensibilities. A close reading of the correspondence suggests that its authors and recipients had no awareness of such a contradiction; if there was, then I have yet to see any concern expressed about it. It would seem, then, that contemporaries subscribed to both these attitudes simultaneously without being unduly troubled by the (notional) differences between them.

Whatever our assessment of their logical consistency, it is difficult to deny that the known realities of the cosmos outlined above framed major aspects of personal and social life within the arena in the eighteenth century. At its core was belief. Shīʿī correspondents stressed its importance, urging their kindred to 'swear by Imām Ḥusayn'[45] and 'be mindful of [his] excellence'.[46] Likewise, an Armenian wrote to his cousin, 'It is desired, O my dear, O my love, [that] the law (*nāmūs*) of *allāh* is always between your eyes and fear of him in your heart.'[47] And this belief could be actively policed, even from afar. Shaykh Dīn in Najaf told Niʿmat Allāh in Bengal that, if there was 'any kind of shortcoming in the belief (*ʿaqīda*)' of a mutual acquaintance, Niʿmat Allāh would be informed of it straightaway.[48] The rationale behind such exhortations and concerns was obvious to contemporaries: their individual and collective self-interest demanded it.

This rather abstract belief in the existence of God and the other godly figures, as well as in their sayings and doings, was accompanied by the duty to be pious and observe the formal precepts of their religious traditions.[49] One element of this duty was highly personal, specific to the individual alone. That is why Sayyid Muṣṭafā could write to his intimates at home, asking them, 'In [your] personal (*khāṣṣ*) time, please do not forget me in [your] prayer.'[50] Prayer seems to have played a central role in approved pious behaviour. A Sufi in Najaf reassured his patron that 'at the threshold of [the Imām's] throne (*ʿarsh*), I do not neglect your sign (*nishān*) in my prayer'.[51] Writing from abroad, a Shīʿī father asked his son 'not to neglect the *fātiḥa* [prayer-ceremony] for the presence Imām Ḥusayn'.[52] Prayer was of such importance to some that its absence was duly noted and condemned. In chastising a kinsman for being

45 BL/Lansdowne/1046, doc. 49. 46 BL/Lansdowne/1046, doc. 58.
47 BL/Lansdowne/1046, doc. 71. 48 BL/Lansdowne/1046, doc. 33.
49 There has been some interesting recent work on Islamic piety in premodern times. As examples, see Shahzad Bashir's *Sufi Bodies: Religion and Society in Medieval Islam* (New York, 2011); Megan H. Reid's *Law and Piety in Medieval Islam* (Cambridge, 2013).
50 BL/Lansdowne/1046, doc. 40. 51 BL/Lansdowne/1046, doc. 25.
52 BL/Lansdowne/1046, doc. 56.

remiss in this regard, ʿAbd al-ʿAṭī b. Yusūf Ḥumṣī reminded him that 'our *rabb* will not allow [a happy outcome] if people (*al-nās*) do not pray'.[53] And when it came to prayer, following correct procedure was crucial. The same Shīʿī father who had written to his son about the *fātiḥa* also placed stress on 'always doing ablution before prayer and praying five times a day'. Through this, he continued, 'You will see how much happiness and purity comes upon [your] *dil*.'[54]

Of course, it was not just prayer that offered opportunities to enact one's piety. Personal engagement in social rituals mattered too. And the social ritual par excellence was pilgrimage to shrine cities, tombs, sacred ground and other places of worship.[55] Karbala was one such place for Shīʿīs. 'Given the desired wind,' wrote Sayyid Muṣṭafā, 'the ship will reach Basra in one month. From Basra to Karbala is a fifteen-day journey. If *allāh* the high wishes, having made the pilgrimages (*ziyārāt*), I will myself have gone in your footsteps and I know that [only thus] may I pass from being extremely weary into a blessed state.'[56]

As the injunctions to pray and to go on pilgrimage suggest, it was not always possible to disentangle acts of personal piety from acts of social piety. And in situations where an individual held a formal rank or office in an organisation imbued with spiritual charisma or authority, disentanglement was essentially impossible; the two kinds of acts were fused, an individual's status and role within the community (or polity) commingled with his personal comportment. Consider the appointment of Sūnī Khān b. ʿĀshiq Khān as *murīd*, or disciple, in 1747 in the Qādirīya brotherhood in Iraq.[57] The *ijāza* that at once recognised and proclaimed this appointment stated his obligations: 'Sūnī Khān . . . came to us and he took the vow (*ʿahd*) and so became our *murīd*. And we charged him to be pious and obey the revealed law (*sharʿ*) and preserve its ordinances (*ḥadūd*) and endure

53 BL/Lansdowne/1046, doc. 71. 54 BL/Lansdowne/1046, doc. 49.

55 BL/Lansdowne/1046, docs. 3, 35, 40. There is good scholarship on Islamic pilgrimage within the region in early modern times. See, in particular, Naim R. Farooqi, 'Moguls, Ottomans and pilgrims: protecting the routes to Mecca in the sixteenth and seventeenth centuries', *International History Review* 10:2 (1988), 198–220; Suraiya N. Faroqhi, *Pilgrims and Sultans: the Hajj under the Ottomans, 1517–1683* (London, 1994); Michael N. Pearson, *Pilgrimage to Mecca: The Indian Experience, 1500–1800* (Princeton, 1996); Robert D. McChesney, 'The Central Asian Hajj-pilgrimage in the time of the early modern empires', in Michel M. Mazzaoui (ed.), *Safavid Iran and her Neighbors* (Salt Lake City, UT, 2003), 129–56; Muzaffar Alam and Sanjay Subrahmanyam, *Indo-Persian Travels in the Age of Discoveries, 1400–1800* (Cambridge, 2007); Alexandre Papas, Thomas Welsford and Thierry Zarcone (eds.), *Central Asian Pilgrims: Hajj Routes and Pious Visits between Central Asia and the Hijaz* (Berlin, 2011).

56 BL/Lansdowne/1046, doc. 40.

57 The Qādirīya brotherhood is the subject of a special issue of the *Journal of History of Sufism* 1–2 (2000).

wrong [from others] and renounce wrong [for himself].'[58] Such considerations were present with even greater force, and more elaborate in form, when appointments were to positions of leadership. The following account, to do with a 'Sufi lodge' (*takīya*), is a case in point.

In a letter dated 10 August 1747, the interim caretakers of a Rifāʿīya Sufi *takīya* in Iraq announced to their brethren in Bengal the choice of ʿAbd al-Rifāʿī as *khalīfa*, or successor.[59] At the same time, he was appointed the *takīya*'s new headman. The authors of the letter stressed that this new headman has endorsed, and will work within, 'the rules and practices (*dastūr va maʿmūl*)' of his predecessor, his recently deceased father. 'He will not permit any shortcoming [in them] . . . and he will in no way excuse himself from working above all in the service of the dervishes (*fuqarāʾ*, sing. *faqīr*) and the fraternity's remembrance [of God] (*dhikr-i ḥalqa*).'[60] These undertakings were described in an accompanying document. Written in the name of Ḥusayn b. Yusūf, a direct descendant of the brotherhood's purported founder, it stated:

> I have authorised him [ʿAbd al-Rifāʿī] to perform the fraternity's remembrance [of God] just as the *khalīfa*s who had preceded him had done. And I appointed him successor to take over the place of his father and that he take control of the *takīya* of his father and in accordance with him, and that he sit in the company of the *faqīr*s and the poor and not act unjustly towards them. And I authorised him [in relation to] everything concerning the fire and the beating of the pins and the devotion to obedience. And none of the [other] *khalīfa*s will encroach upon him unless he commits an [infraction]. And he renounces the atrocious and forbidden things.[61]

It seems that soon after ʿAbd al-Rifāʿī's own appointment as *khalīfa*, he appointed Sayyid Shaʿbān b. Yusūf to the very same rank. The document formally announcing this elevation brims with rich, evocative detail concerning what was required and expected of Sayyid Shaʿbān in his new position. As these requirements and expectations were intimately tied to their known cosmos, the document merits being quoted in full.[62] It opens with a brief account of his appointment: 'Sayyid Shaʿbān b. Sayyid Yusūf was brought to the room . . . And we gave him the oath of the room (*ḥalfa al-ḥujra*) [in the footsteps of] his father. Therefore, no one should deny [his leadership] from [among] the people of the brotherhoods and the

[58] BL/Lansdowne/1046, doc. 81.

[59] On the Rifāʿīya brotherhood, see Alexandre Popovic, *Un ordre de derviches en terre d'Europe* (Lausanne, 1993).

[60] BL/Lansdowne/1046, doc. 20. [61] BL/Lansdowne/1046, doc. 80.

[62] BL/Lansdowne/1046, doc. 79. There are striking parallels between this and appointments made in Ottoman 'guilds' (*esnaf*) in the period. For a suggestive discussion, see H. A. R. Gibb and Harold Bowen, *Islamic Society and the West: a Study of the Impact of Western Civilization on Moslem Culture in the Near East* (London, 1950–7), I, 293–4.

truths (*ahl al-ṭarā'iq wa-al-ḥaqā'iq*) and no one should deny [his leadership] from [among] the people of the succession (*jamī' ahl al-khilāfa*).' There follows a statement of his principal duties and rights:

His consent should be secured for the *rātib* remembrance (*dhikr*) on Friday nights. And [he is authorised to permit] those who want to adhere to the thread of our love. And he will hang the string and the drum and the pin. And no one should disapprove of him. And we have made him swear to be our *khalīfa* and our delegate (*niyāba*). And he will give the pledge (*bī'a*) and vow (*'ahd*) for us to anyone who wishes to adhere to our love. And [that person] will give the *bī'a* and *'ahd* in accordance with the *'ahd* of Sayyid Sha'bān and [be required to] persevere with undertaking the obligatory religious duties in their [appropriate] times and the customary [rituals] which [are related] to them and [perform] whatever is possible of the supererogatory prayers (*nawāfil*) and of the afternoon and evening prayers and be righteous. [Sayyid Sha'bān] should command what *allāh* has commanded and prohibit what *allāh* has prohibited. And he should order the *faqīr* and the body of disciples (*murīdīya*) to behave in a submissive and obliging manner, and to ask for forgiveness in the mornings and in the evenings.

The document closes with the qualities and attributes that, as *khalīfa*, he should aspire to:

He should not change the *faqīr*s for himself. And he should be sweet and not become angry. Indeed, *allāh* alone can be angry. And he should guide the *murīd*s with the excellence of his character. And if he is struck or insulted, he should bear this calmly. He should be content with whatever sustenance *allāh* has given him and praise *allāh* the high in prosperity and in adversity. And he should curb [his] anger and pardon those who wrong him. And he should comfort the *faqīr*s and not assign anything for his own needs without considering theirs. And he should be generous towards the wretched (*gharīb*s) and be humble towards the big and the small (*al-kabīr wa-al-ṣaghīr*). When these laudable qualities and attributes are perfected, [Sayyid Sha'bān] will have received many [divine] favours and excellence and gifts. Then he [will have obtained] the benefits and the intended purpose, and the worshippers (*al-'ubbād*) will return to him time and again.

Charity was an abiding feature of everyday life in India and the Islamic heartlands. Indeed, acts of charity were probably the most common form of social piety within the arena. And there were eminently sensible reasons for it. A son was encouraged by his father from abroad to set aside part of his income for 'the matter of charity (*amr-i khayr*), since from charity comes charity'.[63] A grateful recipient of a charitable donation in Najaf sent his patron in Bengal the rhyming couplet: 'Do for someone a good necessity which does not benefit you / the consolation through *allāh* has another reward (*ajr*)'.[64] The same sentiment was put in prose by a fellow

[63] BL/Lansdowne/1046, doc. 58. [64] BL/Lansdowne/1046, doc. 1.

resident of Najaf: 'Such charitable work brings about the lengthening of lives and progress in good fortune and up the steps of this world and the next leading to an auspicious fate.'[65]

As an act of charity, it was perfectly respectable to donate money to religious institutions, even if the rationale was avowedly utilitarian and self-centred. A father told his son, 'Out of every hundred [rupees] give 1 rupee as the Imam's share (*khazānah*) so that one will never want for money and blessings.'[66] Charity could also take the form of direct material aid for those less fortunate. Muḥammad Adīb, while in Cochin in 1748, was especially keen on this. He instructed Ghulām ʿAlī that 'when he arrives [home], he takes a bundle of the rice which is in the house [and], having cooked it, gives it to the poor'.[67]

The hope was that charity, as well as generosity and kindness – all instances of divinely sanctioned behaviour – would be rewarded by God with a better life in this world and in the world to come. So it is no surprise that this hope was commonly exploited by those seeking the help of others within the intimate community. A debtor, who had already been arrested twice for failure to pay the money he owed, wrote to his nephew in desperation:

> If you give me alms and you free me from this debt and from the oppression of [its] interest, the *rabb* will save you from every difficulty and affliction. And for every good deed that you do for me, the *rabb* will reward you its equivalent in this world and in the next, and in his heavenly kingdom he will put you with his saints. Amen. Since from this world nothing is left to anyone except the good [deeds] that one does. [And] our lord Jesus Christ enjoined [us to behave] in this way regarding the wretched ones. And your reward will not be neglected by *allāh*. And whatever you give me, consider it charity in your favour and [in favour of] the soul (*rūḥ*) of your father and your mother and [in favour of] the soul of your sister.[68]

In a similar vein, a woman pleaded with her long-absent kinsman to help out his mother and their family at home. In return for this, she assured him, God would amply compensate him in this world and, in particular, the next. 'When this letters reaches your hand, send her [your mother] the expenses or high-quality cloth because there is a great need [for it]. The *rabb* will give you [in exchange] the equivalent as repose (*rāḥa*) for 163 [years] in ... the kingdom of heaven.'[69]

As the examples above show, the known realities of the cosmos encouraged contemporaries to petition one another. This tendency exerted a powerful influence on relations between intimates and among members

[65] BL/Lansdowne/1046, doc. 16.
[66] BL/Lansdowne/1046, doc. 56.
[67] BL/Lansdowne/1046, doc. 13.
[68] BL/Lansdowne/1046, doc. 76.
[69] BL/Lansdowne/1046, doc. 77.

of the same confessional group. But the belief that God judged and could dictate the course of human lives, and that life proceeded from divine providence, meant that there were many reasons to petition God directly as well. Most commonly, this took the form of broad, formulaic requests. They were frequently made on behalf of others, asking God to grant, say, current and future health, safety, knowledge, prosperity or comfort. So we see in the correspondence: 'May *allāh* preserve him';[70] 'May *allāh*, the high, keep him safe';[71] 'We are well and in good health . . . and we ask through the generosity of the possessor that you be better than that';[72] 'May the creator keep you fully informed';[73] 'We . . . are praying that your life is completely good and healthy, and [receives] the creator's abundant bounty';[74] 'May our *rabb* prolong your life and dispel for you every misfortune';[75] 'May he keep in his protection and preservation your existence [so that it is safe] from bodily misfortunes and afflictions';[76] 'We are busy praying for your prosperity and long life';[77] 'May the master of the two worlds not deprive you [of anything] . . . may [he] grant cheerfulness to [you, my] dear friend, and free you as soon as possible from sorrows and cause [you] to reach the goals of the two worlds'.[78]

Individuals would also seek divine help or favour for more specific ends. The most forthright of these typically concerned livelihood or business dealings. Consider the following: '[I am] praying night and day for the *rabb*, the godhead, to help you and facilitate your business and increase his bounty for you';[79] 'If *allāh* the high wishes, O my son, may he be with you and protect you in your absence [from me] and may he guide you along the path of success wherever you are headed';[80] 'May the *rabb* take care of you on all the roads [you travel]. We ask that he always takes care of you by means of the essence of his mercies howsoever you have betaken yourself. And we ask by means of the application of his mercies that misfortune does not strike you and he saves you from all misfortunes.'[81]

In keeping with this widespread tendency to petition God and his divine companions, there was frequent acknowledgement of the belief that life and this world are subject to control by divine forces. The belief was captured in God being called the 'omniscient', the 'creator', the 'conqueror', the 'truth', the 'generous', the 'lord', the 'possessor', the

[70] BL/Lansdowne/1046, doc. 68.
[71] BL/Lansdowne/1046, doc. 12.
[72] BL/Lansdowne/1046, doc. 12.
[73] BL/Lansdowne/1046, doc. 68.
[74] BL/Lansdowne/1046, doc. 67.
[75] BL/Lansdowne/1046, doc. 69.
[76] BL/Lansdowne/1046, doc. 37.
[77] BL/Lansdowne/1046, doc. 38.
[78] BL/Lansdowne/1046, doc. 33.
[79] BL/Lansdowne/1046, doc. 67.
[80] BL/Lansdowne/1046, doc. 70.
[81] BL/Lansdowne/1046, doc. 67

'companion', the 'granter', the 'merciful', the 'hearer', the 'witness', the 'giver'.[82] It was thus routine to qualify and preface statements of intent by gesturing to God as the one who had permitted, or will permit, what is to come. The usual pattern was along on the lines of: 'we ask through the generosity of the possessor', 'this through the blessing of God', 'we by the power of God'. Such acknowledgements were invariably conjoined with gratitude when things were good, or when good news was being communicated. A man told a close relative that 'our brother, Khwājā Shammās ʿAbd Allāh, is perfectly well and happy through the mediation of the Virgin (*al-batūl*), the mother of the light'.[83] Similarly, a Shīʿī pilgrim and merchant making his way to Iraq noted that, 'through divine bounty and by the charity of the presence Imām Ḥusayn, peace upon him, in all respects I am well and calm'.[84] More generally, the prevailing attitude was encapsulated in the nostrum that 'well-being [happens] by virtue of praise and thanks' to God.[85] As a result, he was often lauded using stock expressions like 'praise be to God' and 'we thank God'. These furnished the basis for more complex – and more rarely seen – formulations such as: 'We offer thousands of praise and a myriad of thanks to *allāh*.'[86] And their purpose was not just rhetorical. An Armenian in southern Iraq wrote in no uncertain terms, 'What caused your brother suffering was that you do not express the desire we thank our *rabb* for prosperity in our affairs [and that] they are concluded well.'[87]

[82] *ʿallām, bārī, kirdigār, ghālib, ḥaqq, karīm, khudāvand, mālik, mawlā, mujīb, raḥman, sāmiʿ, shāhid, vāhib.*

[83] BL/Lansdowne/1046, doc. 67.

[84] BL/Lansdowne/1046, docs. 49, 50.

[85] BL/Lansdowne/1046, doc. 37.

[86] BL/Lansdowne/1046, doc. 68.

[87] BL/Lansdowne/1046, doc. 71.

3 A familial order: ties of blood, duty and affect

> O my brother and my dear, I hoped of you that your blood would not separate you from your mother and your sisters, even you, for the period of six years. However, it has not come into your consideration whether they have died or moreover whether they are alive since you have not thought about us. We are your sisters. [Regarding] your mother, as far as you are concerned, you are obliged and liable to her by compact and by revealed law.[1]

The power of this passage emanates from verities that are eternal. The sister writing these words in the middle of the eighteenth century was well aware of them. So was her mother. And her brother in far-off India could not in good faith deny them. They are what animate the sister's anger and sadness at her brother's behaviour. We return to this affair later on in the chapter. For the moment, however, the passage matters because it points to a basic commonality between this chapter and the last: both are concerned with features of daily life in the arena that were treated by contemporaries as timeless and inalienable. These features constrained and enabled behaviour in the most fundamental senses, and had enduring consequences for dealings to do with circulation and exchange. But there are significant differences between the chapters too. The preceding one discusses the essential nature of the cosmos, its relationship to man, and the bearing it had on life in this world. In the present chapter, the gaze shifts from the grandest of scales to the humblest. I focus here on the tendencies in social behaviour marked by the greatest of intimacy. Not unlike today, it is within the family household that such intimacy was most widespread, deeply felt and systematically cultivated within the arena. It helped forge and energise among the most meaningful of human relationships. In so doing, it established statuses and roles among kindred, and engendered their sentiments for one another.

Before launching into the details, however, some conceptual tidying up needs to be done. In particular, careful thought must be given to what is

[1] BL/Lansdowne/1046, doc. 77.

meant by the 'family household', and how one can profitably engage with it in light of the source limitations and the paucity of historical scholarship on the subject for India and the Islamic heartlands in pre-modern times. I defer to Chapter 8 a full discussion of the multiple and changing perspectives on the 'family' and 'household' in the scholarly literature, and the principal methods that have been deployed to examine them. For current purposes, and informed by that literature, I adopt a position which is minimalistic in substance and pragmatic in outlook. I take the family to refer to the smallest group of individuals related through descent or marriage – or occasionally through adoption – that was expected to survive from one generation to the next. All of its members belonged to a shared household, which potentially embraced slaves and servants as well. Though the household need not occupy a single building, or even be in a fixed location, it was always situated in an identifiable place. The household provided the material basis of life for at least the dependents within the family, and it was the domicile of the family's leading female member, usually the wife of the paterfamilias. These are the core attributes of what I call the 'family household'. Hopefully, this conception has analytical utility while being flexible enough to take account of the diversity found within the region in our period.

Though the family household per se is not the subject of this chapter – I leave that to Chapter 8 – it furnishes the setting within which were found the realities and the associated patterns of behaviour studied here. The method I use to recover them emphasises the direct and indirect verbal utterances in the correspondence to do with behaviour that was viewed by contemporaries as natural, inherited, given and unchanging. Of particular value are kinship terminology and the feelings close kindred expressed for one another. Within the family household, the realities in question generally manifested themselves in two ways. The first was statuses and roles ascribed to, and played out by, individuals possessing certain well-defined qualities.[2] The second was sentiments vested in, and moulding, particular relationships (which have traditionally been elaborated by scholars under the rubric of affect).[3] While no less formative and consequential than statuses and roles, sentiments tend to be less

[2] It is frequently claimed that an individual cannot be understood apart from his statuses and roles. This claim underpins scholarship which pivots on the notion of 'personhood'. For representative examples, as well as for citations to the relevant literature, see Ákos Östör, Lina Fruzzetti and Steve Barnett (eds.), *Concepts of Person: Kinship, Caste, and Marriage in India* (Cambridge, MA, 1982).

[3] The study of affect and, more generally, emotions has gained in popularity among historians in the past generation. The current state of the field is debated in Nicole Eustace, Eugenia Lean, Julie Livingston, Jan Plamper, William Reddy and Barbara Rosenwein, 'AHR conversation: the historical study of emotions', *American Historical*

predictable and more elusive. It is thus no surprise that their recovery poses a stiffer challenge. As the following pages show, both these patterns of behaviour reveal themselves most openly in the documents in dealings between fathers and sons, and in the treatment of sons by others within their family household.

Choose any community found in Islamicate Eurasia in the eighteenth century and a stark distinction between fathers and their sons would be in evidence.[4] The nature of this distinction may be gleaned from the tone or style in which they interacted with one another. In their letters, fathers generally projected a domineering and exhortative persona to their sons. This seems to have been the case whether or not the son was an adult or married. The key factor was whether or not he still belonged to his father's household.[5] For those who did, we see heavy use of the imperative. Sayyid Muṣṭafā's letters to his son brim with orders in the form of 'you must do this', 'you cannot do that'.[6] Qāsim ʿAbd al-Samīʿ Ṭarabzāwī's letters cleave to a similar pattern. His instructions to his son, Ismāʿīl, were seldom adorned by pleasantries. Statements such as 'do not send us the goods of the people as long as we are constrained', 'do not be idle [in transferring] our Baghdad money to its destination'[7] are characteristic of his tone. Of course, it does not automatically follow that the father was heeded by his son. But obedience does appear to have been the rule, and sons normally submitted themselves to their father with open deference. A son's comportment in relation to his father was, moreover, a matter of broader interest, continually witnessed and reinforced by those around him. Sayyid Muṣṭafā candidly told his son that 'you must remember the desire of my love',[8] that 'you must satisfy your father'.[9] Others in the family household reiterated these strictures. Even as a wife was writing to remind her husband that his son 'venerates you',[10] she was writing to her son: 'A piece of advice for you ... It is possible that your father may say something which restrains you a little. But this is time honoured and so

Review 117:5 (2012), 1487–531. As a very recent contribution, see Ute Frevert *et al.*, *Emotional Lexicons: Continuity and Change in the Vocabulary of Feeling* (Oxford, 2014).

4 Though none of the documents which I have examined talk about adoption, it should not be assumed that it did not occur or that it was uncommon. Until further evidence sheds light on the matter, I reserve judgement about how, if at all, a father's treatment of a biological son would have differed from that of an adopted son.

5 Normative views on rearing children, based on premodern, canonical Islamic texts, are described and analysed in Avner Gilʿadi, *Children of Islam: Concepts of Childhood in Medieval Muslim Society* (London, 1992). The seminal work on the subject is, of course, Phillipe Ariès's *L'enfant et la vie familiale sous l'Ancien Régime* (Paris, 1960).

6 BL/Lansdowne/1046, docs. 49, 56, 58, 60.

7 BL/Lansdowne/1046, doc. 73.

8 BL/Lansdowne/1046, doc. 49.

9 BL/Lansdowne/1046, doc. 58.

10 BL/Lansdowne/1046, doc. 69.

take it with a sweet tongue because he is your father who will not scold you. Do not cause me worry about this matter.'[11] That same son's brother-in-law enjoined him 'to obey your father and to reassure him'.[12]

So the father judged and decreed, while the son listened to him, remembered him, prayed for him, honoured him, loved him, obeyed him and satisfied him. These tendencies point to a larger set of natural rights, expectations, privileges and duties with which the father was invested.[13] The letters show that a father's opinion mattered greatly within his family household. They also show that the formal authority to take major decisions affecting its collective fate was ultimately his alone. This was avowed and accepted by all, which partly explains the exceptional sensitivity displayed for a father's feelings. We see this reflected in the pains taken to treat him with appropriate decorum. We see this in the respect that he demanded as his due. In return, the father was expected to be considerate, kind and generous, and when mistakes happened – and happen they often did – to forgive those under his charge with understanding and compassion. That is why Māralīnā could ask her husband in India to receive his son 'with fatherly tenderness and in a welcoming manner', and what is more to 'accept his apologies'. He was not to 'be furious with him because he is our only son … Rather, show him the love which is not demanded by right'.[14] That is also why ʿAbd al-Qādir in Basra could write to his Calcutta associate Awānīs b. Astūr with the news: 'Your daughter hears that you were travelling in India (*hind*), and yet you do not send her the clothes which she has requested. It is necessary for you to show her consideration because a child (*walad*) is not happy except through having [the attention] of his father.'[15] This consideration for his daughter extended to children acquired through marriage. 'When you send me the expenses,' a wife wrote to her husband, 'send her something to console her because she is your daughter-in-law (*kanna*) and your daughter (*bint*). Don't forget her.'[16]

All this coheres with a primal sense of personal responsibility that the father bore for the current and future well-being of his family household.[17] 'What do you have in this world other than your wife and your son?' ʿAbd Allāh b. Ḥassūn was asked. It was, of course, a rhetorical

[11] BL/Lansdowne/1046, doc. 70. [12] BL/Lansdowne/1046, doc. 71.

[13] These and related concepts are defined in Wesley N. Hohfeld, 'Some fundamental legal conceptions as applied in judicial reasoning', *Yale Law Journal* 23:1 (1913), 16–59.

[14] BL/Lansdowne/1046, doc. 69. [15] BL/Lansdowne/1046, doc. 65.

[16] BL/Lansdowne/1046, doc. 69.

[17] Cf. the discussion of the responsibility that fathers and mature sons had for their dependants at home in Shelomo D. Goitein, *A Mediterranean Society: the Jewish Communities of the Arab World as Portrayed in the Documents of the Cairo Geniza*, vol. I (Berkeley, CA, 1967), 351.

question posed to emphasise the point that 'it is necessary for you to take them in hand'.[18] Being abroad only served to heighten that sense of responsibility. When Thanā' Allāh realised early in April 1748 that he would have to tarry in Cochin because of contrary winds and the Angria pirates, he made it a priority to write home and let his son know: 'Do not be concerned or worried at all. And also you will tell your mother not to be worried [because] no one spends two, four years travelling. If *allāh* wishes, through the kindness of the master, I will certainly reach Bengal in January.'[19]

Again, a father's duty towards his intimate kindred is expressed most openly through his relationship to his son. In large part, the explicitness was necessitated by the generally known fact that the son, in the context of the family household, occupied a special and highly favoured position. As a father, Sayyid Muṣṭafā was typical in this regard. He portrayed himself in his letters as his son's mentor and guide, both in his spiritual life and in his temporal life, both at home and within the broader intimate community. Leading his son and heir towards a godly and virtuous path through life was one of his cardinal duties as a father. It was he more than anyone else who was his son's principal source of trustworthy knowledge and wisdom, because he 'would never wish you [my son] ill, which you must know'.[20] It was he who instructed his son about the material and non-material worlds, about the realities of the here-and-now and the realities of the hereafter. Life, he reiterated, is transient; the only certainty is death. Because one's actions in this world shape one's destiny, he implored his son to embrace God's will and to take as exemplars the Prophet Muḥammad and the Imāms ʿAlī and Ḥusayn. As it is they who determine our fates, only by following their example and teachings would it be reasonable for his son to look forward to a healthy and prosperous future.[21]

But a father's concerns were by no means restricted to the cosmological dimensions; he was equally concerned, and at times more so, with the very mundane, the earthly. Thanā' Allāh encouraged his son – his *bābā* – 'to remain busy reading and writing'. He continued, 'If [God] allows me to remain alive, whatever is in [your] *dil*, I will give [you it].'[22] He also enjoined his son to behave in such a way that 'no one says anything bad'.[23] These concerns were echoed by Sayyid Muṣṭafā, whose son was to 'emphasise reading and writing, [and] to be sensible'.[24] Furthermore, he was to 'spend a part of [his] time ensuring friends are happy and enemies are assuaged',[25] and to 'behave well with everyone'.[26] Despite all the

[18] BL/Lansdowne/1046, doc. 69. [19] BL/Lansdowne/1046, doc. 11.
[20] BL/Lansdowne/1046, doc. 58. [21] BL/Lansdowne/1046, docs. 49, 56, 58, 60.
[22] BL/Lansdowne/1046, doc. 11. [23] Ibid. [24] BL/Lansdowne/1046, doc. 56.
[25] Ibid. [26] BL/Lansdowne/1046, doc. 58.

seeming differences in their backgrounds and circumstances, Māralīnā too subscribed to the responsibilities that the two fathers, Thanā' Allāh and Sayyid Muṣṭafā, were trying to live up to from afar. Even though her son was grown up and married, she was of the opinion that he still had much to gain from his father's ongoing support and instruction. 'Don't leave our dear son alone abroad,' she wrote to her husband. 'Rather, stay together you and he so that paired [with you] we may rejoice in him.' Why? Simply put, 'because we only have *allāh* the high and this son'.[27]

Of course, for a father's care and guidance to have any meaning, the son had to acquiesce. And this is what tended to happen.[28] Moreover, such obligations on the part of the son were not confined to his relationship with his father, even if these were of a special kind. There is evidence that the responsibility which mature sons had for their mother overlapped with the duties of the father, particularly when the latter was away from home for long periods. Despite the delay in Thanā' Allāh's return home, the knowledge that his son was there to take care of his mother must have been a consolation. Even so, the distant father could not forswear giving advice and instructions. The son and mother, he wrote, 'must not suffer with regard to food'. If it proved necessary, the son was to borrow for their expenses 'four [or] five rupees from Shaykh Gul Muḥammad jīyū', or from some other *mahājan*, and Thanā' Allāh would settle accounts with him on his return.[29] He reiterated in a second letter, 'You will spend five rupees or whatever is necessary [and] you will tell your mother not to worry.'[30] Aware of the stresses they might be experiencing because of his delayed return, Thanā' Allāh urged 'both mother and son to remain in agreement'.[31] A son's duty towards his mother was given more forceful expression by 'Abd al-'Aṭī when he charged Shukr Allāh 'always to think about the affairs of your mother because she has a noble right to be taken care of by her loved ones'. He went on:

If *allāh* wishes, she is in want of nothing. But if she sees a single para[32] from [you] . . ., it is known by me that it becomes for her by means of this a consolation which is better than if a thousand kuruş[33] came to her from another source. And

[27] BL/Lansdowne/1046, doc. 69.
[28] For suggestive remarks about the why and the how, see Franz Rosenthal, 'Child psychology in Islam', *Islamic Culture* 26 (1952), 1–22.
[29] BL/Lansdowne/1046, doc. 11. [30] BL/Lansdowne/1046, doc. 48.
[31] BL/Lansdowne/1046, doc. 11.
[32] A silver Ottoman coin. When it was re-issued early in the eighteenth century, the para was worth three akçe.
[33] Introduced in the Ottoman empire around the turn of the eighteenth century, the kuruş, or ghurush, was originally a heavy silver coin equal to forty paras. In the languages of Latin Europe, the kuruş was often called the piastre.

this thing is known by your brothers. And you are informed that her prayer is better for you than treasures galore. And her approval of you shows that *allāh* is pleased with you.[34]

And it was not the mother alone who by right enjoyed such consideration from a mature son; this notion also extended to his sisters. Arsānyūs Alyās, from whom nothing had been heard for several years, was taken to task by his sister Sabīlya. He was condemned for failing to shoulder his filial and brotherly responsibilities. As noted at the beginning of this chapter, she appeared exasperated, even distraught, at her brother's shameful behaviour. In attempting to cajole him back into the fold, she did not mince her words. She invoked in her letter to him the whole gamut of his familial, spiritual and customary duties to his intimate female kindred, duties that were inalienable and unbreakable, duties that bound him to them forever:

O my brother and my dear, I hoped of you that your blood would not separate you from your mother and your sisters, even you, for the period of six years. However, it has not come into your consideration whether they have died or moreover whether they are alive since you have not thought about us. We are your sisters. [Regarding] your mother, as far as you are concerned, you are obliged and liable to her by compact and by revealed law (*shar'*). As far as she is concerned, she is your mother. As far as she is concerned, she nursed you with her milk, she gave you her determination to the extent possible. [You], her son, she carried in her womb for nine months. Rightfully, O my brother and my love, this thing is very difficult [for us]. The one who nursed you considers that you have gone away from her, [that] you will not recognise her from the pain of the separation.[35]

The realities that crystallised in the form of roles and statuses are only one part of the story. These roles and statuses were crosscut by another set of realities that could buttress, undermine or even reverse them. This other set is most apparent in the deepest of emotions which suffused particular relationships. In Sayyid Muṣṭafā's case, his son was 'the light-of-my-eye' (*nūrchashm-i man*),[36] 'my spirit, my life' (*jān-i man 'umr-i man*).[37] These words were no charade; his concern for his son was tender and steadfast. No one else in the family had anything like such attention lavished upon him. In his correspondence, he treated his son at times as a grown-up, at other times as a minor. The overall tone used to address him suggests that the son was old enough to bear social and business responsibilities typically associated with elders, though young enough to be in need of the firm counsel of his elders, especially his father.

[34] BL/Lansdowne/1046, doc. 71. [35] BL/Lansdowne/1046, doc. 77.
[36] BL/Lansdowne/1046, docs. 39, 56, 58, 60. [37] BL/Lansdowne/1046, doc. 49.

But that is not all. The father's letters from abroad bear witness to his distress at his separation from him. Among the arena's people, this distress was often conveyed tellingly – and movingly – through poetic images and allusions. As Muḥammad Mahdī put it to his distant brother, Abū al-Qāsim, in 1747:

> I desire so much to meet you that, like Iskandar [needing] the water of life, I remember you [and] my *dil* is asking [for you]. Bitter tears are falling from my eye. I will not remove the hand from your image until the tulip emerges from my earth. The separation, the separation, if it was in my control, I would remove the separation. My yearning to meet you is so great that, [even] if you come soon, it will be late.[38]

Sayyid Muṣṭafā's way of dealing with the separation was by nurturing his son's image in his mind. 'Not for one instant,' he wrote on more than one occasion, 'do I neglect your memory as *khudā* will testify.'[39] 'Each and every moment, you are in my mind.'[40] 'Night and day, I do not forget your memory . . . Each and every moment, you are in my memory.'[41] And he was adamant that his son respond in kind. 'You also', he insisted, 'must not forget me in [your] blessings.'[42] Sayyid Muṣṭafā tried to assuage his feelings for his far-off son by reminding them both that, 'by means of spiritual and temporal powers, [our] reunion will take place before long'.[43] But until that reunion, they had to make do with correspondence. Even though, as the nostrum had it, this was merely 'equal to half a meeting',[44] it was infinitely preferable to nothing at all. So every opportunity for sending letters had to be seized. Promising to give a full account of himself on reaching Basra, Sayyid Muṣṭafā enjoined his son to do the same, to send him 'details about the reality of your constitution and work'. And he did not stop at his son. He also demanded news 'about the circumstances of the children . . . you must write to me in full detail about what has happened in the period [since my departure both] inside and outside the house concerning [both] the young and the old . . . Do not neglect [to tell me] about the condition of the children'.[45]

A mother's feelings for her son could be just as intense as a father's. Māralīnā's thoughts were constantly attuned to her son, Shukr Allāh, who had recently departed to join his father abroad. Even allowing for rhetorical posturing and formulaic idiom, the sentiments she avowed in her letters to her son and her husband were nothing if not heartfelt. 'Night

[38] BL/Lansdowne/1046, doc. 7. [39] BL/Lansdowne/1046, doc. 56; also see doc. 49.
[40] BL/Lansdowne/1046, doc. 56. [41] BL/Lansdowne/1046, doc. 60. [42] Ibid.
[43] BL/Lansdowne/1046, doc. 49.
[44] MssOcc/NAF/9001: 67–70; MssOcc/NAF/9002: 12–13; MssOcc/NAF/9005: 2–9; HAG/Persian Documents, doc. 27.
[45] BL/Lansdowne/1046, doc. 49.

and day,' she wrote to Shukr Allāh, 'I am praying for you because I do not have solace except in your presence. And I continue to ask our lord Jesus Christ and the truth of his mother that they protect your soul and body, and bring you safe and sound to your father.'[46] To her husband, she confided, 'I do not sleep [at night] because of my thinking of him on his journey [and] through being broken-hearted.'[47] Niʿmat Allāh, a neighbour and close kinsman, reiterated these feelings when he told Shukr Allāh, 'Your mother ... is praying for your life and she has no concern except your separation [from her].'[48]

Māralīnā's feelings for her son thus found expression in her concern for him, which gnawed at her incessantly, and in her frequent entreaties to God to grant him safety and success. This quintessential motherliness, however, was yoked to hard-headed calculations that formed the other side of her relationship with her son. Whenever possible, Māralīnā helped him by faithfully carrying out any instructions he might send her that affected the family's livelihood. She also mediated for him, at times at his behest, at times unbeknownst to him. 'Matters did not go as is desired,' she admitted to her husband. 'Therefore what is in his [your son's] possession is lacking ... This is because of bad luck. He is not to blame.'[49] Such was Māralīnā's attachment to her son that to receive news of his well-being and of his love for her was a cause for rejoicing and gratitude. When Niʿmat Allāh passed on Shukr Allāh's letter to Māralīnā, he observed her reaction. 'She read it and was overjoyed [to learn of] your good health. And she sends you greetings and prayers for continuing [life], and asks *allāh* that he show her soon your face in complete goodness and health.'[50]

It was not unusual for a father and mother to speak with one voice when it came to their son. This commonality can be seen in a mother's demand for news from her son, which could be just as unyielding and forthright as a father's. In 1745, Katarīn wrote to her son from their home in Bengal:

> O my son, you have not informed us about your situation, about what business you are doing or about your state. Send us a letter [in which] you inform us about all of your circumstances in detail so that it consoles our mind concerning you ... O my son, send us a detailed letter concerning the whole of your situation without fail ... And we inform you that we have sent you two letters and this is the third. And send [a letter] to inform us whether you intend to come [home] or not.[51]

Similarly, ʿAbd al-Qādir in Basra informed Awānīs b. Astūr in Calcutta that 'every few days, your mother comes to us in the house (*bayt*) asking

[46] BL/Lansdowne/1046, doc. 70.
[47] BL/Lansdowne/1046, doc. 69.
[48] BL/Lansdowne/1046, doc. 67.
[49] BL/Lansdowne/1046, doc. 69.
[50] BL/Lansdowne/1046, doc. 67.
[51] BL/Lansdowne/1046, doc. 12.

about you, saying he has not sent a letter, he has not sent news about how are things with him. Please would you send each season (*mawsim*) letters by way of Basra and by way of Jidda.'[52]

The commonality is perhaps most readily observed in the shared desire of the father and mother for the son's well-being and future success, or, if away in foreign lands, their prayers for his safety. And the visceral emotions underlying these could not always be contained. Raw and unvarnished, such emotions are documented in a letter written by Ḥannā b. ʿAbd al-Dāʾim. He was writing to his son, from whom he and his wife had received no word for nigh on three years:

> Perhaps the barrier between us is for the best. If *allāh* wishes, may it be good for you. But [consider] how is the state of your father and your mother [at your silence]? We are weeping continuously. If *allāh* wishes, may you be well and [receive] help from the *rabb*. And we apologise if we have been base and made mistakes ... O my son, you should be generous to your parents, [but] you have treated them cruelly since you don't send them a letter even to console us about your well-being. And, O my son, the numerous letters I have written! And I have flung each letter hither and thither devotedly. Now I no longer have the heart and I am left an old man and because of my extreme weakness I feel like an eighty year old. But this is *allāh*'s desire. And also your mother and sisters complain bitterly [because] of their yearning for you. And they send you many greetings and kindness and love all the time. And they kiss your eyes and are praying for you night and day, and in the middle of the night they pray for you and implore you, and they are crying and beseeching the lord of lords (*sulṭān al-salāṭīn*) that he helps you and takes care of you in whatever you do and holds on to your hand. And may your face appear to us soon safe and sound ... And enough of your separation [from us] ... We are like the burning candle so that, by the power of *rabb*, may we still be lit and see you before our life is extinguished and may we die in your presence. Truly the desire, by our *allāh*, is that your face appears to us in complete goodness and health before we die.[53]

This passage leaves us in little doubt about the anguish felt by these parents at the unconscionably long absence and silence of their son. It is also a testament to their enduring love for him.

While such commonalities in the affective tendencies of fathers and mothers were very real, they need to be set against the entrenched differences in their statuses and roles within the family household.[54] Focusing once again on the son, the differences are exemplified by the manner in which a mature son dealt with his father and mother. The letters give no

[52] BL/Lansdowne/1046, doc. 65. [53] BL/Lansdowne/1046, doc. 68.

[54] In a similar vein, see Judith E. Tucker, 'Ties that bound: women and family in eighteenth- and nineteenth-century Nablus', in Nikki R. Keddie and Beth Baron (eds.), *Women in Middle Eastern History: Shifting Boundaries in Sex and Gender* (New Haven, CT, 1991), 233–53.

indication that he was expected to obey a mother's instructions, or that she would even contemplate giving any, at least openly. The contrast with his father is obvious.

We may sharpen our sense of the reigning differences between men and women by considering what was demanded of a husband and a wife in a marriage. Fortunately for us, several of the letters are remarkably candid about the relationship between Māralīnā at home in southern Iraq and her husband, ʿAbd Allāh b. Ḥassūn, then in India. At the time that they were written, the late 1740s, Māralīnā was feeling very frustrated and unhappy. She deemed her husband's ceaseless travelling and longstanding neglect as the proximate cause for her current straitened circumstances. And she resolved to have no more of it. In unburdening herself to him and to her son, we learn much about a wife's situation and her due within the family household and the intimate community. We also learn about how husbands and wives actually interacted with one another.

To Māralīnā's way of thinking, it was unjust that her husband was ignoring her desires and feelings. This insensitivity lay at the root of her lament.

> I say to you, [my] dear, until when must we continue in this condition, with you grumbling and being in a far away country (*bilād*)? I am hard pressed by the situation which has arisen through worries and constraints and low spirits and those difficulties [due to] your separation from me and your absence from me. Is this appropriate, O my lord? And are you satisfied that we spend our lives in this difficult condition? We have now had enough of what we have endured through your absence. I am a poor wife for whom nothing springs forth from my hand without your presence. So until when must we wait for the relief of your arrival? … O my lord … cut short your absence and endeavour to return home so that this unhappiness and worry may come to an end.[55]

Even if not always for the same reasons, Māralīnā felt her husband's absence no less keenly than she did her son's. We have already seen that longing and concern for close kindred, especially for sons, was a commonplace sentiment among the people of the arena, for both men and women. Māralīnā's desire for her husband's physical companionship, however, was linked to her need for the material support that his presence would furnish. Such was the lot of kinswomen, recognised and accepted by all, even if grudgingly. Such was the lot of those in the family household who depended on their often distant husbands and mature sons. Māralīnā was no exception to this. But the manner in which she made her remarks to her husband reveals something else.

[55] BL/Lansdowne/1046, doc. 69.

Māralīnā was formally inferior to her husband within the family household, a reality she frankly acknowledged in a variety of ways. It was quite normal for her – as a wife or a mother – to refer to herself in the presence of her mature son or husband in the first person, as 'I'. She also frequently referred to herself in the third person, defining herself in relation to the person being addressed. With her son, the language she used conveyed respect or endearment, as in 'my soul' (*rūḥī*),[56] or simply gestured to their biological tie. This language certainly does not suggest that her mature son was by right superior to her. Māralīnā's self-image was very different, however, with her husband. Wives commonly described themselves before their husbands in loving, caring and dignified terms, as, say, 'your darling' or 'the noble wife'. Māralīnā did make use of this register. But she also made good use of another that, at least rhetorically, consigned her to the lowest stratum and elevated her husband to the highest. So we see extremely deferential modes of address like 'your slave-girl' (*jārīyatak*), while her husband, in contrast, is 'my sublime honour', 'master', 'lord'.[57]

Such openly avowed inferiority coexisted with the notion of the wife as inviolable, as sacred. This was expressed most clearly when Māralīnā referred to herself as her husband's *ḥurma*.[58] The root meaning of this word is 'that which is holy or a taboo'. This sense of the word is always present even if the primary intent was to convey the idea of a 'woman', 'lady', 'wife'. Māralīnā also confessed in her letters her total material dependence on her husband (and her son). But this dependence was tempered by a powerful drive to preserve her entitlements. She was not afraid to voice and assert her rights to these entitlements if she felt that her husband was failing in his fundamental obligations towards her and his family household. And she was feeling this failure very keenly in 1747.

In the absence of her husband, and being in need of money, Māralīnā turned to her in-laws for help. Niʿmat Allāh, who was both her husband's and her son's brother-in-law,[59] came to her aid. Trying to allay any worries her son might have, he wrote to him,

By the power of *allāh*, we give her whatever expenses she requires, and we do not allow her to turn to anyone else [for help] . . . So whatever expense is desired, we

[56] BL/Lansdowne/1046, doc. 70.

[57] BL/Lansdowne/1046, docs. 69, 77. The references here to slaves and masters derive much of their meaning from the ambient social reality in the period. This is because slavery, alongside servants, formed an integral part of many of the region's households. Citations to the relevant historical scholarship on slaves and slavery may be found in Chapter 4 on the relational order.

[58] BL/Lansdowne/1046, doc. 69.

[59] Two of Niʿmat Allāh's sisters had married Māralīnā brother-in-law and son, respectively.

give it to her. We do not put her in need of anyone [else] and we do not allow her to sell any of your belongings because your belongings are our belongings.[60]

A kinsman confirmed this. 'With respect to expenses, Shammās Niʿmat Allāh does not deny her anything.'[61] Māralīnā herself told her son, 'Niʿmat Allāh does not leave me in want of anything ... Whenever I ask him for expenses, he sends me them without trouble ... O my son, don't forget his good behaviour towards us.'[62]

Māralīnā was grateful for Niʿmat Allāh's help. It allowed her to pay the bills. It also gave her a means to berate her husband.

Behold, O my lord, that we have gained in your place and your affairs a loving man. And his help has arrived as charity in repulsing [my] grief. [His name] is ... Niʿmat Allāh b. Jurūh. And the man does not abandon me when I am in need of someone ... Behold, O my lord, on account of the aforesaid help in your place, there has come to me a bit of relief.[63]

Despite these damning words, there remained limits on the extent to which Niʿmat Allāh could replace her husband. 'O my dear,' Māralīnā continued,

you are informed that whenever I finish the expenses it is embarrassing that I have to ask him [Niʿmat Allāh] again. But the man sends money when it is spent. He even sends other things and oftentimes he sends them to me without a request ... If you came and honoured us with your arrival, how much great[er] joy and true relief we would have.[64]

The counterpart of Niʿmat Allāh's generosity was the husband's egregious neglect of wife and his family at home. 'Consider, O my honoured lord,' his wife wrote, 'that we have not had any joy in our lives. So I ask from your grace that you do not dismiss me from [your] thoughts, but rather you hear this my request.'[65] Now it is conceivable that Māralīnā was unique among wives and mothers in the arena for her bold, uncompromising stance in making such claims on her husband. However, this is unlikely because others too thought likewise. Her son-in-law, ʿAbd al-ʿAṭī, believed that there were certain fundamentals which ʿAbd Allāh as husband owed his wife at home. In a letter to Māralīnā's son, who was at the time en route to his father in India, he noted, 'Keep on trying to persuade him [your father] to return to these parts. It is enough [that] he works hard to return home so that he finds rest and the mind of your mother is put at ease.'[66]

[60] BL/Lansdowne/1046, doc. 67. [61] BL/Lansdowne/1046, doc. 71.
[62] BL/Lansdowne/1046, doc. 70. [63] BL/Lansdowne/1046, doc. 69. [64] Ibid.
[65] Ibid. [66] BL/Lansdowne/1046, doc. 71.

The arena's prevailing realities often generated divergent outcomes for the lives of men and women. Alongside gender, age or generation forms another axis upon which behavioural tendencies may be mapped. As the examples above show, in relation to his son, a father occupied a position of far greater authority and respect. This was accompanied by major differences in responsibilities, especially for the material well-being of the family household and for the education of the children. Though not as sharply defined, the son's behaviour towards his other elders, particularly elder kinsmen, bears comparison with his behaviour towards his father. This points to a clear gap between elders and juniors. A Shīʿī father went so far as to tell his son that 'ending [well in the after-life happens] through the satisfaction of [your] elders (*buzurgān*)'.[67] The notion of *buzurgān*, which I take here to refer to living elders, may be readily stretched to embrace ancestors. This is reasonable given that many of the region's families and communities were proud of their lineage and forebears, and took care to honour and celebrate their deceased kindred. (See Figure 2.) Sayyid Muṣṭafā himself placed a very high value on keeping the memory of his family tree alive. Before embarking on his travels, he was asked by his relatives to get from Iraq 'a genealogy (*nasabnāmah*) for the children'. So precious was this document that he considered it 'more important than a *sanad* for a *manṣab* and a *jāgīr*'.[68] A recipient of money for charitable purposes in Najaf expressed much the same idea in saying: 'You must inform all the [folk] small and big [associated with] that gentleman about the dignity of his lineage (*silsila*).'[69]

An array of known realities and the behavioural tendencies associated with them have been examined in this chapter. These were all embedded in, and constitutive of, intimate relationships characterising the arena's family households. As a rule, great respect was accorded to elders, especially to the father and husband; they expected to be – and usually were – honoured by those around them of humbler status. The latter also tended to acquiesce to the orders and urgings of those above them in an appropriately deferential fashion. Whether low or high, it seems that no one enjoyed what might be described as real personal freedom. Nevertheless, certain individuals by virtue of their status and role did have conferred on them particular rights, privileges and immunities that were far weaker for, or denied to,

[67] BL/Lansdowne/1046, doc. 58.

[68] BL/Lansdowne/1046, doc. 50. A *sanad* was a general term for a document sanctioned by sovereign authority. A *manṣab* referred to a formal rank in the imperial Mughal hierarchy, whose holder was traditionally awarded income from revenues collected from a *jāgīr*, an officially demarcated area of cultivated land.

[69] BL/Lansdowne/1046, doc. 16.

79

هاذي شجرة الحسيب النسيب السيد الجليل السيد

بسم الله الرحمن الرحيم

الحمد لله رب العالمين والصلاة والسلام على رسول
الله صلى الله عليه وسلم وعلى آله الطيبين الطاهرين
اقولوا واعلم ارشدك الله تعالى الى المنهج القديم
وسلك الى طريق المستقيم اما قال النبي صلى الله عليه وسلم
اهل بيتي كمثل سفينة نوح من ركبها نجي ومن تخلف
عنها غرق والاحاديث في ذلك كثيرة كما قال الله تعالى
انما يريد الله ليذهب عنكم الرجس اهل البيت ويطهركم
تطهيرا ورضي الله تعالى عن كل اصحابت رسول الله
اجمعين والاقربا والتابعين قال رسول الله صلى الله
عليه وسلم كل حسب ونسب ينقطع الا حسبي ونسبي
لا ينقطع الا يوم القيامة صدق رسول الله بما قال
قال رسول الله صلى الله عليه وسلم انا مدينة العلم وعلي

بنفسه ويحلم ولا يغضب فان الغضب لله وان يسر
المريدين بحسن خلقه وان يضرب او يشتم يصبر ويقنع
بما رزقه الله من الرزق ويحمد الله تعالى
على السراء والضراء ويكظم الغيظ ويعفو
عن من ظلمه وان يواسي الفقراء ولا يخص
نفسه بشي دونهم وان يكرم الغرباء ويخضع
للكبير والصغير فاذا كملت هاذا الاوصاف والخصال
المحموده حصلت له المنح والفضيله والعطايا
الجزيله ثم احاز الفوايد والمراد واعتاد للعباد
والله الموفق للسداد والله روف بالعباد ان الله
على كل شي قدير برحمتك يا ارحم الراحمين

والحمد لله رب
العالمين
امين

Figure 2. The beginning and end of a letter detailing a genealogy.
Source: BL/Lansdowne/1046, doc. 79.

others. Similarly, there were naturalised differences in liabilities and duties. Women especially were heavily constrained in relation to their husbands, and also to their brothers and sons, even if not always in the same senses. But this did not preclude them from having substantial autonomy at home and within their intimate community, an autonomy which was buttressed by a secure entitlement to the material and affective bases of life. As for sons, they enjoyed special treatment. At the same time, they had to defer with due humility to their fathers in many realms of their lives, and seemingly well into maturity. They were also forever duty-bound to their most intimate kindred, particularly to their mothers and sisters.

Such patterns of behaviour may be correlated to age (or generation), lineage and gender. The fact that individuals within intimate communities were often multiply related in a number of generational dispositions can occasionally throw this correlation into sharp relief. Because of that multiplicity, it was possible to specify relations between kindred using several different terms. However, preference was given to one term over the others in particular contexts. By paying heed to these terms and the contexts in which they were invoked, we learn about the attitudes of kindred towards the structuring of their family, especially with regard to lineage and generational position. For example, with the notable exception of his son, Sayyid Muṣṭafā placed greater weight on the generational position of his close kindred than on their lineage or genealogical proximity to him. As far as he was concerned, authority within his family household was correlated first with age and only then with one's immediate descent group.[70] But correlations of this type had little or no bearing on those behavioural tendencies that manifested themselves as sentiments, to which labels such as anxiety, love, generosity are often applied. All we can say for sure is that the realities fostering such emotions were widespread among intimates of all kinds where personal trust was central, and arguably a defining attribute. The two possible exceptions – for being unusually strong and marked by the most visceral of emotions – were the bonds between a son and his mother, and between a son and his father.

[70] BL/Lansdowne/1046, docs. 56, 58. The case of Sayyid Muṣṭafā's family is discussed in detail in Chapter 8 on flows and interactions.

4 A relational order: intimates, strangers and plurality

> In the land as well as sea . . . business are in the manner as if they were in a burning fire . . . They had no profit at all in the goods from Surat which they laded on board the Armenian, Indian and Dutch ships . . . Sundry persons had freighted for Bassorah a Portuguese ship . . . And without any joking he says that they would not have freighted the ship if he had not promised to come [as] supercargo in it . . . That to please the gentlemen he accepted of the said employment . . . He took these troubles to do good to those of his nation who on account of the war did not dare to lade any thing on board the French or English ships. He hopes that God will favour him on account of the good that he does to those of his nation.[1]

The words above were written by Minas de Eliaz in 1746 while on his way to Basra from Bengal. He would surely have agreed that to survive and make do with one's lot in this world were truisms of life in Islamicate Eurasia. Studying these truisms helps us to grasp how they shaped worldly encounters for Minas, and others akin to him. Pluralistic surroundings, risks to health and property, disparities in access to brute force – such were the undeniable realities that framed everyday behaviour when it came to, say, making a livelihood, sharing information and cajoling partners from afar. This chapter, together with the two that follow, are about realities like these and the behavioural tendencies associated with them. The paired realities and tendencies were apprehended by contemporaries as manmade constructs which imposed eminently practical bounds on what one knew and on one's capacity to act. They also facilitated the acquisition of knowledge and enlarged the possibilities for action.[2]

[1] NA/HCA/42/25 (St Catharina): 77, 79, 82.
[2] There is a sizeable body of scholarship, often in a theoretical vein, on social action or, as it was termed in an earlier generation, structure and agency. For my purposes, those I have found most useful are Amartya K. Sen, 'Rational fools: a critique of the behavioural foundations of economic theory', *Philosophy and Public Affairs* 6:4 (1977), 371–44; Philip Abrams, *Historical Sociology* (Ithaca, NY, 1982); Harrison C. White, *Identity and Control: a Structural Theory of Social Action* (2nd edn, Princeton, NJ, 2008); Peter

The cosmic and familial orders treated in the preceding chapters form a counterpart to the three orders – the relational, the communications, the political – treated in this and the coming chapters. These two sets of orders are exclusive and complementary with respect to one another. Whereas the former was carried within individual persons, the latter emanated from the environment beyond the individual; whereas the cosmic and familial orders were viewed as natural and timeless, in contrast, the relational, the communications and the political orders were viewed as manmade, potentially malleable, artefacts with a past, present and future; whereas one set gestured towards the grandest of scales and the most intimate, the other set pivoted on the vagaries of temporal existence. Construed thus, these orders are two sides of the same coin; in their qualitatively distinct ways, they express the ontology of daily life within the arena in the eighteenth century.

In this chapter, I focus specifically on the relational order. The order is elucidated by examining the three types of relationships that shaped activities central to circulation and exchange in India and the Islamic heartlands. These relationships – those with breadwinners, those within the intimate community and those with strangers – enmeshed individuals in their social context, with formative consequences for their path through life.

Among the most basic challenges that had to be mastered within the arena – challenges that we seldom face today – were those deriving from uncertainties endemic to dealings on regional scales.[3] These uncertainties were themselves a consequence of the extended silences which often punctuated relationships between the arena's people; of the long gestation period for many of their transactions; and of the major constraints on their ability to ensure compliance. As a result, the latest information from a far-off place – for example, a relative's whereabouts or the current price of goods – might well have been overtaken by events since its dispatch. Or perhaps money entrusted to a distant agent might have been used for purposes other than those originally agreed upon. The experience of such

Bearman, Robert Faris and James Moody, 'Blocking the future: new solutions for old problems in historical social science', *Social Science History* 32:4 (1999), 501–33; William H. Sewell, *Logics of History: Social Theory and Social Transformation* (Chicago, IL, 2005).

[3] By endemic uncertainties, I mean those types of uncertainties that were commonly planned for and managed by the arena's participants to *their* satisfaction. There was, of course, another wholly separate category of uncertainties – to do with, say, when and how one will die, unseasonable weather, the outbreak of hostilities, an earthquake – which are inversions of endemic uncertainties. This separate category of uncertainties was simply too unpredictable to be planned for and managed. They are discussed as 'acts of God' in Chapter 2 on the cosmic order.

realities was widespread, and this experience was intimately tied to certain observable tendencies in behaviour.

One such tendency stressed the general value of cultivating interpersonal relationships. Awareness of this may be seen in Sayyid Muṣṭafā's advice to his son that he 'spend a part of [his] time ensuring friends are happy and enemies are assuaged'.[4] The advice was reinforced by his desire that his son 'behave well with everyone'.[5] An obvious rationale for such an attitude was that, because of the endemic uncertainties, it could not be known exactly when and what kind of help might be needed in future. Setting aside the affective motivations studied in the previous chapter, relationships offered several practical benefits to those actively involved in the arena. For one thing, they helped foster a sense of stability and control. To have a personal rapport with someone was to be entwined with a larger social milieu. This diminished the menace of the future by rendering its risks more predictable and thus calculable. For another, with little or no recourse to printed material in the region,[6] few mechanisms could compete with interpersonal relationships as conduits for harvesting new information and ideas, for making enquiries and satisfying curiosity, and for tapping the store of inherited and collective experiences.

But relationships also had value of a more immediate nature. They allowed for the option of calling upon intimates or strangers to help settle disagreements with another party. In 1762, Bernard Picot solicited Ezekiel Rahabi's 'authority' within his Jewish community in Cochin for precisely that end.[7] This was relationships as a kind of insurance, coexisting with the more formal mechanisms for resolving disputes (elaborated in Chapter 6 on the political order). As for the material benefits, they could be rather modest, of value more for the symbolism than anything else. The Gujarati Vindrāvan, for example, regularly sent his partners and clients gifts of locally available produce, typically packets of raisins, small bags of coffee, jars of marmalade and honey.[8] To his associates who happened to visit Mocha, he would offer his home 'to dispose of as [they] saw fit'.[9] Of course, gift-giving was rarely an act devoid of (expectations of) reciprocity.[10] At the same time that Jīvan

[4] BL/Lansdowne/1046, doc. 56. In a similar vein, see BL/Lansdowne/1046, doc. 60.

[5] BL/Lansdowne/1046, doc. 58.

[6] The reasons for the absence of printing in the Islamic world before the nineteenth century are discussed in Francis Robinson, 'Technology and religious change: Islam and the impact of print', *Modern Asian Studies* 27:1 (1993), 229–51.

[7] MssOcc/NAF/9074 (15 July 1762).

[8] MssOcc/NAF/9038: 5, 10, 12, 13, 15, 20, 21, 25, 29.

[9] MssOcc/NAF/9038: 3–6 (August 1767, received in Mahe at the end of September 1767).

[10] A classic work on the subject, which still remains of value, is Marcel Mauss, *The Gift: Form and Reason for Exchange in Archaic Societies*, trans. W. D. Hall (London, 1990).

and Krishan were begging a client on the Malabar coast to accept ten bags of raisins from Mocha as a 'sign of [our] affection',[11] they declared that they wanted him to continue using their services there. Gift-giving frequently merged into requests for special favours that sought to take advantage of the other side's influence or proximity to a certain place. These could be for desirable luxuries. They could equally be for life-and-death necessities. In 1767, Bernard Picot made strenuous efforts to find jewellers for Ezekiel Rahabi and have them sent to him in Cochin. This was not the easiest of favours to fulfil because, as he told Rahabi, 'they have not shown me much desire to travel to Cochin'. If he was still in need of them, however, 'I will send them'.[12] A few years later, it was Isaac Surgun who approached Picot. When Surgun's son fell ill in January 1776, Picot was asked to find particular drugs for him that were not available in Cochin.[13]

Facilitating access to luxuries and necessities points to another general benefit of relationships: to those who were party to them, they made available a wider range of skills and resources. The case study presented in Chapter 8 of the dealings between Nasarvanji Manakji and the brothers Veṅkateśa and Nārāyaṇa Kāmat shows how relationships could be exploited in order, say, to increase the number and value of transactions in which each side had a stake, thereby boosting turnover and profits. They could also be exploited for enhancing rank within the community through, for example, charitable acts. In both instances, reputation and creditworthiness were the main qualities that the individual was seeking to uphold and bolster.[14] This was one of the supreme advantages of being associated with the Kāmat brothers. Their position in Goa and, more broadly, in western India in the middle of the eighteenth century was such that one could quite reasonably expect a word from them on someone's behalf to be widely noted and trusted. This is just what the Portuguese merchant-official Feliciano António Nogueira had in mind when, on having fully settled his accounts with Miguel de Souza and Nasarvanji Manakji in 1785, he asked the Kāmats 'to make it public for the good of my credit'.[15]

The importance that Sayyid Muṣṭafā accorded to relationships in general also reflects a basic feature of the arena of circulation and exchange. In view of the endemic uncertainties, many of the tasks critical

[11] MssOcc/NAF/8992: 87, 88–9.
[12] MssOcc/NAF/9050 (4 July, 16 August, 3 and 9 September 1767).
[13] MssOcc/NAF/8996 (10 February, 1 March 1776).
[14] I consider these qualities at length in Chapter 6 on the political order as central to the existence of that order.
[15] MHR/Correspondence (incoming) (20 October 1785).

to the outcome of a venture required personal initiative. As a practical consequence, this meant that appropriate partners or agents were few in number. Such associates once found could not be readily substituted. In the parlance of economics, they were not very fungible. And so the decision to terminate an existing relationship was never an easy one. Indeed, it was unusual to replace one associate with another performing an identical role; the only exception occurred following death or retirement. As a result, parties to a relationship tended to persevere with their existing ties and work hard on improving them. Vindrāvan is a case in point. Well aware that the French had no realistic alternative to him in Mocha, he knew a failure to meet expectations would not translate into an immediate rupture. After a commercial voyage in 1769 which 'far from being advantageous has been very prejudicial to me',[16] Vindrāvan's principal on the Malabar coast told him that 'the gentlemen last year did not seem satisfied' with him. Nevertheless, their relationship continued, Vindrāvan receiving the gentlest of rebukes: 'it is [incumbent] on you to work in such a way that everyone is happy which I will hear with pleasure because of the interest I take in you'.[17]

The practical need for attentiveness to one's bearing in social life was distilled into aphorisms that were widely aired. It also preyed on the minds of fathers responsible for their sons' education. In the preceding chapter on the familial order, I describe the ties that bound Sayyid Muṣṭafā and Thanā' Allāh – both abroad at the time – to their sons back home in Bengal. Their correspondence makes it clear that they harboured great affection for their sons. However, this sentiment was imbued with hard-headed realism. Their guidance was motivated not just by altruism and an abiding concern for their sons' moral well-being; the fathers were also keenly aware that the relationship of their sons to those around them – within the family household certainly, but beyond its threshold too – had a strategic aspect. Sayyid Muṣṭafā viewed a cheerful demeanour, goodness of character and seemly comportment as cardinal virtues in an upstanding member of his community. To be sociable and genial followed from these.[18] But the matter could not be left at that; directed effort was required as well. For this reason, he insisted that his son, without neglecting to cultivate his inner qualities, be at the same time empathetic and solicitous towards those he met in the round of daily life: if they were happy, he had to ensure that they remained so; if there was

16 He continues, 'Ce à quoi je m'attendais d'autant moins que tous les autres bâtimens Malabars n'ont pas éssuyés de perte'. MssOcc/NAF/9038: 22 (Mahe, 7 March 1770); MssOcc/NAF/9059 (7 March 1770).

17 MssOcc/NAF/9038: 22 (Mahe, 7 March 1770); MssOcc/NAF/9059 (7 March 1770).

18 BL/Lansdowne/1046, docs. 49, 58.

any ill-will, it was his duty to deal with its roots and reconcile their differences.[19] Indeed, to be 'a caresser of friends and an assuager of enemies' appears to have been a commonplace saying.[20] Accomplishing this goal, however, required a thick skin, which underlay Sayyid Muṣṭafā's counsel to his son 'not to listen to the tittle-tattle of people'.[21]

Thanāʾ Allāh echoed much of Sayyid Muṣṭafā's advice – and strictures. His attentiveness to social life at large is most apparent in his sensitivity to the word on the street. So he asked both mother and son to remain in accord, not only for reasons of familial harmony, but also so that 'no one will say anything bad'.[22] The sensitivity was especially acute when it came to perceived slights. His son Gharīb Allāh was duty-bound to keep their intimates at home safe from these. He was to protect Mīr ʿAbd Allāh from insults. But there was more. 'Until I return home,' wrote Thanāʾ Allāh, 'I have charged you that no one wrongs [Shaykh Naẓar Muḥammad]. You personally will remain attentive [to this] ... The pious Gharīb Allāh will continue to take care that no one says anything [bad].'[23] Such injunctions to look out for one's own could extend to the confessional group as a whole. A Muslim in Najaf was reminded in 1747 that 'It is among the cluster of duties (*vājibāt*) that one does not do this injustice to other Muslims and the rights of the [Sufi] dervishes also are not harmed.'[24] The contrast was being made with an Armenian with whom they had been dealing of late. Likewise, a correspondent stressed that, by fulfilling his request, 'no one else will [as a result] treat anyone so badly nor damage the rights of Muslims and the deserving ones'.[25] What these aphorisms and exhortations suggest is that, in communities such as Sayyid Muṣṭafā's and Thanāʾ Allāh's, individuals strove to align disparate elements of their lives in ways that bridged conduct in their personal realm with their bearing in their polity at large.

While certain general orientations regarding interpersonal relationships were independent of the backgrounds of the individuals concerned, the specific cluster of duties, rights and expectations could differ markedly between one type of relationship and another. Relationships among close kindred within the family household are discussed in the previous chapter. We see there that the male heads of family

19 BL/Lansdowne/1046, docs. 56, 58.
20 For example, see BL/Lansdowne/1046, doc. 34, a letter between intimates, possibly from a son-in-law to his father-in-law.
21 BL/Lansdowne/1046, doc. 49. A good case is made for the importance of studying gossip in premodern times in Chris Wickham, 'Gossip and resistance among the medieval peasantry', *Past and Present* 160 (1998), 3–24. This also contains useful references to the scholarly literature on the subject.
22 BL/Lansdowne/1046, doc. 11. 23 Ibid. 24 BL/Lansdowne/1046, doc. 27.
25 BL/Lansdowne/1046, doc. 31.

households – patriarchs, for short – and their mature sons occupied special positions, and the bonds between them were of particular importance. In large part, this stemmed from their role as the chief breadwinners within their community, from their capacity to marshal resources as and when required, and from their personal experience of the ways of the world. They were recognised as critical for the present well-being, ongoing unity and future prosperity of their family households, and of their immediate community. This was a near universal attribute of the arena's people. As a result, patriarchs and mature sons were treated with considerable respect, and ties with them assiduously cultivated. While there is no denying the comparable, or even greater, significance of other relationships, the unique quality of patriarchs and their mature sons was that it was only they who could *expect* to command authority throughout their communities by virtue of their status.

The exceptional nature of these individuals was expressed rhetorically through the epithets and titles with which they were addressed. These are all instances of relational markers detailed in Chapter 1 on cognitive patterns, with common examples being 'devoted [to you]' (*mukhliṣ*), 'most generous' (*akram*), '[your] dignity' (*janāb*). Some of these markers referred to the author himself in relation to the addressee. Others referred solely to the addressee. The main purpose of such terms was not to communicate actual information about, say, genealogical or generational distance between the pair. Rather, their prime function appears to have been to signal – or assert – the degree of affection between two individuals or their relative status within the community.

Fictive kinship, especially claims to and reminders of brotherliness, was another means of cultivating relations with mature sons and their fathers. Male kindred between whom there existed a close bond could refer to one another in fraternal terms, whether or not they were real brothers. Niʿmat Allāh, for example, was very partial to this sentiment, and its emotional bedrock. He invoked it frequently in talking about, and addressing, kindred beyond his own nuclear family. To Shukr Allāh, who was both his uncle and brother through separate marriages,[26] he wrote: 'We are lovers and guardians of the affection, and bread and salt [that we have shared]. By the power of *allāh*, our love is eternal and [our] love brotherly. You know this. Don't ever worry about this matter.'[27] In his relations with Shukr Allāh's father, the feelings avowed by Niʿmat Allāh, though more muted and deferential, still conveyed intimacy. He asked Shukr Allāh

[26] Niʿmat Allāh was doubly related to Shukr Allāh. His sisters were married to Shukr Allāh and Shukr Allāh's paternal uncle, respectively.
[27] BL/Lansdowne/1046, doc. 67.

that, on meeting his father in India, he 'embrace our revered brother, your father, and kiss him for us in our absence, and present him our many greetings and respects and eternal, forever love and night-and-day prayers'.[28]

Such assertions of brotherly relations were meaningful for several reasons. That they expressed deeply held sentiments should not be gainsaid, unless, that is, we have evidence to the contrary. But it is also true that they had a tactical value; they could be employed in reinforcing an individual's claims on his 'brother' by throwing into sharp relief his moral obligation towards him. Again, Niʿmat Allāh offers us a good example. When it was useful, he had little compunction about exploiting his (partially fictive) brotherly ties with Shukr Allāh and the (real) brotherly ties between Ḥannā and Shukr Allāh's father, ʿAbd Allāh. This tactic is seen at work in his letter to Shukr Allāh. As noted above, Niʿmat Allāh asked Shukr Allāh to find out what had become of Ḥannā's son, Anṭūn, whose arrival was long overdue. He made a point of reminding Shukr Allāh to 'be very attentive to [this matter] because [Anṭūn] is the son of your uncle [and] because his father and your father are [brothers]. Your father asked to relay to you that we [and] his brother are [brothers].'[29]

The bonds that individual members of the community had with patriarchs and with mature sons were crucial for the community's well-being. But so was the relationship *between* mature sons and their fathers. This patrifilial bond was especially important for those who depended most on it for their material survival and future prospects, above all, the wife, the mother, the sister. The interaction between a father and his mature son thus formed one of the central axes around which the family household pivoted. While obviously of great significance to their immediate kinswomen, this relationship also mattered greatly to the community at large. That is why it was not just individuals within the nuclear family who were attentive to its dynamic and concerned about its health. In Chapter 3 on the familial order, letters are quoted which bear witness to direct intervention by dependants and by others in the community. This could be to shore up the patrifilial relationship in a general sense, or it could be to help resolve the particular difficulties under which the father and his mature son were labouring at the time.

The concern evidenced for patrifilial relationships was paralleled by the responsibility of husbands, fathers and mature sons for the survival of their immediate dependants, usually their closest kindred. Chapter 3 also examines the inalienable duties of a husband towards his wife, as well as of a mature son towards his mother and sisters. This is done in terms of the

[28] BL/Lansdowne/1046, doc. 67. [29] Ibid.

behavioural tendencies characterising their bonds. It follows that kinsmen had to have some kind of livelihood in order to fulfil what was required of them. But which one? And having made the choice, how to go about it?[30]

The actual choice of livelihood was, of course, framed by an individual's background and the prevailing context. Usually he had little or no control over the matter, and, indeed, may not even have been fully cognisant of the fact. The choice was sculpted by his community's traditions and the character of their ambient polity, a matter to which I return in Chapter 6 on the political order. Such restrictions, however, still left open the issue of what were the principles that determined in practice the prosecution of a livelihood. In the case of trade on regional scales, some aimed for the greatest possible return in any given transaction. The rationale for the transaction would then be based on its relative profitability. But this objective was tempered by reigning attitudes towards risk and expediency; given the well-known uncertainties endemic to the region at the time, the arena's participants were usually satisfied if the proceeds from the transaction met their current working and living costs, and covered the fundamental needs of their dependants. This is reflected in the manner in which accounts were typically kept. As elaborated in the discussion of practices later in the book, priority was given to income and cash flow over longer-term indicators such as assets and liabilities.[31]

I have made liberal use of the word 'community' thus far without having defined it. In this section, I begin the process of recovering its substance and form. Core to my understanding of community in eighteenth-century India and the Islamic heartlands lies the notion of an intimate.[32] To the

[30] For recent work on livelihoods in India and the Islamic heartlands in our period, see Abdul-Karim Rafeq, 'Making a living or making a fortune in Ottoman Syria', in Nelly Hanna (ed.), *Money, Land and Trade: an Economic History of the Mediterranean* (London, 2002), 101–23; Muzaffar Alam and Sanjay Subrahmanyam, 'Making of a munshi', *Comparative Studies of South Asia, Africa and the Middle East* 24:2 (2004), 61–72; Rosalind O'Hanlon and C. Minkowski, 'What makes people who they are? Pandit networks and the problem of livelihoods in early modern western India', *Indian Economic and Social History Review* 45:3 (2008), 381–416.

[31] Cf. the accounting calculus discussed in Shelomo D. Goitein, *A Mediterranean Society: the Jewish Communities of the Arab World as Portrayed in the Documents of the Cairo Geniza*, vol. I (Berkeley, CA, 1967), 200–9, 263.

[32] While the manner in which the intimate community is construed here overlaps with the notion of a moral community, I allow for more openness and do not confine it to a single culture or ethnicity. Among the classics in anthropology that centre on the notion of a moral community, see in particular John K. Campbell's *Honour, Family and Patronage: a Study of Institutions and Moral Values in a Greek Mountain Community* (Oxford, 1964) and Paul Stirling's *Turkish Village* (London, 1965). My understanding of an intimate community also overlaps with Robert C. Ellickson's conception of a close-knit group in his *Order without Law: How Neighbors Settle Disputes* (Cambridge, MA, 1991). Interestingly,

people of the arena, it would have been clear who was an intimate. Shāh Kawthar had no doubts about it as far as Sayyid ʿĪsā was concerned. A correspondent was informed, 'Always between me and ... Sayyid ʿĪsā and the [other] presences, there has been and remains an intimacy and connection. And they have always been attentive to my affairs.'[33] Niʿmat Allāh put it in more earthy terms. An intimate for him was someone with whom one shared 'affection and bread and salt',[34] whereas for Sayyid Muṣṭafā, it was an individual whom one remembered in one's 'personal (*khāṣṣ*) time'.[35]

While who was an intimate may have been obvious to contemporaries, this is not so for us; the subjectivity inherent in that very assessment renders the notion of an intimate, and more generally of an 'intimate community', elusive. We can, however, discern some of its core features. Despite the great variety on display, which often reflected local circumstances, the bonds among intimates could be as formative as any other. The bonds might be between kindred through marriage, friends living in the same quarter, devotees of the same shrine, masters and their slaves (or servants).[36] This variety, however, was threaded through by several

there appears to be a resonance between how I understand an intimate community and the loyalty, allegiance and affection that existed between the Mughal emperor and his nobles, at least as articulated by John F. Richards in his 'The formulation of imperial authority under Akbar and Jahangir', in John F. Richards (ed.), *Kingship and Authority in South Asia* (Delhi, 1998 [1978]), 285–326.

[33] BL/Lansdowne/1046, doc. 51.

[34] BL/Lansdowne/1046, doc. 67. The symbolism of bread and salt, and the importance ascribed to them, is touched upon in Nile Green, 'Blessed men and tribal politics: notes on political culture in the Indo-Afghan world', *Journal of the Economic and Social History of the Orient* 49:3 (2006), 344–60.

[35] BL/Lansdowne/1046, doc. 40.

[36] There is growing interest among scholars on the subject of slaves and slavery in the region in our period. Among the recent contributions, note in particular Shaun E. Marmon (ed.), *Slavery in the Islamic Middle East* (Princeton, NJ, 1999); Janet J. Ewald, 'Crossers of the sea: slaves, freedmen, and other migrants in the northwestern Indian Ocean, *c.*1750–1914', *American Historical Review* 105:1 (2000), 69–91; Scott C. Levi, 'Hindus beyond the Hindu Kush: Indians in the Central Asian slave trade', *Journal of the Royal Asiatic Society of Great Britain and Ireland* (third series) 12:3 (2002), 277–88; Pedro Machado, 'A forgotten corner of the western Indian Ocean: Gujarati merchants, Portuguese India and the Mozambique slave trade, *c.*1730–1830', *Slavery and Abolition* 24:2 (2003), 17–32; Sussan Babaie, Kathryn Babayan, Ina Baghdiantz-McCabe and Massumeh Farhad, *Slaves of the Shah: New Elites of Safavid Iran* (London, 2004); Ghislaine E. Lydon, 'Slavery, exchange and Islamic law: a glimpse from the archives of Mali and Mauritania', *African Economic History* 33 (2005), 117–48; Indrani Chatterjee and Richard M. Eaton (eds.), *Slavery and South Asian History* (Bloomington, IN, 2006); William G. Clarence-Smith, *Islam and the Abolition of Slavery* (Oxford, 2006); Terence Walz and Kenneth M. Cuno (eds.), *Race and Slavery in the Middle East: Histories of Trans-Saharan Africans in Nineteenth-Century Egypt, Sudan, and the Ottoman Mediterranean* (Cairo and New York, 2010); Bruce S. Hall, 'How slaves used Islam: the letters of enslaved Muslim commercial agents in the nineteenth-century Niger Bend and Central Sahara', *Journal of African History* 52:3 (2011), 279–97. Cf. the account of slaves and slave girls in Goitein, *A Mediterranean Society*, I, 130–47.

constants: intimates were characterised by having multiple ties to each other, by deep attachment to the same locality and by a sense of personal responsibility for the well-being of the collective as a whole. The main advantage of belonging to such a collective was, of course, mutual aid in a world whose uncertainties were accentuated by large distances and long silences.

Bonds among intimates find observable expression in the correspondence in two ways. One is through the pains taken over the language used in their letters. In particular, authors strove to communicate their feelings for each other in a pleasing, beautiful, touching, imageful register. It appears to have been almost de rigueur to note that the addressee was always in the writer's mind. A father-in-law was told, 'Not one moment and one breath passes without remembering and praying for all the friends, especially [you, who are] the just appreciator of the powerless.'[37] This point could also be made through the motif of dreams.[38] In his response to a letter just arrived in Najaf in the late 1740s, Shāh Kawthar wrote, '[Your letter] made evident the facts of the well-being of [your] temperament [and] spirits, and of all the incidents and stories of [your] dreams . . . Your dreams indicate future contentment.'[39] Such sentiments were frequently expressed in poetic form, especially as couplets. 'I entrust to you my capital / [because] you know its [every] up and down.'[40] Couplets such as this could be the author's own or, what was commonplace, they could be drawn from the rich literary canon available to them.[41] Ḥāfiẓ was a popular choice. The same Shāh Kawthar who talked about dreams also quoted Ḥāfiẓ in the same letter: 'Yūsuf being lost will come back to Canaan. Do not grieve. / The house of sorrows will become one day a rose-garden. Do not grieve.'[42]

The reference to the rose-garden gestures to an important quality marking correspondence between intimates: powerful, sentient imagery.

[37] BL/Lansdowne/1046, doc. 34.

[38] On dreams and dreaming, see Özgen Felek and Alexander D. Knysh (eds.), *Dreams and Visions in Islamic Societies* (Albany, NY, 2012) and, more generally, David Shulman and Guy G. Stroumsa (eds.), *Dream Cultures: Explorations in the Comparative History of Dreaming* (Oxford, 1999).

[39] BL/Lansdowne/1046, doc. 25. [40] BL/Lansdowne/1046, doc. 44.

[41] *Sabk-i hindi* was a dominant style in the Persian poetry of the period. A good introductions to it may be found in Shamsur Rahman Faruqi, 'Stranger in the city: the poetics of Sabk-i Hindi', *Annual of Urdu Studies* 19 (2004), 1–93. Also see Paul E. Losensky, *Welcoming Fighānī: Imitation and Poetic Individuality in the Safavid-Mughal Ghazal* (Costa Mesa, CA, 1998). For a discussion that situates *Sabk-i hindi* in its historical setting, see Muzaffar Alam, 'The culture and politics of Persian in precolonial Hindustan', in Sheldon I. Pollock (ed.), *Literary Cultures in History: Reconstructions from South Asia* (Berkeley, CA, 2003), 131–98.

[42] BL/Lansdowne/1046, doc. 25.

This imagery was frequently metaphorical, its potency stemming from widely understood analogies. The rose and the garden figured prominently among them. As another author put it, 'May the sought-after roses bloom continuously in the rose-garden of hope.'[43] 'The rose in the meadow has opened,' wrote yet another, 'and the birds in the courtyard of the garden cry that your place is empty.'[44] Just as prominent was the imagery of intoxication. 'Without premeditation, we are drunk in the wine of your love.'[45] Elsewhere, playing on the tension between a valued end and a proscribed means: '[Drunk in] the purest wine of [our] faceless friend is our unlawful act / see the beauty of the excellence of our loyalty.'[46]

However, the imagery marshalled by intimates need not always be so metaphorical. It could also have highly personalised elements that suggested, or encouraged, a literal reading. These elements were perhaps most palpable when yoked to the body.[47] We see this conceit, for example, in a letter by Sayyid Muṣṭafā. He told an intimate at home, 'Having been favoured by your personal blessings, there will come your fragrance. Having allowed it on my face, I will inhale your aspects which will [then] pass into [my] *dil*.'[48] The following passage, written in Najaf, draws on bodily images in an even more visceral fashion:

> May [God] keep in his protection and preservation your existence [safe] from corporeal misfortunes and afflictions. My pivot, I am at such a loss since the date that I boarded the blessed ship *Munzal* until now which has been nearly forty or fifty days. Because of the great separation [between us], [my] endurance has been exhausted and [my] *jān* is close to leaving the frame of my body. I have no sleep at night and no peace [during] the day. I am at such a loss that not speaking is better. The tongue in one's mouth is the guardian of one's head.[49]

The second way in which bonds among intimates find observable expression in the correspondence is in the manner in which they apologised for, or alternatively tried to explain away, their perceived failings. Knowledge of the fact that they could not be readily cut loose from each other coupled with the knowledge of their moral and sentimental attachments to one another to produce a special situation: the consequences for an individual of his failings tended to take longer to reveal themselves in

[43] BL/Lansdowne/1046, doc. 34. [44] BL/Lansdowne/1046, doc. 59.
[45] BL/Lansdowne/1046, doc. 34. [46] BL/Lansdowne/1046, doc. 30.
[47] A homoerotic, perhaps even homosexual, sensibility is in evidence here. The subject is discussed in Sabine Schmidtke, 'Homoeroticism and homosexuality in Islam: a review article', *Bulletin of the School of Oriental and African Studies* 62:2 (1999), 260–6 and Kathryn Babayan and Afsaneh Najmabadi (eds.), *Islamicate Sexualities: Translations across Temporal Geographies of Desire* (Cambridge, MA, 2008).
[48] BL/Lansdowne/1046, doc. 50. [49] BL/Lansdowne/1046, doc. 37.

his intimate relationships than in those with strangers, allowing him greater opportunity to correct for them, both for his own sake and for the collective good. Apologies made for expectations not being met could be terse. Because he was unable to send a more fulsome letter, Shāh Kawthar in Najaf asked the recipient to 'grant me forgiveness for my shortcomings and may you treat my incomplete work sympathetically'.[50] To be so terse, however, was unusual; apologies to intimates were normally elaborate affairs. When an agent in Najaf informed his principals in Bengal that their instructions had yet to be undertaken, he explained the matter as follows:

> [God] is aware that in this season in no way was it possible to execute [the task]. And in this regard, concerning [my] work for all the gentlemen, I am ashamed. But very soon, with divine might and power . . ., I will take care of and prepare the many special pearls as gifts for the small and the big of the sort that you have ordered. And if *allāh* wishes, please know [that] I will send [them] either by way of Surat through Mīr Abū Ṭālib Ṣāḥib Ṭālqānī or [they] will reach you by another way. And please do not consider me guilty. Rather, please ask on my behalf for forgiveness from the other gentlemen.[51]

Another correspondent stressed that the failing was not typical of him and, indeed, 'making an excuse and indolence are not my traits . . . I was not able to order the pearl shavings and other items. On this occasion, however, may my shortcoming in relation to you be forgiven and may you even pardon everything by virtue of your sublime patronage.'[52] And even as forgiveness was being sought, it was not uncommon to ask for help, highlighting the complexity of dealings between intimates. '[My] hope is that, having directed them, they will forgive my shortcomings,' an unnamed individual wrote from Cochin in 1748. 'In the time that I have spent in your service, there happened great rudeness and incomplete work from me. And yet concerning me, you have not denied me the good offices that come from you . . . In exchange, may [God] favour you with rewards.'[53]

As I have already noted, one of the chief benefits of having ties to intimates was the option of requesting – and the expectation of obtaining – aid on favourable terms, at least to begin with. Chapter 3 on the familial order gives several examples of intimates coming to one another's help, of Thanā' Allāh guaranteeing funds from afar to cover the daily expenses of his wife and son at home, of Niʿmat Allāh stepping in for Māralīnā's distant husband and giving her the material support that she so sorely needed. These are supplemented here with one more example. The latter

[50] BL/Lansdowne/1046, doc. 25.
[51] BL/Lansdowne/1046, doc. 35.
[52] BL/Lansdowne/1046, doc. 21.
[53] BL/Lansdowne/1046, doc. 38.

is worth noting because of its unusual subject and the extraordinary mix of factors that brought it into being.

From his home in Iraq in 1747, an uncle sent a letter to his nephew, who was at the time based in Bengal. The uncle had decided to take this initiative only because 'you reminded me ... to have the courage to write about [my] circumstances'. He had some good news to relay. 'Your little sister has been [born] and she is akin to a magnificent jewel around my neck.' However, the arrival of his daughter meant big changes for him personally, since 'it is not possible for anyone to be uplifted through [such] responsibility when at night he is destroyed because of worry'. The worry was well founded because the uncle was mired in an impossible situation. 'I am an opium addict,' he admitted. This meant high expenses, due to which 'I am suffering from very bad health.' He was desperate for 'a remedy for [my] hidden pain'. Though he did not ask his nephew for money, he did request a favour of him; the uncle asked his nephew to intercede on his behalf with his father-in-law. 'In [your] letter to Shāh Bahāī, please write that what has happened with respect to me is like someone who is an opium addict and your daughter is [as a result] without a husband.'[54] In this man's plea for help, we see the intimate community at work.

For such reasons and in a likewise fashion, the intimate community was a fact of life for the arena's people. But because often it did not coincide with formally recognised organisations and groups (producing tensions which are discussed later in Chapter 6), the entity is not easily discerned in the documents from the period. There is, however, one fairly reliable point of access. And this is to be found in the closing part of many letters exchanged between intimates. Clustered here are the greetings directed from named individuals, or categories of individuals, at the author's end to named individuals, or categories of individuals, at the addressee's end. Even when brief, they convey a sense of the collective within which both sender and recipient were enmeshed. From Najaf, Shāh Kawthar hoped that his prayers would reach 'the brother-*ṣāḥib* and all [his] big and small [ones]' in Bengal, as well as 'the mother-*ṣāḥiba* and all [her] little [ones]'.[55] Commonly, however, those who were invoked transcended close kindred and the family household. They could be denoted as their mutual 'big and small friends'.[56] But to be so generic was unusual among intimates; when friends were mentioned – which happened frequently enough – it was much more usual to mention others in their intimate

[54] BL/Lansdowne/1046, doc. 34. A good recent work on the subject is Rudolph P. Matthee's *The Pursuit of Pleasure: Drugs and Stimulants in Iranian History, 1500–1900* (Princeton, NJ, 2005).

[55] BL/Lansdowne/1046, doc. 25. [56] BL/Lansdowne/1046, doc. 30.

community alongside them. Muḥammad ʿAlī Majhalibandarī was asked to kiss the eyes of the children (*nūrchashmanān*), and to pass on blessings from his intimates in Najaf to 'all the brother-*ṣāḥib*s and kindred (*khvīshān*) and acquaintances (*āshināyān*), near and far'.[57] In a similar manner, ʿInāyat Allāh in Najaf requested his regards be passed on 'to ʿAlī Ḥaḍrat Mīrzā Shukr Allāh Ṣāḥib and Mīr Muḥammad ʿAlī, and to the remainder of the acquaintances and friends [in Bengal] who asked about the conditions on this side'.[58]

The closing part of their correspondence sometimes permits us to go beyond the broad outlines of the intimate community and grasp some of its substance. I will confine myself to three examples here, all from the 1740s, whose juxtaposition is instructive. In the first, Muḥammad ʿAlī Khān in Bengal was informed that the author's brother sends greetings, and 'my son, Muḥammad ʿAbbās ʿAlī, who is now six years old and his sister, who is three-and-a-half years old, kiss [your] hand and foot. And all the devoted small and big ones submit [their greetings].' Shifting focus to the recipient's end, the letter's author expressed the hope that Muḥammad ʿAlī Khān's sons, Muḥammad Kāẓim and ʿAlī Taqī, 'and the other sons and children of the great *mīr ṣāḥib*' are prosperous. The letter ended with the author praying for ʿAlī Riḍā and for 'the kind gentlemen and acquaintances and friends, far and near'.[59]

Friends are prominent figures in the second example. A nephew asked his uncle, Āqā Mahdī, to pass on his greetings to Muḥammad Ḥusayn. He went on:

> Please send [my] prayers to Ḥājī Abū al-Ḥasan Ṣāḥib and to Āqā Ibrāhīm Ṣāḥib and to Mīrzā Muḥammad Ṣāḥib and to Āqā Ṣāliḥ Ṣāḥib and to Mīrzā Aḥmad Ṣāḥib and to [my dear] friends that are known to me ... And please send [my] prayers to the kind sister with a *jān* equal to [that of my] dear brother Muḥammad Ḥusayn.[60]

The third example is the most detailed of the lot and is drawn from a letter written in 1745 by Katarīn in Bengal to her son, Isrāyīl, then residing not far from Basra. More than half of it is taken up by a succession of brief messages relaying the best wishes of intimates at home. At the top of the list were Abū Naṣr Allāh and uncle Bahna and his four children, and aunt Maryam and her three children. There followed the recipient's sister and brother-in-law, Mūsā, and their children; his brothers, Shamʿūn, Isṭifān and Jarjī; and his sisters, Haylāna and Sayyida. Broadening out, Katarīn went on to mention his grandmother Maryam; the children of his aunt; Tawāziya, the daughter of his uncle, and her

[57] BL/Lansdowne/1046, doc. 35. [58] BL/Lansdowne/1046, doc. 29.
[59] BL/Lansdowne/1046, doc. 21. [60] BL/Lansdowne/1046, doc. 37.

husband and children; his aunt Khātūn; Ḥanna and his mother; uncle Niʿmat Allāh and 'the people of his house, and his son, ʿAṭā Allāh, and the rest of his children'. The scribe, who evidently wrote up the letter in neat on Katarīn's behalf, is noted as well. He was Isrāyīl's uncle, Yūsuf, and he together with his daughter, Shamūna, sent their best wishes too. Katarīn brought matters to a close by letting her son know that 'our neighbour, Yūsuf, and the people of his house, wish you well, and all the acquaintances and friends ... send you many greetings'.[61]

The assumption that in times of need an individual could always turn to his intimates at home for help – and in the normal run of things receive it – had a corollary. And that was the restrictions placed on his personal freedoms. Indeed, it was on the plane of the intimate community that the potential conflict between personal freedoms and collective obligations erupted most frequently.[62] In the most extreme scenario, individuals – always men, seldom married – might try to vanish while abroad, causing great distress to intimates at home.[63] But to vanish was not as easy as might be imagined. Such was the density and extent of the web of ties between intimates active in the arena, not keeping to the planned itinerary or failing to arrive at the agreed-upon destination was noted and the fact quickly disseminated among them. Purposeful action was then taken to locate the individual. Though we do not know the reason for Anṭūn's disappearance in the late 1740s, the response of his intimates is telling. In an earlier letter from western India, Shukr Allāh had informed Niʿmat Allāh, at the time at home in southern Iraq, that Anṭūn 'has not reached his place'. Niʿmat Allāh wrote back,

> O my brother, by your life, send us information about whichever place he may be in and whatever is the difficulty causing this impediment. For as long as you tell us that he has not reached his place, O my brother, continue informing us about which place [he may be in]. And if your hand reaches him, take from him a letter and send it to us.[64]

Such disappearances were, as a result, quite rare. In any case, for those who chafed under the strictures imposed by the intimate community, there were normally enough provisions for individual autonomy and

[61] BL/Lansdowne/1046, doc. 12.

[62] The subject is discussed to telling effect in Avner Greif, 'Cultural beliefs and the organization of society: a historical and theoretical reflection on collectivist and individualist societies', *Journal of Political Economy* 102:5 (1994), 912–50 and Nicolas Michel, 'The individual and the collectivity in the agricultural economy of pre-colonial Morocco', in Nelly Hanna (ed.), *Money, Land and Trade: an Economic History of the Mediterranean* (London, 2002), 15–36.

[63] BL/Lansdowne/1046, docs. 68, 77. Cf. the attempts to escape wife, family and/or community noted in Goitein, *A Mediterranean Society*, I, 58–9.

[64] BL/Lansdowne/1046, doc. 67.

advancement to persuade them of the merits of remaining within the fold. The options available to a youth on the verge of manhood were at best confined to the livelihood in which his family was engaged or the occupation dominated by his community. In due course, with the gain of knowledge, acumen and working capital, together with an assiduously cultivated reputation, he might branch out by himself. He could set up a merchant house or seek to establish his own partnerships.[65] But even if successful, his freedom as an individual was almost always circumscribed by the steadfast expectations of, and duties towards, his intimates, expectations and duties which accompanied him for life. It appears that the pursuit of self-interest was permitted as long as an individual's actions did not transgress the intimate community's basic principles concerning mutual aid. On one level, these principles were of a piece with the era's prevailing uncertainties. On another, an upbringing within the community generated feelings of affection for one another. Reinforced by the teachings of elders, as described earlier in the account of the familial order, this fostered an inner compulsion and manifest desire for the common good, buttressed by the knowledge that others too felt and thought likewise.

Owing to these considerations, an individual's pursuit of his personal goals would usually yield to the collective interests of his intimate community in the event of a conflict. This is why there was never any real doubt that Minas de Eliaz, whose words crown this chapter, would actually permit his own affairs to compromise his ultimate loyalty to his brethren. That principle was put to the test by the situation in which he found himself entangled in the 1740s. Having debated the matter, he resolved to put the well-being of his intimate community ahead of his own personal interests by consenting to travel on the *Santa Catharina* as its supercargo for its freight voyage to Basra. While en route, he reflected on the circumstances that had convinced him to take this course of action. 'In the land as well as sea ... business are in the manner as if they were in a burning fire.' The immediate cause for this was that 'the goods from Surat [for Bengal] which they laded [the previous season] on board the Armenian, Indian and Dutch ships' had 'had no profit at all'. In an attempt to cover their losses, 'sundry persons had freighted for Bassorah a Portuguese ship', the *Santa Catharina*. 'And without any joking ... they would not have freighted the ship if he had not promised to come [as] supercargo in it.' One of the reasons for accepting 'the said employment' was 'to please the gentlemen'. But that was not all; Minas was aware of his

[65] Cf. the discussion of credit, debts and loans in Goitein, *A Mediterranean Society*, I, 197–200, 250–62.

moral duty to his beleaguered community. He declared that 'he took these troubles to do good to those of his nation who on account of the war [of the Austrian Succession] did not dare to lade anything on board the French or English ships'. At the same time, it was hoped that this selfless act would not go unrewarded. 'God will favour him on account of the good that he does to those of his nation', for having taking upon himself 'to make this voyage for the benefit of his poor people'.[66]

So intimates dealt with each other on a regular and frequent basis. But where the parties to a relationship were not intimates, they were invariably 'strangers'. In other words, to be an intimate was *not* to be a stranger – and to be a stranger was *not* to be an intimate. From an individual's standpoint, the two were exclusive, and to a large extent defined in negation to one another. Strangers were those with whom one interacted as a matter of course in the arena but who were situated outside one's intimate community.[67]

Encountering such strangers, and developing ties with them that endured, was in keeping with the variegated ethnic mosaic of the arena. We see in the correspondence ʿAbd al-Qādir, a Muslim, probably a Shīʿī, maintaining relations with several Armenians, locally in Basra, as well as in Aleppo and Bengal. He also employed a 'broker' (*dallāl*) called Manbūr, who was very likely a *baniyā* from Gujarat.[68] A Christian 'gentleman merchant' (*khvājah*) played a key role in transferring a sum of money from Bengal to a Sufi brotherhood in Najaf.[69] The family of the Armenian ʿAbd Allāh b. Ḥassūn, living in southern Iraq, made use of the French merchant-official Jean Dumont to convey their goods between Surat and Basra in the late 1740s.[70] At the same time, one of their kinsmen was employed as an 'interpreter' (*turjumān*) for the Dutch traders in Basra.[71] A Shīʿī Muslim, Muḥammad Adīb, sent instructions from Cochin in 1748 to his sons in Bengal to recover the 200 rupees that were owed them by his Hindu associate, Bābū Rādhā Krishan.[72] And as shown in detail in Chapter 8, a Gauḍ Sārasvat Hindu family in Goa kept up relations throughout the eighteenth century with a diverse array of merchants, officials, clients, brokers, agents and bankers in western India and around the Arabian Sea littoral.[73]

[66] NA/HCA/42/25 (St Catharina): 77, 79, 82.
[67] For a tantalising account of how the 'stranger' has been conceptualised in premodern Arabic literature, see Franz Rosenthal, 'The stranger in medieval Islam', *Arabica* 44 (1997), 35–75.
[68] BL/Lansdowne/1046, docs. 65, 66. [69] BL/Lansdowne/1046, doc. 51.
[70] BL/Lansdowne/1046, doc. 67. [71] BL/Lansdowne/1046, docs. 70, 71.
[72] BL/Lansdowne/1046, docs. 8, 13, 23.
[73] The family papers are found in XCHR/MHR. For much of the eighteenth century, the firm was managed by Suba Kāmat. After his death in the 1760s, his sons Veṅkateśa and Nārāyaṇa Kāmat took over the reins.

Excluding members of their own confessional group, many of their correspondents in the last third of the century were Portuguese or Luso-Indians. But the family also had several Parsi, Armenian and Jewish associates, and was in active communication with the French together with members of other Hindu communities based on the Malabar coast.

These instances testify to the ethnically kaleidoscopic nature of the world of the arena's people. Good evidence for how entrenched this diversity was can be found among those who manned and travelled on the caravans and ships linking up different parts of Islamicate Eurasia. I offer two of the most insightful examples preserved in the documents examined for this book.[74] The first concerns 'the men of the blessed ship *Munzal*'. Managed by a medley of individuals, the ship was on a voyage from Bengal to Basra in 1748. It was crossing the Arabian Sea when, owing to contrary winds and currents, and the threat posed by the Angria pirates lurking in the area, it was forced to turn back and seek refuge in ports along the Malabar coast.

While biding their time, the ship's officers and passengers composed a formal document, an *ʿarḍdāsht*, for their principals. They outlined in this their current predicament. The body of its text is written in Persian, and contains their names, along with their ranks or occupations. Their personal signs – in the form of a signature, seal or symbol – are given in the margin, beside which their names are stated once again, some in Arabic script, some in Latin script. The document shows clearly that several distinct backgrounds were represented among the ship's officers and passengers.[75] The captain was a Frenchman and the same Muḥammad Adīb noted above was the *nākhudā*, or ship's master. As for the officers, they included Thanāʾ Allāh, who went as a *kirānī* ('clerk' or 'accountant'), and two *muʿallim*s ('pilot' or 'mate'), the Dutchman Peter Willeboorts and the Luso-Indian Christian Stephen. The three passengers on board – the Armenian Kāspār and the Muslims Mīr Muṣṭafā and Mīr Muḥammad

[74] For this part of the world in premodern times, there are very few extant sources that give the names of *all* those who actually manned and travelled on ships and caravans. They are almost non-existent for ventures not owned or managed by the European East India companies, with the Ottomans as a possible exception. On those populating Ottoman ships, see Giancarlo Casale, 'The ethnic composition of Ottoman ship crews and the "Rumi challenge" to Portuguese identity', *Medieval Encounters* 13 (2007), 122–44. Details on ships and shipping in the Indian Ocean and the Islamic world may be found in Robert B. Serjeant, *Farmers and Fishermen in Arabia: Studies on Customary Law and Practice* (Aldershot, 1995); Hassan S. Khalilieh, *Islamic Maritime Law: an Introduction* (Leiden, 1998); David Parks and Ruth Barnes (eds.), *Ships and the Development of Maritime Technology in the Indian Ocean* (London, 2002).

[75] Unfortunately, no information is given about the ordinary seamen.

Shafīʿ, both probably Shīʿī – are described merely as 'merchants' (*savdāgarān*).[76]

It would appear that this ethnic (and confessional) diversity was no bar to consensus on the ship, at least when it came to the big decisions. This is just as well because, prior to their return to the Malabar coast, the ship's officers and passengers had faced a very big decision indeed: whether to persist with their original itinerary and run the gauntlet of the Angria 'grabs and gullivats', which were about to encircle them, or to cut their losses and make for the nearest safe haven. After some deliberation, prudence won the day. As the pirates got closer, the name of the port-town of Tellicherry started being 'heard on the tongues of the people'. 'What were we to do since the suitable wind was not blowing?' asked Muḥammad Adīb. '[So] hurriedly, because of our terror, the wood and the merchandise (*takhtah va māl*) were thrown overboard and, out of fear of [losing our] lives, everyone being in agreement with each other, [the ship] turned back from there [and] once again reached … Tellicherry.'[77] The *ʿarḍdāsht* stressed that this decision had been taken by consensus. Once the ship's officers and passengers became aware of the imminent threat posed by the Angria pirates, '[they] were at a loss and confused. Accordingly, the captain asked the whole group [of officers and passengers] and they [decided] for the welfare of one another' to return to the Malabar coast.[78]

The second example harks back to the story of the *Santa Catharina* recounted in the prologue. It deals in particular with the ill-fated final stretch of the ship's return voyage, during which it was captured by the British squadron off the Coromandel coast. Those on board at the moment of its capture in May 1748 display a spectrum of backgrounds comparable to the example above. There is, however, an important difference: the documents are much more forthcoming with respect to the background of the *Santa Catharina*'s officers and passengers, and, what is remarkable, allow us to

[76] A copy was made of the original text. It does not carry the signatures and there are some minor differences in the spellings of the names and their ranks or occupations. In the original, BL/Lansdowne/1046, doc. 5, the officers and passengers style themselves as:

مایانکه کپتان موسی نخیلی [پهنلی] و ناوخدا شیخ محمد ادیب و خواجه کاسپار ارمنی و میر محمد شفیع و میر مصطفی
سوداگران کرانی سید ثناء الله و پتر معلم بزرگ و استان معلم کوچک و معلم محمود بوسمان جوزه کوله انداز نکلاو و قطب
سارنک و فخرو تندیل و دوکهی تندیل و لعل ناوخدا کسب و غیره مردمان جهاز مبارک منزل ایم

In the copy, BL/Lansdowne/1046, doc. 4, they are styled as:

مایانکه کپتان پهنلی [نخیلی] و ناوخدا شیخ محمد ادیب و خواجه کاسپار ارمنی و میر مصطفی و میر محمد شفیع سوداگران و
کرانی سید ثناء الله و پتر معلم بزرگ و استیون معلم کوچک و معلم محمود و بوسمان جوزهٔ و نکلا و کولنداز [گوله انداز] و
قطب سارنک و فخرو [فخر و] تندیل و دوکهی تندیل و لعل ناوخدا کسب و غیره مردمان جهاز مبارک منزل ایم

[77] BL/Lansdowne/1046, doc. 2. [78] BL/Lansdowne/1046, doc. 4.

glimpse its crew and ordinary seamen. The documents which enable us to reconstruct the ship's population while on the high seas are among those that were confiscated by the British[79] and transcripts of the subsequent interrogations of the ship's captain and several of its officers, passengers and crewmen.[80]

On being halted, the *Santa Catharina* had on board forty-nine officers and crewmen, and around fifteen passengers and servants. The captain was João de Faria Leitão. A part-owner of the *Santa Catharina*, he was a subject of the Portuguese crown and claimed Goa as his permanent residence, even though his current domicile was in Chandannagar in Bengal.[81] While he bore the title of captain with pride, there was little else about him that suggested captain; it was generally acknowledged that Leitão had no experience or knowledge of navigating a ship on the high seas.[82] This task was entrusted instead to the Frenchman Pierre Louis Perdiguier. A native of Brest and a subject of the French crown, Perdiguier made his living as a mariner and merchant. He had originally embarked as an ordinary passenger at Basra, with the aim of returning home to Chinsura in Bengal. But as the *Santa Catharina* just then was missing a navigator – the previous one had died while the ship had been at anchor in Basra – he was persuaded to take on the late navigator's job. Once the terms had been agreed, Leitão 'called all the officers and men aft [before setting sail from Basra] and told them to obey Perdiguier in all that related to the navigating and working the ship. He thus took charge and every night gave the officer of the watch orders to steer such a course as he thought proper.' In carrying out these functions, though the documents do not state it openly, Perdiguier would have been aided by the ship's *nākhudās*, the indigenous master navigators who knew that part of the world intimately.[83]

79 NA/HCA/42/25 (St Catharina). 80 NA/HCA/42/26 (St Catharina).

81 Most of the officers, passengers and crew of the *Santa Catharina* had close ties to Bengal's commercial settlements, many of which in the 1740s were under the formal or effective control of one or another of the European East India companies. For example, the Dutch governed Chinsura, the French Chandannagar (and Pondicherry on the Coromandel), and the British Calcutta (and Madras on the Coromandel and Bombay on the west coast). Those who were born locally or gained permanent resident status in the European-dominated settlements were normally considered subjects of the relevant European sovereign.

82 It appears that João de Faria Leitão's chief role in this venture was to lend credence to the claim that the *Santa Catharina* sailed under Portuguese protection.

83 For a recent study of the meanings ascribed to the term *nākhudā* in western maritime Asia before the opening of the maritime route via the Cape of Good Hope, see Ranabir Chakravarti, 'Nakhudas and nauvittikas: ship-owning merchants in the west coast of India (*c.* AD 1000–1500)', *Journal of the Economic and Social History of the Orient* 43:1 (2000), 34–64. This article also surveys the operations of these 'ship-owning merchants' on land and on sea, and their relationship to the coastal polities of western India before the appearance of the Portuguese.

Apart from the captain, it is notable that all the ship's purported officers were French subjects and several of its seamen French-speakers. The chief mate, who was also described as the second captain, was Etienne de Bris. He had been born in Europe (in Havre de Grace) and was of no fixed residence, 'having been at see [*sic*] for the past seven years'. Aside from de Bris and Perdiguier, the other officers were 'Indian Frenchman' – Indian by birth and of part-French ancestry – or they were Luso-Indians – of part-Portuguese ancestry – or they were local converts to Catholicism. For example, the second mate, André Delneuf, was the son of a Frenchman and a Bengali woman from Bandel. He had been born in Chinsura 'under Dutch colours', but moved with his parents to Chandannagar when he was very young. Yet to marry, he divided his time between the French settlements of Pondicherry and Chandannagar. Delneuf's immediate subordinate, Jacques La Guerre, had been born in Pondicherry, where he still resided. He had originally joined the ship's company as a passenger, but was appointed mate half-way into the journey (for which he was paid 30 rupees a month). Last among the officers to be mentioned was the boatswain, Paulo de Rozario. He was a Luso-Indian Christian and a native of Chandannagar.

The ship's crew exhibited more variety than its officers. Frustratingly, however, we possess much less information about them as individuals; the documents allow us to describe their backgrounds merely in broad strokes. The *Santa Catharina*'s crew numbered about forty in total. With three exceptions, they were all Muslims or Luso-Indian Christians, and subjects of the Mughal emperor, or of one of his eighteenth-century successors. Their homes lay in different parts of India. While most were indigenous to Bengal, a significant proportion came from the Coromandel and the Malabar areas.[84] Mirroring the officers, the crewmen were organised hierarchically. The lowest rung was occupied by ordinary seamen, the lascars and rowers, who were the most numerous group within the ship's population. Some of them would have been employed as individuals on mutually agreed terms; others would have been there as members of communities with a recognised proficiency in the job; and yet others would have been slaves. Above the ordinary

[84] On Tuesday, 5 December 1747, a month before the ship's departure from Basra, a list was drawn up of the *Santa Catharina*'s crewmen, most probably by André Delneuf, the second mate. It noted the following: carpenter Gonsalve; steersman Bastian; guards Gaspar and Roustom; Raphael, Soucour, Abdoul Houssen casa/d [?]; lascars Asen Dada, Joudy, Marcar, Din Mamet, Quèvou, Etouary, Callé, Neamot, Naran, Mondy, Morat, Antoinne, Janou, Chian, Badou, Faquira, Abdoulla Malaye and Latif; Paul, Josique and Mingue; boatswains Tom and Leandre; master Giomalgy Galfats; rowers Monbaree Malay, Pir Mamet, Gyhoman, Moula, Mamot Gyhoma and Francisque Biche Bosman. NA/HCA/42/25 (St Catharina) (3 October 1747).

seamen were ranged *sarhangs* ('boatswain' or 'head of a group of lascars'), *tandīls* ('boatswain'), carpenters, steersmen and the *nākhudās*. The three members of the crew who did not quite fit into this scheme had some kind of tie to Europe or to the European presence in the region. Boutad was a French-speaking Luso-Indian seaman and native of Chandannagar; Francisco a gunner originally from Venice; and Aculment de Rozario a Luso-Indian Christian born in Cossimbazar, but who had lived with a European – a Mr Findlay – at Chandannagar for the past fourteen years. Aculment de Rozario, who was single, is of particular interest because, when asked about his sovereign, he replied that he did not know. Three Armenian passengers made up the remaining individuals on board the *Santa Catharina*. The most senior among them was Minas, the supercargo and a member of the Armenian 'company' that had hired the ship for the freight voyage. The others were Johannes de Nazar, Minas's clerk and brother-in-law, and Johannes de Gregory, who was trading on his own account and acting as agent for several of his brethren in Bengal and Iraq.

This and similar evidence suggests that ethnic, religious, linguistic and occupational diversity, and diversity by place of origin, current residence and subjecthood, were innate to life in the arena. But this diversity was not a choice. Rather, and this is the crucial point, the diversity was a state of being for the arena's participants, an aspect of the reality of their world in their times that simply could not be ignored. This reality, however, did not translate into plurality in the sense of some harmonious multiculturalism. What plurality there was was highly qualified.[85] Sovereign power within the polities of India and the Islamic heartlands was, as elaborated in Chapter 6, the preserve of a tiny fraction of the population, often determined by lineage. Moreover, communal or confessional boundaries were rarely breached when it came to marriage or adoption. So there was little by way of political or cultural plurality. There *was*, however, considerable plurality in material and logistical dealings, and in urban living arrangements. Individuals belonging to many different types of associations – and rooted in a remarkably diverse array of traditions – were by necessity in continuous interaction for the purposes of trade, finance, communication, intelligence, travel and transport. Similarly, members of many different ethnic groups resided together in the region's urban settlements, even if they tended to cluster in their own quarters. It is in

[85] The modern scholarship on diversity, plurality, multiculturalism and cosmopolitanism is vast. As a guide to it, I have found useful the essays in Carl W. Ernst and Richard C. Martin (eds.), *Rethinking Islamic Studies: From Orientalism to Cosmopolitanism* (Columbia, SC, 2010).

these partial senses that I use the word plural to characterise the daily lives of those who were mobile, literate and worldly.[86]

This diversity and plurality was inflected through the arena's associations, which existed in a state of mutual dependence because of their possession of valued but scarce resources and skills. Together, they served to reinforce certain behavioural tendencies. At a minimum, dealings with strangers crucial for pursuing one's livelihood were widely tolerated, trumping any dogma to the contrary. Such tolerance merely required acknowledgement and acceptance of difference. However, the arena's people often went beyond this. We also see in the documents conscious adaptation to the fact of difference. The result was a form of coexistence among strangers that was purposefully maintained.[87] This cohered with the prevailing attitude of pragmatism or expediency in interactions between them. The benefits to be had from any such interactions were evaluated dispassionately in general. Over time, however, these could develop into what we might call friendships.

Though quite different from friendships among intimates, friendship and the figure of the friend were prominent tropes in correspondence between strangers.[88] Letters regularly opened with the recipient being described as 'the most dear of friends (*aṣdiqāʾ*) and loved ones'.[89] The notion of friendship was also marshalled as an ideal worth striving for. This was rendered explicit in 1747 by a correspondent in Najaf who framed his complaint in just those terms: 'seemingly, no letter or anything else came to me [from you] . . . which would have improved our friendship (*yārī*)'.[90] In a separate letter sent at about the same time, another Najafi stated, 'I have always written [to you] wanting in this world friendship (*dūstī*) and goodness.'[91] But friendships did not exist merely on the plane

[86] This qualified plurality may be correlated to the presence, or otherwise, of sites of sociability in public. For useful insights, see Paulina B. Lewicka, 'Restaurants, inns and taverns that never were: some reflections on public consumption in medieval Cairo', *Journal of the Economic and Social History of the Orient* 48:1 (2005), 40–91.

[87] My understanding of tolerance and coexistence is indebted to Marc Baer, Ussama Makdisi and Andrew Shryock, 'Tolerance and conversion in the Ottoman empire: a conversation', *Comparative Studies in Society and History* 51:4 (2009), 927–40.

[88] There are strong resonances between friendship as invoked in the examples that follow and the juristic notion of 'informal cooperation' (*ṣadāqa, ṣuḥba*) and the political notion of *hamsāyah*. For a stimulating discussion of friendship and informal cooperation, see Shelomo D. Goitein, 'Mediterranean trade in the eleventh century: some facts and problems', in Michael A. Cook (ed.), *Studies in the Economic History of the Middle East from the Rise of Islam to the Present Day* (Oxford, 1970), 51–62 and his *A Mediterranean Society*, vol. i, 164–9. On *hamsāyah*, see Shah Mahmoud Hanafi, *Connecting Histories in Afghanistan: Market Relations and State Formation on a Colonial Frontier* (Stanford, CA, 2008), 9, 49–50.

[89] BL/Lansdowne/1046, docs. 65, 66. [90] BL/Lansdowne/1046, doc. 21.

[91] BL/Lansdowne/1046, doc. 16.

of rhetorical tropes or aspirational ideals. They actually meant something in everyday life. This is most apparent when the notion was individualised. So in a letter to Muḥammad ʿAlī b. Jaʿfar Bahāī in Surat, Jawhar Darankal took care to send greetings from Basra to 'those who ask about us from among the friends and the loved ones'.[92] Also writing from Basra, the Muslim ʿAbd al-Qādir expressed the hope in his letter to the Armenian Sulaymān in Calcutta that his prayers will reach 'our friend Khvājah Anṭūn'.[93] And from Najaf, Shāh Kawthar waxed lyrical about his gratitude for his correspondent's friendship, noting that, in whatever he does on his behalf, he 'takes into account [his feelings] of closeness and affection for him'.[94]

But even in such instances of friendship, uncommon though they might have been, caution was always exercised in ways felt unnecessary when dealing with close kindred or members of the intimate community at home. The salient differences in relations among strangers as opposed to relations among kith and kin may be understood as a function of the quality of trust embedded within them. Now trust is a big word which in its various guises lies at the centre of much of the historical scholarship on non-state actors in premodern times.[95] Rather than assess the pros and cons of this weighty literature so as to arrive at a definition of trust, I approach the word in a simple, minimalist fashion and let the evidence flesh out its substance. Trust here is marshalled as a potential attribute of all relationships, be they between two individuals, or between an individual and an organisation. Construed thus, relationships may be classified – and differentiated – in terms of the quality of the trust embedded within them. If that was it, however, trust would be an attribute of all relationships. But it can also be used to elucidate the mechanisms actually deployed (or *not* deployed) by the parties involved in order to achieve one or more desired ends. The particular character of these mechanisms allows trust to be subdivided into two major types: personal and impersonal. In varying measures, both contributed to the trust marking a given relationship. At the same time, the two types

[92] BL/Lansdowne/1046, doc. 72. [93] BL/Lansdowne/1046, doc. 66
[94] BL/Lansdowne/1046, doc. 51.
[95] Trust has figured most prominently of all in studies of mercantile communities and networks. These have sought to explain, inter alia, how trust in such communities and networks was generated and sustained. A range of factors and mechanisms have been proposed, not least reputation, contract enforcement, legal norms and collectivist values. For an account of this historical scholarship, and as a recent contribution to it in its own right, see Jessica L. Goldberg, 'Choosing and enforcing business relationships in the eleventh-century Mediterranean: reassessing the "Maghribī traders"', *Past and Present* 216 (2012), 3–40. More generally, from both a historical and a sociological perspective, see Charles Tilly, *Trust and Rule* (Cambridge, 2005).

sprang from different origins and had different implications for the kinds of transactions that could be realistically entertained. The share of these two types in the overall trust was ultimately a function of the risk appetite of each individual, the trajectory of their relationship and the mechanisms available to increase the chances of a transaction being crowned with success. In the case of personal trust, as shown in Chapter 3, central to it was the role of affect or sentimental attachments, and an intuitive sense of a person's nature. These normally derived from a shared upbringing within the same household, family or neighbourhood, and were invariably confined to members of the same intimate community. It follows that personal trust more likely featured in relationships in which the individuals concerned belonged to the same linguistic or confessional group, thought of themselves as emerging from the same corner of the world, believed in the same founding stories and could imagine themselves joined to one another through kinship.

But if trust were solely personal, we would not be able to account for many of the arena's observed activities. In particular, it would be very difficult to make sense of the mutual dependencies that crossed communal boundaries and, by extension, of the regional-scale, deferred transactions in which the stakes were held by individuals who were essentially strangers. This is where the role of impersonal trust comes most forcefully into view. It compensated for the potential fragility of relationships – due to, say, lack of current information about what the other party was doing or limitations on one's ability to implement a decision – by helping to engender fidelity to the original agreement; in the event of unexpected developments, it encouraged initiatives that were in their shared interest. This basic idea was stated by ʿInāyat Allāh in 1747. 'If bidden, there is trust (*amānat*) [between us],' he wrote to his principal in Bengal. 'The rule (*ḍābita*) of trust is that we are aware of every aspect of your interest.'[96] Critical to the functioning of this rule was access to dispersed knowledge about an individual's reputation or creditworthiness, the presence of effective tribunals for arbitrating disputes, and the existence of robust networks of couriers to help supervise and manage a transaction's progress. Relationships with those beyond the intimate community, even relationships that approximated to modern notions of friendship, needed the support provided by such mechanisms to enhance trust within them. In their absence, many dealings either would not have taken place or would have been sharply curtailed. The mechanisms in question formed

[96] BL/Lansdowne/1046, doc. 26.

part of the reigning political order, and it is within that framework they are examined in a later chapter. For the moment, however, it will suffice to note that the elements of the minimal troika of tolerance, pragmatism and impersonal trust reinforced one another. In so doing, they made conceivable dealings that were the stuff of daily life within the arena.

5 A communications order: language, writing and couriers

Correspondence is equal to half a meeting.[1]

There were major uncertainties endemic to regional-scale activities in the eighteenth century. The way that contemporaries preferred to handle them was through face-to-face meetings. Unfortunately, such meetings were often impractical, if not impossible. As the saying above has it, correspondence went much of the way towards filling that breach. The uncertainties that most worried contemporaries stemmed from the large distances and the long silences which characterised normal dealings within the arena. They also stemmed from the known risks to persons and property. The passage of information and execution of tasks were thus frequently marked by delays and, moreover, were routinely discounted for possible inaccuracies or shortcomings. In order to render uncertainties like these manageable, care was taken, as the previous chapter shows, to cultivate relationships, among intimates for sure, but also with strangers. As the following chapter shows, this attentiveness to relationships was complemented by efforts to preserve the autonomy of the arena's organisations and groups, and shore up the mechanisms that facilitated impersonal trust. There is also a third level on which uncertainties were confronted: responsive engagement with the prevailing technologies of the time. At the level of infrastructural realities, the most relevant of these pivoted on communication, transport and health.

Before the arrival of printing, the steam engine, electric telegraph and pasteurization, it was realities of age-old provenance that dictated the passage and safe-keeping of objects and people, and shaped the movement of ideas and information. While these realities were often hindrances, they were certainly not insurmountable. So we see in the period a significant fraction of the region's inhabitants corresponding with one another, pilgrims and merchants embarking on journeys that

[1] MssOcc/NAF/9005: 2–9. For other examples, see HAG/Persian Documents, doc. 27; MssOcc/NAF/9001: 67–70; MssOcc/NAF/9002: 12–13.

lasted a year or more, and a sizeable trade in both luxury and bulk goods. The fact that such activities were taking place means that the technologies for communication, transport and health must have been sufficiently resilient, affordable, versatile and accessible. But this needs to be reconciled with another fact, that much of India and the Islamic heartlands was beset by acute insecurity in the middle of the eighteenth century. As summarised in the introduction, that is the received wisdom in modern scholarship. Many contemporaries were of the same opinion.[2] ʿInāyat Allāh was 'apprehensive' in Najaf in 1747 because 'this world is in conflict'.[3] Qāsim ʿAbd al-Samīʿ wrote from Basra that same year, 'The world is troubled and scary in every place.'[4] And yet transactions characterised by large distances and long silences were a commonplace. How can we make sense of this apparent conundrum?

The answer to this question is to be found in the region's infrastructure. Unfortunately, our current knowledge of its infrastructure in this period of such remarkable changes is patchy at best. With the exception of the few sectors and territories in which sovereign regimes or Europeans had a direct stake, the literature does not shed much light on the technologies with an immediate bearing on communication, transport and health before the nineteenth century. Instead, we must make do with isolated clusters of studies of varying quality and detail that explore particular elements of this infrastructure.[5]

I focus specifically on communication in this chapter. This is because the technologies of communications, much more so than for transport and health, were largely under the control of the arena's people themselves. So in the pages to come, I offer an account of the givens of written communication in India and the Islamic heartlands in the eighteenth century. This entails an examination of its regional, community and local languages, as well as of the lingua francas and the 'languages' based primarily on touch and secret codes. There follows a discussion of the principal scripts employed for activities to do with circulation and exchange, of the widely used substrates on which they were preserved – especially palm-leaves and paper – and of the tools used for writing on them. After detailing the several means of conveyance available for transporting packages of low weight and high value within

2 Good studies of contemporary opinion include John F. Richards and Velchuru Narayana Rao, 'Banditry in Mughal India: historical and folk perceptions', *Indian Economic and Social History Review* 17:1 (1980), 95–120 and Patricia Risso, 'Cross-cultural perceptions of piracy: maritime violence in the western Indian Ocean and Persian Gulf region during a long eighteenth century', *Journal of World History* 12:2 (2001), 293–319.

3 BL/Lansdowne/1046, doc. 24.

4 BL/Lansdowne/1046, doc. 74.

5 Citations to these studies may be found in the relevant parts of this and subsequent chapters.

the region, I round off the chapter by considering the behavioural patterns associated with the prevailing realities.

Pared down to its essentials, communication over large distances was restricted to word of mouth or symbols preserved in material form. Because the extant contemporary sources rarely document actual conversations, there is little we can say about the former. This is a major handicap given the central role played by orality at a time when functional literacy, even among the purportedly educated, was limited to a tiny minority.[6] In Iran in the 1740s, for example, a visitor noted that 'many of the Persians in high offices could not write'.[7] And in Surat and Bombay, we have evidence that oral contracts were preferred to written contracts until at least the third quarter of the eighteenth century.[8] While the details of conversations have almost without exception been lost to posterity, it is still possible to reconstruct their broad outlines through commentaries and retrospective accounts by litigants, biographers, notaries, historians and travellers as chroniclers of their present and past.[9] I tap into these where available. But it is undeniable that the surviving sources direct our attention mainly to writing and communication mediated by the written word. As a result of this heavy constraint, there is always the risk of overstating the importance of the written word in the movement of information and ideas within the arena. The best we can do is to be aware of this risk and make allowance for it as and when appropriate.

While it is not possible to determine precisely the relative importance of the spoken word and the written word in interactions over large distances,

[6] Literacy in the Islamic world in premodern times, and the state of the scholarship on it, is surveyed in Nelly Hanna, 'Literacy and the "great divide" in the Islamic world, 1300–1800', *Journal of Global History* 2:2 (2007), 175–93.

[7] Jonas Hanway, *Historical Account of the British Trade over the Caspian Sea ...*, vol. I (London, 1753), 317. Hanway lived in and travelled across Russia and Iran in the 1740s while undertaking a range of commercial ventures. The tone in which this observation is relayed indicates surprise. It would seem that these illiterate elites tended to dictate their messages to clerks or secretaries and then affix their seals to them once they had been written up in neat.

[8] Indeed, oral contracts retained their significance in some sectors, notably insurance, through to the end of the century. See, for example, IOR/G/36/76: 794; MSA/Misc/HCR/MRC/27: 373–6; MSA/Misc/HCR/MRC/31, 149; IOR/P/416/119: 54–9.

[9] There is some good work on orality in relation to writing. In particular, see Brinkley Messick, 'Legal documents and the concept of "restricted literacy" in a traditional society', *International Journal of the Sociology of Language* 42:1 (1983), 41–52; Gilles Veinstein, 'L'oralité dans les documents d'archives ottomans: paroles rapportés ou imaginées?', *Revue du monde musulman et de la Méditerranée* 75–76 [special issue on *Oral et écrit dans le monde turco-ottoman*] (1995), 133–42; Boğaç A. Ergene, 'Evidence in Ottoman courts: oral and written documentation in early-modern courts of Islamic law', *Journal of the American Oriental Society* 124:3 (2004), 471–91.

the written word was without doubt central to them.[10] And by far the most popular vehicle for communicating it was the letter. Despite appearances, communicating via letter was far from a simple or straightforward act. It required training in, and experience of, the relevant handwriting styles, visual aesthetics, epistolary forms and genre identifiers. These constituted a widely dispersed practice, which is detailed in a later chapter. But before such a practice could be entertained, there was the matter of the language and the script, and the tool for writing on a given substrate. Technologies like these were crucial for everyday life in the arena, and decisions regarding them were made on a daily basis.[11]

Islamicate Eurasia in the eighteenth century was home to a cornucopia of languages, many oral, some written, a few tactile. Its linguistic map may be likened to a polka-dotted patchwork quilt: local and community languages interleaved by regional languages and undergirded by a wadding of lingua francas.[12] (See Map 5.) Arabic in its many forms was the language that enjoyed the greatest physical reach within the region. It included many dialects, which, in the opinion of the intrepid Carsten

[10] On writing and the culture of writing in the region, see Brinkley Messick, *Calligraphic State: Textual Domination and History in a Muslim Society* (Berkeley, CA, 1993); George N. Atiyeh (ed.), *The Book in the Islamic World: the Written Word and Communication in the Middle East* (Albany, NY, 1995); Baber Johansen, 'Formes de langage et fonctions publiques: stéréotypes, témoins et offices dans la preuve par l'écrit en droit musulman', *Arabica* 44 (1997), 333–76; Veena Naregal, 'Language and power in pre-colonial western India: textual hierarchies, literate audiences and colonial philology', *Indian Economic and Social History Review* 37:3 (2000), 259–94; Nelly Hanna, *In Praise of Books: a Cultural History of Cairo's Middle Class, Sixteenth to the Eighteenth Century* (Syracuse, NY, 2003); Houari Touati, *L'armoire à sagesse: bibliothèques et collections en Islam* (Paris, 2003); Sheldon I. Pollock, 'Literary culture and manuscript culture in precolonial India', in Simon Eliot, Andrew Nash and Ian Willison (eds.), *Literary Cultures and the Material Book* (London, 2006), 77–94; Adrian Gully, *The Culture of Letter-Writing in Pre-Modern Islamic Society* (Edinburgh, 2008); Ghislaine E. Lydon, 'A paper economy of faith without faith in paper: a reflection on Islamic institutional history', *Journal of Economic Behaviour and Organization* 71 (2009), 647–59; Graziano Krätli and Ghislaine Lydon (eds.), *The Trans-Saharan Book Trade: Manuscript Culture, Arabic Literacy, and Intellectual History in Muslim Africa* (Leiden, 2011); Konrad Hirschler, *The Written Word in the Medieval Arabic Lands: a Social and Cultural History of Reading Practices* (New York and Edinburgh, 2012); Rosalind O'Hanlon, 'Performance in a world of paper: Puranic histories and social communication in early modern India', *Past and Present* 219 (2013), 87–126.

[11] Among these technologies, printing is conspicuously absent. Though several attempts were made to introduce it beforehand, printing did not establish itself in the region until the nineteenth century. For details on its reception and consequences, see Francis Robinson, 'Technology and religious change: Islam and the impact of print', *Modern Asian Studies* 27:1 (1993), 229–51.

[12] The situation may also be described as a linguistic cosmopolis. This is a subject of growing interest among scholars. For an introduction and survey, see Sheldon I. Pollock, 'The cosmopolitan vernacular', *Journal of Asian Studies* 57:1 (1998), 6–37 and 'Cosmopolitan and vernacular in history', *Public Culture* 12:3 (2000), 591–625.

Niebuhr, exhibited such variety that they were not always mutually intelligible. Based on information gathered during his travels through Arab countries (and India) in the mid-eighteenth century, he observed:

> There is perhaps no other language diversified by so many dialects as that of Arabia . . . Even in the narrow extent of the Imam of Sana's [Ṣanʿāʾ] dominions [in western Yemen], this diversity of dialects is very considerable. Not only does the language of the Tehama [Tihāma] differ from that spoken in the highlands, but, even in the same parts of the country, people of rank use words and phrases entirely unknown to the rest of the people. These dialects of Yemen differ still more widely from those used by the Bedouins in the desert, than from one another.[13]

This diversity was found both in pronunciation – where that 'of one province differs equally from that of other provinces' – and in writing – where 'letters and founds [fonts] are often changed in such a manner as to produce an entire alteration upon the words'.[14] Notwithstanding this diversity, the common forms of the language seen in personal correspondence and official documents were tolerably familiar, at least for the region's worldly and literate individuals, Muslims or otherwise. These forms meshed elements of the classical version (*fuṣḥa*) and the local spoken vernacular, producing what is nowadays called Middle Arabic.[15]

Outside the personal realm, Arabic was supplanted by one of several Turkic languages across much of Anatolia and Inner Asia, while it vied with Persian for dominance in Iraq and the Persian Gulf area. In Iran and Afghanistan, however, battle was never joined; beyond the theological and juristic fields, Persian was virtually unchallenged as the language of polite discourse. Furthermore, Shīʿī communities whose roots lay in Iraq and Iran would often continue to have Persian as their preferred language even when resident elsewhere in the region. As for the Indian

[13] Carsten Niebuhr, *Travels through Arabia and Other Countries in the East*, trans. Robert Heron, 2 vols. (Edinburgh, 1792), II, 254–5. He believed that 'the language of the Koran . . . differs so widely from the modern language of Arabia, that it is now taught and studied in the college of Mecca just as the Latin is at Rome . . . The old Arabic language is, through all the East, just like Latin in Europe, a learned tongue, to be acquired only in colleges, or by perusal of the best authors' (II, 254). As for his rationalisation for this dialectical variety: 'The [Muslim or Arab] nation having extended their conquests, and sent out colonies through great part of Asia, and almost over the whole coasts of Africa, the different people conquered by them have been obliged to speak the language of their new masters and neighbours. But those people retained at the same time terms and phrases of their former language, which have debased the purity of the Arabic, and formed a diversity of dialects' (II, 254–5).

[14] Ibid., II, 255. Niebuhr goes on to write: 'I found the pronunciation of the Southern Arabs more soft, and better adapted to European organs, than that of the inhabitants of Egypt and Syria' (II, 255–6).

[15] For more details, see Joshua Blau, *A Handbook of Early Middle Arabic* (Jerusalem, 2002), 14–15, 19.

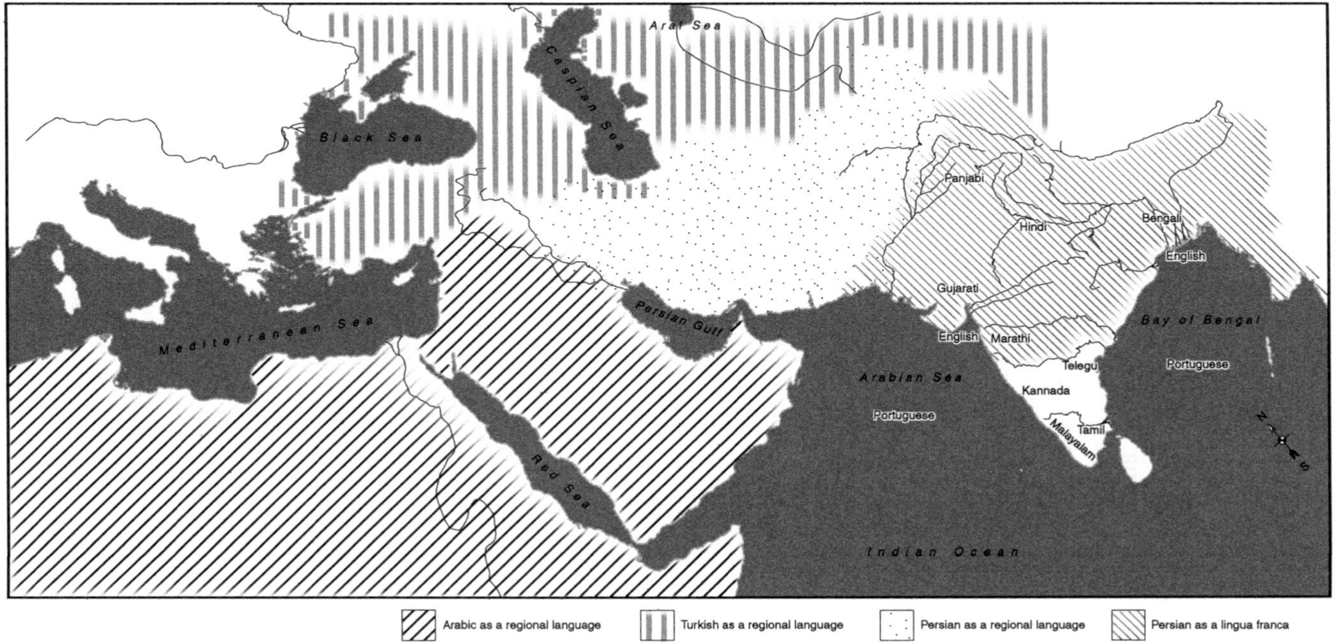

Map 5. Regional languages and lingua francas.

subcontinent, observers agreed that Persian was the sole language which one could expect to find in every major settlement whether in speaking or in writing.[16] Abraham-Hyacinthe Anquetil-Duperron, the celebrated French orientalist, remarked that, with the exception of the extreme south, Persian was in 'common use' throughout the country,[17] at least, so Niebuhr added, among 'all people of distinction'.[18] Pierre Sonnerat noted that, while Hindi too was present over much of India,[19] it was mostly confined to oral communication.[20]

In comparison with the Maghrib, Levant, Arabia, Iraq and Iran, where Arabic or Persian reigned supreme outside the personal realm, India showcased a much greater variety. Travellers there, even if seldom able to grasp their details, were impressed by the array of languages on display. A small number of them, in trying to make sense of their ambient surroundings, sought to elucidate India's linguistic cosmopolis. Sonnerat, who spent several years in southern India in the 1770s, observed that Tamil was spoken in all the coastal areas of southern India, from Orissa in the east to Cochin in the west. He noted that in Orissa Telegu too was

[16] The situation of Persian in Mughal India is described in Muzaffar Alam, 'Pursuit of Persian: language in Mughal politics', *Modern Asian Studies* 32:2 (1998), 317–49, which appears in revised form as 'The culture and politics of Persian in precolonial Hindustan', in Sheldon Pollock (ed.), *Literary Cultures in History: Reconstructions from South Asia* (Berkeley, 2003), 131–98.

[17] Abraham-Hyacinthe Anquetil-Duperron, *Voyage en Inde 1754–1762: relation de voyage en préliminaire à la traduction du Zend-Avesta*, ed. Jean Deloche, Manonmani Filliozat and Pierre-Sylvain Filliozat (Paris, 1997), 175.

[18] Niebuhr, *Travels through Arabia and Other Countries in the East*, II, 405.

[19] Pierre Sonnerat, *Voyage aux Indes Orientales et à la Chine . . .*, vol. I (Paris, 1782), 125. 'Hindi' is noted by Anquetil-Duperron as a major language in India, though he does not give details about its geographical reach. Anquetil-Duperron, *Voyage en Inde 1754–1762*, 174–5. For documentary evidence regarding the use of Hindi at the court of Haidar Ali at Mysore, see IOR/G/37/3: 175–8.

[20] In Mughal India, *hindī* appears to have been used in Persian texts as a generic term to refer to non-Persian languages. The term *hindavī*, or *hindvī*, also figures in Persian texts, though this tends to pre-date the Mughal period. For details on the history of Hindi and its variants, see Christopher Shackle and Rupert Snell (eds.), *Hindi and Urdu since 1800: a Common Reader* (London, 1990); David Lelyveld, 'Colonial knowledge and the fate of Hindustani', *Comparative Studies in Society and History* 35 (1993), 665–82; Shamsur Rahman Faruqi, *Early Urdu Literary Culture and History* (New Delhi, 2001); Shamsur Rahman Faruqi, *The Flower-Lit Road: Essays in Urdu Literary Theory and Criticism* (Allahabad, 2005); Shantanu Phukan, '"Through throats where many rivers meet": the ecology of Hindi in the world of Persian', *Indian Economic and Social History Review* 38:1 (2001), 33–58; Allison Busch, *Poetry of Kings: the Classical Hindi Literature of Mughal India* (New York, 2011); Tariq Rahman, *From Hindi to Urdu: a Social and Political History* (Karachi, 2011). In the eighteenth century, documents were seldom written in Hindi, even though the language was in widespread use as a lingua franca in oral communication. A rare exception to this is contained in a note sent by a British merchant to his Hindu associate at Goa in the 1750s or 1760s. Though it is mostly in English, it opens with several lines in Hindi written in Latin script. XCHR/MHR/Other Documents (undated): 2.

commonplace and, moreover, the working language of nearly all the merchants on the Coromandel coast. Malayalam dominated the Malabar coast and, to its north, 'in the direction of' Gujarat, Marathi was the principal language of its residents.[21]

Anquetil-Duperron, endowed with a rare faculty for yoking careful observation to trenchant analysis, has left us with an informative, if incomplete, account of the distribution of languages spoken by India's inhabitants. Based on his residence there in the late 1750s and early 1760s, during which time he learnt Persian, Anquetil-Duperron divided the subcontinent into five linguistic zones, moving from south to north. The first zone coincided with the extreme south. This was dominated by Tamil and Malayalam. These same languages also prevailed in the second zone, encompassing present-day Tamil Nadu and Kerala above the districts of Tirunelveli (Tinnevelly) and Thiruvananthapuram (Trivandrum). He noted that Malayalam was widely used along the coast between Kollam (Quilon) and Ezhimala (Elimala) in the Kannur district of Kerala. Karnataka and Andhra Pradesh constituted the third zone, within which Kannaḍa and Telegu were the chief languages. The domain of Kannaḍa specifically stretched from the coast at Hosdurg (in the Kasargod district of Kerala) to the territories of the ruling Bhonsle family (part of the Maratha confederacy). Marathi was the language of the fourth zone, which overlapped with the territories of the Maratha confederacy and extended to Surat in Gujarat. The fifth zone covered the remainder of India to the north, where Gujarati, Bengali and Hindi dominated.[22]

Of course, in any settlement of note, regional languages were entangled with other languages which, though vibrant, were often restricted to the personal realm and to particular ethnic communities. As Niebuhr observed in relation to the Maghrib, the Levant and the Fertile Crescent, 'Although the Arabian conquerors have introduced and established their language in the countries which they conquered, yet their

[21] Sonnerat, *Voyage aux Indes Orientales et à la Chine . . .*, I, 125–7. Though the author uses the verb 'parler' when specifying the language in general use by the residents of specified areas, it is clear from the context of the passage that his remarks apply to both the oral and written medium.

[22] Anquetil-Duperron, *Voyage en Inde 1754–1762*, 174–5. Anquetil-Duperron was well aware that his zonal linguistic map only sufficed as a first approximation. In addition to languages, he remarked on the widespread use of what he called 'jargons ou dialectes' along stretches of western India's coastal areas. He observed the presence of a 'corrupted' (*corrumpu*) Malayalam, which he described as the 'patois' of the coast of Tirunelveli; Tulu, closely related to Kannaḍa, was current among 'fishermen, Pulayars and other low castes, [who live in the coastal region stretching] from Elimala to two days' [journey] north of Mangalore'; Konkanī was spoken at Goa; and Maharashtri was in common use between Bombay and Surat.

subjects have not always left off the use of their mother tongue.'[23] The relative significance of these more localised languages was usually correlated with the broader influence of the community's specialised vocation. This could be considerable in situations where it exercised an effective monopoly over trade in certain goods or services. A telling example of this was the widespread use of Gujarati in credit transactions, minting and the movement of capital via *hundis*.[24] Its use was predicated on the domination of these sectors in many of the region's settlements by *baniyās*, who maintained strong ties to their ethnic communities at home in Gujarat.

It would be reasonable to think that, just to survive, any visitor would have had to pick up at least the rudiments of the locally dominant regional or community language. However, this often proved unnecessary because of the presence of recognised lingua francas.[25] Persian may be viewed as one such lingua franca in the Indian subcontinent, where it was 'received at the courts ... [and was] very useful for the dispatch of business'.[26] Portuguese covered an even bigger area, no doubt because of its critical role in mediating commerce. Across the region, Niebuhr wrote, 'in trade corrupt Portuguese is the language used'. In India, it was described as 'a

[23] Niebuhr, *Travels through Arabia and Other Countries in the East*, II, 256. His account proceeds to give interesting details on these subject languages: 'In Syria and Palestine, indeed, no language is to be heard but the Arabian, and yet the Syriac is not absolutely a dead language, but is still spoken in several villages in the Pachalick of Damascus. In many places, in the neighbourhood of Merdin and Mosul, the Christians still speak the Chaldean language, and the inhabitants of the villages who do not frequent towns, never hear any other than their mother tongue. The Christians born in the cities of Merden and Mosul, although they speak Arabic, write in the Chaldean characters, just as the Maronites write their Arabic in Syriac letters, and the Greeks the Turkish in Greek letters ... In Natolia [Anatolia], these nations [the Greeks and Armenians] speak their own languages in several different dialects ... The Kurdes, who are nearly independent, have preserved their ancient language, of which there are in Kurdistan three principal dialects ... ' (II, 256–7). At the same time, Niebuhr recognised 'many people living under the dominion of the Arabians and Turks have lost the use of their mother tongue' or that its use was preserved only for special occasions, such as religious ceremonies. He gives as examples the Greek and Armenian residents of Egypt and Syria, who 'speak Arabic and the services of their public worship are performed in two languages at once' (II, 256–7).

[24] BL/Lansdowne/1046, doc. 62.

[25] Much of the historical scholarship on lingua francas (and creoles) centres on the Mediterranean basin, though the Indian Ocean is gaining in popularity. See Henry Kahane, Renée Kahane and Andreas Tietze, *Lingua Franca in the Levant: Turkish Nautical Terms of Italian and Greek Origin* (Urbana, IL, 1958); Guido Cifoletti, *La lingua franca mediterranea* (Padua, 1989); John E. Wansbrough, *Lingua Franca in the Mediterranean* (Richmond, Surrey, 1996); Karlfried Knapp and Christiane Meierkord (eds.), *Lingua Franca Communication* (Frankfurt am Main, 2000); Jocelyne Dakhlia, *Lingua franca: histoire d'une langue métisse en Méditerranée* (Arles, 2009); Pier M. Larson, *Ocean of Letters: Language and Creolization in an Indian Ocean Diaspora* (Cambridge, 2009); Eric R. Dursteler, 'Speaking tongues: language and communication in the early modern Mediterranean', *Past and Present* 217 (2012), 47–77.

[26] Niebuhr, *Travels through Arabia and Other Countries in the East*, II, 405.

corrupt lingo' (*un mauvais jargon*),[27] on par with 'what the Lingua Franca is in the Levant'.[28] Portuguese was commonly spoken by 'servants' (*domestiques*) in Mocha;[29] it was the default language for conducting trade in Dutch Cochin;[30] Portuguese was so widespread in Calicut that some were reluctant to use it for writing letters containing sensitive information;[31] and it was the only language, alongside English, which had legal status in the eyes of the authorities in British Madras.[32]

In addition to travel accounts, there is a wealth of documentary evidence that testifies to the use of Portuguese across many different ethnic and linguistic boundaries. The personal and business correspondence of a Hindu merchant house based in Goa and of a French merchant-official resident in Mahe offer insightful examples. For much of the eighteenth century, the merchant house was managed by Suba Kāmat, a Gauḍ Sārasvat Hindu, and, following his death, by his sons Veṅkateśa and Nārāyaṇa. Deeply enmeshed in the trade and finance of western India and the Arabian Sea area, their house maintained relations with a wide range of individuals active in regional circulation and exchange. Though a large proportion of these were Portuguese and Luso-Indians, many other backgrounds were also well represented. With members of their own linguistic group, they used Marathi (or Konkani), their native tongue. In communicating with their other associates, who included Parsis, Gujarati *baniyā*s, the French and British, their preferred language was Portuguese; recourse to English occurred only as a last resort.[33]

27 Sonnerat, *Voyage aux Indes Orientales et à la Chine . . .*, I, 125–7.
28 Niebuhr, *Travels through Arabia and Other Countries in the East*, II, 405.
29 Ibid., I, 10.
30 Cochin's Dutch governor, Adriaan Moens, wrote to his French associate in 1779 to say that he was being forced to deal with French affairs in Portuguese because there remained no more French speakers in his settlement. MssOcc/NAF/9013: 45–9.
31 Antonio de Quental at Calicut asked his principal to forgive him for not writing his letter, which dealt with a highly sensitive issue, in a language other than Portuguese because 'he p[a] ser impossivel achar hua pessoa p[a] fazer'. MssOcc/NAF/9003: 104.
32 This status of Portuguese was not a formal one. Rather, it was tacitly acknowledged by the authorities because of its widespread use among the residents of Madras and the Coromandel coast. Its privileged status is demonstrated by the fact that Portuguese was the only language, alongside English, in which depositions could be exhibited in Madras's Mayor's Court. This was the case even though litigants who came before the bench hailed from many different linguistic backgrounds. For examples of depositions in Portuguese, see TNSA/Mayors Court Records/Pleadings/5: 356–73; TNSA/Mayors Court Records/Pleadings/5: 383–96; TNSA/Mayors Court Records/Pleadings/18B: 418–37. Depositions in all other languages had to be translated into English (or, much more rarely, Portuguese) before they would be accepted as evidence by the court.
33 Writing in 1787 to Nasarvanji Manakji, a Parsi broker and merchant resident in Bombay, the Kāmat brothers told him that 'quando a VM[ce] impossibilite de escrever em Portuguez, bastarà nos em Inglez, por qualquer de sua poessoas'. XCHR/MHR/Correspondence (outgoing) (4 December 1787).

Like the Kāmats, Bernard Picot, a French merchant-official based on the Malabar coast between the 1740s and the 1770s, had interests all around the Arabian Sea rim (and elsewhere in maritime Asia too). Though he used French with his fellow countrymen, Portuguese was his language of choice in corresponding with his Jewish, British, Indian and Dutch associates, who made up nearly half of his regular correspondents.[34] Indeed, in 1771, he went so far as to instruct Isaac Surgun, a Jewish landowner, merchant and diplomat living in Cochin, to reply to him in a manner that was 'well expressed in good Portuguese'.[35] When Picot received letters in a language other than French or Portuguese – which generally meant English, Arabic, Marathi or Persian – he would get it translated into Portuguese or, more rarely, French.

Arabic and English, though less widespread than Persian or Portuguese, also served as lingua francas. In the case of Arabic, educated Muslims, whatever their background, were expected to have some familiarity with it, if only because of its incomparable prestige as the language of the Qur'ān, the sharia and the traditional Islamic sciences. English, in comparison, was a parvenu. Starting almost from scratch, its popularity began its extraordinary rise only from the second half of the eighteenth century. Largely confined to places such as Basra, Surat, Bombay, Madras and Calcutta and their hinterlands, places where the British had an established presence, its rise was bound up with their growing commercial and political clout in maritime Asia and the Indian subcontinent.[36]

In general, those for whom lingua francas were not their native tongues used them in a simple and functional way, adopting a pragmatic, conversational approach to their grammar. Although Portuguese, when marshalled as a lingua franca, was normally articulated in keeping with metropolitan standards, despite numerous inconsistencies in spelling, written Arabic could diverge greatly from its classical form, cleaving much more to the local vernacular. The most extreme cases that I have come across are messages composed in Latin script but in a language that is a melange, or fusion, of several Romance languages. This is evidenced in a series of letters written in the 1760s and 1770s by

[34] Picot's regular correspondents (142 in total) were distributed as follows: French 72 (50.7%), Portuguese or Luso-Indian 25 (17.6%), 'Hindu' or non-Muslim Indian 19 (13.4%), British 15 (10.6%), Muslim 5 (3.5%), Dutch 3 (2.1%), Jewish 2 (1.4%), Armenian 1 (0.7%).

[35] MssOcc/NAF/9054: 245 (26 October 1771).

[36] On the rise of English in India, to begin with as a lingua franca and later as a literary language, see Vinay Dharwadker, 'The historical formation of Indian-English literature', in Sheldon Pollock (ed.), *Literary Cultures in History: Reconstructions from South Asia* (Berkeley, CA, 2003), 199–267.

Gujarati *baniyās* in Mocha to their French associates in Mahe and Pondicherry.[37] The 'language' that they used shared a great deal with contemporary Italian, French and Portuguese on the syntactic and lexical levels. Even though at first sight it appears a strange, mysterious amalgam, their message may be comprehended if formal knowledge of its languages is suspended and the text spoken aloud.

Linked to lingua francas, there was an intriguing and little-known class of what may be called private or specialised languages. These were most often found in situations where maintaining secrecy was of paramount concern, and appear to have been of two broad types. The first derived from ordinary languages. Niebuhr claims to have 'seen more than once educated Arabs who praised the secret of writing to a friend without a third person being able to read it'.[38] Families too were known to have their own forms of communication, with many of the trappings of a language, and to which only they and their closest associates were privy. This was true, for example, of 'a distinguished Iranian family of merchants' at Shiraz, with whom Niebuhr was personally acquainted and 'who . . . had among themselves a special language'. It is difficult for us to discern whether or not this was a real language because no details are given about its character. Niebuhr himself appears to have been sceptical, viewing it as akin more to a secret lexicon than a language per se when he added the qualification: 'at least they had given to several things names of their invention so that they could speak in front of others without the latter understanding them'.[39]

The languages belonging to the second type were tactile. Dependent on touching fingers, they were often found in discussions conducted in the open between prospective buyers and vendors (or intermediaries acting on their behalf).[40] The aim of these tactile languages was twofold: to facilitate effective negotiations and to allow the negotiators to reach an agreement in the open without others being aware of its details.[41] Mediated by touch, deals for the sale and purchase of goods, which could be sizeable, were conducted between the interested parties 'with the greatest calm and in complete good faith'.[42]

[37] MssOcc/NAF/8992: 1–3, 4–8; MssOcc/NAF/8998: 150–3, 155.
[38] Carsten Niebuhr, *Description de l'Arabie, d'après les observations et recherches faites dans le pays même . . .*, vol. I (Paris, 1779), 144.
[39] Ibid., I, 144.
[40] Tactile languages are technically known as dactylonomy and, in the Islamic world, as *ḥisāb al-ʿaqd*. Their role in negotiations is examined in Chapter 7 on everyday practices.
[41] Niebuhr, *Description de l'Arabie*, I, 145.
[42] Anquetil-Duperron, *Voyage en Inde 1754–1762*, 360.

The value of these languages derived from their simplicity and their strict focus on prices and quantities. Anquetil-Duperron described the usual manner in which a typical negotiation was conducted in Surat in 1758 as follows:

> The merchant states the price without lengthy preliminaries. The purchaser responds by putting his hand inside that of the other . . . He indicates by the number of bent or extended fingers how much below the asking price he is prepared to pay and sometimes the deal is concluded without any word being said.[43]

Niebuhr came across negotiations of a similar type during his travels in Arabia in the 1760s. In his account, 'The two parties make it known, on the one side, what he desires, on the other, what he is willing to pay, by touching each other's fingers or the joints of the hand, which signify 100, 50, 10, etc.'[44] In both cases, the 'languages' are portrayed as functional and efficient, well suited to the task of relaying useful information rapidly between the negotiators.

Tactile languages also had the advantage of restricting knowledge of the discussion's contents to the two sides directly involved, keeping in the dark any employees and others who might be in the vicinity. Unlike the first type of languages noted above, this was not done by controlling their dissemination. Indeed, if that were the case, tactile languages would have been rendered obsolete since their value was strongly correlated to the number of individuals conversant with them. The point is made by Niebuhr, who remarked, 'One does not make a mystery of this art which, if it were a secret, it would not be of great utility.'[45] Secrecy, an essential ingredient in such transactions, was maintained instead by covering 'the hand with the end of one's cape'[46] or, alternatively, by placing the hands 'under a shawl or some other cover'.[47] This usually worked so well that 'it allows the broker or agent to deceive his principal [on whose behalf he is conducting the negotiations], even in his presence'.[48]

After its language, the foundational attribute of any text is the script in which it is composed.[49] In India and the Islamic heartlands in the

[43] Anquetil-Duperron, *Voyage en Inde 1754–1762*, 360.
[44] Niebuhr, *Description de l'Arabie*, I, 145. [45] Ibid. [46] Ibid.
[47] Anquetil-Duperron, *Voyage en Inde 1754–1762*, 360.
[48] Niebuhr, *Description de l'Arabie*, I, 145.
[49] A clear distinction is made here between a written text's script, style and handwriting. A script is defined as the set of graphemes that embody the definitive or universal characteristics of the language's writing system. The style, in contrast, is the conventionalised manner in which individual symbols – also known in the literature as glyphs, characters or signs – are formed and combined with each other while still recognised as members of the same script or, equivalently, derived from their root graphemes. Thus, one script may be associated with multiple writing styles, and the variant symbolic representations of each

eighteenth century, the text's script was almost always dictated by the choice of its language. This was because each of the region's languages with an established literary heritage was commonly associated with a particular script. Several of these were current at the time, based on either the alphabetic or syllabary systems.[50] Of course, any one script could, with relatively minor variations – say, an extra letter or two, different styles or the use of additional diacritics – be the vehicle for languages belonging to more than one linguistic family. So the Arabic script was conventionally used for writings in Persian, Ottoman Turkish and Arabic, which embrace the Indo-European, Turkic and Semitic families.[51] As for English, Portuguese, Dutch and French, all members of the Indo-European family, they were normally written in the Latin script.[52]

But several exceptions to these broad generalisations are worth noting. Languages that were young or undergoing rapid transformations, or those that were predominantly oral in their usage, could be associated with multiple scripts. This state of affairs is exemplified by Hindi.[53] Widespread across India, especially in the north, it experienced major changes in the eighteenth century. Its grammar was derived largely from *Khaṛī bolī* ('the standard dialect') and its lexicon drew heavily on several regional languages, notably Arabic, Persian and Sanskrit. Though within the arena it was mostly restricted to everyday speech, Hindi was sometimes seen in business and political correspondence. In such cases, it was written either in a modified Arabic script[54] or in the Kaithi or Devanāgarī (Nāgarī) script;[55] the Latin script could also be used, though this was rare.[56]

grapheme in these styles are termed its allographs. In the act of composing a text, of course, the conventional style adopted by its author is modified by and fused with the idiosyncrasies of his handwriting.

50 For general accounts of writing, writing systems and their evolution, see Marcel Cohen, *La grande invention de l'écriture et son évolution* (Paris, 1958); Ignace J. Gelb, *A Study of Writing* (rev. edn, Chicago, 1963); David Diringer, *Writing* (London, 1982); Geoffrey Sampson, *Writing Systems* (Stanford, CA, 1985); Jack Goody, *The Logic of Writing and the Organization of Society* (Cambridge, 1986).

51 The chief difference in the use of the Arabic script by these languages is that the Persian and Ottoman Turkish alphabets have four letters – [p] (پ), [ch] (چ), [zh] (ژ), [g] (گ) – in addition to the standard Arabic alphabet.

52 These languages all have the same the alphabet but, owing to differences in their phonology, each has recourse to distinctive sets of diacritical marks.

53 See above for citations to the scholarly literature on the history of Hindi.

54 HAG/Persian Documents, doc. 24.

55 It has been claimed that until the nineteenth century the Kaithi script was more commonly used in schools in northern India for writing Hindi than either Devanāgarī or Nāgarī. In this thesis, it is only from the latter half of the nineteenth century that the Kaithi script was successfully marginalised by Devanāgarī. For an account of the 'contest' between the two scripts, see Alok Rai, *Hindi Nationalism* (London, 2001).

56 There is an example of Hindi written in Latin script in XCHR/MHR/Other Documents (undated): 2.

Even among the more canonical and less obviously dynamic languages, there was occasional use of multiple scripts. Consider the case of Arabic. Certainly by the eighteenth century, we seldom find Arabic sources composed in any script but the Arabic. This is true whether the language was native to the author and his audience, or a lingua franca, whether the author and his audience were Muslims, or adherents of some other religious tradition. Nevertheless, there were special circumstances in which older traditions resurfaced that used other scripts for composition in Arabic, especially if rooted in a rich literary heritage. The best-known instance is recourse to Hebrew characters. This tradition, which has a venerable genealogy stretching back to Abbasid times, was widely adopted by the settled Jewish communities of the Near East and the Mediterranean basin.[57]

While the tradition had attenuated by the eighteenth century, it was certainly not lost. In 1776, that very fact proved a godsend for Jīvan and Krishan. At the time, they were making a living as brokers in Mocha and they were confronted by a linguistic conundrum. When writing to their non-Gujarati correspondents in India, Jīvan and Krishan's lingua franca was Arabic. Ordinarily, the language would be written in the Arabic script.[58] But 1776 was no ordinary year. That year all of their usual clerks were indisposed and none of those who were available knew how to write in the Arabic script. Evidently such was their need, the brokers could not wait for the return of their usual clerks. So they cast around for a substitute. The best that they were able to come up with was an individual, almost certainly Jewish, who, while he could comprehend spoken Arabic, was only able to write the language in Hebrew characters. From the circumstances in which the letter was composed, it is clear that the Gujarati brokers dictated their message to the Jewish writer in Arabic, which he then wrote up in neat in the Hebrew script. At the very end of the letter, Jīvan and Krishan apologised to their correspondent, asking him not 'to pay any attention to this being written in the Hebrew script because no other writers could be found.'[59]

[57] A significant proportion of the Cairo Geniza documents were written in Arabic in the Hebrew script. For more details, see Shelomo D. Goitein, 'The documents of the Cairo Geniza as a source for Mediterranean social history', *Journal of the American Oriental Society* 80:2 (1960), 91–100 and Colin F. Baker, 'Judaeo-Arabic material in the Cambridge Genizah collections', *Bulletin of the School of Oriental and African Studies* 58 (1995), 45–54.

[58] An example of their usual practice, namely, drafting or dictating their letters in Gujarati or Arabic to a clerk who would then write it up in neat in Arabic in the Arabic script, may be found in MssOcc/NAF/9005: 64–7. The letter was translated into a language with which recipient was familiar at his end of the chain of communication.

[59] MssOcc/NAF/8992: 88–9.

Though literary languages cannot do without scripts, the reverse is not the case; not all scripts current in Islamicate Eurasia were tied to languages. This was especially true of those employed for accounting and coding. In accounting, there was a well-established script – variously termed *siyāq* or *raqmī* – that was familiar to the region's merchants, banks, scribes and administrators down to at least the nineteenth century.[60] The numbers in this script were generated by glyphs combined according to standard orthographic rules.[61] The glyphs for the numbers one to ten were, in effect, simple and functional logograms of the words for the same numbers written out in Arabic that had over time been deformed and abbreviated. Additional glyphs denoted tens, hundreds, thousands and so on, and the orthographic rules specified how these glyphs were supposed to be combined and oriented with respect to one another.[62] Even if one were fluent in Arabic, Persian or Ottoman Turkish, without formal training this script was (and remains) opaque for the uninitiated. However, the effort required for gaining mastery over *siyāq* was more than offset by the greater efficiency thus obtained in drawing up and maintaining simple accounts in it, certainly as compared with Arabic or Hindi numerals. Once he had gained sufficient familiarity with *siyāq* – which, as with ordinary languages, was mostly a matter of practice and perseverance – the writer was able to compose accounts at high speed because the symbols representing the numbers are very concise and articulated in sympathy with the natural movements of the fingers and wrist. (See Figure 3.)

[60] Despite longstanding knowledge and development by indigenous mathematicians, astronomers and astrologers of the Hindi-Arabic (or positional decimal) numeral system, the extant sources in Arabic and Persian show that *siyāq* for bookkeeping remained in use until as recently as the turn of the twentieth century.

[61] Though these glyphs were standardised in any given place, different *siyāq* scripts were in currency in different parts of the region. So it cannot be assumed that the practioners of one would have been conversant with the other. Two of these variants, common to Iran and India in the period, are illustrated in William L. Hanaway and Brian Spooner, *Reading Nastaʿliq: Persian and Urdu Hands from 1500 to the Present* (Costa Mesa, CA, 1995), 24–5. Compare these with illustrations of the *siyāq* 'alphabet' used by the tribes of southern Iran in the early part of the twentieth century in H. Kazem Zadeh, 'Chiffres siyāk et la comptabilité persane', *Revue de monde musulman* 30 (1915), 1–51.

[62] For further details about this accounting system, see Edward Henry Palmer and F. Pincott, *Oriental Penmanship: Specimens of Persian Handwriting* (London, 1886), 39–40; Kazem Zadeh, 'Chiffres siyāk et la comptabilité persane'; Muḥammad Ṣāliḥ, 'Siyāqnamah (Dastūr al-siyāq)' (only available in manuscript); Muḥammad Mahdī Furūgh Iṣfahānī, *Furūghistān: Dānishnāmah-yi fann-i istifa va siyāq*, ed. Irāj Afshār (Tehran, 1999); ʿAbd al-Vahhāb b. Muḥammad ʾAmīn Ḥusaynī Shahshahānī, *Baḥr al-javāhir fī ʿilm al-dafātir va sarrishtah-yi siyāq-i ḥisāb* (Tehran, 1271/1854; Isfahan, *c.* 1880). The EI2's article on 'siyāqat', though useful in places, is of limited value for the Islamic world as a whole because of its brevity and its focus on *siyāq*'s application in the Ottoman empire.

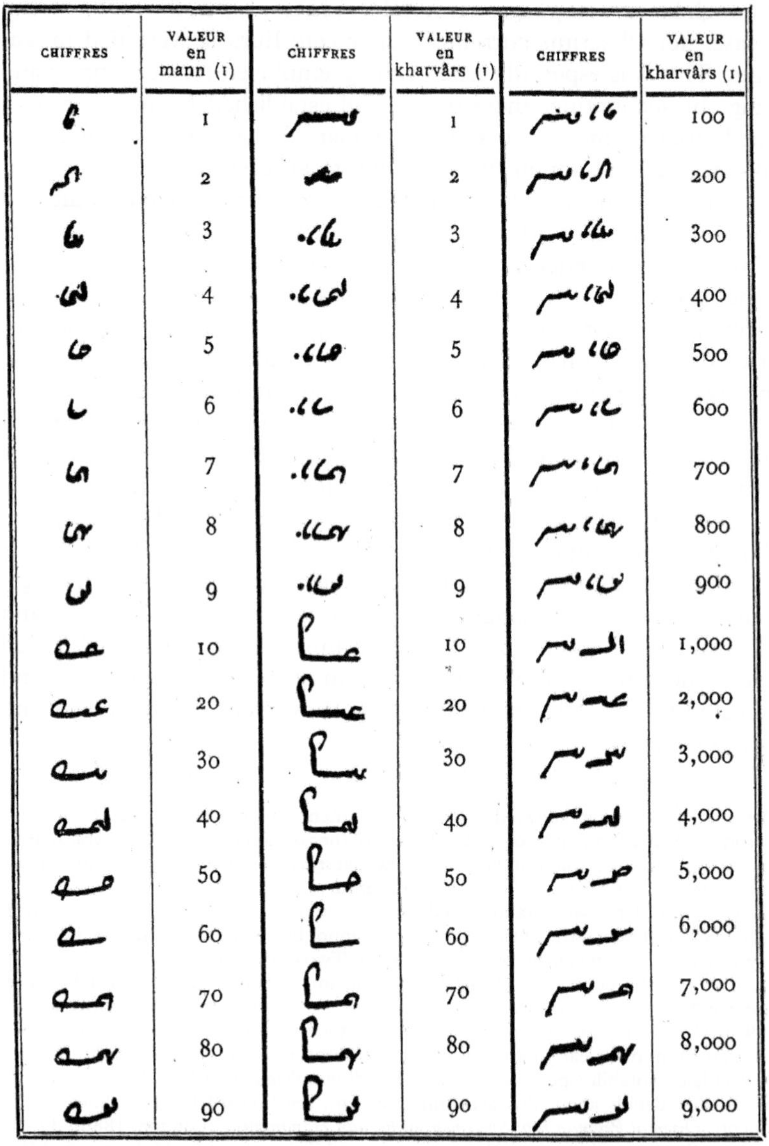
CHIFFRES
VALEUR en mann (1)
CHIFFRES
VALEUR en kharvârs (1)
CHIFFRES
VALEUR en kharvârs (1)
1 2 3 4 5 6 7 8 9 10 20 30 40 50 60 70 80 90
1 2 3 4 5 6 7 8 9 10 20 30 40 50 60 70 80 90
100 200 300 400 500 600 700 800 900 1,000 2,000 3,000 4,000 5,000 6,000 7,000 8,000 9,000

Figure 3. *Siyāq* in Persian bookkeeping.
Source: H. Kazem Zadeh, 'Chiffres siyâk et la comptabilité persane', *Revue de monde musulman* 30 (1915), 1–51.

It was also not uncommon to keep accounts in scripts – or, more properly, codes – based on ad hoc systems that were the author's construction. This was the wont of the Shirazi 'family of merchants' noted earlier by Niebuhr, who 'used, in their account-books, symbols known to themselves alone'.[63] Though not scalable and much less versatile than *siyāq*, let alone Hindi, Arabic and European numerals, such scripts were perfectly serviceable for the simple purposes for which they were marshalled. Furthermore, if secrecy was a consideration, they offered an additional layer of security. Niebuhr remarked upon 'the [Armenian] cook of an English merchant at Aleppo [who] kept the accounts of the expenses of his master and only knew how to write ordinary numbers'. In order to keep his accounts secret, he created his own private code composed of 'glyphs': 'a circle designated a pudding, a spiral line a pâté, a straight line crossed by smaller lines small birds'.[64] Having a private code for keeping accounts appears to have been a widespread phenomenon, for even 'chauffeurs, artisans, labourers all had their symbols'. In their case, the rationale was probably convenience more than secrecy since they were required to present their accounts to their superiors or the authorities for inspection on a regular basis. To facilitate this, they would 'read their accounts every Saturday or every fortnight to a clerk and have them drawn up in neat'.[65]

No less foundational than languages and scripts to the arena's communications order were the writing substrates and the writing tools by which symbols were preserved in material form. The choice of the two was in practice entwined; settling on one effectively determined the other if only because the tools adapted to the particular material qualities of each substrate were few in number. In the case of India and the Islamic heartlands, the available substrates were more or less restricted to palm-leaves and paper.[66]

The parts of the region in which palm-leaves remained in common use were by the eighteenth century confined to Sri Lanka and certain areas of India.[67] In these places, however, the millennium-old tradition

[63] Niebuhr, *Description de l'Arabie*, I, 144. [64] Ibid., I, 144–5. [65] Ibid.

[66] In earlier periods, papyrus, leather and parchment as writing substrates had been commonplace too. For a good overview, see Albertine Gaur, *Writing Materials of the East* (London, 1979). References to the scholarly literature on the nature, production and history of writing substrates in the Middle East, South Asia and Southeast Asia may be found in R. Teygeler (ed.), *Preservation of Archives in Tropical Climates: an Annotated Bibliography* (Paris, 2001).

[67] Palm-leaves were also widely employed as a writing substrate in the countries of Southeast Asia historically influenced by Indian culture. For more details, see John Guy, *Palm-leaf and Paper: Illustrated Manuscripts of India and Southeast Asia* (Melbourne, 1982).

was vibrant, assiduously cultivated by the local literati. Pierre Sonnerat travelled to southern India in the 1770s and took a keen interest in the preparation of palm-leaves and the writing techniques appropriate to them. He observed that the source of the palm-leaf pages was 'the leaf of a type of palm tree [called palmyra]'.

This leaf, [when] splayed out like a fan, is thick and dry. The strips that one separates from it are called olles ... In order to form the characters, the authors put the olle on one hand and write with the other [using an] awl ... They write on both sides and then put black ink on the letters which they have just etched. In order to make a book, they stack the olles on top of each other and at each end make a hole which cuts through all the sheets. They pass through it a string which, in this way, binds all the olles.[68]

Perhaps the most significant constraint on the broader use of palm-leaves, even in places where it was still widespread, was its intimate association with Indic languages. Elsewhere in India, especially in the north, which had long been exposed to Perso-Islamic and Mughal influences, writing on palm-leaves had given way to paper well before our period. In Sonnerat's opinion, which has been echoed in modern scholarship, this substitution occurred because the Mughals preferred 'paper to palm-leaves'.[69] Though weaker, a similar dynamic was at work in the south of the country. Within the area's several nominally Muslim polities, above all in Hyderabad and Arcot, the secular trend was against the use of palm-leaves and in favour of paper. And this was occurring not just at court; there was pressure to adopt paper even for revenue accounts and other kinds of records that had traditionally been kept on palm-leaves. The main force for change was the lack of familiarity of the Muslim rulers and their officials with the scripts and languages associated with palm-leaves; they were far more at home with Persian and Hindi, which were conventionally written on paper.[70] This trend away from palm-leaves was reinforced by the dominance of paper in corresponding with elsewhere in Islamicate Eurasia, where palm-leaves seldom figured as writing substrates.

[68] Sonnerat, *Voyage aux Indes Orientales et à la Chine* ..., I, 136. Though Sonnerat limits his description of writing on palm-leaves to incision by a stylus, it was also standard practice to write with brush and ink.

[69] Ibid.

[70] An example of this may be seen in a request by the nawab of Arcot for accounts of certain goods freighted on his vessel, *Safinat Allāh*, sailing from Maḥmūd Bandar to Jidda in the 1794. The official responsible for maintaining them informed him that these accounts, which had originally been written on palm-leaves, had been destroyed. Nevertheless, he had been able to recover much of the information from other sources which, on being translated into Persian and written down on paper, would be sent to him. TNSA/Persian Records/111: 26.

Outside the Indian subcontinent, paper was the preferred medium for almost every community and textual genre related to activities vested in circulation and exchange. Invented in China in the first or second century BC, the use of paper had gradually spread westward over the following millennium.[71] Paper manufacturing was quickly taken up in certain areas of the region, most enthusiastically in Iran, after its introduction in the eighth century. But in India, there was resistance to this trend. Though India must have been exposed to paper very early by Buddhist monks returning from China, the manufacture of paper only began in the fifteenth century in the north; the south had to wait longer still.[72] The spread of paper mills within the region at large was checked in the sixteenth century when paper started being imported in significant quantities from Europe, with Italy in the vanguard. Such was its success that indigenous paper manufacturing was curtailed, and increasingly so with time.[73]

Despite this competition from Europe, Iran and India continued to host major centres of paper manufacturing in the eighteenth century. These catered for local demand and demand from other parts of the region. In keeping with prevailing requirements and tastes, Indian paper was often thinner and had a smoother finish than that imported from Europe. Sonnerat remarked that paper in India was generally 'made from wet rags of linen [or] cotton'.[74] Similarly, based on his travels through Iran in the 1740s, Jonas Hanway noted, 'the Persians make their paper of cotton and silk-rags'.[75] In both places, glossed and coloured paper appears to have been popular.[76] This was made in southern India by coating the base paper 'with rice paste which gives it coherence and a

[71] For more details on the manufacture and use of paper in the Islamic world, see D. Baker, 'Arab paper making', *The Paper Conservator* 15 (1991), 28–35; Yves Porter, *Peinture et arts du livre: essai sur la littérature technique indo-persane* (Paris, 1992), 21–60; and the sumptuously illustrated study by Jonathan Bloom, *Paper before Print: the History and Impact of Paper in the Islamic World* (New Haven, 2001). The classic modern account of the history of paper is Dard Hunter's *Papermaking: the History and Technique of an Ancient Craft* (2nd edn, New York, 1947), which may be complemented by the more recent Lucien Polastron, *Le papier: 2000 ans d'histoire et de savoir-faire* (Paris, 1999).

[72] Bloom, *Paper before Print*, 217. Sonnerat wrote: 'les Indiens écrivent aussi sur du papier, dont je crois que l'usage a été introduit chez eux par les Mogols ... Il n'y a pas long-tems qu'ils se servent de papier, puisque tous les ouvrages anciens sont écrits sur des olles.' Sonnerat, *Voyage aux Indes Orientales et à la Chine ...*, I, 136.

[73] Bloom, *Paper before Print*, 217.

[74] Sonnerat, *Voyage aux Indes Orientales et à la Chine ...*, I, 136.

[75] Hanway, *Historical Account of the British Trade over the Caspian Sea ...*, I, 317

[76] The various types of coloured and glossed paper, and how they are prepared for writing, are discussed in Ḥabīb Allāh Faḍā'ilī [Fazā'ilī], *Ta'līm-i khaṭṭ* (Tehran, 1356/1977–8), 355–402 and Porter, *Peinture et arts du livre*, 41–60.

varnish similar to that [of paper] from China',[77] whereas in Iran, 'after it is manufactured[,] they set a gloss upon it with a smooth stone or shell'.[78] As this paper was 'soft and smooth ... [it] is very liable to be torn or broken', which was why, again in Iran, 'they always roll it up'.[79] Paper was also manufactured in a range of colours and 'often ... [inlaid with] gold and silver'.[80] This latter type, though obviously a luxury, was the norm in circumstances where etiquette, protocol and ceremony required it. That was invariably the case when it came to petitioning the sovereign, his courtiers or members of his household;[81] correspondence between rulers[82] or requesting burial of deceased relatives in sacred ground.[83] For general use, however, Indians 'like best paper with a greyish tint. They seldom write on white, which they only use to wrap goods.'[84]

The shape and size of such paper, apart from being rectangular, did not conform to any universal standards.[85] It seems that individual vendors or would-be authors cut the paper, which was initially produced and sold as large sheets, to the dimensions best suited to its intended purpose. Once acquired and cropped to the desired width and height, the writing could then begin. If using locally made paper, the author would use a quill- or reed-pen, holding his 'fingers far away from the top of the pen'.[86] For European paper, which tended to be heavier and coarser, preference was given to the sharper-tipped goose-quill pens.[87] The ink in which these

[77] Sonnerat, *Voyage aux Indes Orientales et à la Chine ...*, I, 136.
[78] Hanway, *Historical Account of the British Trade over the Caspian Sea ...*, I, 317.
[79] Ibid. [80] Sonnerat, *Voyage aux Indes Orientales et à la Chine ...*, I, 136.
[81] TNSA/Persian Records/113: 3, 15.
[82] TNSA/Persian Records/113: 4, 7; TNSA/Persian Records/114: 12, 25, 45.
[83] TNSA/Persian Records/113: 5, 6 14, 16, 22, 33; TNSA/Persian Records/114: 7.
[84] Sonnerat, *Voyage aux Indes Orientales et à la Chine ...*, I, 136.
[85] It may well be the case, however, that paper intended for those who wrote in Arabic-script languages was normally longer in one dimension than the other in comparison to paper bought by those who wrote in Latin-script languages. The reason for this possible difference stems from the distinctive textual aesthetics associated with the individual scripts. Any such aesthetic had a direct bearing on the manner in which paper was folded, sealed and addressed before being dispatched. These matters are elaborated in Chapter 7 on everyday practices.
[86] In southern India, Sonnerat observed that 'ils écrivent avec une plume de roseau, en tenant les doigts fort éloignés de la taille de la plume'. Sonnerat, *Voyage aux Indes Orientales et à la Chine ...*, I, 136. In Iran, 'they use pens made of reeds brought from the southern parts of Persia'. Hanway, *Historical Account of the British Trade over the Caspian Sea ...*, I, 317. For details on the various types and preparation of reed-pens and quills and their correct usage by an accomplished medieval scholar and administrator in the Mamlūk chancery, see vol. II of the magnificent and encyclopaedic work on secretaryship by Aḥmad b. ʿAlī al-Qalqashandī (1355–1418), *Ṣubḥ al-aʿshā fī ṣināʿat al-inshā* ʾ (ms., 7 vols., completed 1412; ed. Muḥammad ʿAbd al-Rasūl Ibrāhīm, 14 vols., Cairo, 1331–8/1913–20). This may be usefully compared with the much more recent work by the well-known Iranian calligrapher, Ḥabīb Allāh Faḍāʾilī [Fazāʾilī], *Taʿlīm-i khaṭṭ*, 55–70.
[87] Bloom, *Paper before Print*, 7.

pens were dipped was invariably black, obtained by mixing either carbon with oil or gall-nuts with ferrous minerals.[88]

Southern India excepted, paper was the dominant medium for record-keeping and correspondence among all literate groups operating in the arena. It had several qualities in its favour: relatively low cost and weight, physical versatility and durability, ease of manufacture, and availability in a panoply of colours, textures and thicknesses. As a result of its popularity, there was an active trade in paper in all of the region's principal settlements. Some was imported from European mills; much of it was produced in India and Iran. If individuals at smaller settlements ran short of paper, their associates elsewhere would procure fresh supplies for them.[89] In most places, however, paper was one of the items that both wholesale and pedlar merchants normally kept in their portfolio of goods for sale on demand.[90]

Without means of conveyance, communication within the arena would, of course, have been moot.[91] That it was not was because of the region's transport infrastructure and the practices allied to it.[92] A great deal of communication on regional scales was sustained, organised and managed

[88] 'Midād', EI2, VI, 1031b.

[89] For example, Antonio de Quental, a Luso-Indian clerk and agent based at Calicut, asked his employer to send him some paper in 1776. MssOcc/NAF/8998: 26.

[90] There was a dispute in 1766 over a transaction in paper at Madras between a local merchant and a clerk. It tells us a lot about paper in Madras. TNSA/Mayors Court Records/Pleadings/18B, 418–37. For paper as one among several items ordered by a French merchant-official from Goa-based Hindu merchants in 1789, see XCHR/MHR/Correspondence (incoming) (25 December 1789).

[91] Communication over large distances would also have been moot without adequate health provision. On the subject of precolonial medicine, see Seema Alavi, *Islam and Healing: Loss and Recovery of an Indo-Muslim Medical Tradition, 1600–1900* (Ranikhet, 2007) and Alavi, 'Medical culture in transition: Mughal gentleman physician and the native doctor in early colonial India', *Modern Asian Studies* 42:5 (2008), 853–97.

[92] There is sizeable corpus of historical scholarship on the region's physical infrastructure and an increasing amount on beasts of burden. Of particular relevance are Halford L. Hoskins, *British Routes to India* (New York, 1928); Holden Furber, 'Overland route to India in the 17th and 18th centuries', *Journal of Indian History* 29:2 (1951), 105–34; Usha Agarwal, 'Roads from Surat to Agra in the seventeenth and eighteenth centuries', *Quarterly Review of Historical Studies* 5:3 (1965–6), 148–55; Usha Agarwal, 'Historical account of the roads from Kabul to Calcutta during the seventeenth and eighteenth centuries', *Quarterly Review of Historical Studies* 9:3 (1969–70), 147–60; Maxime Siroux, 'Les caravanserais routiers safavids', *Iranian Studies* 7:1–2 (1974), 348–75; Abul Khair Muhammad Farooque, *Roads and Communications in Mughal India* (Delhi: Idarah-i Adabiyat-i Delli, 1977); Suraiya N. Faroqhi, 'Camels, wagons, and the Ottoman state in the sixteenth and seventeenth centuries', *International Journal of Middle East Studies* 14:4 (1982), 523–39; Eric Macro, 'South Arabia and the overland route to India', *Proceedings of the Seminar for Arabian Studies* 12 (1982), 49–60; Jean Deloche, *Transport and Communications in India prior to Steam Locomotion*, vol. I: *Land Transport*, vol. II: *Water Transport* (New Delhi, 1993–4); Colin Heywood, *Writing Ottoman History:*

in two particular ways: by a given organisation or group internally ('in-house communication')[93] and on an ad hoc basis underpinned by pre-existing ties of intimacy ('relational communication'). For both these mechanisms, which are discussed in Chapter 7, the only technology required was an effective means for physically conveying individuals and their effects. Intermediation too was important for the viability of such communication. No less important were hearsay and the word on the street. In 1747, the letters arrived which Shāh Kawthar in Najaf had long been expecting. But owing to the delay in reaching him, Shāh Kawthar was unsure whether his replies would reach Basra before 'the time and season for the departure of the ships' for India. However, he received 'a hint' that gave him hope and so his decision was made and he proceeded as originally planned.[94] Such hints were, of course, no substitute for hard evidence. Another individual, whose name we are not given, had also been waiting in Najaf for his letters from India. When he 'heard through hearsay the first news of the arrival of the letters [in Basra], I remained anxious until, by whatever means, praise be to *allāh*, [they] reached Najaf from Basra'.[95]

Keeping an ear cocked for the word on the street must have been an ingrained trait among those engaged in circulation and exchange. And its benefits were enhanced for expectant recipients who were proactive. This is what we see in the documents. The anxiety of the individual above at not knowing 'what has happened to the letter' of his correspondent in Bengal was such that he had considered 'inquiring into this so that [the matter] is clarified'.[96] A contemporary of his went beyond considering and actually tried to do something about it. As he recounted later:

> Both the Surati and Bengali ships arrived [in Basra] on the 18th of July. Although I was searching [for it], the reply to my letters did not arrive. And having gone [to] Khvājah Istifān, I demanded [from him] the reply to my letters. Khvājah Istifān remarked that 'the letter from the *mīr ṣāḥib* has not arrived because [he] has gone to the province of [Ghanasam]. And my brother could not take [the letter in] Bengal [from him] since where the *mīr ṣāḥib* is [even] birds do not fly.'[97]

These practices joined with the transport infrastructure to make in-house and relational communication highly significant for the movement

Documents and Interpretations (Aldershot, Hampshire, 2002); Suraiya Faroqhi (ed.), *Animals and People in the Ottoman Empire* (Istanbul, 2010); Alan Mikhail, 'Unleashing the beast: animals, energy, and the economy of labor in Ottoman Egypt', *American Historical Review* 118:2 (2013), 317–48. Cf. Goitein, *A Mediterranean Society*, I, 211–14, 275–352.

93 Jarjī, Shukr Allāh's employee (*khidmatkār*), was used for this purpose, among others, for the family's interests. BL/Lansdowne/1046, doc. 67.

94 BL/Lansdowne/1046, doc. 51. 95 BL/Lansdowne/1046, doc. 35. 96 Ibid.

97 BL/Lansdowne/1046, doc. 3.

of ideas and information within the arena. At the same time, there were many instances in which recourse to these modes of communication was not possible or desirable. This could be for reasons of availability, cost, secrecy, reliability or speed. In such cases, there were two conceivable alternatives, sovereign postal services and specialised couriers.

The region in our period had nothing akin to the scheduled, fixed-price postal service open to all who could afford it which was to emerge in the following century.[98] That is not to say postal services did not exist in earlier periods.[99] However, those that did differed in two respects from their modern successors. On the one hand, as facilitating sovereign rule was a primary concern, access to them was often limited to those engaged on official business or to those who enjoyed the patronage of the governing elites. On the other hand, as these services were under the direct control of the sovereign regime, they seldom operated beyond the confines of the territory over which the ruler nominally presided; they certainly did not operate on regional scales.

It is for these reasons that sovereign postal services did not play a significant role in communication within the arena in the eighteenth century. The demand that there was for such services was met instead by a medley of specialist couriers. Couriers took responsibility for personally transporting packages of high value and low weight, which entailed importantly the acquisition of the necessary licences and passports from officials.[100] Those who specialised in this occupation were, in effect, commissionaires, employed to convey these packages securely in return for a payment. The distinctive characteristic of this mechanism was that the specialist courier and the sender were normally strangers in a non-hierarchical relationship. Their relationship appears to have been grounded in convenience, the expectation of monetary gain and the prospect of ongoing collaboration. While it is possible that specialist couriers received and undertook commissions as individuals, the

[98] For India, see Chitra Joshi, 'Dak roads, dak runners, and the reordering of communication networks', *International Review of Social History* 57:2 (2012), 169–89.

[99] The main works on the subject for the region are Usha Agarwal, 'An account of the postal system in India from 1650 to 1750', *Bengal Past and Present* 85 (1966), 40–57; Goitein, *A Mediterranean Society*, I, 282–4; M. A. Nayeem, *The Evolution of Postal Communications and Administration in the Deccan (from 1294 AD to the Formation of the Hyderabad State in 1724 AD)* (Hyderabad, 1969); M. A. Nayeem, *The Philatelic and Postal History of Hyderabad*, 2 vols. (Hyderabad, 1970); Irfan Habib, 'Postal communications in Mughal India', *Proceedings of the Indian Historical Congress*, 46th Session (Delhi, 1986), 236–52; Adam J. Silverstein, *Postal Systems in the Pre-Modern Islamic World* (Cambridge, 2007).

[100] BL/Lansdowne/1046, doc. 43. Cf. the account of passports and letters of safe conduct in Goitein, *A Mediterranean Society*, I, 347.

historical record suggests otherwise. It seems that it was far more common for them to operate within the framework of well-defined indigenous organisations or groups. These associations of, say, the Aiyangar pattamars in southern India,[101] the 'Zamindari Dak' in northeastern India[102] or the *chāpārs* in central and southern Iran[103] had the expertise to ensure the safe transport of packages within the domain that was familiar to them. The provision of this service depended on their pre-existing ties with the relevant local power-brokers. As a result of these ties, such associations often exerted oligopolistic control over the occupation within their particular domain. Their presence in postal communication was, moreover, one aspect of a broader engagement with the domain's informational fabric.[104]

The employers and clients of the foregoing couriers tended to be wealthy, powerful and well connected. In practice, this meant government officials, the European East India companies, and the region's larger family firms and merchant houses. As exemplified by the Aiyangar pattamars, these specialist couriers and their managers belonged to autonomous or wholly independent associations, usually defined by residence and kinship. In exchange for expenses, wages and fees, they promised the secure and timely delivery of packages within their domain. The groups were presided over by headmen who determined whether or not to accept a commission or to enter into the permanent service of a would-be employer. These headmen were respected and honoured for their knowledge. They were often well-off and occupied high social status. They oversaw and protected their charges, and formed the main link between them and their employers and clients. They were also entrepreneurs, with substantial interests in sectors beyond the provision of postal services, extending to intelligence, diplomacy and trade.

This chapter has been about the infrastructural realities most salient to circulation and exchange on specifically regional scales. Those whose livelihoods pivoted on such activities had a deep appreciation of the ways in which their everyday behaviour was both constrained and enabled by these ambient realities. They engaged purposefully with them not merely to survive but also to profit from what they made possible. In the

101 A case study of the Aiyangar pattamars is presented in Gagan D. S. Sood, 'The informational fabric of eighteenth-century India and the Middle East: couriers, intermediaries and postal communication', *MAS* 43:5 (2009), 1085–116.
102 Mohini Lal Majumdar, *The Postal History of Zemindari Dawk (1707–1906)* (Calcutta: Ṛddhi-India, 1984).
103 BL/Lansdowne/1046, doc. 3.
104 This broader engagement is detailed in Sood, 'The informational fabric of eighteenth-century India and the Middle East.'

pains taken to minimise, or at least render manageable, the potentially harmful consequences of the communications infrastructure, we can infer certain basic orientations that guided daily life within the arena. These manifested themselves most openly in the course of individual transactions. For those involved in the circulation and exchange of objects, knowledge or people, the factors that dominated their calculations may be readily enumerated: cost, speed, reliability, duration, flexibility, secrecy, risk of failure and investment of effort. But the precise weight ascribed to each one, and how they actually moulded a particular decision, are not so readily specified; they depended on the temperaments of those involved, the specifics of the venture and the reigning circumstances. While a search for hard-and-fast algorithms or formulae would probably be misplaced, it is possible to discern at least two widely held behavioural tendencies intimately bound up with the region's infrastructural realities. One encouraged the arena's people to cultivate a holistic outlook. The other fostered an entrepreneurial spirit.

The holistic tendency took the form of, what was for the age, an agnostic, inquisitive, even adventurous, approach to knowledge and, more pointedly, to education and self-improvement. As seen in Chapter 3 on the familial order, Sayyid Muṣṭafā counselled his son to focus on reading because it would make him wiser and more sensible. That was in keeping with the formative aspects of this tendency.[105] It was in keeping too with the absence of dogmatic restraints on ideas and information. But perhaps the holistic tendency expressed itself most forcefully in the unquenchable thirst for news displayed within the arena. Shāh Kawthar was typical in this regard. 'I had been in a state of expectation,' he informed a patron in Bengal, 'when the river of love came bearing your news. I had long been without your news. My cry was that your letter is my greatest desire.'[106]

The value to us of an explicit avowal of such principles lies not just in its insights into the prevailing attitudes to news within the arena. They also tell us about how knowledge of the world more generally, and people's experiences of it, was accessed and made sense of. In our world today, there are certain spheres of social life that are viewed as distinct. The most obvious of these are the economic, political, cultural and social. Echoing and elaborating a point made in Chapter 1, the boundaries between these spheres in the eighteenth century were highly porous or, as is more likely, non-existent. That is to say, the signal divisions in everyday life were constructed on a very different set of foundations to those familiar to us nowadays. This follows quite naturally from the need felt by the arena's

[105] BL/Lansdowne/1046, doc. 60. [106] BL/Lansdowne/1046, doc. 16.

participants to situate their daily affairs within sufficiently broad parameters so that news received by their correspondents would still be of sufficient utility on arrival. Those whose livelihoods were framed by the arena thus depicted a world shaped at once by social, political, economic, private and public dynamics which, to their minds at least, were inextricably entangled with one another.

This holistic tendency reinforced and was, at the same time, reinforced by a second characteristic tendency. And that was entrepreneurship. If entrepreneurship is defined as the capacity to respond creatively to unexpected changes – entrepreneurship as judgement[107] – then this trait was true of most individuals whose livelihoods were rooted in regional-scale circulation and exchange. It was as true of those labouring on their own account as for those working in partnership with strangers or intimates. This trait may be interpreted as an inevitable reflection of the uncertainties endemic to activities marked by large distances and long silences. Though the language of the documents that I have studied does not contain a term which refers specifically to entrepreneurship, there is no doubt that the notion itself was widely understood by contemporaries and, more importantly, embraced. The matter is revisited in Chapter 7. For the time being, what needs to be borne in mind is that entrepreneurship was a widely dispersed trait within the arena.

[107] Different scholars emphasise different attributes as central to entrepreneurship. Among the most prominent are management, imagination or creativity, innovation, alertness or discovery, charismatic leadership and judgement. For a useful survey of modern views on entrepreneurs and entrepreneurship, see Joergen R. Elkjaer, 'The entrepreneur in economic theory: an example of the development and influence of a concept', *History of Economic Ideas* 13:6 (1991), 805–15.

6 A political order: temporal authority and governance

> The situation of the government in Baghdad and Basra has changed. The keeper of the seal Kūr Wazīr came to Baghdad, where previously there was Aḥmad Pasha. And in Basra there came Ilchī Pasha Aḥmad Pasha, the companion of the sultan. And he sent the mandate to Muṣṭafā Pasha [who] resided in the court ... And the former *mutasallim* went back and forth ... seizing from people a lot of money. And they were forced to give him many loans, and seemingly whether or not they can fulfil them.[1]

Everyday life in the arena was framed by its ethnic and religious diversity, and by the array of ties that existed between strangers and among intimates. These realities are discussed in Chapter 4 on the relational order. Just as important was the region's communications infrastructure, the subject of the previous chapter. But still left open is the matter of the exercise of temporal authority beyond the confines of the intimate community. As indicated by the quote above, the ways in which this authority was exercised had consequences for livelihoods enmeshed in circulation and exchange. Despite its obvious importance, the matter is not easily discerned in the sources. One exception is to be found at the juncture of the arena with the polities of India and the Islamic heartlands. Marked by chronic tensions, this juncture is where temporal authority was most acutely felt. The factors underlying these tensions derive from the very qualities that made the arena distinctive. Those who participated in it were collectively mobile and worldly, cultivating ties which crossed the horizons bounding their immediate surroundings. In contrast, the great majority of the region's inhabitants led more sedentary lives; they were subject to more comprehensive surveillance and control by their polity's sovereign regime, and were less likely to breach the established political and cultural frontiers.

This chapter pivots on a question that has troubled rulers down the ages: how to maintain stability within the region's individual polities when

[1] BL/Lansdowne/1046, doc. 73.

the arena's core activities transcended polities as a matter of course.[2] The answer was found in several widely dispersed characteristics. These characteristics – corporatism, hegemony and precedence – helped reconcile those engaged in regional-scale activities to life within a given polity. The characteristics were also tied to certain tendencies in behaviour. These tendencies reveal themselves to us most clearly in conflicts over succession and over individual ventures. By studying a number of such conflicts, this chapter gives an account of the emphasis placed on self-regulation, of the importance accorded to reputation and creditworthiness, and of the preferred means – at the centre of which lay customs – for handling everyday disputes.

The differences in outlook between the arena's participants and the polity's ruling elites undoubtedly generated tensions. At the same time, these tensions, while chronic, seldom exceeded manageable bounds. This dynamic is reflected in three general characteristics of the arena, which I set out here in a stylised manner.[3] The first characteristic was *corporatism*. Each settlement of note in the region was home to a population of permanent, long-term and transient inhabitants. Those active in circulation and exchange were affiliated to one or more associations. Examples seen in the documents include Sufi brotherhoods, companies of specialist couriers and family-based merchant houses. Within the region's polities, associations like these were the basic building-blocks for organising and managing social life. Their members exhibited self-awareness of the fact of their

[2] In thinking through this issue in general terms, I have found the following works of particular help: Ernest Gellner, *Plough, Sword and Book: the Structure of Human History* (Chicago, 1988); Patricia Crone, *Pre-Industrial Societies* (Oxford, 1989); Kirti N. Chaudhuri, 'Reflections on the organizing principle of premodern trade', in James D. Tracy (ed.), *The Political Economy of Merchant Empires: State Power and World Trade, 1350–1750* (Cambridge, 1991), 421–42.

[3] The main text in effect outlines my model of the region's polities in relation to the arena of circulation and exchange. The model has been sharpened through engagement with Shelomo D. Goitein, *A Mediterranean Society: The Jewish Communities of the Arab World as Portrayed in the Documents of the Cairo Geniza*,(Berkeley, CA, 1967), I, 59–70, 75–80, 266–72; Irfan Habib, 'Merchant communities in precolonial India', in James D. Tracy (ed.), *The Rise of Merchant Empires: Long-Distance Trade in the Early Modern World, 1350–1750* (Cambridge, 1990), 371–99; Michael N. Pearson, 'Merchants and states', in Tracy (ed.), *The Political Economy of Merchant Empires*, 41–116; Christopher A. Bayly, *Empire and Information: Intelligence Gathering and Social Communication in India, 1780–1870* (Cambridge, 1996); Basim Musallam, 'The ordering of Muslim societies', in Francis Robinson (ed.), *Cambridge Illustrated History of the Islamic World* (Cambridge, 1996), 164–207; Louise Marlow, *Hierarchy and Egalitarianism in Islamic Thought* (Cambridge, 1997); Farhat Hasan, *State and Locality in Mughal India: Power Relations in Western India, c. 1572–1730* (Cambridge, 2004); Karen Barkey, *Empire of Difference: the Ottomans in Comparative Perspective* (Cambridge, 2008). For a comparable stylised model, albeit specific to the Ottoman world, see H. A. R. Gibb and Harold Bowen, *Islamic Society and the West: a Study of the Impact of Western Civilization on Moslem Culture in the Near East* (London, 1950–7), 208–16, 276–81.

belonging. Their belonging was also widely recognised and supported in their host polities, contributing greatly to corporate solidarity and cohesion. Many of them had, moreover, a homogeneous and finite membership restricted to particular families or lineages. These criteria were commonly reinforced by identification with specific neighbourhoods or quarters. In these particular senses, the associations were thus closed and exclusive. But they did not exist in isolation; they had ongoing dealings with one another. Because of their possession of locally established rights, duties and freedoms, they frequently exerted oligopolistic (or even monopolistic) control over valued resources or livelihoods. As a result, the communities and organisations found in each settlement needed one another for their individual well-being.

But this corporatism was not played out on a level playing field. Rather, it was differentiated by a hierarchy which situated the associations in a partial order. That is to say, one's relative proximity and access to sovereign power was commonplace knowledge within the locality, even if ready comparisons could not be made between different localities. Furthermore, recourse to brute force in maintaining this order was the exception. These facts point to *hegemony* as a second characteristic of how temporal authority was exercised. In each settlement, there was a clear separation between ruler and ruled. The former would usually belong to the same close-knit group, often a numerical minority. This, together with the state of technology being what it was at the time, meant that it was impossible for the ruling group to assert its dominance over the rest of the populace in the long run if too many of their subjects objected to their subjecthood. The rulers could not sustain the hierarchy over which they presided by coercion – or the threat of coercion – alone. The maintenance of this hierarchy thus required the active and voluntary support of others on its lower rungs, some as clients, some as allies. The instrumental or material rationale for such support is fairly obvious. In return for upholding their ambient order, each individual association's duties, grants and exemptions were guaranteed. These in turn ensured a reliable source of employment and income for a significant fraction of their members. The benefits usually took the form of preferential rates of taxation, of monopolies over the cultivation of certain agricultural items or the production of specific manufactures, or of permission to trade in restricted goods or services. These benefits were, of course, distributed unequally. Less unequal – though only relatively so – was the promise to all those who embraced the order of a modicum of protection of life, limb and property, on land and at sea. This was coupled to the theoretical option of recourse to the sovereign's justice to right egregious wrongs if the more normal channels did not give satisfactory redress.

However, more than self-interest was needed to preserve this status quo. If self-interest were all, the situation would have been inherently unstable, with each individual association always fearful of arbitrary exploitation by a coalition of others. Such instability was the exception because self-interest was complemented by the existence of *precedence*, a third characteristic feature of the arena. This refers to a generalised respect for what permanent and long-term residents considered the established procedures, rules and principles. Understood as inherited from past generations, and hallowed through widespread usage, these procedures, rules and principles held sway over jurisdictions ranging from the local neighbourhood to the region at large. And it was by virtue of them that the hegemonic order in any one polity retained its integrity. As long as the authorised space of action for each social unit was preserved and the constraints under which they laboured not deemed excessive, most participants were reconciled to the prevailing order, whatever their position in it. These spaces and constraints were ultimately specified and legitimated by precedence.

Such are the concerns that Sultan Abū Bakr had in mind in 1755. At the time, he was the ruler of the Arabian Sea port of 'Bata' and had just written to the governor of Portuguese Goa.[4] In 'a period of increasing affection', he believed the moment was now ripe to foster commerce between their respective settlements. He urged the governor 'to send one ship from Goa or to write a letter to Daman and Diu to send a ship to our port in order to trade'. If this were to happen, 'we ... will send ships every year to the Christian port'. Security would not be a problem. The Portuguese need not fear 'the Arabs or others because, [in] all of the land that is under my control (*mulkī*), no one will ever harm you even to the smallest extent'. 'If your ships come [to our port],' he promised them, 'they will be [respected as] the property (*haqq*) of the Portuguese.' But there was more:

> If your ships were to come to our port in order to trade ... we would treat them with even more decency (*al-ḥishma*), consideration (*al-riʿāya*) and honour (*al-nāʿmūs*) than the French and English because we and you are friends from old times, from the time of our fathers and grandfathers.

And if these reassurances did not prove quite enough, Sultan Abū Bakr dangled before the governor the prospect of special material privileges. Every year, six or seven ships owned by the French, English and 'the people of Surat' arrived, laden with cowries, and departed at 'the beginning of the season'. Appealing directly to their baser competitive instincts, Sultan Abū

[4] All quotes in this paragraph are from HAG/Persian Documents, doc. 27. The reading of the settlement's name is uncertain. While I have opted for 'Bata', 'Taba' is also a possibility.

Bakr told the Portuguese that 'if your ships were to come from Goa or Daman or Diu to our dear place ... they can bring cowries ... and other goods. And they [may take in exchange] ivory and *qurūs*, and we will dispatch [their ships] at the start of the season before the ships of the others'.

In this settlement, then, as in all settlements that were hubs for circulation and exchange, corporatism, hegemony and precedence were signal characteristics of how authority was exercised beyond the personal realm. Though real, these characteristics are not easily observed. Easier to observe are certain widely dispersed tendencies in behaviour with which they were enmeshed. These tendencies came out into the open in two kinds of situations above all. One was the moment a relationship ended or was bequeathed. High stakes were frequently at issue since that moment could initiate a major redistribution of wealth, status and prestige. The other was during disputes over dealings that extended beyond the frontiers of any one polity in the region. It is through attempts to contain the tensions intrinsic to these two kinds of situations that the prevailing tendencies revealed themselves, usually to be reinforced as orthodoxy, occasionally to be called into question. Conflict is thus at the heart of this chapter's analysis. By focusing on the manner in which conflicts were handled, we learn about the prevailing modes of acting, thinking and feeling that cohered with the sovereign realities of the period.

Arguably, the behavioural tendency that dominated all others in the arena pointed towards self-regulation. The main evidence for this is the fact decision-making authority outside the family and household was wielded mostly on the plane of communal groups and social organisations. Rulers, and their courtiers and officials, were generally kept at arm's length from these associations; access to their internal affairs was heavily restricted and, when permitted, it was kept within strict parameters. There were several very good reasons to cultivate self-regulation. While guarantees of the sovereign's protection and justice were certainly of value in everyday life, they were not to be relied upon in general by his regime's inconspicuous majority. Personal and collective experience gave ample evidence that unpredictability and arbitrariness were not uncommon traits in the behaviour of the sovereign and his governing elites.[5]

[5] For historical details and general reflections on the matter, see John R. Perry, 'Forced migration in Iran in the seventeenth and eighteenth centuries', *Iranian Studies* 8:4 (1975), 199–215; Charles Tilly, 'War making and state making as organized crime', in Peter Evans, Dietrich Rueschemeyer and Theda Skocpol (eds.), *Bringing the State Back In* (Cambridge, 1985), 169–91; John F. Richards, 'Warriors and the state in early modern India', *Journal of the Economic and Social History of the Orient* 47:3 (2004), 390–400.

In this regard, the middle of the eighteenth century was certainly no exception. The final years of Nādir Shāh's regime in Iran appear to have been especially difficult for the country's population.[6] In a letter sent to his nephew in 1747, Mīrzā Muḥammad wrote,

If you are interested in knowing more about the state of this country, the truth of the matter is that for two successive years Nādir Shāh has entered Isfahan during the winter and he brought [with him] every kind of oppression and harm [imaginable]. And when he arrived this year, he decreed that the people of the villages and [their] kindred plunder all the houses of the city. They struck everywhere in Isfahan.

Nādir Shāh finally left Isfahan on 24 January 1747, 'heading towards Khorasan by way of Kerman. And everywhere he went, there was much killing.'[7] Muḥammad Mahdī's account is more expansive, and more personal:

Twice, the august retinue of... Nādir Shāh passed through Isfahan. And whatever was connected to oppression and injustice, he undertook [it]. He slayed nearly forty thousand people and, after he left, several thousand [of those who had survived] were afflicted by famine and scarcity, and they also perished through that. From among the incidents to have befallen our house ..., he demanded fifty tomans on the basis of the revenue assessment (*amlāk-i mulkī*) of the villages of Būrān and Ascharī... He arrested me and [threatened to] pull out my nails ... my uncle, Mīrzā Muḥammad ʿAlī... after a great deal of effort borrowed [the money] from the head of the chancellery (*sarkār-i dīvān*).[8]

There were hopes that with Nādir Shāh's death in 1747 – news of which was met with widespread relief, if not joy – the situation would improve.[9] But it did not; life seems to have gone on much the same as before. Something very similar was afoot at about the same time in Iraq.[10] Soon after the death also in 1747 of Aḥmad Pasha, the Ottoman governor of Baghdad, Qāsim ʿAbd al-Samīʿ wrote to his son in Surat. He informed him about the current state of the market in Basra and how their

[6] On Iran under Nādir Shāh and his immediate successors, see Michael Axworthy, *The Sword of Persia: Nader Shah, from Tribal Warrior to Conquering Despot* (London, 2006); Ernest S. Tucker, *Nadir Shah's Quest for Legitimacy in Post-Safavid Iran* (Gainesville, FL, 2006); Jos J. L. Gommans, *The Rise of the Indo-Afghan Empire, c. 1710–1780* (Leiden, 1995); John R. Perry, *Karim Khan Zand: a History of Iran, 1747–1779* (Chicago, 1979).

[7] BL/Lansdowne/1046, doc. 28. [8] BL/Lansdowne/1046, doc. 7.

[9] BL/Lansdowne/1046, docs. 14, 29.

[10] For recent accounts of Iraq in the period, see Tom Nieuwenhuis, *Politics and Society in Early Modern Iraq: Mamluk Pashas, Tribal Shaykhs and Local Rule between 1802 and 1831* (The Hague, 1982); Hala Fattah, *Politics of Regional Trade in Iraq, Arabia and the Gulf, 1745–1900* (Albany, NY, 1997); Dina R. Khoury, *State and Provincial Society in the Ottoman Empire: Mosul, 1540–1834* (Cambridge, 1997); Thabit A. J. Abdullah, *Merchants, Mamluks, and Murder: the Political Economy of Trade in Eighteenth-Century Basra* (Albany, NY, 2001).

commercial ventures were faring. He informed him too about the state of the country more generally, and the series of changes in the highest echelons of the governing regime provoked by Aḥmad Pasha's death. Kūr Wazīr was now in control of Baghdad, Muḥammad Pasha Īlchī of Basra, and Sulaymān Kāhiya of Adana. Just as in Iran, this transfer of power created opportunities for the new ruler and his officials – and problems for the 'people'. Qāsim ʿAbd al-Samīʿ noted, 'The former *mutassalim* [Kūr Wazīr] went back and forth . . ., seizing from people (*nās*) a lot of money. And [they were forced to give him] many loans, and seemingly whether or not they can fulfil them.'[11] And this was not a one-off. He reminded his son with an air of resignation, 'These years, we have suffered a lot [on account of] the governors (*al-ḥukkām*), all of us. The money has vanished, for us and for you.'[12]

Experiences like these militated against blind faith in a ruler's assurances. It is because of them that further guarantees were sought by subject communities. And paramount among these guarantees was autonomy in handling their internal affairs. By minimising sovereign access and agitating for greater self-regulation, intrusions by the governing elites were kept in check. This allowed them in turn to keep in check the risks of disruption and exactions that often accompanied such intrusions.[13]

Of course, self-regulation at the corporate level conferred other, more positive advantages. It helped subjects to demarcate and police their association. One consequence was to make it easier for them to determine suitable marriage partners and uphold contemporary notions of spiritual or cosmological purity. Furthermore, self-regulation helped to preserve the existing dominance of select groups over particular skills and occupations; it authorised current members to decide who could – and who could *not* – gain the necessary training or draw on privileged resources. But the advantages were not solely in favour of the polity's subject groups and organisations; the ruling elites too benefited from self-regulation as a widely dispersed orientation. In exchange for formal recognition of a community's status and role in the polity, the sovereigns often received 'gifts' which contributed materially to the maintenance of

[11] BL/Lansdowne/1046, doc. 73. [12] BL/Lansdowne/1046, doc. 74.

[13] This tendency towards self-regulation was paralleled, and reinforced, by the tendency to keep the internal affairs of an association secret, especially from strangers. For a stimulating discussion of this, albeit in a very different context, see Igor Kopytoff, 'The internal African frontier: the making of African political culture', in Igor Kopytoff (ed.), *The African Frontier: the Reproduction of African Traditional Societies* (Bloomington, IN, 1987), 3–84. As strangers had little or no knowledge of the current state of such associations from within, the importance accorded to dispersed knowledge of their reputation and creditworthiness was correspondingly enhanced.

their regime.[14] Some of these gifts took the form of money advanced to the government or to individual members of the ruling elites on favourable terms. Self-regulation also enabled the ruling elites to govern the polity more easily by spreading out the burden of governance. This is seen in the many instances where subject associations had responsibility for keeping order within their domains. What this meant in practice was that disagreements between their own members were handled internally. The collection of government revenue too – and its payment into the treasury – was to a significant extent managed by associations autonomous of the ruling group. Finally, self-regulation had as a corollary the acceptance of the sovereign as occupying the pinnacle of the local order. This enhanced his prestige and, by extension, the legitimacy of his rule.

While the benefits normally accrued to both sides – to the rulers and to the ruled – it is also the case that de jure acknowledgement of self-regulation within the polity often formalised a de facto situation. This situation resulted from the limited capacity of the ruling group to impose effectively its will on, let alone directly manage, the subject population. The reality is thrown into sharp relief by the many communities who made themselves indispensable for the material prosperity of the town or port by their control of scarce resources or skills. These communities were in a powerful bargaining position; if their demands for, say, autonomy were not granted or respected, they could halt their activities, refuse to cooperate or, in extremis, migrate to another settlement. Whatever the specifics of the response, it would be to the detriment of the polity, not least its ruler. For all these reasons, it is seldom possible to discern the specific motives that informed the commitment to self-regulation on the part of the diverse corporate elements of any given polity, let alone their relative weighting. The best we can say is that self-regulation was a generally observed principle framing life in the settlements of Islamicate Eurasia throughout our period.

We can be more precise, however, about the manner in which self-regulation was formally acknowledged. After being appointed in 1747 as the Ottoman *turjumān* for the Dutch community (*ṭāʾifa*),[15] Niʿmat Allāh

[14] The function, symbolism and genealogy of this exchange are discussed in Ann K. S. Lambton, 'Pīshkash: present or tribute?', *Bulletin of the School of Oriental and African Studies* 57:1 (1994), 145–58; Stewart Gordon, 'Robes of honour: a "transactional" kingly ceremony', *Indian Economic and Social History Review* 33:3 (1996), 225–42; Stewart Gordon, 'Legitimacy and loyalty in some successor states of the eighteenth century', in John F. Richards (ed.), *Kingship and Authority in South Asia* (Delhi, 1998), 327–48; Stewart Gordon (ed.), *Robes of Honour: Khil'at in Pre-Colonial and Colonial India* (New Delhi, 2003); Albrecht Fuess and Jan-Peter Hartung (eds.), *Court Cultures in the Muslim World: Seventh to Nineteenth Centuries* (New York, 2011).

[15] BL/Lansdowne/1046, docs. 70, 71.

remarked to his kinsman, 'Two months ago, the sultanic patent (*barāt*) in translation reached us [in southern Iraq]. And we put on the fur cap and we dressed our children [to celebrate].'[16] Variations on Niʿmat Allāh's account occurred in all of the region's polities. The local ruler, frequently the delegated embodiment of a distant sovereign, would affirm or grant to an individual acting on behalf of a social group or organisation – here, by way of a sultanic *barāt* – a cluster of privileges, duties and exemptions. While the details of each cluster could differ considerably between associations and between polities, their spirit invariably pointed towards self-regulation. The attendant ceremony would usually take place in a setting accessible to those invested with sovereign power. It would also be re-enacted on a regular, often annual, basis, and generally had to be confirmed upon the accession of a new sovereign.

So much for formal recognition. But what did self-regulation actually mean for those groups and organisations that exercised it? In broad terms, it meant that their members were allowed to live according to their own norms – religious, linguistic, familial – and govern themselves in the manner of their (collective) choosing. This was so as long as they did not undermine the sovereign's core prerogatives or impinge upon those of other associations. Self-regulation necessarily entailed structures for monitoring and administration internal to each association. These structures had to cope with disagreements among their members, sustain their collective distinctiveness and cohesion, and ensure their current and future well-being. Inevitably, this produced a situation within the polity in which its associations had many features in common. Each polity was thus marked by a great deal of replication, if not redundancy. These commonalities, however, went hand in glove with self-regulation, and cannot be understood apart from it.

In an environment imbued by such self-regulation, a small number of individuals, families or lineages were recognised as the leaders or representatives of the polity's associations. By virtue of their charisma, experience or wealth, they were the usual conduits through which major grievances were aired to the local ruler and his officials. They were also the conduits through which the sovereign's decisions concerning their brethren were communicated and implemented. Though rare, some of these individuals had sufficiently close ties to the sovereign, or were powerful enough in their own right, to be accorded the status of, say, a courtier or nobleman that elevated them into the ruling elites. Another far-reaching consequence of self-regulation derived from the

16 BL/Lansdowne/1046, doc. 67.

responsibility that associations had for the sector or occupation dominated by their members. Minimal interference by sovereign authorities and others in the polity meant that each association as a collective bore the lion's share of the risks undertaken by their individual members in going about their businesses.

The foregoing sums up the senses in which I claim that self-regulation was a central feature of the arena of circulation and exchange, expressing one of its most salient behavioural tendencies. But for it to be true of everyday life, it could not operate in a vacuum; it required other complementary orientations in behaviour similar in scope and significance. Indeed, in a context without an authoritative and invasive centre able to impose itself systematically and at will, and in which there was little or no opportunity – or desire – to cultivate affective bonds between strangers, it could hardly be otherwise. For self-regulation to persist in such a context, there was need of mechanisms capable of generating and maintaining impersonal trust. If nothing else, without impersonal trust, the barriers to exploitation of one another in the arena would have been too low, making tolerance, let alone coexistence, impossible. It is impersonal trust which made possible dealings between individuals from different backgrounds that went beyond the short term and the small scale; it is impersonal trust which enabled transactions characterised by large distances and long silences.[17]

In Chapter 4 on the relational order, I discuss impersonal trust within the framework of relationships between strangers. Specific conditions had to be met in order to create and preserve this type of trust. It was predicated on an effective region-wide transport and communications infrastructure; on the availability of practices, such as recordkeeping and intermediation, which permitted supervision, management, verification and signalling of behaviour from afar; and on organisations capable of arriving at, and implementing, decisions in ways that were generally accepted. But impersonal trust was also predicated on two particular behavioural tendencies that were widely dispersed within the arena. The first tendency was to pay close heed to the knowledge disseminated about an individual or the association represented by him. This normally took the form of reputation or creditworthiness. Its counterpart was, of course, the great pains taken to protect and, if at all possible, enhance reputation and creditworthiness, both for oneself and for the associations to which one belonged. The second

[17] For an interesting set of musings on the subject of trust, especially in relation to social networks, see James S. Coleman, *Foundations of Social Theory* (Cambridge, MA, 1990). Also see my discussion of trust in Chapter 4.

tendency proclaimed itself most clearly in the event of disputes. They elicited a strong preference for mediation or arbitration based on established procedures, rules and principles. Whatever the precise details of these procedures, rules and principles, they were invariably recognised as legitimate by those party to the dispute, and deemed sufficient for achieving a successful resolution. The remainder of this chapter examines these two tendencies in turn.

By the very nature of the activities that characterised the arena, regular and frequent dealings occurred between strangers from diverse backgrounds. Given that they did not belong to the same intimate community, this begs the question: how were strangers initially brought into contact with one another? For those not present in the same place, one option was to make a direct approach via letter. This option was exercised by Hirji Jivanji. Out of the blue, Bernard Picot received a letter from Bombay in 1775 in which Hirji Jivanji offered to purchase some goods that he had heard were in Picot's possession. Though Picot was unable to sell him the goods, he left open the possibility of collaborating in future.[18] Such a direct approach, however, was uncommon. The more usual practice was for contact to be mediated by a third party already known to both sides. But for a relationship to be put on a firm basis more was required than finding about one another's existence and getting in touch. This is because there was no universally accepted mechanism for communicating the imprimatur of an authoritative body concerning a particular individual's attributes, such as his experience, training, aptitude or reliability. In its absence, there was an obvious need for some other kind of mechanism that would allow a stranger to make a reasonable assessment of the risks of entering into an undertaking with that individual, and so be able to craft terms appropriate to it. The mechanism that existed depended on prior knowledge of their reputation for being 'correct in their dealings'[19] or, what amounted to the same thing, the creditworthiness of that individual *and* of the associations to which he belonged. Such knowledge was already dispersed throughout the networks within which both were situated, and played a crucial role in determining with whom strangers interacted and the manner in which they did so.

Reputation is seldom mentioned explicitly in the letters. But on the occasions that it is, the importance accorded to it by the author and recipient is evident. Hoping to spur on his associate in Bengal, Shāh Kawthar in Najaf wrote, 'It is repeated that the quicker and better you work, it will augment your good name (*nīknāmī*) and my gratitude. And I

[18] MssOcc/NAF/9060: 91 (22 December 1775). [19] BL/Lansdowne/1046, doc. 27.

am so completely satisfied by [your] manner that there is no need [for me] to exhort [you].'[20] Reputation was not just of concern to those active in the arena. Members of the ruling elites too could be highly sensitive about how they were generally perceived, so much so that for some it was a key factor in their decisions. This was Muḥammad Adīb's experience in 1748. He and his fellow passengers were seeking a safe berth for their ship and cargo along India's Malabar coast. Tellicherry proved unsatisfactory and so they tried Calicut. Muḥammad Adīb recounts what happened in a report for his principal written up a little while later: 'We approached the raja of the aforesaid port, [Calicut]. We asked [him] for space. He replied, "There is conflict between me and another raja. How can I give you space if *khudā* does not want [it]? At this time, something very bad might happen [which] may then cause [me] a bad name (*badnāmī*)."'[21]

Given the centrality of reputation, a stranger was in a real bind if his was blemished, or as a newcomer he had yet to acquire one. In such instances, a recommendation by a reputable figures was invaluable for opening doors.[22] The initiative might be taken by the referee himself. Writing in 1747 on behalf of Shaykh Niʿmat Allāh, who had just arrived in Bengal from Najaf, an associate was informed that Shaykh Niʿmat Allāh

> has behaved in a very sincere and assured [manner] with me [in Najaf]. In expectation of the favours which you will afford him because of all [your] types of kindness and consideration and love, you will ensure for him success and the fulfilment of [his] desires. I also know for sure that whatever happens, you will not fall short.[23]

This referee's underlying message was: if he is good enough for me, he ought to be good enough for you. The point is made openly in another letter sent from Najaf that same year. Its author stated, '[Concerning] whomever I suggest to you for your affairs, if I like the person for his work, I will also introduce the same person to you.'[24]

In the cases above, details are lacking about what precisely endeared (or might endear) the person in question to the referee. The Gujarati *baniyā* Mulgy Raganath was, in contrast, more forthcoming. Introducing an associate to the Kāmat brothers in Goa in the late 1780s, he wrote, 'For your greater convenience, I suggest a merchant who is [called] Natu Samuji.' He offered several reasons why Samuji was worthy of the Kāmats' consideration. 'He has all the offices of Daman factory in his hands. He also undertakes all the orders of this place as of other ports.

[20] BL/Lansdowne/1046, doc. 51. [21] BL/Lansdowne/1046, doc. 2
[22] Cf. the brief account of letters of introduction in Goitein, *A Mediterranean Society*, I, 347.
[23] BL/Lansdowne/1046, doc. 16. [24] BL/Lansdowne/1046, doc. 30.

And he has [as] his clients men [who wear] hats (i.e., Europeans). For them, he does everything here to the extent that they would not be able to do any trade here [without him].'[25] By bringing the two sides together, whatever the amount of detail furnished, the referee was allowing the stranger to tap his own reputation. In effect, he was casting himself as the stranger's guarantor or bondsman.

In a variation on the theme above, a stranger who opted to make the initial contact himself might name specific individuals willing to vouch for him. Joze Francisco Anello, for example, introduced himself to Veṅkateśa Kāmat in 1786 by mentioning that Essu Śeṇvī, 'your correspondent and tobacco farmer[,] can tell you that I have served him in whatever he has ordered me and that I do not cease to [serve him] whenever he orders me, whether as a merchant or for his own [personal] affairs'.[26] Only then did he proceed to outline his proposal. However, names alone were not always enough. In 1769, Bernard Picot asked Gabriel Menezes, a French merchant who had been living in Masqat for much of the previous decade, to 'assure all the Masqatis who would like to come here [to Mahe] to trade that they will receive all possible help, advantages and facilities'. But there was a caveat: this support would only be given to those bearing 'letters of recommendation for me' written by Menezes himself.[27]

What ultimately accounts for the centrality of reputation in impersonal trust was the tendency for the arena's people to keep their eyes peeled and ears cocked for new information *and* to solicit it actively whenever the opportunity presented itself. In turn, this depended on the capacity – and willingness – of individuals to pass on information to their associates in a suitable fashion. It might seem that this mechanism had a competitor in handwritten or printed manuals that sought to prepare novices for life in one or another of the region's settlements. These manuals contained guidance on how they might go about their business, which extended to brief accounts of communities and individuals worth developing ties with or, alternatively, to beware of or avoid. Such manuals were available in at least some of the major towns and ports in the period.[28] On the specific matter of communities and individuals to be found locally, consider the handwritten manual owned by John Pybus. This was first composed in

[25] XCHR/MHR/Correspondence (incoming) (October 1789).
[26] XCHR/MHR/Correspondence (incoming) (3 November 1786).
[27] MssOcc/NAF/9059 (17 March 1769).
[28] Those I have found thus far were all written by Europeans who resided in maritime Asia, or had spent a considerable period of time travelling and working in the region. Examples from the eighteenth century include Charles Lockyer, *Account of the Trade in India* ... (London, 1711); a manuscript handbook from the mid-eighteenth century, owned and perhaps written by the British merchant-official John Pybus (IOL/Mss Eur/F110/11); Pierre Blancard, *Manuel du commerce des Indes Orientales et de la Chine* (Paris, 1806).

about 1740, and then regularly updated thereafter. For Masqat, it noted, 'You have liberty of Chusing your own Broker (*dallāl*) and Shroff (*ṣarrāf*).'[29] It also alluded to the presence in Masqat of 'two Fellows call'd Hillow and Gaussey, who talk good English and may be of use'.[30] These remarks are typical of such manuals. Despite their typicality, however, it is difficult to judge how representative they are of the views that prevailed within the arena. This is because manuals like Pybus's had a very limited readership; they were essentially confined to settlements in maritime Asia with a significant European presence.

Much more popular and influential as a channel for the dissemination of the kind of information contained in these manuals were existing relationships. The information conveyed through relationships had the great advantage of being more current. Especially pertinent were ties between a principal and his agent, or between a broker and his client. These are studied in the next chapter as signal features of the practice of intermediation. For present purposes, they are significant because they helped disperse knowledge about reputations within their networks. The Kāmat brothers of Goa make the point. By virtue of their established reputation, and their many correspondents who spanned a broad spectrum of backgrounds, the Kāmats were famed for their ability to disseminate information quickly and widely. And as this information carried their imprimatur, the expectation was that it would be noted and given credence. This is clearly what Feliciano António Nogueira, a Portuguese merchant-official, was hoping for when, on having settled his accounts with Miguel de Souza and Nasarvanji Manakji, he asked the Kāmats in 1785 'to make it public for the good of my credit'.[31] Finding out that someone had a good reputation could make a relationship. Conversely, finding out that someone had a bad reputation could break a relationship, or prevent it being formed in the first place. In 1776, a pair of Gujarati Hindu brokers at Mocha informed their French principal that the governor there, whom they knew personally, was 'a cheat in his accounts'. They brought this fact to the attention of a captain who had recently arrived from Surat in the company of one of the governor's ships. On being told, the captain assured them that he would no longer deal with 'similar people'.[32]

It follows quite naturally from the above that individuals who populated the arena were sensitively attuned to their perceived reputation, and were prepared to go to considerable lengths to protect and augment it.

[29] IOL/Mss Eur/F110/11: 41. [30] Ibid.
[31] XCHR/MHR/Correspondence (incoming) (20 October 1785).
[32] MssOcc/NAF/8992: 87, 88–9.

While I have referred solely to individuals in discussing reputation thus far, this does not mean that reputation was a quality associated with them alone. The reality was that few, if any, of the individuals active in the arena had reputations vested in their person in isolation. Rather, they were shaped by the groups and organisations of which the individual was a recognised member. In this sense, reputationally at least, an individual never acted for his own account; others related to him as a representative of one or more collectives, enmeshing his creditworthiness with that of his collectives. That an individual's reputation could not be readily distinguished from the reputation of the collective with which he was primarily associated was explicitly addressed in instances of succession.

Vindrāvan and Jīvan were in charge of a merchant house with branches in Gujarat and the Ḥijāz in the middle of the eighteenth century. When they both passed away in 1778, the breach that they had left was quickly filled. The first act of the new headmen was to inform their clients of these deaths and to reassure them that the house would continue to operate as before. The responsibility for managing French interests in Mocha fell to Cūrjī and Jūpā.[33] They introduced themselves to the French governor of Mahe, on the other side of the Arabian Sea, as 'your two brokers in the house'. They explained that, following the recent deaths of Vindrāvan and Jīvan, 'the governor of Mocha took a lot of money from us because of [us being] the French brokers'. But 'as long as you remain [our clients], compensation will follow'. Though still awaiting formal confirmation as brokers to the French, they had 'provided service to the Frenchmen from Mauritius and they departed thanking [and] praising us'.[34] They expressed the wish that the French would continue to avail themselves of their services because, even though control of the house had passed to new headmen, the house remained the same.

A very similar approach was taken by Bīljī and Dhāma on the death of their father, Sīkrān Hīrjī, at the end of 1789.[35] In response to a letter from the agents of the nawab of Arcot, they wrote from Mocha, 'We will not hide from you that our father, Khvājah Sīkrān Hīrjī, during the month of Rabīʿ al-Awwal [November or December], left this world, which is the fate of all

[33] I have transliterated their names as Cūrjī and Jūpā but it is likely that this is only an approximation to their real names. The reason for this uncertainty is that their names are not fully vowelled in their letter to Picot, which was written in Arabic, and they are spelt differently on the two occasions that they are mentioned. In the main body of the text, they are written as: كورجي and جوپا. On the envelope, however, they appear as: كودرجي and جويلاله. This difficulty is compounded by the fact that the names were written in a script that does not readily express the full register of sounds that characterise their native linguistic environment (probably Gujarati or Sanskrit).

[34] MssOcc/NAF/9011: 36–7 (13–14 August 1778).

[35] An alternative possible reading of the first name is Bīlḥī.

that lives.' But they were quick to let the nawab's agents know that there was no need to worry. 'We have succeeded him in all of his affairs and the house is flourishing as it was before and even more.' They hoped that the nawab would retain them as his brokers in Mocha, in the same capacity as their late father. 'We only have good intentions. We are established to serve you in every way and, if *allāh* wishes, by your leave, this will be clear [to you].'[36]

Reinforcing a point made in the last chapter, the importance accorded to reputation tied an individual to his collective which, as a result, constrained his personal freedoms. In whatever he did, he had to take into account the views of others in the collective and behave in keeping with their expectations. This is because the latter in effect operated as gatekeepers; by determining who might tap their collective reputation and share in their resources, they defined the qualifications required of would-be and existing members. At the same time, the very fact of belonging to the collective opened up possibilities which would otherwise have been denied to the individual on his own. He was able to draw upon the track record, the physical capital and the relational assets already possessed by the collective, and in so doing benefit from a ready-made reputation and enjoy the credit that went along with it. In time, the collective too would gain from the experience, skills and resources acquired by him. If, however, he had chosen to remain outside its framework, he would have faced difficult, probably insurmountable, obstacles to building up a good reputation.

So dispersed knowledge of one's reputation and credit was a major factor in creating trust between strangers. It was certainly an abiding concern to all parties contemplating a joint venture. At the same time, this knowledge conferred no guarantees that the venture would work out as agreed, expected or desired. In that event, differences might arise on how to proceed. These differences would very often be ironed out through consensus, grudging or otherwise, as part of the normal push and pull of human interactions. Ezekiel Rahabi's 'authority' in Cochin within his community was often invoked for this end. In 1762, Bernard Picot, who was in 'desperate need' of funds for his own use, asked Rahabi to persuade Isaac Surgun to pay him the sum of money that he was supposed to have sent him some time ago. He suggested that 'this will not give you much difficulty because this man is subordinate to you; he will carry out punctually what you order him'.[37] But when the likes of Rahabi proved unequal to the task, relationships could sour to the extert the two sides

[36] TNSA/Persian Records/110: 10.
[37] This debt arose as a result of Surgun failing to remit to Picot, in accordance with their prior agreement, the proceeds received in Cochin from the sale of Picot's goods in Masqat by his broker there, Narotum. MssOcc/NAF/9074 (15 July 1762).

lost any realistic hope of sorting out their differences through further discussion. Although rare, everyone in the arena knew that such an outcome could be his lot at the start of any venture involving strangers, even between those who held each other in high regard. To convince him to proceed, he needed assurances that, in case of a complete breakdown in relations, there were options available which would help them patch things up or, failing that, allow him to survive a total loss. These assurances were provided by mechanisms intended to resolve disputes among strangers in a manner that was sufficiently accessible, definitive, quick, inexpensive and fair.

When disagreements reached a point where talking no longer served any useful purpose, there were two possible options. Both involved the good offices of a third party. One was to reach a mutually acceptable settlement through mediation. The other was to seek adjudication that would decide in favour of one side or the other. The resolution of such disputes between members of, say, the same household or extended family must have almost always occurred informally. This would explain the rarity in the official legal record of litigants who were also close kindred. Presumably, disputes were not especially uncommon among close kindred, and no doubt they could be just as contentious and intractable as any other – or perhaps even more so. But the indirect evidence suggests that disputes between intimates were seldom aired outside their collective, and outsiders were seldom asked to help resolve them; they were invariably handled from within. Where the parties to the dispute were strangers, however, the failure rate of informal attempts at mediation or adjudication was much higher. When this happened, more formal mechanisms would typically be invoked.

One possible mechanism was to approach the ruler or his personal delegate, usually a minister or high official, and ask him to deal with the issue.[38] The provision of justice was, of course, core to the exercise of sovereignty by a ruler over his domains. It was at once an inalienable duty that he had towards his subjects and a reaffirmation of his position at the apex of the regime.[39] The duty and reaffirmation were institutionalised in each settlement as courts or tribunals in the sovereign legal order. The

[38] See, for example, James Baldwin, 'Petitioning the sultan in Ottoman Egypt', *Bulletin of the School of Oriental and African Studies* 12:3 (2012), 499–524.

[39] The theories of sovereignty found in the region in premodern times are discussed in Aziz al-Azmeh, *Muslim Kingship: Power and the Sacred in Muslim, Christian and Pagan Polities* (London, 1997); John F. Richards (ed.), *Kingship and Authority in South Asia* (Delhi, 1998); Ram Prasad Tripathi, 'The Turko-Mongol theory of kingship', in Muzaffar Alam and Sanjay Subrahmanyam (eds.), *Mughal State 1526–1750* (New Delhi, 1998), 115–25; Boğaç A. Ergene, 'On Ottoman justice: interpretations in conflict (1600–1800)', *Islamic Law and Society* 8:1 (2001), 52–87; Patricia Crone, *God's Rule: Government and Islam*

highest forum in this order was the one constituted by the ruler himself and his closest advisors. In this sense, the *dargāh* of the *imām* of Yemen and the court of the governor and council of Bombay Presidency were equivalent. Judgement in this type of forum was nominally dispensed by the ruler in person; in theory, he was the arbiter of final instance. One way of gaining an audience was to petition the ruler directly. Another way was to appeal from a court or tribunal lower down in the order.

Most settlements had several such forums. These were normally attached to the array of officials to whom sovereign authority had been delegated by the ruler. Though their nomenclature varied between polities, these officials bore the main responsibility for everyday governance. This meant, among other things, the provision of justice. So we see legal forums throughout the region presided over by *ṣāḥib*s of the *shurṭa*, by *qāḍī*s, *faudār*s, *muḥtasib*s and *kotwāls*.[40] And that is just for starters. Soon after Sayyid Hidāyat Allāh's death in 1744 in Baghdad, a dispute arose between his chosen executor, Muḥammad b. ʿAlī, and his eldest son, Sayyid Ṣāliḥ, over the division of the estate. The executor claimed that, ten days before he passed away, Sayyid Hidāyat Allāh had bequeathed 'a third of [my] assets for the well-being of the threshold of Ḥaḍrat Imām ʿAlī', with the remainder to be distributed to his family in Iraq and Bengal. His son claimed, however, that his father had made no such bequest, and so the whole estate ought to be transferred to his family. The dispute was heard in the name of 'the governor (*wālī*) of Baghdad and Basra', and was decided in favour of the executor in 1745.[41] Officially, the personal court of this governor, at the time Aḥmad Pasha, had jurisdiction over all his subjects in the polity. But, as seen here as elsewhere, it was in forums on the lower rungs of the order that the real business of sovereign justice was handled. Though these forums supposedly had narrower jurisdictions, the reality was they had great flexibility over what kind of disputes to hear and who could make use of them. In part, this resulted from their overlapping

(New York, 2004); Hakan T. Karateke and Maurus Reinkowski (eds.), *Legitimizing the Order: the Ottoman Rhetoric of State Power* (Leiden, 2005).

40 The institutions of law from a sovereign's perspective are described in Émile Tyan, *Histoire de l'organisation judiciaire en pays d'Islam*, 2 vols. (2nd edn, Leiden, 1960 [1938]); Muhammad Basheer Ahmad, *Judicial System of the Mughal Empire* (2nd edn, Karachi, 1978); Hervé Bleuchot, *Les institutions traditionelles dans le monde arabe* (Paris, 1996); Willem Floor, 'The secular judicial system in Safavid Persia', *Studia Iranica* 29:1 (2000), 9–60. A detailed account of a sovereign forum that gained considerable influence from the latter of the eighteenth century is given in Gagan D. S. Sood, 'Sovereign justice in precolonial maritime Asia: The case of the Mayor's Court of Bombay, 1726–1798', *Itinerario* 37:2 (2013), 46–72.

41 BL/Lansdowne/1046, docs. 82, 83.

jurisdictions, which injected creative ambiguity into the sovereign legal order. In part, it reflected the particular needs and demands of the local populace.

While dogma might suggest that these forums were reserved for the polity's largest community, or for the group from which the ruling elites hailed, the practice was seldom so clear-cut. Several recent studies have shown that members of non-Muslim communities living in settlements ruled by Muslims occasionally preferred the 'Islamic' justice rendered by government officials to that of their own brethren, even for matters wholly personal in nature.[42] This could be because they felt unable to gain redress through the normal channels, or because they were appealing to a higher forum in search of, as Ghulām ʿAlī ibn Darwīsh Muḥammad put it, the ruler's 'more ample justice'.[43] It is easy to understand why. By virtue of their access to coercive force, rulers were able to issue and impose decisions on an entirely different basis to their subjects. Their decisions could potentially supersede all others that ran counter to them, as well as superseding the rules and principles that framed them. The preference for the ruler's justice was also occasionally found among the headmen of communities as a whole. This is exemplified by the Parsi *panchāyat* of Bombay in the middle of the eighteenth century.[44]

[42] It follows that the jurisdiction of a polity's dominant forums cannot be assumed to be limited to specific groups. A more faithful account of the situation would convey the notion that boundaries between legal forums were often blurred and contested. Such 'transgressions' have been explored in greatest detail for the Anatolian and Levantine provinces of the Ottoman empire. See, for example, Ronald C. Jennings, 'Zimmis (non-Muslims) in early seventeenth century Ottoman judicial records: the sharia court of Anatolian Kayseri', *Journal of the Economic and Social History of the Orient* 21:1–3 (1978), 225–93; Najwa al-Qattan, 'Dhimmis in the Muslim court: legal autonomy and religious discrimination', *International Journal of Middle East Studies* 31:3 (1999), 429–44; Najwa al-Qattan, 'Litigants and neighbours: the communal topography of Ottoman Damascus', *Comparative Studies in Society and History* 44:3 (2002), 511–33; Ze'ev Maghen, 'Theme issue: the interaction between Islamic law and non-Muslims', *Islamic Law and Society* 10:3 (2003), 267–75; Leslie P. Peirce, *Morality Tales: Law and Gender in the Ottoman Court of Aintab* (Berkeley, Los Angeles and London, 2003); Iris Agmon and Ido Shahar, 'Theme issue: shifting perspectives in the study of Shariʿa courts: methodologies and paradigms', *Islamic Law and Society* 15:1 (2008), 1–19; Boğaç A. Ergene, *Local Court, Provincial Society and Justice in the Ottoman Empire: Legal Practice and Dispute Resolution in Çankırı and Kastamonu (1652–1744)* (Leiden and Boston, 2003); Boğaç A. Ergene, 'Social identity and patterns of interaction in the sharia court of Kastamonu (1740–44)', *Islamic Law and Society* 15:1 (2008), 20–54.

[43] MSA/Misc/HCR/MRC/31: 807.

[44] For more details on the community, especially in relation to the European presence, see David L. White, 'Parsis in the commercial world of western India, 1700–1750', *Indian Economic and Social History Review* 24:2 (1987), 183–203; Amalendu Guha, 'More about the Parsi Sheths: their roots, entrepreneurship and comprador role, 1650–1918', in Dwijendra Tripathi (ed.), *Business Communities of India* (New Delhi, 1984), 109–50.

The right to deal with disputes among Parsis in western India was traditionally a prerogative of the relevant *panchāyat*. To the extent that the historical record documents such matters, this organisation functioned autonomously, accountable to no one but members of their own community. This remained the case in Bombay until the middle of the eighteenth century, when 'the *panchāyat* of Bombay found it could no longer rule the Parsi community with its old authority'.[45] Previously in Bombay, as in other settlements in Gujarat where Parsis resided, one of the punishments commonly decreed for those found guilty was to be beaten with a shoe. This was considered a grave humiliation. But with Bombay's rapidly growing Parsi population, and their close involvement with British administration and trade from the 1730s, the *panchāyat* there found it increasingly difficult to enforce this penalty. It resolved to claw back some of its 'old authority' by requesting the formal sanction of Bombay's government. In 1778, the *panchāyat* petitioned the governor of Bombay, William Hornby. His reply was encouraging. He empowered the *panchāyat* 'to meet and inquire into all matters that are committed by your caste, contrary to what has been agreed to by the majority of the caste, and to punish the offender agreeably to the rules of your caste, so far as not permitting them to come to your feasts, or beat them with shoes, but no other corporal punishment'.[46] By taking this step, the Parsi *panchāyat* of Bombay sought to recover its authority over the local community by subordinating itself to the ruler's authority.

As this example shows, even in situations where the ruler was invited to intercede, this need not bring into play the dominant forums of the sovereign legal order. The exceptions notwithstanding, these forums were primarily concerned with disputes involving those belonging either to the polity's ruling group or to its largest resident community. Those active in circulation and exchange rarely figured among their number. And this was for two very good reasons. First, use of these forums might offer the sovereign opportunities to intervene elsewhere in their internal affairs. Intervention was generally unwelcome owing to the problems it might cause for their livelihoods. To wit, Banaji Limji, a Parsi residing in western India, noted in the early 1770s that litigation in Bombay's Mayor's Court often gave more 'trouble' than independent arbitration.[47] Second, the sovereign and the ruling elites too were chary of getting mixed up in the internal affairs of their subjects, even if all parties to the dispute ardently desired it. This is because it might upset the current balance within their polity. As a result, they often refused to hear such cases.

[45] Dosabhai F. Karaka, *History of the Parsis*, vol. I (London, 1884), 218. [46] Ibid., 219.
[47] MSA/Misc/HCR/MRC/31: 806.

These reasons underlie the strong presumption on the part of both ruler and ruled that, in the event of a dispute among the latter, the initial recourse would be to mediation or arbitration within the appropriate communal or occupational forums. These forums could be openly and systematically incorporated into the sovereign legal order. Or if not, they might have the tacit recognition and support of the ruling elites.[48] Much more commonly, however, such forums were wholly independent of the sovereign legal order, situated outside the ruler's purview.[49] It is in these independent forums that the overwhelming majority of disputes within the arena were resolved. But not everyone active in the arena was keen on this presumption. ʿAbd Allāh Pesseker was one such individual. In the mid-1770s, he complained to William Taylor, a Justice of the Peace in Bombay, that he had been defrauded by Bhikhaji, a Muslim ship-owner, and he wanted his help in gaining redress. When Bhikhaji was confronted by Taylor, Bhikhaji asked that their dispute be resolved privately. ʿAbd Allāh Pesseker, however, was not convinced. Taylor sought to overcome his reservations by arguing that 'if he persisted in his refusal of such an equitable proposition, the world would conceive he had preferred his complaint from motives not the most truly honest'.[50] The dispute was eventually referred 'to the consideration of four arbitrators'.[51]

48 This subject has been discussed mostly under the rubric of state-sanctioned legal pluralism. A range of perspectives and interpretations are on offer. See, for example, M. Barry Hooker, *Legal Pluralism: an Introduction to Colonial and Neo-Colonial Laws* (Oxford, 1975); Lauren Benton, *Law and Colonial Cultures: Legal Regimes in World History, 1400–1900* (Cambridge, 2002); Lakshmi Subramanian, 'A trial in transition: courts, merchants and identities in western India, circa 1800', *Indian Economic and Social History Review* 41:3 (2004), 269–92; Ido Shahar, 'Legal pluralism and the study of Shariʿa courts', *Islamic Law and Society* 15 (2008), 112–41; Paolo Sartori and Ido Shahar, 'Legal pluralism in Muslim-majority colonies: mapping the terrain', *Journal of the Economic and Social History of the Orient* 55:4–5 (2012), 637–63.

49 These independent forums may be interpreted as being part of a self-regulating legal regime that existed outside formal sovereign control. By self-regulating I mean that, notwithstanding the absence of an authoritative centre, the forums interacted with one another in a coherent and stable manner. Evidence and arguments in favour of this interpretation may be found in Abraham L. Udovitch, 'The "Law Merchant" of the medieval Islamic world', in G. E. von Grunebaum (ed.), *Logic in Classical Islamic Culture* (Wiesbaden, 1970), 113–30; Abraham L. Udovitch, *Partnership and Profit in Medieval Islam* (Princeton, 1970); Robert C. Ellickson, *Order without Law: How Neighbors Settle Disputes* (Cambridge, MA, 1991); Murat Çizakça, *Comparative Evolution of Business Partnerships: the Islamic World and Europe, with Specific Reference to the Ottoman Archives* (Leiden, 1996); Hassan S. Khalilieh, *Islamic Maritime Law: an Introduction* (Leiden, 1998); Ghislaine E. Lydon, 'Contracting caravans: partnership and profit in nineteenth- and early twentieth-century trans-Saharan trade', *Journal of Global History* 3:1 (2008), 89–113; Ghislaine E. Lydon, *On Trans-Saharan Trails: Islamic Law, Trade Networks, and Cross-Cultural Exchange in Nineteenth-Century Western Africa* (New York, 2009).

50 MSA/Misc/HCR/MRC/42: 203. 51 MSA/Misc/HCR/MRC/42: 198, 203.

That resolving disputes within the arena through independent means was the preferred option is illustrated by Banaji Limji's dealings with his former partner, Rangaji Ramseth. Once their dispute had escalated to the point that 'it appeared impractical to bring them to any satisfactory conclusion . . . , [the partners] agreed [in 1770] to refer the adjustment of their accounts and disputes to the decision of arbitrators'.[52] This was a sensible move because of the several benefits associated with it. In the first place, it was probable that the litigants were familiar with the procedures of the forum. This was so even if they were not habitués of the port or town where the dispute was to be adjudicated. Babu Lambatia made that very argument in 1747. Describing himself as 'a merchant from another country entirely unacquainted with the custom of this place [Bombay] and the rules of this Ho[nourable Mayor's] Court', he requested his dispute with Ram Bhawani Shankar, a Bombay resident, 'be put upon arbitration'. He stressed that he was 'entirely ignorant of the method of procedure' of the Mayor's Court, unlike that of independent arbitration.[53] Equally important for those who sought justice in independent forums was their relative ease of access, speed and low cost. These qualities were highlighted by Babu Lambatia. He wrote of his wish that 'any disputes betwixt him and [Ram Bhawani Shankar] might be decided by merchants in the way of arbitration, rather than engage themselves in a process at law so much to the detriments of their trade and concerns by loss of time, expence, &c.'.[54]

Whatever the de jure status and reach of the forums available for resolving disputes, their jurisdictions were never perfectly demarcated or comprehensively ordered in relation to one other. The forums could have exclusive, joint or even competing jurisdictions over particular subsets of a settlement's population. Thus we must assume a certain degree of permeability between forums, as well as an ongoing struggle over who could have recourse to their justice and what kind of dispute could be heard by them. In particular, we must not be overly strict in maintaining distinctions between sovereign and independent justice, or between subservient and dominant forums.[55] Having said that, it does seem to have been the case that the procedures for litigating were well established for each individual forum.[56]

[52] MSA/Misc/HCR/MRC/35: 1813. [53] IOR/P/417/2: 409. [54] Ibid.

[55] The porous nature of the boundaries between independent and sovereign legal forums is exemplified in a dispute that played itself out at Bombay and Surat in the late 1730s. For details, see IOR/P/416/115: 323–35.

[56] My analysis in this section is based on examples drawn mainly from towns and ports in western India, especially Surat and Bombay. It is worth noting that, as these settlements had in the period ties spanning the region at large, the findings presented here have a broader relevance than might appear to be the case at first glance.

If there is a meaningful distinction to be made among the forums that typically resolved disputes within the arena, it is in terms of the character of their litigants, mediators, arbitrators, umpires and judges: in one type, these individuals generally made their livelihoods through the same occupation; in the other type, they belonged to the same community. Of course, the two modes of self-identification could amount to the same thing in practice – as evidenced by many of the region's Sufi brotherhoods. Even in these instances, however, there existed a noticeable difference in orientation, with one of the shared attributes having primacy over the other. It is by means of their orientation that I distinguish between these two types of forums, referring to one as 'occupational' and the other as 'communal' forums.

As discussed in Chapter 1, individuals active in the arena were apprehended through the filter of the social collectives – *ahl*, *ṭā'ifa*, *jamā'a*, *panchāyat* – of which they were part. These could be designated in confessional or ethnic terms, or in terms of subjecthood. The forums for resolving disputes among their members were invariably situated within such collectives. It follows that the function of the communal forum was merely one of many for which the collective took responsibility. Collectives could also be defined in terms of the livelihood pursued by their members, like the money-lending *mahājan*s of northern India, the artisans of the guild-like *ṣinf*s of Iran or the caraveneers who transported coffee bales in the Ḥijāz.[57] These occupational collectives tended to require less of their members than did their communal analogues; they were more narrowly focused on issues directly relevant to their livelihoods. At the same time, because background was downplayed, occupational forums could have a more diverse body. So the central difference between these two types of forums – the communal and the occupational – pivoted on those aspects of an individual's behaviour that their collectives made a claim on, one being more comprehensive and dogmatic, the other more circumscribed and (notionally) agnostic. Since the basic procedures followed in both types had much in common, I focus below on similarities in their procedures, pointing out differences as and when appropriate.[58]

[57] Cf. the associational nature of craftsmen discussed in Goitein, *A Mediterranean Society*, I, 80–92.

[58] It may be useful to compare my account of these procedures with the scholarly literature on procedures in Islamic law. Of particular relevance are Robert Brunschvig, 'Le système de la preuve en droit musulman', *Etudes d'Islamologie* 2 (1976), 201–19; Ronald C. Jennings, 'Kadi, court, and legal procedure in 17th-century Ottoman Kayseri', *Studia Islamica* 48 (1978), 133–72; Baber Johansen, 'Formes de langage et fonctions publiques: stéréotypes, témoins et offices dans la preuve par l'écrit en droit musulman', *Arabica* 44 (1997), 333–76; Boğaç A. Ergene, 'Evidence in Ottoman courts: oral and written

Occupational and communal forums were not continuously active entities in general. Rather, they were ad hoc, called into being when disagreements became intractable. The deliberations within them would take place in a venue dictated by custom and circumstance. Those who sat in judgement, or sought to bridge the two sides, were not permanent appointees, nor was a permanent record maintained. Despite such transient qualities, mediation and arbitration were recognised as established – and effective – means of overcoming entrenched opposition.[59] So when the insurers of a ship, much of whose cargo had been stolen in 1743 by residents of Kholgar, refused to honour their policies, the Gujarati freighters' immediate response was to ask the 'principal merchants' of Bombay to intervene and settle their dispute.[60]

While the specifics of how their dispute would have been handled – its formal initiation, the appointment of the forum's headmen, the investigation, deliberation and resolution – varied considerably from settlement to settlement, and from forum to forum, certain patterns appear to have been widely dispersed across the region. To begin with, there were a number of stages which preceded the formal start of the process. Litigants were obviously aware that the decisions taken in these stages might be critical to the final outcome. Therefore, they were given careful thought. The very first was the proposal. The documents do not reveal any fixed procedure for this. Resolving a dispute through formal means could be proposed in person or through some intermediary. In Bombay in the mid-1740s, Babu Lambatia and Muhammad Ismail presented their proposal to Ram Bhawani Shankar by combining these approaches. They asked him to accompany them to the house of David Medley, a local resident who earned his keep as an attorney at the Mayor's Court and through private trade. In his presence, they urged Ram Bhawani Shankar to allow the dispute between them to be put to private arbitration. This he

documentation in early-modern courts of Islamic law', *Journal of the American Oriental Society* 124:3 (2004), 471–91; Ron Shaham, *The Expert Witness in Islamic Courts: Medicine and Crafts in the Service of the Law* (Chicago, 2010).

59 There are interesting resonances with the stress placed here on arbitration and mediation and the notion of *ṣulḥ* in Islamic law. For more details on the latter from a historical perspective, see Abdülmecid Mutaf, 'Amicable settlement in Ottoman law: Sulh system', *Turcica* 36 (2004), 125–40; Aida Othman, '"And amicable settlement is best": *Ṣulḥ* and dispute resolution in Islamic law', *Arab Law Quarterly* 21 (2007), 64–90; Işık Tamdoğan, '*Sulh* and the 18th-century Ottoman courts of Uskudar and Adana', *Islamic Law and Society* 15 (2008), 55–83; Paolo Sartori, 'The evolution of third-party mediation in Sharīʿa courts in 19th- and early 20th-century Central Asia', *Journal of the Economic and Social History of the Orient* 54:3 (2011), 311–52.

60 IOR/P/416/118: 201.

finally 'comply'd with ... after much solicitation and at the request of the said Mr. Medley'.[61]

The oral agreement was merely the opening gambit. For occupational forums at least, attention then turned to the bond. This set out the basic parameters of the forthcoming suit. Three issues dominated here: the amount to be forfeited by the parties if they failed to abide by the forum's decisions; instructions and guidance on how the inquiry would be undertaken and the decision reached; and the choice of who was to preside over the forum as its headmen.

Litigants recognised the penalty value had to be high enough to compel all sides to respect the terms of the bond dictating the forum's conduct. But there was reluctance to hand over to the forum, or the designated third party, more money than was absolutely necessary. The evidence suggests that these countervailing tendencies gave rise to penalties that were of the same magnitude as the value of the disputed transaction. In a dispute which took place in Bombay and Surat in the late 1730s over the amount a principal had authorised his agent to spend on a vessel, it was agreed to set the value of the penalty at 5,000 rupees. This was comparable to the ship's base value, which was put by its previous owners at 7,025 rupees.[62] Similarly, in a 1747 case pivoting on a respondentia bond with a face value of 650 rupees, the litigants agreed upon a penalty worth 500 rupees.[63]

Reaching consensus on the basic procedural issues beforehand enabled the forum to minimise future uncertainties and additional disagreements, and ultimately facilitate a successful resolution. Bonds often stated 'in what manner the award is to be delivered' and the 'limited time ... within which it ought to be deliver'd to both the partys concerned'.[64] It was also common to find remarks on what constituted permissible evidence. Indeed, litigants who were dissatisfied with the forum's procedures or outcome could use the absence of such terms to have the whole process nullified. So standard was their presence that bonds without these terms were described in the 1730s as having 'irregularities'.[65] But these terms were not the final word on the matter. They could always be trumped by the forum's headmen, who retained considerable latitude to pursue the course deemed best suited to the reigning circumstances. To ensure this, they were given 'ample authority to determine on their disputes'.[66]

It is thus not surprising that an issue of supreme concern to litigants in these preliminary stages was the choice of the forum's headmen. In

[61] IOR/P/417/2: 405. This is described again, in more or less the same terms, in subsequent depositions in IOR/P/417/2: 407, 408.
[62] IOR/P/416/115: 323–35. [63] IOR/P/417/2: 392. [64] IOR/P/416/115: 334.
[65] IOR/P/416/115: 333–5. [66] MSA/Misc/HCR/MRC/35: 1813.

almost every instance, the authority to arbitrate or mediate disputes lay with a select group of prominent and reputable individuals locally respected for their knowledge, wisdom or charisma. They had inherited or earned this by virtue of their wealth, experience or age, or because they belonged to particular families or cleaved to lineages with ancestors who were venerated. Those who presided over the forums were typically community elders and patriarchs of influential households; *ʿālim*s, clerics and scholars; Sufi *shaykh*s and *pīr*s; and the masters of a recognised occupation. Whatever their precise background or status, they all had in common the quality of being leaders in their respective domains. This is why I refer to them as 'headmen'.

The manner in which the forum's arbitrators or mediators – its headmen – were selected gestures to what is perhaps the starkest difference between communal and occupational forums. In the former, litigants usually had little or no say in their selection. In the latter, by contrast, the litigants' views frequently mattered, sometimes greatly. For all the suits heard in occupational forums in western India that I have examined, either the headmen were selected by the mutual consent of the litigants or the same number of headmen were selected by each litigant independently of the other. Where the first situation prevailed, the number was usually one per party,[67] though to have each accorded two was not abnormal.[68] This notional equality, coupled with the assumption that the headmen would be sympathetically inclined to their selectors, was clearly intended to pre-empt charges of a priori bias.[69] In addition, an umpire could be nominated. His main duty was to break any deadlock between the arbitrators or mediators. But he was also there to help them reach a consensus or, failing that, a majority decision.[70] The headmen were expected to be knowledgeable about the issues surrounding the dispute. As a result, they were usually local residents with sufficient experience of their chosen livelihood. These are some of the reasons that lay behind Babu Lambatia's avowed preferences. A Muslim shipowner and merchant who got embroiled in a dispute in Bombay in the 1740s, he stated that he was 'averse to any Englishmen being arbitrator in the affair' because 'he was an utter stranger to all the English upon the island' and 'not versant in the English tongue'. Even though he did not have 'any manner of acquaintance upon' Bombay, he demanded instead that his dispute be 'decided by some of the principall merchants natives of

[67] There are many instances of this in the records of Bombay Mayor's Court. See, for example, MSA/Misc/HCR/MRC/35: 1813.
[68] MSA/Misc/HCR/MRC/42: 196–231. [69] MSA/Misc/HCR/MRC/35: 1814.
[70] IOR/P/417/2: 410.

the place'. At least, so he argued, he understood 'their language' and 'could have the benefit of giving the full information in the affair'.[71]

As long as everyone was satisfied that the headmen had been appointed in the correct manner, their pronouncements, once the forum was in session, appear to have been binding. Perhaps the most compelling evidence for this is the absence of any case in which a resolution by a majority was subsequently overturned. This is reinforced by the views of the headmen themselves. Responding to accusations of partiality in his deliberations and conduct, Ram Shenoy stated in 1774 that 'he was properly authorized' as an arbitrator. Thus, he 'cannot deem himself answerable for his actions as such to ... any body whatsoever'.[72] Confident that the bond had been negotiated in the proper way and that the suit had followed the correct procedures, Ram Shenoy felt his reputation, and that of his forum, was safe from charges of impropriety. His self-belief would have been bolstered by the prevailing custom that, in the event of an arbitrator's decision being challenged, the burden of proof lay on the complainant. There was also a strong presumption that the headmen were men of credit who acted in good faith. To call this into question could have grave consequences. This perhaps explains Ram Shenoy's indignant tone. By virtue of the 'penalty bond ... himself [the plaintiff] and [his] partner [had] entered into', they had undertaken 'to abide by the arbitrement of your defendant [Ram Shenoy] ... [And see] how far he has cancelled that obligation by his gross impeachment of your defendant's intention and principles.'[73]

Once the terms of the bond had been settled, it was drawn up and a copy given to each party. These copies were then signed or sealed as appropriate, but would not be 'mutually given'[74] until the two sides had deposited the value of the penalty written into the bond with the forum's headmen, or some other named third party. This could take place at the moment the bond was issued, or several days after the event. Only then were the copies exchanged between the litigants, marking the commencement of the forum's work. This exchange was not merely a symbolic gesture; the whole process pivoted on it. Before then, no matter how far discussions had progressed, any party to the dispute seems to have had the right to withdraw unilaterally without suffering a penalty. But after the exchange had occurred, the costs of unauthorised withdrawal, or a breach of any of the terms specified in the bond, could be forbiddingly high. Towards the end of 1739, in a case pitching Ḥājī Baqil against Nathu Madhuji, a certain 'Mr Say was appointed by [the] consent of both partys

[71] IOR/P/417/2: 409. [72] MSA/Misc/HCR/MRC/35: 1817.
[73] MSA/Misc/HCR/MRC/35: 1818. [74] IOR/P/416/115: 334.

and bonds drawn'.[75] But when the bonds 'went to be signed', for reasons that are unfortunately not stated, Nathu Madhuji refused to sign them. As a result, discussions had to be re-opened and new arbitrators found who were acceptable to both sides.[76] This act of Nathu Madhuji's would have met with Babu Lambatia's approval. Babu Lambatia was of the opinion that any party engaged in preliminary negotiations always has 'a liberty, even when they may have given their word, to recede from [the forum] upon better advice before ... obligatory writtings are passed between them'.[77]

The bonds detailed the framework within which the mediators and arbitrators conducted their investigation into the facts of the dispute and debated the various arguments set forth by the litigants. However, much of the procedure, especially the applicable rules and principles, were merely hinted at or left unstated. There was no one template to which all forums were expected to conform; indeed, attempts to fashion or impose such a template would have been vitiated by the highly circumstantial and pragmatic nature of dispute resolution. Despite this variety, there were nevertheless certain tendencies that appear to have had general applicability within the arena. Headmen would give prior notice to the litigants concerning when they planned to meet to consider the suit. Not to do so was thought unusual.[78] Their inquiry and deliberations could require 'many meetings',[79] and would take place either in the home of a litigant[80] or in that of one of the headmen. In these meetings, the headmen would 'carefully ... look over and consider'[81] the 'papers, letters and other vouchers'[82] that had been presented by the litigants as evidence. It was their prerogative to declare which documents were relevant to the case; they were under no obligation to give any justification for their decisions.[83]

The conclusion of the forum's work paralleled its start, and the rationale for it was similar. After the final judgement was announced in oral or written form, a 'written' or 'general' release was drawn up. This contained the terms of the resolution. A copy was given to each of the parties to the dispute and to each of the forum's headmen.[84] The litigants endorsed their copies – usually with a personal seal or signature – and handed them to the headmen for safe-keeping. For as long as the terms of the release remained unfulfilled,[85] the forum remained in existence. At this point, a third party could be introduced. When this occurred, it was frequently at

[75] IOR/P/416/115: 327. [76] Ibid. [77] IOR/P/417/2: 411. [78] IOR/P/416/115: 332.
[79] IOR/P/416/115: 327, 332. [80] IOR/P/416/115: 333. [81] IOR/P/416/115: 333.
[82] IOR/P/416/115: 327, 332. [83] IOR/P/416/115: 333. [84] IOR/P/416/115: 334–5.
[85] There could be many reasons for this. A common example was awaiting the delivery from one party of a sum of money awarded to the other as compensation. IOR/P/416/115: 327.

the instigation of one of the litigants, especially if sensitivities were acute. Third parties were particularly useful in situations where a long delay was expected before the terms of the resolution would be met, or where further assurances of the forum's impartiality and reliability were required. Gangadas Rupji was invited to perform just this role in the late 1730s. It occurred during the arbitration of a dispute between Ḥājī Baqil, a Surat-based merchant and ship-owner, and Narayandas Tuckidas and Nathu Madhuji, both merchant-brokers. The releases had been drawn up and endorsed by the two sides, but the forum's judgement had yet to be fully implemented. In the meantime, two releases were entrusted to Gangadas Rupji by the arbitrators, 'charging him not to deliver the same to either party without the other party's consent first had',[86] and not until the affair had been 'equitably adjusted'.[87]

Once the terms had been fulfilled to everyone's satisfaction, the releases were exchanged and the forum dissolved. The fact that all sides tended to adhere to the proposed resolution suggests that the forum's procedures contained enough checks and balances for its decisions to command widespread acquiescence. This normally marked the end of the affair. It is also presumably why most of the arena's forums did not provide for appeal. Of course, a disgruntled party might seek to overturn a decision by petitioning a forum thought to have greater prestige or superior authority.[88] But such petitions were seldom made – and when they were, they rarely met with success.

The main focus above has been on what I term occupational forums. There is, however, every reason to believe that resolving disputes through communal forums was just as prevalent. Frustratingly, because of their nature and the self-regulating communities within which they were embedded, the extant sources are such that we are never likely to discover much about how the latter actually functioned. Nonetheless, we can gain insights from documents that allow us to piece together individual disputes. This section gives an account of one such dispute. It involves members of the Armenian community of New Julfa, and is preserved in letters written after the event by one of the participants. In relation to the foregoing analysis of occupational forums, it is worth highlighting the resonances between the two types of forums in their constitution and procedures, and the fact that those making a living through a specific occupation could be – and often were – ethnic brethren.

[86] IOR/P/416/115: 333. [87] IOR/P/416/115: 334.
[88] An example of this may be found in IOR/P/416/115: 334–5.

From the era of Shāh ʿAbbās's rule (r. 1587–1629) to the latter half of the eighteenth century, the spiritual home of many Armenians dispersed throughout Islamicate Eurasia was New Julfa, a suburb of Isfahan.[89] The place was also an administrative centre for the community's wide-ranging activities. When disputes arose among them, they were invariably settled from within. By custom, reputable members present in the locality at the time would choose between themselves the arbitrators or mediators. Once they had carried out their inquiries and deliberated on their findings, their decision was deemed final and binding on all parties. Minas de Eliaz's personal correspondence dating from the 1740s permits us a series of glimpses into the progress of a dispute and its attempted resolution.[90] It conveys a sense of how an ordinary communal forum was set up and went about its business. For this alone, the dispute merits being recounted in full.

As described more fully in the prologue, the *Santa Catharina* dropped anchor off Basra in the middle of 1747. The ship had been hired the previous year by a 'company' of Armenians then living in Bengal for a freight voyage to Basra and back. One of them, Tenisuas de Paulo, had invested 2,000 rupees of the money placed in his charge by his Armenian principal, Sheriman of Isfahan. The capital was used to purchase one of ten shares into which the venture was divided. At the same time, so it was alleged, Tenisuas had freighted on the ship thirty bales of piece-goods for his own personal account. However, these had been purchased not with his own money but with the unspent portion of Sheriman's capital. If true, then Tenisuas had broken the terms of his agreement; the money was to have been used solely for the principal's benefit. The allegation continued that, in order to mask its real owner, Tenisuas claimed to have bought the piece-goods on behalf of another Bengal-based Armenian, Shahin de Giabre, and they were to be consigned in Basra to Mexita de Tarus. Minas de Eliaz, the *Santa Catharina*'s supercargo, agreed to deliver these items to Mexita on Tenisuas's behalf. After the ship reached Basra, owing to an unexpected need for money, Sheriman's agents there applied 'to Mr Minas for him to declare the goods he had on board of his ship on account of the said Tenisuas as also the share he

89 On the Armenian diaspora in early modern times, see Ina Baghdiantz McCabe, *Shah's Silk for Europe's Silver: the Eurasian Trade of the Julfa Armenians in Safavid Iran and India (1530–1750)* (Atlanta, GA, 2002); Vahan A. Bayburdyan, *International Trade and the Armenian Merchants in the Seventeenth Century* (New Delhi, 2004); Sebouh D. Aslanian, *From the Indian Ocean to the Mediterranean: the Global Trade Networks of Armenian Merchants from New Julfa* (Berkeley, CA, 2010).

90 This is contained in a large bundle of documents, relating primarily to the affairs of the Armenian community of eighteenth-century Iran and maritime India, in NA/HCA/42/25 (St Catharina).

had in the ship. To which Mr Minas answered that without taking thereupon the merchants opinion first, he could say nothing about it.' After this was 'proposed to the merchants[,] they agreed'.[91] Sheriman's Basra agents evidently had doubts over Tenisuas's fidelity. But Minas was reluctant to divulge the requested information because he was beholden to his client.

A forum was duly set up. It was presided over by Satur de Agamal, Petrus de Waistcan, Menazacan de Piratam, Zacaria de Sheriman and Johannes de Parcelius, all Armenians present in Basra at the time. In the course of their inquiry, Minas's books were examined to identify Tenisuas's interest in the ship and its cargo. It was confirmed that Tenisuas had one share in the ship worth 2,000 rupees that had been purchased on Sheriman's account and for his principal's interest. But there was uncertainty over the true ownership of the thirty bales of piece-goods, and over the provenance of the money used for their purchase. Sheriman's local agents reminded the arbitrators that 'according to the Law of Julpha when a master delivers any money to his servant, he has a right to take and make use of the same wherever he can find them whenever he is in want of them'.[92] The arbitrators concurred and, on 31 December 1747, they ordered Minas to deliver up to Sheriman's Basra agents the 2,000 rupees that Tenisuas had invested in the *Santa Catharina* on behalf of, and at risk of, Sheriman.[93] Minas agreed to abide by this decision, but 'as to what relates to the thirty and odd bales he could say nothing because he had delivered the bills of lading to the persons that laded them [i.e., Shahin] and had received the freight for the same so that he was obliged to deliver the goods to the persons whom the same were consigned to [i.e., Mexita]'.[94] In the absence of further evidence, it appears the arbitrators were unable to decide whether or not Tenisuas was their owner. The forum ultimately accepted the bills of lading as valid, in effect dismissing the charge of embezzlement against Tenisuas.

The actual procedures that governed the execution of a suit in the arena's occupational and communal forums were crucial to dispute resolution. As we have seen, they shaped how a case was initiated and how the inquiry into its facts was conducted; they shaped the manner in which it was prosecuted and defended, and the manner in which the final decision was pronounced and implemented. While there were many similarities between forums, the specific set of procedures embraced by each forum was unique to it, and thus distinguished it from all others in the arena.

[91] NA/HCA/42/25 (St Catharina): 269–71. [92] Ibid.
[93] NA/HCA/42/25 (St Catharina): 203. [94] NA/HCA/42/25 (St Catharina): 269–71.

This was less true, however, of the other major elements of the law used to articulate contractual agreements and to deal with any disagreements that might arise later. These other elements were the binding rules and principles that determined the essence of the rights, obligations and immunities of those who fell under a forum's jurisdiction. It was on their basis that the headmen discerned the substantive laws most applicable to the dispute at hand.

While the evidence is incomplete, there are very good reasons to interpret the rules and principles that framed the attempted resolution of disputes as having, if not identical form and function, then at least a familial resemblance in the region's ports and towns. The ongoing exposure of individuals to the arena's plural character was central to this convergence. Moreover, judicial commonalities that transcended sovereign frontiers were a prerequisite for activities like travel, communication and trade, which were regularly and frequently conducted over large distances, bridging polities and executed in ethnically diverse contexts. They were thus the cumulative result of generations of movement between far-flung places by agents, traders, bankers, pilgrims, scholars and clerics. The ideas and experiences that accompanied such individuals helped engender a set of rules and principles which spanned India and the Islamic heartlands. The forums responsible for resolving disputes reflected the needs and demands of their clients by adapting themselves to rules and principles recognised across jurisdictions.

These rules and principles could potentially derive from various sources. The sources could be a sovereign's decrees, government statutes, canonical treatises or established traditions.[95] Despite scholarly attention

[95] There is a large body of historical scholarship on these sources of law. I have found most useful the following works: John D. M. Derrett, *Religion, Law and the State in India* (London, 1968); John Makdisi, 'Legal logic and equity in Islamic law', *American Journal of Comparative Law* 33:1 (1985), 63–92; Brinkley Messick, 'The mufti, the text and the world: legal interpretation in Yemen', *Man* 21:1 (1986), 102–19; Haim Gerber, *State, Society, and Law in Islam: Ottoman Law in Comparative Perspective* (Albany, NY, 1994); Muhammad Khalid Masud, Brinkley Messick and David S. Powers (eds.), *Islamic Legal Interpretation: Muftis and their Fatwas* (Cambridge, MA, 1996); Haim Gerber, *Islamic Law and Culture 1600–1840* (Leiden, 1999); Muzaffar Alam, '*Shari'a* and governance in the Indo-Islamic context', in David Gilmartin and Bruce B. Lawrence (eds.), *Beyond Turk and Hindu: Rethinking Religious Identities in Islamicate South Asia* (Gainesville, FL, 2000), 216–45; Dina R. Khoury, 'Administrative practice between law (Shari'a) and state law (Kanun) on the eastern frontiers of the Ottoman empire', *Journal of Early Modern History* 5:4 (2001), 305–30; Donald R. Davis, jr, 'Intermediate realms of law: orporate groups and rulers in medieval India', *Journal of the Economic and Social History of the Orient* 48:1 (2005), 92–117; Muhammad Khalid Masud, Rudolph Peters and David S. Powers (eds.), *Dispensing Justice in Islam: Qadis and their Judgements* (Leiden, 2005); Timothy Lubin, Donald R. Davis jr and Jayanth K. Krishnan (eds.), *Hinduism and Law: an Introduction* (New York, 2010).

having focused predominantly on these, by far the most important source of substantive law for dispute resolution within the region was customs.[96] By customs, I mean the modes of behaviour that were understood by contemporaries as legitimate and timeless, even if the truth is they were impermanent expressions of social forces in constant flux. Customs were ubiquitous, sanctioned on multiple scales and levels; they were enmeshed with collective memory, solidarity and consciousness; and they were products of both inherited patterns and recent innovations.[97] A subset of them underpinned the rules and principles embraced by the arena's communal and occupational forums. While customs were the dominant source of law in these contexts, it is worth bearing in mind that they were in continuous interaction with the other potential sources. Designated by a variety of terms in our period – *'urf, ta'āmul, 'āda, ta'āruf, qanūn* are some of the most common – many elements of the prevailing customs were gradually incorporated into, and codified, within government statutes. Even sharia was adapted to take account of this situation. Though customs were never formally admitted as one of the principal sources of Islamic law (*aṣl*, pl. *uṣūl*), attempts were made, especially by jurists in the *Ḥanafī* school, to confer upon them doctrinal respectability by rearticulating them in keeping with canonical dogma.[98]

So the importance of customs in general, and law in particular, was recognised and supported at all levels of the region's polities. But this does not make the task of recovering them any the easier. The main difficulty stems from the very nature of customs as contested and shifting. Whatever their specific details, the genealogy of customs, especially their origins, was at best hazily remembered by their adherents. This is so even though customs were central to the vernacular repertoire. They were continuously talked about, enacted, assumed, respected. These are the ways in which they were continuously injected with vitality. These are

96 My understanding of customs is indebted to Edward P. Thompson, *Customs in Common* (New York, 1991).

97 Robert B. Serjeant has made notable contributions to our knowledge of customs in the region. In particular, see his 'Maritime customary law off the Arabian coasts', in Michel Mollat (ed.), *Sociétés et compagnies de commerce en Orient et dans l'Océan indien: actes du huitième Colloque international d'histoire maritime (Beyrouth, 5–10 septembre 1966)* (Paris, 1970), 195–207; *Studies in Arabian History and Civilisation* (London, 1981); *Customary and Shari'ah Law in Arabian Society* (Aldershot, 1991); *Farmers and Fishermen in Arabia: Studies on Customary Law and Practice* (Aldershot, 1995); *Society and Trade in South Arabia* (Aldershot, 1996). More recent contributions include Ron Shaham (ed.), *Law, Custom, and Statute in the Muslim World: Studies in Honor of Aharon Layish* (Leiden, 2006); Ayman Shabana, *Custom in Islamic Law and Legal Theory: The Development of the Concepts of* 'urf *and* 'ādah *in the Islamic Legal Tradition* (New York, 2010).

98 The ways in which customs were legitimised and incorporated into sharia is discussed in Gideon Libson, 'On the development of custom as a source of law in Islamic law', *Islamic Law and Society* 4:2 (1997), 131–55.

the ways in which they were negotiated and propagated, from place to place, and from generation to generation. All this occurred, however, without the mediation of the written word; customs were almost entirely expressed orally or through corporeal behaviour. The one situation in which we might expect customs to be verbalised on paper was during a dispute resolution. Unfortunately for us, it was rare for any headman who heard, investigated and pronounced on disputes to document his deliberations for posterity. On the contrary, the presumption was that to do so would be inappropriate. As Bhikhaji noted in 1775,

> It is ever recommended an award should never contain more than is absolutely necessary to explain the determination of the arbitrators or umpire in the clearest, shortest, and most explicit manner possible for language to convey such determination or decision. Nor is it the custom to set forth the reasons and motives of the arbitration in any proper award whatever.[99]

The customs which actually prevailed in the arena of circulation and exchange have thus left traces that are barely perceptible in the extant historical record. In fact, it is remarkable how seldom contemporaries were motivated to state explicitly the importance of reigning customs in their formal agreements. This is probably because the feature was simply taken for granted and treated as obvious by the parties involved; the customary terms that they were obliged to obey and uphold, particularly in relation to unexpected developments, were left implicit owing to their familiarity to all concerned. Detailing them in writing would have served no useful purpose. One of the very few exceptions to this is a contract drawn up in Portuguese in Goa in 1789. It proclaimed that the corvette *Salvamento*, owned jointly by José Francisco Anello, Veṅkateśa Kāmat and Nārāyaṇa Kāmat, was about to sail from Goa on a commercial venture. An agreement was negotiated by the ship's owners and José Joaquim de Vasconcelos, who was to travel as the ship's captain, first pilot and supercargo, all at once. In the signed contract, we see the word 'costume' invoked repeatedly. It makes its first appearance on Vasconcelos agreeing to forgo certain privileges concerning the passengers, 'which, following . . . custom, he would have had in the corvette'. He was compensated with a gratuity. Other perquisites established by custom are also noted in the document. Vasconcelos had personal use of the ship's audience room, with which came servants paid for by the owners. And the owners accepted that, if the captain suffered any illness or unforeseen accident not covered in their agreement, they were duty-bound to take care of him in the customary manner. The document

[99] MSA/Misc/HCR/MRC/42: 208.

concluded with the owners and Vasconcelos committing themselves 'to carry out to the full this agreement, not only in what is stated explicitly but also by good and approved custom that must be observed'.[100]

The specific nature and function of customs varied according to the type of transaction. There seems to have been, however, a positive correlation between the significance of customs in an agreement and the regularity and frequency with which transactions occurred that were underpinned by agreements of that kind. This correlation is borne out by dealings that criss-crossed the Arabian Sea area in the eighteenth century. Some of the most commonplace were based on formal agreements with a sizeable customary component. These included agreements for insurance, freight and credit.[101] I close this chapter by looking at a series of such agreements in order to apprehend how customs operated in practice.

The simplest kind of agreements for maritime insurance dealt with small-scale commercial ventures. The resulting policies were issued to the ship-owners or freighters for a specified itinerary by one or more merchants or bankers. These latter normally belonged to the same close-knit community or occupational group. The liability of each insurer was individually specified in the policy. In return, a premium was paid. So on 17 September 1739, when Govind Kessu, Wassanji Narad and Sambo Ransor drew up a policy in favour of Muḥammad Ibrāhīm for the return voyage of his shybar *Tokeley* from Bombay to Masqat, it was stated that Govind Kessu was liable for 50 rupees, Wassanji Narad for 25 rupees and Sambo Ransor for 25 rupees.[102] Capped by the overall value of the policy, valid causes for receiving a pay-out were shipwrecks, losses at sea and seizure by pirates, minus any sums that the policy-holder was able to recover through salvage.

Agreements for insurance were generally short and concluded orally. One of the principal reasons for their brevity must have been widespread familiarity with the main constraints to which the policies were subject

[100] XCHR/MHR/Other Documents (1 December 1789).

[101] For recent work on such agreements in premodern times, see Vardit Rispler-Chaim, 'Insurance and semi-insurance transactions in Islamic history until the 19th century', *Journal of the Economic and Social History of the Orient* 34:3 (1991), 142–58; Daniel Panzac, 'L'economie-monde Ottomane en question: les clauses monétaires dans les contrats d'affretèment maritime au XVIIIe siècle', *Journal of the Economic and Social History of the Orient* 39:3 (1996), 368–78; Mohd. Masum Billah, 'Islamic insurance: its origins and development', *Arab Law Quarterly*, 13:4 (1998), 386–422; Daniel Panzac, 'Le contrat d'affrètement maritime en Méditerranée: droit maritime et pratique commerciale entre Islam et Chrétienté (XVIIe–XVIIIe siècles)', *Journal of the Economic and Social History of the Orient* 45:3 (2002), 342–62.

[102] IOR/P/416/115: 22–6. For another example, see MSA/Misc/HCR/MRC/7: 76–82.

and with the procedures to be followed in the event of an undesirable outcome. Perhaps the most severe customary term was that, unless explicitly stated otherwise, insurance policies only covered accidents or losses which happened during the voyage itself; the ship and its cargo were entirely at the owner's, or the freighter's, risk while anchored in port. This rule was applied by the insurers of maritime ventures at the port-town of Porepatam (Porbandar) in Gujarat. In the early 1740s, a vessel by the name of the *Jenny* was insured for a voyage from Bombay to Masqat. The holder of the policy, Muʿallim Daud, demanded that the insurers pay out its face value after the *Jenny* had been plundered in Masqat by Nādir Shāh's army, which had recently seized control of the place. Much of the other local and foreign shipping in Masqat was plundered as well at the same time. But aside from Muʿallim Daud, no one else who had been similarly insured sought compensation from their insurers. They seem to have accepted that, by the 'known custom in these countrys', the losses would have to be covered by them alone.[103] The rationale for this custom was twofold: to reduce the temptation for the local ruler to seize a ship and its cargo, and to limit the insurers' liabilities. Many insurers feared, and with reasonable justification, that, if insured while in harbour, the ruler might give in to the temptation to impound the vessel until its insurers agreed to ransom it. This was an oft-heard complaint of merchants, ship-owners and insurers with interests on the west coast of India in the 1730s.[104]

The itinerary for a voyage covered by an insurance policy was usually specified in the contract, together with any permitted deviations. However, the amount of detail varied. The benefit of minimal detail accrued mainly to the policy-holders; it gave tactical flexibility to the managers of the venture. This was of particular value in the event of unforeseen developments. At the same time, lack of detail gave rise to the possibility of conflicting interpretations if circumstances did not allow the full voyage to come to term as planned or if the itinerary had to be altered without the knowledge or consent of the insurers, and the vessel was subsequently lost.[105] In every port, it was custom that determined the latitude given to the captain or supercargo to alter the original itinerary as specified in the agreement, and for the policy to remain in force.

Even if an insurance policy had not been taken out, compensation could be awarded for losses suffered, at least for seizures on the high seas. In such cases, the relevant customs determined the amount to be

[103] IOR/P/416/119: 54–5. [104] MSA/Misc/HCR/MRC/7: 155–6.
[105] There are examples of such disputes in IOR/P/417/2: 373–411 and MSA/Misc/HCR/MRC/7: 76–82.

paid, by whom and to whom, thus effectively furnishing a kind of safety net. In Bombay in the middle of the eighteenth century, the view was that the amount of compensation a freighter could claim from the ship-owner if his goods were plundered 'under[, say,] the pretence of pass money and the like[,] by Malvons and other petty rajas', was linked to the amount he had paid to freight his goods.[106] When several vessels from Bombay had their cargos seized by pirates in 1740, a number of disputes erupted between the ship-owners and the freighters over the compensation due to the latter. Though no formal insurance policies had been drawn up, the Bombay-based merchants selected to arbitrate these disputes decreed that all freighters who had paid 5 rupees per morah or candy should bear the totality of their losses, while those who had paid 6 rupees should be compensated to the tune of half the value of their losses. As for those who had paid 7 or 8 rupees freight money, 'the [ship-]owners should make good and pay for such plunder'. The freighters argued that, by custom, any merchant who paid as much as 8 rupees had a right for his goods to be guaranteed against any losses, 'as if he had written [a] contract'.[107] This dispute shows that, though the custom had its detractors, the general sentiment was that the payment of higher freight charges ought to confer greater protection.

Local customs often tilted the balance in favour of one side or the other in situations of contested claims over the proceeds of a transaction. This offered a resolution by defining the order of precedence of these claims upon liquidation of the assets. A ship-owner who in the late 1760s had leased his vessel to a merchant for a freight voyage and also extended credit to him benefited from these customs.[108] The agreement framing the transaction had not stated how the credit related to bonds that had subsequently been taken up by the ship's leaser upon respondentia and bottomry from local residents.[109] It was custom that stepped in to fill this breach. In much of western India at the time, 'it was always the custom . . . to discharge the debt for freight before debt due upon respondentia bonds'.[110]

However, it is in unpredictable environments – where it was difficult, if not impossible, to calculate risk – that the salutary influence of customs

106 MSA/Misc/HCR/MRC/12: 78. 107 MSA/Misc/HCR/MRC/12: 78–9.

108 MSA/Misc/HCR/MRC/31: 502.

109 *Respondentia* is a loan to an individual secured against his goods that are being transported by a vessel. The loan is repayable only on the safe arrival of the vessel and its cargo at the destination specified in the contract. In case of loss or harm, the risk is borne by the lender. *Bottomry* is a loan to an individual secured against his share in the vessel. The loan is repayable only on the safe arrival of the vessel at the destination specified in the contract. In case of loss or harm, similar to respondentia, the risk is borne by the lender.

110 MSA/Misc/HCR/MRC/31: 499.

was felt most acutely. Customary protections and guarantees gave an individual the confidence to negotiate agreements for transactions that would otherwise not have been considered. This was common when past experience was of little or no use as a reliable guide for present or future action. Uncertainties were typically fanned by political chaos, the outbreak of war or arbitrary exactions by local officials. Customs helped tame these. Their value may also be seen through their capacity to extend an agreement's life-span in exceptional or unusual situations beyond what had originally been agreed. In 1776, in one of the first attempts by a British ship to sail up the Red Sea to Suez, the Calcutta-based Parsi Manakji Shapurji engaged John Shaw to purchase sundry goods in Cairo for his account.[111] Their agreement did not limit Shaw 'to any specific time for the performance of the said contract as it was not possible to provide against the eventual accidents of a voyage'. Nevertheless, it was understood, as Manakji claimed later, the goods should be delivered to Calcutta the next season or as soon as possible thereafter, with Shaw at liberty to deliver them in person or through someone else. Otherwise, he continued, 'if the time of delivery was not fixed to the period herementioned it would be impossible to limit the expiration of the contract to any time whatever'.[112] We see at the heart of this dispute a custom that compensated for enough of the unpredictability to allow a risky and innovative undertaking to be entertained – and attempted.

[111] For further details about this agreement and the venture, see MSA/Misc/HCR/MRC/045: 456–80.

[112] MSA/Misc/HCR/MRC/45: 474.

7 Everyday practices: indispensable skills and techniques

> The broker states the price without lengthy preliminaries. The purchaser responds by putting his hand inside that of the broker ... He indicates by the number of bent or extended fingers how much below the asking price he is prepared to pay and sometimes the deal is concluded without any word being said. In order to confirm the deal, they hold hands a second time, and it is concluded by a gift presented to the purchaser by the seller in proportion to the transaction and the status of the contracting parties.[1]

The orientalist and traveller Anquetil-Duperron made these observations during his stay in India in the middle of the eighteenth century. His observations gesture to some of the everyday skills and techniques – the practices – that were indispensable for circulation and exchange in the period. What linked these practices together were certain shared qualities: they were eminently useful and reliable; they satisfied common wants and needs; and they were readily available, to be learnt and deployed.[2] Though found in many realms of daily life within the region, their value – their indispensability – is thrown into starkest relief in ventures characterised by large distances and long silences, ventures that typically bore the imprint of individuals hailing from diverse backgrounds and that transcended the boundaries of any one polity as a matter of course.

To grasp the historical meaning of the practices noted in Anquetil-Duperron's observations, we need to analyse them in light of the subjects treated in the preceding chapters. In particular, they need to be related to

1 Abraham-Hyacinthe Anquetil-Duperron, *Voyage en Inde 1754–1762: relation de voyage en préliminaire a la traduction du Zend-Avesta* (Paris, 1997), 360.

2 This formulation of practices owes much to the notion of 'useful and reliable knowledge'. On the latter, see Ian Inkster, 'Potentially global: "useful and reliable knowledge" and material progress in Europe, 1474–1914', *International History Review* 28:2 (2006), 237–86 and the working papers produced under Patrick K. O'Brien's direction by the *Useful and Reliable Knowledge in Global Histories of Material Progress in the East and the West* project (London School of Economics, 2010–14). Also relevant is Peter Howlett and Mary S. Morgan (eds.), *How Well do Facts Travel?: The Dissemination of Reliable Knowledge* (Cambridge, 2011).

the concepts and images by means of which the arena's surroundings were accessed and made sense of, and the prevailing realities which constrained and enabled how the people of the arena confronted their world. These features of the arena existed in mutual dependence with the practices discussed in the present chapter. Indeed, practices may be viewed as actualisations, in line with reigning modes of thinking and imagining, of widely dispersed behavioural tendencies. What distinguishes practices from the cognitive patterns and the five orders examined earlier in the book is their instrumentality and inclusivity; they were oriented towards highly specific ends and employed by a broad range of individuals. Given how many of the arena's participants had to deal with similar functional challenges in pursuing their livelihoods, that these practices were held in common is only to be expected.

There were many different kinds of skills and techniques central to daily life within India and the Islamic heartlands. This chapter is about that particular subset which was especially germane to the arena of circulation and exchange. In the sections to follow, I discuss the rhetorics of correspondence and the epistolary templates underlying them; intermediation by far-off agents and brokers; the art of negotiation; and settling deferred transactions from a distance. The chapter concludes by situating these practices in the context of the region in the eighteenth century.

The composition and comprehension of letters

The separation of individuals by large distances was a fact of life for those active in the arena. When to this was joined the need to remain apart for long periods, certain realities gained a significance that they would not otherwise have had. These realities, and the tendencies in behaviour associated with them, are detailed in the preceding chapters. In one way or another, the issue of communication lies at their base. The documents reveal that only two modes of communication were in frequent use. One was to entrust the message orally to a traveller, who would relay it to the recipient on meeting him. Another was to entrust the message to a letter, which would then be carried to the addressee by a courier or friend or associate. The focus of this section is on the second of these modes.[3]

[3] For details on letter-writing more generally in the Islamic world, see Adrian Gully, *The Culture of Letter-Writing in Pre-Modern Islamic Society* (Edinburgh, 2008). Citations to the modern scholarly literature on writing, textuality and literacy may be found in Chapter 5 on the communications order.

The present section complements Chapter 5, where I examined the givens of communication by means of symbols preserved in material form – languages, scripts, substrates and tools – and the holistic and entrepreneurial patterns of behaviour which these realities constrained and enabled. Here, I examine the skills and techniques that were embedded in the composition and comprehension of letters. The resulting practice sufficed to make correspondence over large distances possible. But it did so in ways that reveal differences and similarities among those engaged in regional-scale activities, which, to the best of my knowledge, have not previously been commented on by scholars. I elaborate this practice by juxtaposing personal letters written in the middle of the eighteenth century in Arabic-script languages with those written at the same time in Latin-script languages. By doing so, I aim to reconstruct the ways in which the practice was realised within the arena.

My account is framed by the most challenging kind of situation commonly faced by an individual wishing to write to a far-off associate. This occurred when the correspondents did not have a language in common. For that situation, I examine the main features of the process by which a letter was typically composed and comprehended. These features are its visual aesthetic, the physical act of its creation, its underlying templates, the rhetorical mechanisms for dealing with the prevailing uncertainties, its markers of identity, the logistics of sealing and addressing, and its reception on arrival.[4]

Each of the scripts used in letters circulating within Islamicate Eurasia was characterised by an identifiable and distinct visual aesthetic. The main elements of the aesthetic of any text are its morphology, directionality and writing style. As the articulation of these elements was often specific to a given literary or documentary genre, I restrict the discussion here to one genre – personal correspondence – in languages written in the arena's most popular scripts, the Latin and the Arabic.[5]

Letters in English, French and Portuguese normally had a block of space at the top of the opening page which was left empty, save for a few words hovering above the preamble. (See Figure 4.) The main body of the text was invariably composed of lines directed horizontally, extending from the left edge of the page to its right edge, maintaining the same

[4] Although for a different period, Brinkley Messick examines similar topics in his *Calligraphic State: Textual Domination and History in a Muslim Society* (Berkeley, CA, 1993). Of greatest relevance are chapters 11 and 12.

[5] The description that follows is based on a study of personal correspondence in Arabic, English, French, Hindi, Ottoman Turkish, Persian and Portuguese dating from the middle decades of the eighteenth century. Other genres dispersed within the arena that could have been studied include those associated with petitions, contracts, receipts and notarised documents.

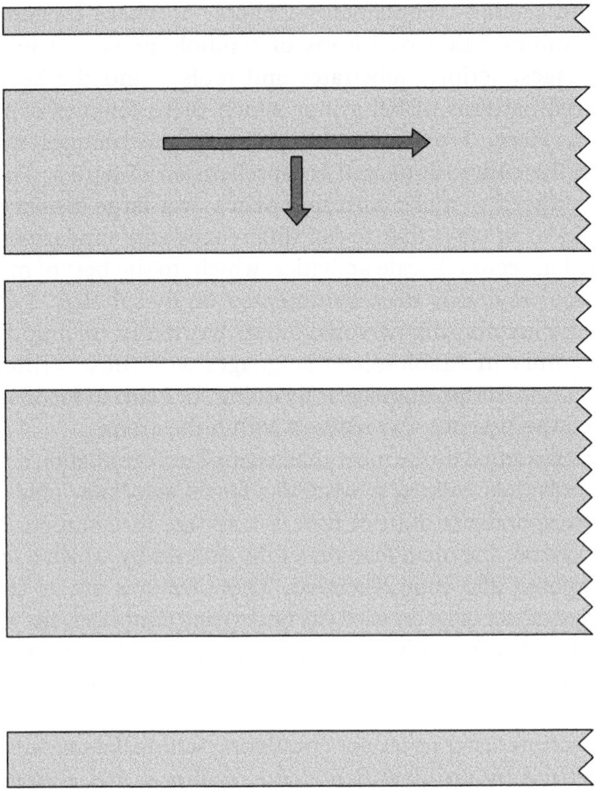

Figure 4. Basic template for Latin-script letters.

distance between the page's left edge and the first letter of each line. Each new line was started immediately below the most recently completed line. On reaching the bottom edge of the page, the writer might continue as before, either on its reverse side or on a new sheet of paper. The closing was generally separated from the main body of the text, and characterised by more liberal use of indents and empty spaces between its lines. Aside from the preamble and closing, the text as a whole adopted the shape of a block or a series of blocks, with straight edges along the top, bottom and left-hand side, and a jagged edge along its right-hand side; indents or line spaces to indicate paragraphs were usually absent.

In terms of their visual aesthetics, there were only two major affinities between letters in Latin-script languages and letters in Arabic, Persian and Ottoman Turkish, the main Arabic-script languages of the time. (See

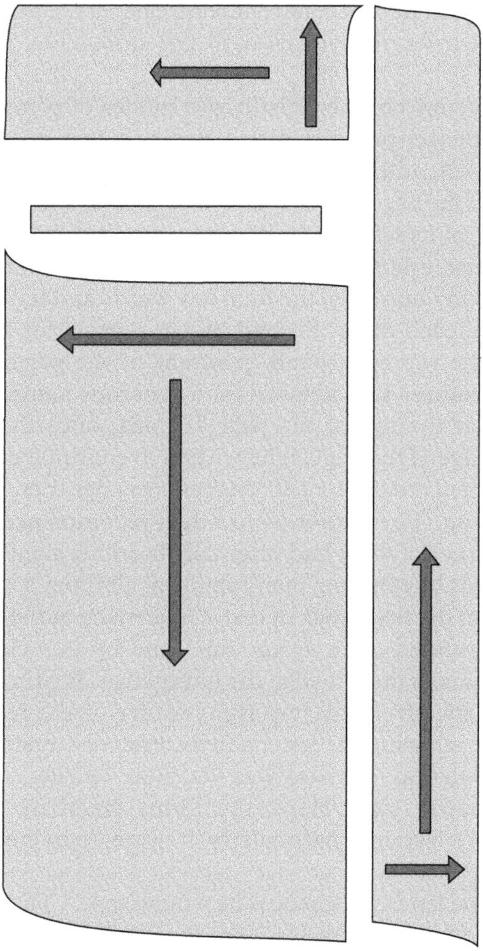

Figure 5. Basic template for Arabic-script letters.

Figure 5.) One was composition in horizontal lines that succeeded each other in a downward direction. The other was the presence of a block of near-empty space marking the beginning of the letter, which need not be – and often was not – at the top of the page. Aside from these two affinities, the aesthetic of letters in the Arabic script was quite different. Some of these differences are rooted in orthography: the Arabic script does not distinguish between upper and lower cases; the start of a new idea in the letter was signalled not, as in Latin-script letters, by a new sentence or paragraph, but by well-known linking characters, formulas or stock phrases; special markers were used to flag quotations from the Qur'ān or poetry.

Other differences stem from their distinctive modes of composition. Three aspects of Arabic-script letters stand out in this regard. First, in moving from right to left, authors always kept a constant distance from the right-hand edge of the page and the start of each line, and continued writing until the edge of its left-hand side was reached. Sometimes the writing deviated consistently from the horizontal level on approaching the edge, the line curving upwards, the final few words and letters piled precariously on top of each other. Second, it was normal for letters to begin at a point in the top right-hand quadrant of the page, not far from its geometrical centre. This allowed for a generous margin on the right-hand side and at the top of the page.[6] Third, once the author reached the bottom edge of the page, if he wished to continue the letter, the page would be turned around by 180°, its bottom edge thereby being transformed into its top. The author would then recommence writing from the top-right corner of what had originally been the right margin, progressing downwards line by line, maintaining at all times a small but constant distance from the first block of text. On arriving at the bottom, the letter would be rotated once again, this time by 90° clockwise, making what was originally the left edge the lower edge. Writing usually started a certain distance from the top-right corner of the remaining block of empty space, allowing the letter's invocation or superscription to float in pristine isolation. If there was yet more to say, the letter continued on the reverse side. Here, the forms taken by the text expressed much more variety, particularly if little remained to be written.[7]

Another feature of the letter's aesthetic is its writing style.[8] Though each script – Latin or Arabic – could in theory be represented in many different styles, individual languages were historically associated with a small subset of them. Some styles were by convention reserved for particular genres, say,

[6] Only in cases where the letter was brief did the writing start close to the right-hand edge of the page.

[7] For further details on the aesthetics of various genres of documents composed in the Arabic script, see William L. Hanaway and Brian Spooner, *Reading Nasta'liq: Persian and Urdu Hands from 1500 to the Present* (Costa Mesa, CA, 1995); Yves Porter, *Peinture et arts du livre: essai sur la littérature technique indo-persane* (Paris, 1992), 61–72.

[8] The writing style is to be distinguished from the handwriting of its author; writing styles are conventional, learnt and recognisable, while an author's handwriting is unique to that author. From this perspective, any text is characterised by a particular writing style inflected through the author's handwriting.

poetry or official pronouncements.[9] Regarding correspondence within the arena, the choice of the style appears to have been determined largely by the background and personal inclination of the writer. Among the most prevalent in the eighteenth century were copperplate French, italic Portuguese, Arabic *naskh*, and Persian *nasta'līq* and *shikastah*. (See Figure 6.) The remarkable persistence of individual styles was in all likelihood a consequence of the similar training received by the clerks and linguists who resided in a given place. Their penmanship could be exquisite, with great care lavished on the thickness and curvature of the individual letters and words and their orientation with respect to one another. More often, however, the overriding concern for the author was to write rapidly while maintaining a minimum level of legibility for his readers. That must be one of the factors behind the popularity of the *shikastah* ('broken') style in Persian correspondence. (See Figure 7.) In this style, symbols usually kept separate elsewhere were combined, and many diacritical marks omitted, allowing scribes to keep the pen on the surface of the paper for longer.

In the simplest scenario, the author would write the letter himself in its final form in a single sitting. But the ambient realities did not always permit such luxuries. Especially for those who maintained and cultivated a large number of relationships, the letter was normally composed over several stages. It was first drafted in the author's own hand or by dictation to a scribe. If there was no need for translation, it was then written up in neat, usually by a clerk in the author's employment or one commissioned specifically for the task. The draft was presumably kept by the author for his own records, while the neat version was sealed, addressed and dispatched to its intended recipient.

Recourse to a clerk was standard procedure. Depending on the language and the place, a clerk was referred to as a *kātib*, *nivīsandah*, *munshī*, *écrivain* or *escrivão*.[10] Clerks are often noted in the sources, though

[9] Classic works on the subject include Ḥabīb Allāh Faḍā'ilī [Fazā'ilī]'s *Aṭlas-i khaṭṭ: Taḥqīq-i dar khaṭūṭ-i Islāmī* (Tehran, 1350/1971–2) and *Ta'līm-i khaṭṭ* (Tehran, 1356/1977–8). Also see Adam Gacek, *Arabic Manuscripts: a Vademecum for Readers* (Leiden, 2009).

[10] The topic of clerks in their various manifestations is of renewed interest among scholars. See Muhammad Zameeruddin Siddiqi, 'The intelligence services under the Mughals', in *Medieval India: A Miscellany*, vol. II (London, 1972), 53–60; Michael H. Fisher, 'The office of Akhbar Nawis: the transition from Mughal to British forms', *Modern Asian Studies* 27:1 (1993), 45–82; Cornell H. Fleischer, 'Between the lines: realities of scribal life in the sixteenth century', in Colin Heywood and Colin Imber (eds.), *Studies in Ottoman History in Honour of Professor V. L. Ménage* (Istanbul, 1994), 45–61; Muzaffar Alam and Sanjay Subrahmanyam, 'Making of a munshi', *Comparative Studies of South Asia, Africa and the Middle East* 24:2 (2004), 61–72; Kumkum Chatterjee, 'Scribal elites in Sultanate and Mughal Bengal', *Indian Economic and Social History Review* 47:4 (2010), 445–72; Rosalind O'Hanlon, 'The social worth of scribes: Brahmins, Kayasthas and the social order in early modern India', *Indian Economic and Social History Review* 47:4 (2010), 563–95.

Ta'līq

Dīwānī

Shikastah

Scribal *naskh*

Ruq'ah

Siyāqat

Nasta'līq

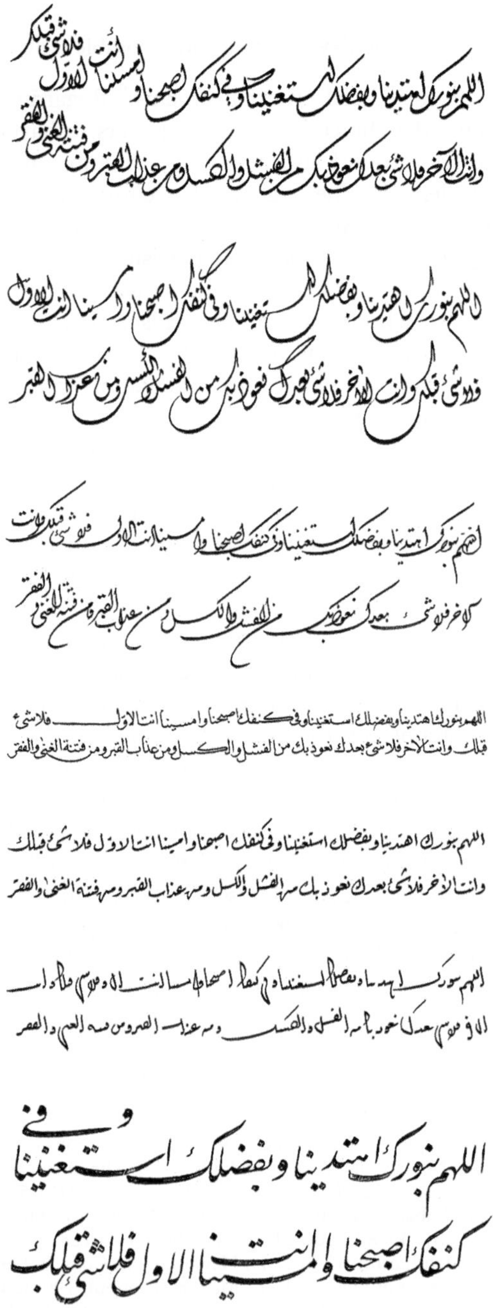

Figure 6. Typical writing styles in the Arabic script.
Source: Nabil F. Safwat, *The Art of the Pen: Calligraphy of the 14th to 20th Centuries* (with a contribution by Mohamed Zakariya, Oxford, 1996) / The Nasser D. Khalili Collection of Islamic Art, CAL 471 / © Nour Foundation. Courtesy of the Khalili Family Trust.

Figure 7. Persian letter in *shikastah-nastaʿlīq*.
Source: BL/Lansdowne/1046, doc. 52.

invariably in passing. That they were constitutive for this practice is suggested by the fact authors could legitimately blame them for any tardiness in keeping up their end of the correspondence. Authors excused themselves by claiming clerks were scarce,[11] or indisposed owing to illness,[12] or temporarily away on a visit.[13] Further evidence for their widespread use is found in the handwritings on display in the letters sent from a particular settlement. The documents show that, among those composed at roughly the same time, the number of distinct handwritings is far fewer than the number of their purported authors.[14] This indicates that the same clerk was employed by multiple authors (or that, alternatively, one author doubled as a clerk for others).

The process of composition was at its most complex in instances where the final version of the letter was to be written in a language not known by its putative author. If this was a lingua franca, or one of the local languages, the author would have been able to find a translator with relative ease. For other languages, however, few residents, if any, were available who were conversant in them. Locating a competent translator for these languages, especially in the smaller settlements, was thus no trivial task. This was the situation with Arabic in many of the ports of western India in the middle of the eighteenth century, a fact that Bernard Picot had come to appreciate all too well. Picot was a French merchant-official based in Mahe on the Malabar coast, who in the 1760s and 1770s regularly sent letters to correspondents in the Maldives and Oman.[15] These had to be dispatched in Arabic. In order to get his French or Portuguese drafts translated into suitably elegant and idiomatic Arabic, he followed a tried and tested procedure. An account of this procedure illustrates nicely how the arena's people were able to resolve the kind of difficulties typically encountered in crafting letters that crossed languages.

Picot's correspondence for the Maldives and Oman was first drafted by him in person or by a clerk in accordance with his instructions. It was written either in French or Portuguese, though the latter was preferred because the clerks in Picot's employment were better acquainted with it. These clerks, all indigenous to the Malabar area, were fluent in Malayalam and Portuguese; only one or two of them knew any French.

[11] MssOcc/NAF/8992: 87, 88–9. [12] MssOcc/NAF/8996: 66.
[13] MssOcc/NAF/8997: 131.
[14] See, for example, the letters composed in Cochin or Basra or Najaf in BL/Lansdowne/1046.
[15] These correspondents included Sultan Khaqān in the Maldives and the Imām and Amīr at Masqat. For the original drafts in French, Portuguese and Arabic, see MssOcc/NAF/9002: 22, 23; MssOcc/NAF/9002: 75–7; MssOcc/NAF/9003: 56–9.

As for Arabic, it would seem that there was no one in Mahe who could read or write it. Since Portuguese, alongside Persian, was the most widespread lingua franca in the Malabar area, the translator of the draft into Arabic was much more likely to have known Portuguese over French. So as to facilitate the translation and minimise the risk of errors, it was important that the text presented to him was already in that language. This is why a draft originally drawn up in French was generally translated into Portuguese by one of the clerks who knew both languages *before* it left Mahe in search of a translator.

The task now was to find someone able to convert that draft into Arabic and, importantly, rewrite it in a register appropriate to the language, its contents and the intended recipient. Only then could the letter be written up in its final form. Such expertise was usually confined to settlements that maintained relations with Arabic-speaking areas; in western India in the eighteenth century, among the most promising candidates would have been Calicut and Surat.[16] The translator, once commissioned, produced a draft in Arabic. The neat version was written up either by the translator himself or by a scribe. At last, the letter was ready to be dispatched to the addressee, leaving the French, Portuguese and Arabic drafts behind to be preserved by Picot in his records.

This account shows that, in situations where translation was necessary, a letter had as many as four incarnations before being entrusted to a courier. With each additional stage, the practicalities of composing the document gained in complexity. The most elusive were innate to the very act of translation. Even if the author insisted that the dispatched letter be faithful to the original draft, translations could not be literal because of the expectations of the recipient. As every genre in each language had its distinctive idiom, formulas and rhetorical texture, translation necessarily entailed the reworking of the author's message to make it conform to what would have been familiar and comfortable for the recipient. Failure to do so increased the likelihood of misunderstandings; it might even be cause for offence.

Translations were undertaken by linguists who could be in the permanent service of the author or his organisation, borrowed from or shared between associates or friends, or commissioned as and when the need arose.[17] Though each lingua franca and regional language had a number of terms – *interprète, língua, tarjumān* – that referred specifically to this activity, it was also very common (as seen below) for the individual to

[16] Dwijendra Tripathi, *Oxford History of Indian Business* (New Delhi, 2004), 23.

[17] MssOcc/NAF/9003: 27; TNSA/Persian Records/111: 27; XCHR/MHR/Correspondence (incoming) (4 February 1778).

perform other roles in the realms of communication and trade. Such individuals were generally referred to as *dubashis* or *gumāshtahs* in India and Iran. These broader terms encompassed an array of livelihoods, from a clerk, responsible for recordkeeping, drafting and translation, via an agent, concerned with interpreting, money-lending, news provision, remittances and negotiations, to a freelance intermediary or broker. Furthermore, it was not uncommon for such individuals to be merchants or landowners in their own right.

Whether in Latin- or Arabic-script languages, personal letters composed as above exhibited the same overall threefold division into a preamble, main body and closing. The contents of the preamble and closing were mostly governed by protocol and etiquette. It was also in these two parts that the letter's principal identifiers – its date of composition, author and recipient – were normally located. In other respects, however, the template underlying letters in the Arabic script differed from that found in letters in the Latin script. For this reason, I treat them separately.

In personal letters in the Latin script, the preamble and closing were generally brief.[18] They were also relatively simple in style. Many of the same expressions could be found in either part. The preamble would begin with a superscription that announced the letter's recipient. This sometimes took the form of the family name alone, at other times the family name with the given name. The name was invariably preceded by a title, often abbreviated, that gestured towards the individual's status in the polity. Common examples include 'Sir', 'Senhor', 'Monsieur', 'Negociante'. This could be accompanied by a simple epithet, such as 'Meu' or 'Honourable'. On occasions when the name was omitted, the title alone signalled the addressee. There usually followed a series of pithy and formulaic declarations in which the author wished the recipient good health and success, expressed his desire to please and serve him, professed his friendship, or gave thanks for having remembered him. It was also common to remark here on letters recently arrived from him, noting their dates and itineraries.

The transition to the main body of the letter was abrupt. Likewise, the departure from it to the closing tended to occur without ceremony. Similar to the preamble, the closing would generally be brief, composed largely of stock phrases, perhaps echoing those found earlier in the letter.

[18] The scholarly literature on the history of epistolary practices in Latin-script languages in Europe is extensive. As examples, which also contain citations to other work in the field, see David Barton and Nigel Hall (eds.), *Letter Writing as a Social Practice* (Philadelphia, 2000); Roger Chartier, Alain Boureau and Cécile Dauphin, *Correspondence: Models of Letter-Writing from the Middle Ages to the Nineteenth Century*, trans. Christopher Woodall (Cambridge, 1997); Pierre Albert, *Correspondre: Jadis et naguère* (Paris, 1997).

The author reiterated his devotion to the addressee, and his willingness to fulfil his orders promptly. He assured him of his continuing respect, requested his friendship and wished him perfect health. Often, he would insist on regular and detailed correspondence, expressing the hope that the recipient would continue to have faith in his sincerity. Such sentiments were usually deferred to the letter's closing, though exceptions abound. The end of the letter was marked by a subscription. This contained a formal and self-deprecatory statement of the author's fidelity, often in abbreviated form. Variations on 'your very humble and obedient servant' were popular in letters in Portuguese, English and French. The closing was always rounded off by the author's signature, followed not infrequently by a short postscript.

The letter's date and place of composition, often set apart in some obvious fashion, tended to be near its start or its end, either by the addressee's name or the author's signature. It is notable that the contents of the preamble and closing were generally devoid of references to the cosmos or divine figures. Only letters in Portuguese deviated from this pattern. In these, realms beyond the mundane might be invoked in the main body, the preamble or closing, as expressions in the vein of 'I ask God to protect you [so as to] see you again in this place in good condition.'[19] Normally, however, references to divine figures were confined to a terse formula at the letter's very end. This immediately preceded the closing statement and signature, and were usually modelled on: 'may God preserve you' (*Deus guarde*) or 'may God preserve you for many years' (*Deus guarde a vossa magestade muitos anos*).

In contrast to personal letters in the Latin script, divine figures were prominent in correspondence written in Arabic and Persian.[20] The preamble, in particular, was God's special domain. Generally much more elaborate and regimented than in Latin-script letters, the preamble extended from the opening character (or words) of the letter to the

[19] MssOcc/NAF/9003: 104.

[20] All the major Arabic-script languages of the region have a long tradition of writing about epistolography and ornate prose, variously called *inshā'* and *tarassul*. Good studies of this tradition include Momin Mohiuddin, *Chancellery and Persian Epistolography under the Mughals: From Babar to Shah Jahan (1526–1658)* (Calcutta, 1971); Riazul Islam, *Calendar of Documents on Indo-Persian Relations (1500–1750)*, vol. I (Tehran, 1979), 1–54; Ishtiyaq Ahmad Zilli, 'Development of *Inshā* literature till the end of Akbar's reign', in Muzaffar Alam, Françoise Delvoye and Marc Gaborieu (eds.), *The Making of Indo-Persian Culture: Indian and French Studies* (New Delhi, 2000), 309–50; Antoine-Louis-Henri Polier, *A European Experience of the Mughal Orient: the I'jaz-i arsalani (Persian letters 1773–1779) of Antoine-Louis-Henri Polier*, trans. and intro. by Muzaffar Alam and Seema Alavi (New Delhi, 2001), 13–17.

formulaic transition to its main body.[21] Non-Christian authors tended to start it with an invocation. This could be a single character – the letter *alif* – or word – *huwa* (he) – that intimated God's presence, or it could be a chain of words, normally in Arabic, praising him.[22] Such invocations were often absent in correspondence between Christians indigenous to the region, as well as by sojourning residents from western Europe. There would follow the initial specification of the addressee, frequently accompanied by a short blessing, in which God was asked to protect him or grant him success.[23] This could be written in a superscription – which might begin immediately or with a linking term, typically *ilā* (to) or *ba'd salām* (after peace). It was just as common, however, for it to be merged, at least visually, with the main body of the text.

The addressee's name was noted at this point, if it was noted at all. Surrounding it would be his titles and respectful or intimate epithets, common examples of which are listed in Chapter 1 on cognitive patterns. The titles and epithets highlighted the recipient's genealogy, his achievements and standing within the community or polity, and gestured towards the author's understanding of their relationship. These, and the blessings, were repeated and elaborated in the next portion of the preamble, which was usually initiated by a brief linking term.[24] It was here that the author presented himself. This was often done indirectly by means of his ties to the correspondent.[25] The author might begin this portion of the preamble by declaring his desire to meet the addressee[26] and expressing the hope that he is in fine health.[27] God would be

[21] The preamble often constituted a large fraction of the letter. It made up the bulk when the main aim of the letter was to maintain personal relations between the correspondents. Preambles as the dominant motif were thus common in letters of thanks, blessings or congratulations, or messages enquiring after the recipient's health, yearning for a speedy reunion or conveying feelings for him.

[22] The tradition of using *huwa* to signal God is generally associated with Sufi traditions. Expressions that were commonly used to invoke and praise God include: الحمد لاالله (praise to *allāh*); الحمد لاالله مستحقه (praise to *allāh* to which he is entitled); هو الله (he is *allāh*); هو الله وحقه (he is *allāh* and this is his right); هو الله تعالى (he is *allāh* the high); بسم الله الرحمن الرحيم (in the name of *allāh*, the merciful, the compassionate); باسم الله الرحمن الرحيم وبه مستعين (in the name of *allāh*, the merciful, the compassionate and through him one seeks assistance).

[23] Examples may be found in Chapter 2 on the cosmic order.

[24] The correspondence reveals a number of terms could be used as the link, such as غب (after); اولا (first); امين (amen); بعد هذا ,بعده or بعد از (after); سبب تسطير الحروف (the reason for writing these letters); ميرساند (it is submitted).

[25] One of the very few instances of a letter in which the author names himself explicitly at this point is BL/Lansdowne/1046, doc. 11.

[26] 'Let it be known [that I have] eagerness for a meeting [with you].' BL/Lansdowne/1046, doc. 49.

[27] '[I have a] great desire [to see] your auspicious vision completely well and healthy.' BL/Lansdowne/1046, doc. 68.

repeatedly invoked, in order to be praised and beseeched. Especially in letters between intimates, the author might ask his correspondent not to forget him or neglect him in his prayers; the author in turn reassured the recipient that he was thinking of him and praying for him.[28] Frequently, he would comment on his own health and affairs, perhaps noting that he had been prompted to do so by his correspondent's own concern in his previous letter to him.[29] Thanking God that all is well, he might add 'may your condition not just be like that but better than that'.[30] The preamble was also where the author could remark on any recently arrived letters, or on letters expected that had yet to arrive. Soon after receiving a letter, a father wrote to his son:

> You are informed that ... on the date that I set off from Isfahan to go to [my] uncle, no letter had arrived from you. I was extremely upset when, praise be to *allāh*, on the fourth day of the month Sha'bān of the year 1160 (11 August 1747), [your letter] arrived [just as] my sad heart was seeking [news of] your circumstances.[31]

However, it was rare for an author to give details here of their correspondence's contents, provenance, itinerary or date of receipt (though they might appear later in the main body).[32] The preamble was used instead to relay other kinds of information. For this purpose, writers had a wide range of models available for them to select and adapt to their particular needs. Despite being constrained by rules of etiquette, preambles in personal letters in the Arabic script exhibited great diversity. They could be simple and brief – or long, intricate and florid. They presented the writer with a stage on which to display his rhetorical skills, establish his credentials and proclaim his relationship to the addressee. The information that a preamble communicated helped assure the recipient of the letter's authenticity.

The transition to the main body of the letter was indicated by one of several well-known characters, words or phrases.[33] There was no upper

[28] BL/Lansdowne/1046, doc. 60. [29] BL/Lansdowne/1046, docs. 68, 72, 73.

[30] BL/Lansdowne/1046, docs. 68, 72. [31] BL/Lansdowne/1046, doc. 9.

[32] An exception to this may be found in BL/Lansdowne/1046, doc. 7, which notes the date of receipt in the preamble.

[33] Among the commonly used characters and words in Arabic were: وقد (And); ويا (And O ...); انه (That); هو انه (It is that); امين انه (Amen. That); وبعده (And after that). As for phrases in Arabic and Persian, they centred on the notion of informing the recipient: وثاني تعلم يا ... ان (And secondly you are informed, O ..., that); ثم نخبر سعادتكم (Then we inform your grace); ونعرفكم بان (And we inform you that); والذي نعلم به جنابكم السعيد اعلمكم الباري بكل خير بان (And that we inform your felicitous honour – may the creator inform you fully – that; BL/Lansdowne/1046, doc. 67); بخدمت ... ميدارد كه (I submit to ... that); معلوم بوده باشد (It is made known); مخفى نماند (Let it not be hidden); براى اطلاع معروض ميدارد (To inform [you], I submit); بموفق عرض بندگانحضور ميرساند (For giving success through a report for the servant's presence, I submit; BL/Lansdowne/1046, doc. 39).

limit to the length of this part; the letters I have examined show that the main body could range from a few short lines to several long pages. The end of this part, and the shift to the closing, was normally abrupt, without any of the fanfare associated with the earlier transition from the preamble to the main body.[34] The only common exceptions that I have seen are cases where the author was asking a superior for a favour. So as to highlight his humble status in such cases, he might mark the shift with: 'to say anything more would lack civility'[35] or 'I am not able to express its meaning and [to attempt] to write it would lack civility'.[36] A formulaic apology for penning the letter itself performed a similar function: 'But hopefully I will be forgiven. How can I [truly] write about the condition of my *dil*? [Only] *khudā* is the possessor and witness.'[37]

Unlike the preamble, the closing tended to be simple and short. This rule was not followed only in instances where the author chose to dwell on greetings, a frequent occurrence in correspondence between intimates. Indeed, as discussed in Chapter 4, this provided an opportunity to mention kindred, friends and neighbours – both at the addressee's end and the author's own – who had not previously been noted. These greetings tended to be short and stylised, patterned on 'he salutes you',[38] 'he sends you greetings',[39] 'he blesses you',[40] 'may our love reach you'.[41] They would be extended, however, if the author, or those relaying their salutations via the author, wished to communicate a personalised message. Their recipients could be named explicitly, though often with a nickname rather than the given name. It was as common, however, to refer to them in kinship terms, or by means of their relationship to the addressee. If the correspondents were working associates, the author might announce his willingness to undertake any commission the recipient might have for him. At the same time, the correspondence suggests this sentiment was more muted the higher the author's status relative to the recipient.

The closing of the letter ended with a brief prayer or salutation, to which the author's personal seal was often added. The prayer stated, or gestured towards, the writer's desire for the addressee's long life and prosperity.[42] The salutation was seldom more than a word or two in length, and usually abbreviated or, especially in Persian, took the form

[34] Though in one Persian letter, the end of the main body is announced by the formulaic 'what more do I need to write' (زیاده چه نویسم).
[35] BL/Lansdowne/1046, doc. 18. [36] BL/Lansdowne/1046, doc. 50.
[37] BL/Lansdowne/1046, doc. 40. [38] یسلم علیک [39] یهدیک السلام
[40] بخدمت . . . دعا و سلام, دعا خواند
[41] کسی را سلام برسد, کسی را دعا برسد, بلغ دعاءنا الی, بلغ محبتنا الی
[42] This was often signalled by simply writing 'more' or 'what is more' (زیاده, زیاده چه). When expressed more fully, we find 'what more [needs to be submitted save] may you live long

of a logogram. Typical examples include: ‘peace’ (*salām*), ‘blessing’ (*duʿā*), ‘eternity’ (*bāqī*), ‘what more’ (*ziyādah chih*), ‘what more needs submitting’ (*ziyādah chih ʿarḍdāsht*), ‘what more need I write’ (*ziyādah chih nivīsad*). Even after its formal end, letters might continue with one or more ‘postscripts’. These were set apart from each other, and from the main body of the letter, by empty space or the unusual directionality of their writing. Finally, there was no clear-cut rule about the location of the letter’s date and place of composition (if present, that is). Some dates were noted at the very end of the letter, others at its beginning or middle, in the centre of the page or close to an edge. They could also be found on the envelope. Their mobility notwithstanding, dates were usually distinguished in some obvious fashion.[43]

Unsurprisingly, the contents of the main body of letters in the Arabic and Latin script were as varied as the situations in which the writers found themselves. But amidst this variety there were two topics seldom passed over in silence: the regularity and frequency of correspondence was one, and the quantity of news communicated was the other.[44] Formulaic requests for regular, frequent and detailed correspondence could be found in the main body of the letter or in its closing. Authors could be very forthright in making these requests of those lower in status. More often, however, they would be couched in terms of a gentle but insistent plea: ‘don’t be slow in [sending your] letters for us’,[45] ‘don’t cut us off from your letters’,[46] ‘don’t hold back your letters from us’.[47]

These requests were complemented and reinforced by complaints that the recipient was being remiss in keeping up his end of the correspondence.[48] The resulting silence and absence of news was, so it was often claimed, a

and be prosperous’ (زیاده چه عمر و دولت باد); ‘what more [needs to be submitted save] may your life and prosperity always increase’ (زیاده چه عمر و دولت در ترقی باد); ‘may you and your prosperity continue’ (باقي و عمرکم باقي); ‘what more needs to be submitted [save] may the whole sun shine brightly on [your] life [and] prosperity’ (زیاده چه عرض تمام افتاب عمر دولت تابان باد).

43 Within BL/Lansdowne/1046, docs. 9, 28 provide the only instances of the date of composition being written into the body of the text.

44 Cf. the account of the contents of letters exchanged between merchants in Shelomo D. Goitein, *A Mediterranean Society: the Jewish Communities of the Arab World as Portrayed in the Documents of the Cairo Geniza*, vol. I, *Economic Foundations* (Berkeley, CA, 1967), 164–9.

45 BL/Lansdowne/1046, doc. 77.

46 BL/Lansdowne/1046, docs. 65, 72.

47 BL/Lansdowne/1046, doc. 68.

48 ABdR/J/01J/138 (9 September 1776); BL/Lansdowne/1046, docs. 65, 66, 68, 77; MssOcc/NAF/9004: 164–5; MssOcc/NAF/9005: 64–7; MssOcc/NAF/9038: 2–27, 29–36, 38–9; TNSA/Persian Records/114: 19; TNSA/Persian Records/112: 4; XCHR/MHR/Correspondence (outgoing) (22 January–9 November 1779); XCHR/MHR/Correspondence (outgoing) (5 March 1785); XCHR/MHR/Correspondence (outgoing) (13 January–15 April 1791).

perpetual source of worry, unhappiness and pain for his intimates. As he could so easily assuage them by being more conscientious, the responsibility and guilt was thus the recipient's.[49] Authors would bemoan the fact that their correspondent's letters, even when sufficient in number, did not contain enough information[50] or neglected discussion of key subjects.[51] Whether or not they were justified in levelling such complaints, authors invariably stated their desire that letters be dispatched to them on a regular basis.[52] When they further demanded that correspondence be exchanged as frequently as possible,[53] this meant at least once a season (*mawsim*).[54] And only if the letter conveyed news about the current situation in the most fulsome detail – a common enough wish[55] – would the recipient be able to rest easy,[56] maybe even derive pleasure from reading it.[57] Collectively, these rhetorical techniques served as powerful reminders to both recipient and author of the foundational role of regular, frequent and detailed correspondence in sustaining relationships over large distances, and of the concomitant need for active effort on both sides. This was symbolised by a resident of Najaf in 1747. Despite the pain being caused by his injured hand,[58] he forced himself to 'write these two words in my own hand in order to remove [any possible] worry' on the recipient's part.[59] The effort was well worth it, whatever the limitations of the written word.[60] As several authors put it, 'correspondence is [equal to] half a meeting' (*al-mukātabāt niṣf al-mulāqāt*).[61]

These rhetorical techniques were complemented by specific items of information so as to facilitate communication. The receipt of any letter would almost always be acknowledged.[62] This acknowledgement was sometimes accompanied by a statement giving its date of arrival at the final destination,[63] perhaps with a note of its

[49] BL/Lansdowne/1046, docs. 65, 66, 68, 77; MssOcc/NAF/9011: 36–7; MssOcc/NAF/9005: 64–7.

[50] BL/Lansdowne/1046, docs. 65, 71.

[51] BL/Lansdowne/1046, doc. 71.

[52] BL/Lansdowne/1046, doc. 78; MssOcc/NAF/9005: 2–9; MssOcc/NAF/9038: 2–27, 29–31, 33–5.

[53] MssOcc/NAF/9011: 36–7.

[54] BL/Lansdowne/1046, docs. 65, 71.

[55] BL/Lansdowne/1046, docs. 12, 74, 78; MssOcc/NAF/9005: 2–9; MssOcc/NAF/9038: 2–27, 29–31, 33–5.

[56] BL/Lansdowne/1046, doc. 12.

[57] MssOcc/NAF/9038: 2–27, 29–30, 32–3, 36, 38–9.

[58] BL/Lansdowne/1046, docs. 22, 25, 33.

[59] BL/Lansdowne/1046, doc. 22.

[60] Shāh Kawthar, for example, noted that 'language (*zabān*) is incapable of properly thanking the just appreciator'. BL/Lansdowne/1046, doc. 1.

[61] MssOcc/NAF/9005: 2–9. For other examples, see HAG/Persian Documents, doc. 27 (الكتاب نصف الملاقات); MssOcc/NAF/9001: 67–70; MssOcc/NAF/9002: 12–13.

[62] BL/Lansdowne/1046, docs. 12, 65, 69, 71, 75, 78; MssOcc/NAF/9005: 2–9; MssOcc/NAF/9005: 64–7; MssOcc/NAF/9009: 43; MssOcc/NAF/9038: 2–27, 29–31, 33–5; TNSA/Persian Records/112: 10a; TNSA/Persian Records/113: 18.

[63] MssOcc/NAF/9059 (6 March 1769); TNSA/Persian Records/110, 34; XCHR/MHR/Correspondence (incoming) (5 December 1777); XCHR/MHR/Correspondence

date of composition[64] and brief remarks on the latter stages of its journey,[65] on the courier who delivered it[66] or on the intermediary who had passed it on.[67] Details might also be given about previous letters that had been written and dispatched,[68] letters that ought to have arrived by now but which had failed to do so,[69] plans for writing further letters in the near future,[70] and letters recently, or soon to be, sent to others of interest to both parties.[71]

Markers that uniquely identified a letter to the recipient's satisfaction were integrated into the epistolary templates discussed above. One of the most important was the date of composition. Several calendars were available in the region for the purposes of dating.[72] While the great majority of letters were given a single date, it is not uncommon to find the equivalent dates given in different calendars, especially in correspondence between individuals hailing from different backgrounds. In the eighteenth century, letters in the Latin script normally adopted the Julian or Gregorian (solar) calendar. Dates in Arabic-script letters, in contrast, were usually written in the Hijri (lunar) calendar. But even in correspondence between Muslims, Arabic-script letters could be dated in calendars other than the Hijri, in conformity with, say, a local tradition. This may be seen in the use of calendars that started with the accession (*julūs*) of a new sovereign. For correspondents who were not Muslims, other calendars were

(incoming) (27 September 1778); XCHR/MHR/Correspondence (incoming) (14 June 1789); XCHR/MHR/Correspondence (outgoing) (18 October 1782).

64 BL/Lansdowne/1046, doc. 10.

65 BL/Lansdowne/1046, docs. 71, 78; MssOcc/NAF/9011: 36–7; MssOcc/NAF/9038: 2–27, 29–30; TNSA/Persian Records/114: 18; XCHR/MHR/Correspondence (outgoing) (1 April 1779); XCHR/MHR/Correspondence (outgoing) (4 February 1791).

66 BL/Lansdowne/1046, docs. 65, 67, 69; MssOcc/NAF/9005: 2–9; MssOcc/NAF/9038: 1, 2–27, 29–30; MssOcc/NAF/9059 (6 March 1769–2 April 1770).

67 MSA/Misc/HCR/MRC/31: 359–85.

68 BL/Lansdowne/1046, doc. 12; MssOcc/NAF/9038: 2–27, 29–30; MssOcc/NAF/9059 (6 March 1769–2 April 1770).

69 BL/Lansdowne/1046, doc. 67; MssOcc/NAF/8992: 87, 88–9; MssOcc/NAF/9011: 36–7; MssOcc/NAF/9038: 32–7, 38–40.

70 BL/Lansdowne/1046, docs. 13, 44, 73, 74; MSA/Misc/HCR/MRC/31: 373; MssOcc/NAF/8996: 46, MssOcc/NAF/9059 (6 March 1769–2 April 1770); XCHR/MHR/Correspondence (incoming) (11 November 1777); XCHR/MHR/Correspondence (incoming) (16 January 1788).

71 BL/Lansdowne/1046, docs. 65, 66, 78; MssOcc/NAF/9038: 2–27, 29–30; MssOcc/NAF/9059 (6 March 1769–2 Apr 1770); XCHR/MHR/Correspondence (incoming) (27 March 1780); XCHR/MHR/Correspondence (incoming) (25 November 1788).

72 Details on some of the main calendars that have been current in the Islamic world are given in S. H. Taqizadeh, 'Various eras and calendars used in the countries of Islam', *Bulletin of the School of Oriental and African Studies* 9:4 (1939), 903–22 and 10:1 (1939), 107–32. Though very useful for its technical details, the list of calendars discussed is not exhaustive.

commonplace. Among Armenians from southern Iraq who wrote in Arabic, for example, letters could be dated in Hijri alone,[73] in both Hijri and the Julian calendar,[74] or solely in the Julian.[75]

As fundamental as dates were the markers that specified the letter's nominal author and intended recipient. The manner in which this was done, however, varied considerably between scripts. In Latin-script correspondence, the author was almost invariably identified by his personal signature composed in his own hand. This was always located underneath the formulas signalling the end of the message. If the author did not have writing literacy in the relevant language, the signature might take the form of a symbol of some kind, like a cross or a circle, or be his fingerprint; otherwise, the signature was his name, perhaps embellished, abbreviated or distorted to such an extent that in effect it became a logogram. Even if the letter was drawn up by a clerk, it would still be its purported author who was expected to sign it in his own hand.[76] Without a signature, aside from the potential difficulties in identifying its authorship, the letter would have been considered incomplete and probably viewed with suspicion by the addressee.

This practice was at its most complex in situations where the stated author was unfamiliar with the language and script of his letter. It is only letters whose main body is in the Latin script, and which were written up by a clerk at the behest of its author, that I have found something akin to signatures in the Arabic script. In such cases, the signature could be accompanied by its transliteration in Latin script. Once Muḥammad Shafīʿ Balūmār's letter in Portuguese for the Kāmat brothers in Goa was ready, he added his signature in Arabic script below the Latin transliteration of his name.[77] Similarly, in situations where the putative author was ignorant of the Arabic-script language in which the document had been composed, he would identify himself in his native language in the manner appropriate to it. The officers, merchants, agents and mariners responsible for a commercial voyage to the Persian Gulf wrote from Cochin in 1748 a collective statement in Persian (see Figure 8). By means of this, they sought to inform their Bengali principals of the current state of affairs. The authors of the documents, together with several local officials, identified themselves in the margin. Those who were conversant with Persian or Arabic used their personal

[73] BL/Lansdowne/1046, doc. 12. [74] BL/Lansdowne/1046, docs. 67, 68.
[75] BL/Lansdowne/1046, docs. 69, 70, 71, 77.
[76] This is most obvious where the text of the letter is in a different handwriting (and pen) from the signature.
[77] The author wrote his name as محمد شفيع بلومار. This is transliterated in the letter, most probably by the clerk, as 'Mahomed Xefy Palamar'. XCHR/MHR/Correspondence (incoming) (2 May 1784).

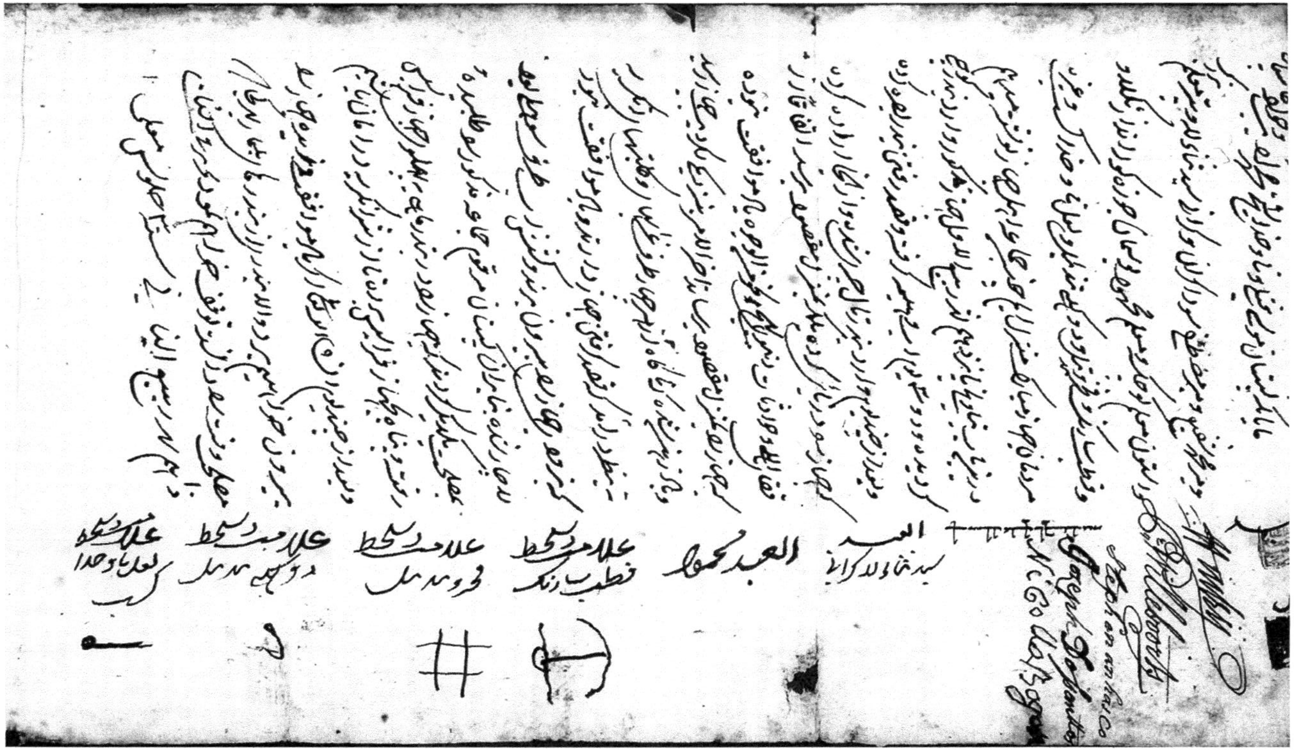

Figure 8. Different kinds of authorial identifiers.
Source: BL/Lansdowne/1046, doc. 5.

seals (containing Arabic-script inscriptions). The others, not being able to write in Persian, opted for other identifiers with which they were more familiar. Two Dutch officials and two Portuguese or Luso-Indian mariners, for example, added their signatures in the Latin script, while an Armenian merchant printed his name in Armenian characters. The remaining 'authors' – all mariners – did not have writing literacy. They preferred to identify themselves through designs of varying intricacy, from what appears to be a stylised anchor to a short line rolled up at one end.[78]

In general, the way in which authorship was ascertained in letters written in Arabic-script languages was very different from those in Latin-script languages. What is abundantly clear is that, in personal correspondence in Persian and Arabic, the authors did *not* reveal themselves through a logographic representation of their names. Moreover, they did not limit themselves to a single type of marker in order to declare or signal their identity. They could choose from among several possibilities which enabled the reader to determine the letter's provenance and authenticity. The name of the author, in keeping with the ambient writing style, might be inserted into the text itself. This would normally be in the preamble that immediately followed the invocation and the specification of the addressee. Commonly, however, the name was found in an eye-catching location away from the main text, say, in the corner of the page or on its reverse side or on the envelope.

A widely accepted and authoritative expression of authorship in Islamicate Eurasia – and the only option for those without literacy – was the seal or signet. This was generally fashioned out of a semi-precious stone, such as garnet, jacinth or agate, which, if worn on the finger, was set in a silver or copper ring. Otherwise, it was mounted on a handle and carried in a pocket or suspended around the neck. The stone, frequently carved into a simple shape like an oval or a square, was engraved with a short inscription. This could be the author's name alone or his name accompanied by a brief motto or pious saying.[79] Take the example of Shāh Kawthar's seal. We find in it the expression: 'The cupbearer of Kawthar like Muḥammad is ʿAlī.'[80] Based on what the Arabist Edward Lane saw while living in Egypt in the early nineteenth century, this kind of seal would have been prepared for use by dabbing 'a little ink . . . upon it with one of the fingers'. The seal would

[78] BL/Lansdowne/1046, doc. 5.

[79] 'Ils portent ordinairement leur nom ou leur devise au doigt, gravée sur une pierre.' Carsten Niebuhr, *Description de l'Arabie, d'après les observations et recherches faites dans le pays même . . .*, vol. I (Paris, 1779), 143. Hanway noted that 'in their rings they wear agats, which generally serve for a seal, on which is frequently engraved their name, and some verse from the Khoran'. Jonas Hanway, *Historical Account of the British Trade over the Caspian Sea . . .*, vol. I (London, 1753), 317.

[80] BL/Lansdowne/1046, doc. 43.

then be 'pressed upon the paper, the person who uses it having first touched his tongue with another finger, and moistened the place in the paper which is to be stamped'.[81] Seals were often added next to their owner's name written out in full, and could be found in the margins, after the closing of the text, on the reverse side of the page or on the letter's cover, alongside the address. (See Figure 9.)

A third type of marker avoided explicit identifiers altogether in favour of invocations or oblique (to us) phrases that sufficed to communicate the letter's authorship. In such instances, the recipient would be able to infer the author's identity by means of the relationship avowed between the two of them within the text. This could range from the simple and obvious ('my son')[82] via the honorific ('the pivot of the two worlds')[83] to the intimate ('the light-of-my-eye, my darling, my life').[84]

Shifting from the author to the recipient, the specification of the individual for whom the letter had been composed was more straightforward in Latin-script languages, and this was true regardless of the author's background. The intended recipient's name would normally be noted at the very top of the page and be repeated on the letter's cover. In a similar fashion, many letters written in Arabic-script languages followed the invocation with an explicit statement of the addressee's name. The name would often be mentioned again on the cover. In the many cases where the addressee's name per se is not given, the chain of attributes marshalled in reference to the recipient – titles, epithets, benedictory formulas – must have sufficed to define his status and relationship to the author, and so identify him uniquely.

Whatever its language or script, once the letter had been written up in neat, its contents were hidden from view and secured. Directions were then added to its cover for delivery to its final destination. (See Figure 10.)

The simplest method in which this was done was by folding up the letter so that its text was no longer visible. Glue or gum was then applied at one or more junctures (which would have to be prised apart by the recipient in order to read it).[85] According to the traveller Carsten Niebuhr, 'the Arabs' folded letters by rolling them up to the desired circumference and then flattening them.[86] After folding, Arabic-script letters were about an inch in height and seldom more than six inches in length. Letters in Latin-script

[81] Edward W. Lane, *Account of the Manners and Customs of the Modern Egyptians ...* (London, 1860), 31.
[82] BL/Lansdowne/1046, doc. 12. [83] BL/Lansdowne/1046, doc. 8.
[84] BL/Lansdowne/1046, docs. 49, 56, 60. [85] ANOM/CdI/A/15 (1755).
[86] Niebuhr, *Description de l'Arabie*, I, 143

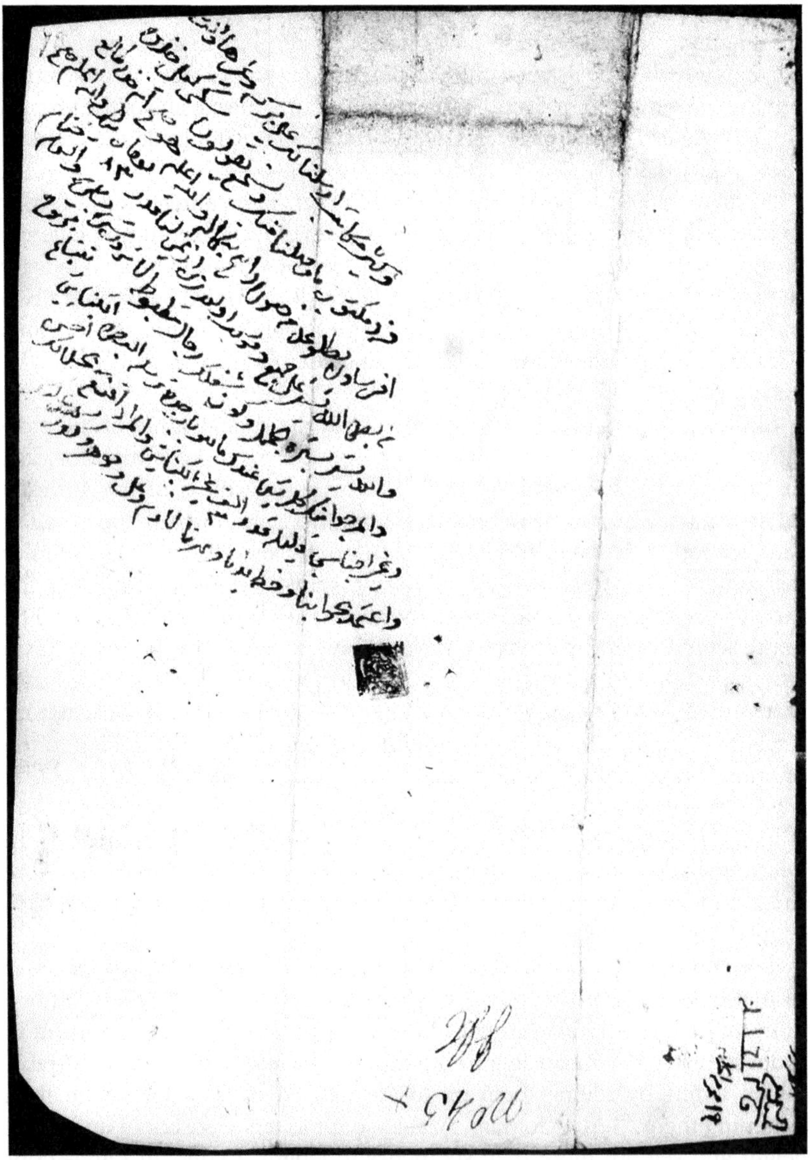

Figure 9. Seal at the end of a letter.
Source: BL/Lansdowne/1046, doc. 74.

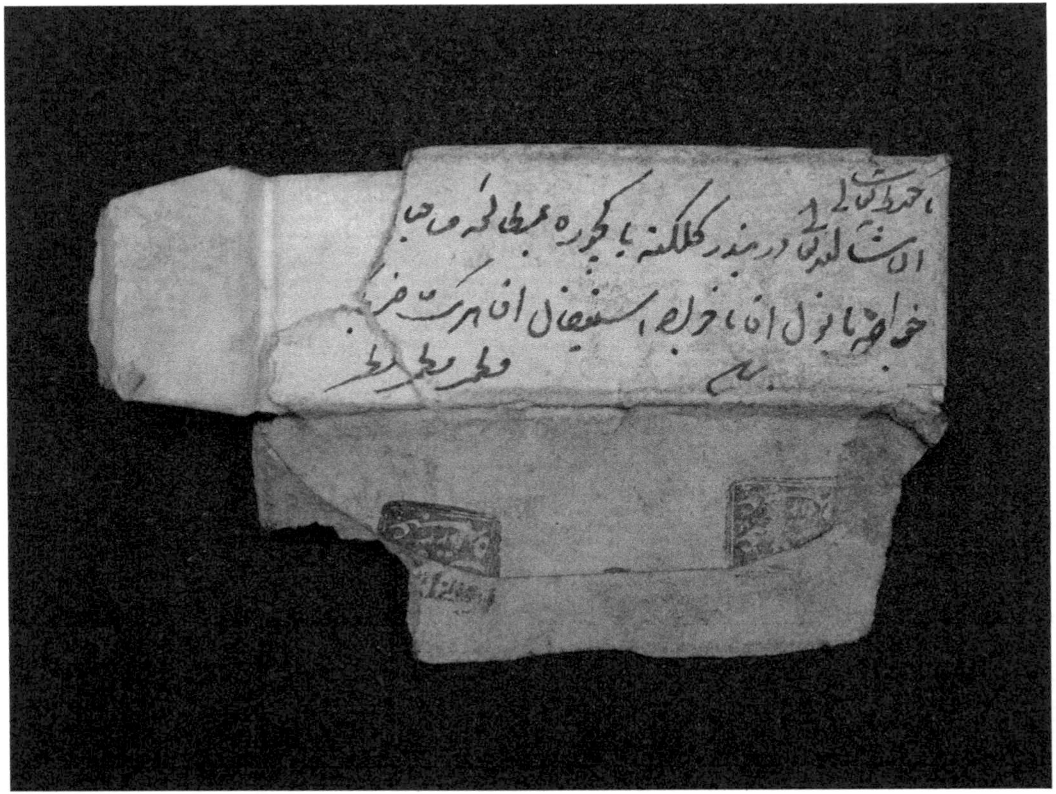

Figure 10. Letter cover, bearing seals and an address.
Source: NA/HCA/32/1833.

languages were on the whole less tightly folded. Of course, this option was available only if there was little or no writing on the reverse side. If there was writing on the reverse side, the practice seems to have been to wrap the folded letter in another piece of paper before securing it.[87] For both Latin-script and Arabic-script letters, this cover was closed by using some kind of glue or by applying a gum at points along its trailing edge. The same gum, which was 'composed of a mixture of galls, burnt rice, and gums' in Iran,[88] could also double as the substrate on which the author's personal seal was imprinted. 'In the temperate provinces of Iran', red or 'Spanish' wax (*cire d'Espagne*) was available as an alternative. The wax was not used elsewhere in the area because, 'in hot countries ... [it] softens and loses it impression'.[89] For letters secured with glue alone, especially for those in the Arabic-script, a standard technique was to print in ink the author's personal seal along the edges that would have to be torn on opening it.

There were several different methods for organising the dispatch of letters. They could be inserted within other documents. The covering document would then be expected to contain guidance for the intermediary on how to deliver the enclosed item to its final destination.[90] Sayyid Muṣṭafā, for example, took care to point out, 'I have written the name of [the recipient] on their letters at the top of [their] address ... To repeat: the letters are enclosed within your letter. It is necessary that you send them to Mīrzā Qubād Beg, son of Mīrzā Murād Beg, who will forward them [to their destination] wherever it may be.'[91] Such instructions might be foreshadowed in the letters themselves. Ḥannā b. ʿAbd al-Dāʾim remarked to his son, 'This letter [which] we have sent you was inside the letter for Khvājah Shukr Allāh ... In the same way, send us your letter inside his letter [for us].'[92] If the courier responsible for transporting these letters had in his charge many such items, they could be placed in separate purses, bundles or boxes,[93] and tied up with string, the knot frequently being stamped with the owner's seal. The name and location of the individual authorised to open it could also be written or etched on the surface.

The differences notwithstanding, the various modes of addressing shared the goal of imparting sufficient detail to enable the recipient, and his current whereabouts, to be correctly ascertained. Latin-script letters

87 It is rare for envelopes to survive; most recipients discarded them after having opened the letter. For an exception, see the collection of envelopes in NA/HCA/32/1833.
88 Hanway, *Historical Account*, I, 317.
89 Niebuhr, *Description de l'Arabie*, I, 143.
90 BL/Lansdowne/1046, docs. 68, 70, 71.
91 BL/Lansdowne/1046, doc. 55.
92 BL/Lansdowne/1046, doc. 68.
93 For examples of different types of packaging, see BL/Lansdowne/1046, doc. 45; MssOcc/NAF/8998: 13; XCHR/MHR/Correspondence (incoming) (27 March 1780); TNSA/Persian Records/111: 32.

rarely carried anything more than the barest statement of the recipient's name and his present location. In the 1780s, a Portuguese merchant directed his Hindu associates in Goa to address any correspondence for him with: 'To Salvador Francisco Cardozo in the Portuguese factory in Surat.' He assured them that this would be enough.[94] In contrast, the modes employed by those who wrote in Arabic-script languages tended to be more elaborate. The address was usually written out in one or more full sentences. It often began with an invocation to God that the letter be conveyed safely to its destination. There would follow a brief account of the intended recipient, who was specified either directly by name or indirectly by means of a series of titles and epithets. In the late 1740s, Sayyid Murtaḍā was given clear instructions in this regard from his father, who was at the time en route to Iraq. 'It is necessary', he wrote from Cochin, 'that on the address of the letter is my name and the name of my father, who is Nāṣir ʿAlī Khān, and that the names of Basra and Karbala are written.'[95]

In situations of uncertainty over the addressee's current location and future itinerary, the author might specify multiple destinations, and give instructions on how to deliver the letter to its final recipient. Shaykh Dīn, who knew only that the recipient was somewhere in Bengal, addressed his 1747 letter from Najaf in the following manner: 'May [this arrive] for the honourable consideration of ... Niʿmat Allāh in Murshidābād or Shāhjahānābād or ʿAẓīmābād or wherever he may be.'[96] Multiple recipients too could be specified. On a purse sealed in Basra in the 1740s, the author had written that it was being sent to Hugli 'for the consideration of... Mīr Sayyid ʿAlī b. Mīr Abū Ṭālib or... Mīrzā Muḥammad Riḍa. And if they are not present, you will deliver [it] to Mānāvīl Aghā ... if it seems that I will not come and collect it myself'.[97] Similarly, Muḥammad Adīb told his son,

May the letter of Sayyid Thanā' Allāh the *kirānī* reach his home by whatever way possible. You will give it either to the hand of Shaykh Bāb Allāh or to the hand of Shaykh Dīn Muḥammad jīyū. By whatever way possible, may [it] reach [its destination]. His son's name is Sayyid Gharīb Allāh. The place [is called] Gharībah, near the *haveli* of... Hidāyat Allāh.[98]

Authors might also name one or more individuals as temporary guardians, in the hope that, with their more up-to-date knowledge of the intended recipient's whereabouts, they would be able to forward the letter

[94] 'Ao Salvador Francisco Cardoza na Feitoria portugueza en Surate – e nenhum titulamario' MHR/Correspondence (incoming) (3 June 1788).
[95] BL/Lansdowne/1046, doc. 56. [96] NA/HCA/32/1833. [97] Ibid.
[98] BL/Lansdowne/1046, doc. 13.

to him. Failing that, it would be waiting for him when he next passed through.[99]

Not infrequently, the cover bore the letter's date of composition and author's name. A 1747 letter in Persian had as its address: 'If *allāh* wishes, may [this letter] arrive for the noble consideration of the prosperous Miyān Aghā Muḥammad Ṣāḥib and Ghulām ʿAlī. The necessary submissions of Muḥammad Adīb were written on the date of sixteenth of the month of Rabīʿ al-thāni. May [God] the high cause [it] to arrive safe and sound from the port of Cochin.'[100] The cover might also contain brief remarks concerning its passage and delivery. On an otherwise blank reverse side of a letter in Arabic written in 1745, the address was given as: 'If *allāh* wishes, may [this letter] reach Basra [and] be received by the hand of Khvājah Masʿūd and through his bounty, may he send it on to Calcutta for the hand of Isrāyīl b. Shakīr Shamʿūn al-Ḥalabī.'[101]

The arrival of a letter was a notable event. It could be a cause for joy too. 'With thanks to [God] ... your illustrious letter arrived. My *jān* was so happy. When my eye fell on your letter, my *dil* was freed from sorrow.'[102] In a similar vein, a kinsman recounted, 'Verily, since your noble, precious letter for your mother reached us with the courier from Basra, it has been the most blessed of moments and most glorious of hours. We have read it and understood its meaning and we have thanked him the high for the soundness of your well-being which is our ultimate desire.'[103]

After the letter had at last found its way to its intended recipient, as long as it was in a familiar language, all that remained to be done was to decipher the text. But this was not always a trivial matter. Bad handwriting, unusual spelling or idiosyncratic grammar could pose major challenges for the reader. Vindrāvan, a Gujarati working as a broker in Mocha in the 1760s, was acutely conscious that his own handwriting and manner of composition left much to be desired. To compensate for this, he would recommend to his non-Gujarati correspondents individuals at their end who would be able to help them make sense of his letters.[104] If the language was *not* familiar to the recipient, however, the letter had to be translated into one that the recipient could read. The task might be undertaken on an ad hoc basis either by a linguist who specialised in such work or by a local resident who happened to know the language. This was routine in situations where it was rare to receive such letters. But if a significant proportion of the correspondence was in unfamiliar

[99] BL/Lansdowne/1046, doc. 45; XCHR/MHR/Correspondence (outgoing) (20 June 1779).
[100] BL/Lansdowne/1046, doc. 13. [101] BL/Lansdowne/1046, doc. 12.
[102] BL/Lansdowne/1046, doc. 22. [103] BL/Lansdowne/1046, doc. 78.
[104] MssOcc/NAF/9038: 6.

languages, and their contents of high enough value, the recipient might well have linguists in his employment, or at least have arrangements in place to ensure ready access to them as and when necessary.

This procedure is illustrated by the experience of Bernard Picot, whom we met earlier in the chapter. In the 1760s and 1770s, Picot received a succession of letters in Arabic. Those that have been preserved were mainly from his brokers and agents in Mocha[105] and Masqat,[106] and from ruling members of the sovereign regime in Oman.[107] As ships from these and other Arabian ports seldom included halts in Mahe or Tellicherry, ports within easy reach of Picot's residence, any correspondence that they might be carrying for him would be delivered by the *nākhudā*, or captain, to an intermediary in one of the larger, more frequented, ports in western India. These could be Bombay, Surat, Cochin, Goa or Calicut, in each of which Picot either maintained an agent or had an agreement with a local associate.

After taking delivery of his letters from Arabia, the intermediary was quick to notify Picot of their arrival.[108] If unable or unauthorised to find a linguist, these were forwarded to him straightaway. As Picot himself did not have anyone capable of translating the letters into French or Portuguese, the only languages that he knew, they would be sent to a settlement which did possess translators with the appropriate linguistic skills. The Luso-Indian Antonio de Quental occasionally served him in this capacity in Calicut, which was at the time home to several communities conversant with both Arabic and Portuguese. Quental's exchange with Picot also reveals that there could be other, less predictable, difficulties associated with translation. A commission received in 1778 proved especially trying in this regard. He explained to Picot,

> It was necessary for four people to read [the letter for him from his brokers in Mocha] because it is so badly written. The letter is in Arabic, but whoever wrote it does not know the language well. You must not mind the fact that some words cannot be expressed with greater clarity. It was necessary to translate according to what was written and you must make sense of it as [best] you can.[109]

[105] Jīvan, Ḥabisha, Candu Qugu and Jabel. MssOcc/NAF/9005: 64–7; MssOcc/NAF/9011: 36–7.
[106] Narayandas. MssOcc/NAF/9005: 2–9.
[107] Imām Aḥmad b. Sa'id b. Aḥmad b. Muḥammad al-Bū Sa'īdī and Amīr Khalfān b. Muḥammad b. Abd Allah al-Bū Saīdī. MssOcc/NAF/9001: 67–70; MssOcc/NAF/9005: 2–9.
[108] MssOcc/NAF/9011: 68; XCHR/MHR/Correspondence (outgoing) (5 March–2 December 1777).
[109] MssOcc/NAF/9011: 67.

On being translated into Portuguese or French, the letters were dispatched, accompanied by their originals, to Picot with the next pattamar travelling to Mahe or Tellicherry.[110] If in Portuguese, the letters were then translated into French by a linguist either in Picot's service or borrowed from his British associates in nearby Tellicherry. Some of the French translations were then entered into a letter book.[111] As for the Arabic originals, they were preserved elsewhere, together with their translations into Portuguese or French.[112]

The foregoing account of the epistolary techniques and conventions dispersed within Islamicate Eurasia reveals that they were embedded in a dense communicative web. In being a conduit through which information about a letter's current status was transmitted, in having the strength and malleability to withstand the shock of unexpected developments, in relaying the paramount importance of diligence on all sides – by virtue of these qualities, this web played a critical role in reducing many of the risks attending the passage of correspondence to manageable levels.

The analysis of the letters written in Arabic-script and Latin-script languages has resulted in two findings which are worthy of note. The first is that, despite the diversity in the backgrounds of those active in the arena, there are only a couple of systemic differences in their approach to corresponding over large distances. One difference is that, whatever the author's ethnicity or subjecthood, letters composed in the Latin script invariably terminated with his signature written in his own hand. In contrast, the authors of Arabic-script letters were identified by their personal seals, or by their name inscribed within the body of the text, or by the relationship avowed by them to the recipient. The other difference pivots on the manner in which correspondence was addressed; letters composed in the Arabic script bore addresses that were substantially more elaborate and detailed than those in the Latin script. These two differences aside, the choice of script seems to have exerted no meaningful influence on the techniques commonly used to signal, monitor and verify the letter's passage, on the role played by drafts, clerks and translators, or on the ensemble of markers normally deployed for ascertaining the recipient. In other words, there was an outstanding degree of

110 XCHR/MHR/Correspondence (outgoing) (15 July–5 August 1777).

111 MssOcc/NAF/9038. From among the several thousand letters received by Picot during his residence on the Malabar coast, only those from his associates who corresponded in Gujarati, Persian or Arabic, and which had to be translated into a language that he could comprehend, had their French translations entered into a letter book. I presume that their special treatment was due to their rarity and the linguistic challenges involved in getting them translated.

112 MssOcc/NAF/9001: 67–70; MssOcc/NAF/9005: 2–9, 64–7; MssOcc/NAF/9011: 36–7.

similarity among letters characterised by scripts formally of very different provenance.

Perhaps more extraordinary is the second finding to emerge from this section's analysis: the vehicle for the differences that *did* exist in the letters from the period was the script. The vehicle was not, as one might expect, the ethnicity or subjecthood or indeed any other cultural trait of the author. Nor was it the language in which the letter was composed. Rather, the evidence suggests that, notwithstanding his native language, the author readily adopted the visual aesthetic, rhetorical norms and epistolary template of the script – Arabic or Latin – in which the final version of the letter was to be written. Where the script of the target language differed from the author's own, the original draft underwent several transformations before being dispatched; in the course of its phased composition, it was extensively re-articulated, in both form and content.

Intermediation by brokers and agents

Recourse to intermediation was one of the quintessential attributes of circulation and exchange over large distances. India and the Islamic heartlands in the eighteenth century offer plenty of support for this claim. Staying with the topic of the previous section for a moment, the passage of letters was monitored by intermediaries who informed their authors, and sometimes the intended recipients too, about their past and future movements. This was possible because intermediaries had privileged access to several kinds of information. Communicating this information to their principals was among their most crucial duties. Intermediaries might be required to notify them of their letter's safe delivery,[113] or of its arrival and onward journey.[114] Details might also be given about letters that happened to be in transit, and in the care of others in the area.[115] And if there were any unforeseen difficulties in the letter's passage, principals would be told as soon as possible.[116]

These were the ways in which intermediaries were integral to communication within the arena. But their significance ranged far beyond communication. This stems from their particular qualities: they were well versed in the locally dominant languages and lingua francas; they

[113] BL/Lansdowne/1046, docs. 67, 71, 78; TNSA/Persian Records/109: 62; TNSA/Persian Records/114: 18; XCHR/MHR/Correspondence (incoming) (20 November 1788).

[114] BL/Lansdowne/1046, doc. 67; MssOcc/NAF/9004: 164–5; MssOcc/NAF/9038: 2–27, 29–30, 32–3, 36, 38–9; TNSA/Persian Records/114: 18.

[115] MssOcc/NAF/9009: 62, 67, 75–7.

[116] MssOcc/NAF/9007: 169–70.

were familiar with the conventions governing commercial dealings where they resided; they had good ties with the relevant power-holders and money-men; and they were acquainted with the most recent intelligence. For these reasons, intermediaries could – and often did – perform multiple roles for their principals.[117] The intermediaries who figure most prominently in the modern scholarly literature were members of ethnic communities which formed far-flung diasporas.[118] But not all of them need be so far flung. The Parsis of Bombay exemplify this.[119] By the 1770s, a sizeable fraction of them had developed close relations with the English East India Company, and with many British merchants and ship-owners. Owing to dispersed knowledge of their ties, they were sought out by foreigners and locals alike who wanted a partner, buyer or seller from within the British community. One such Parsi was Burjorji Shapurji. In 1770, the Bombay resident Dorabji Fadonji asked him to find out whether David Bristow, the purser on board an East Indiaman, could be persuaded to freight a cargo of ginger to Mocha and sell it there for his account. A few days later, accompanied by Burjorji, Bristow went to Dorabji's warehouse in order to examine the ginger. During the ensuing negotiation, Burjorji acted as both match-maker and interpreter.[120] A number of Gujarati associations occupied an analogous

[117] As a result of their particular advantages, intermediaries also acted as interlockers between the ruling elites and those elements of their polity of interest to them that did not fall within their purview. The topic is discussed in Christopher A. Bayly, 'Knowing the country: empire and information', *Modern Asian Studies* 27:1 (1993), 3–43; Christopher A. Bayly, *Empire and Information: Intelligence Gathering and Social Communication in India, 1780–1870* (Cambridge, 1996); Muzaffar Alam and Sanjay Subrahmanyam, 'Witnesses and agents of empire: eighteenth-century historiography and the world of the Mughal *munshī*', *Journal of the Economic and Social History of the Orient* 53:1–2 (2010), 393–423.

[118] As the scholarly literature would have it, the diasporas par excellence in the early modern world were Jewish and Armenian. The recent work on them includes Jonathan I. Israel, *Diasporas within a Diaspora: Jews, Crypto-Jews and the World Maritime Empires, 1540–1740* (Leiden, 2002); Francesca Trivellato, *The Familiarity of Strangers: the Sephardic Diaspora, Livorno, and Cross-Cultural Trade in the Early Modern Period* (New Haven, CT, 2009); Ina Baghdiantz McCabe, *Shah's Silk for Europe's Silver: the Eurasian Trade of the Julfa Armenians in Safavid Iran and India (1530–1750)* (Atlanta, GA, 2002); Sebouh D. Aslanian, *From the Indian Ocean to the Mediterranean: the Global Trade Networks of Armenian Merchants from New Julfa* (Berkeley, CA, 2010). On diasporas more generally, see Ina Baghdiantz McCabe, Gelina Harlaftis and Ionna Pepelasis Minoglou (eds.), *Diaspora Entrepreneurial Networks: Four Centuries of History* (Oxford, 2005).

[119] The importance of the Parsi community as intermediaries is discussed in Amalendu Guha, 'More about the Parsi Sheths: their roots, entrepreneurship and comprador role, 1650–1918', in Dwijendra Tripathi (ed.), *Business Communities of India* (New Delhi, 1984), 109–50; David L. White, 'Parsis in the commercial world of western India, 1700–1750', *Indian Economic and Social History Review* 24:2 (1987), 183–203.

[120] MSA/Misc/HCR/MRC/29: 575–6.

situation in Surat.[121] In 1773, the British merchant-official George Perrot instructed his broker, Kirparam Bhairam, to arrange a deal on his behalf with Maulana Fakhr al-Dīn, a local Shī'ī worthy. The negotiation that followed was undertaken entirely by Kirparam: he discussed terms with the Maulana, conveyed messages between the two sides and formalised the agreement without the principals ever needing to meet in person.[122]

Most intermediaries confined themselves to dealings with those who did not exercise sovereign power. But settlements also had residents who had carved out an expertise in acting as a bridge between outsiders and the local ruling elites. This subset of intermediaries, who were often formally recognised as such, seldom belonged to the same community as the rulers. Their relationships were instead founded on their status and experience, and their patient nurturing of contacts, not uncommonly over several generations. In return for a fee, they would help their principals negotiate with the sovereign and his officials. The brothers Veṅkateśa and Nārāyaṇa Kāmat, leading members of an established family of merchants-brokers and landowners in Goa, inherited an array of ties from their father in the 1760s. One of them was with José Teixeira de Mendouça, a Portuguese merchant based in Mangalore. Mendouça leveraged his privileged across to the governing cadre in order to convey messages between the Kāmats and the settlement's higher officials. He also supplied his Goan principals with current information about local prices, and kept them abreast of any other news that might have a bearing on their interests. He was not, however, given authority to negotiate with Mangalore's officials for the purchase of pepper, the area's major cash crop. For this task, the Kāmats preferred to send one of their agents directly from Goa.[123]

The variety exhibited by the relationships between intermediaries and their principals means that they cannot be reduced to simple patterns. Principals could select as intermediaries those who were close to them. If so, they would frequently be members of the same family: brothers

[121] For further details, see Ashin Das Gupta, *Indian Merchants and the Decline of Surat, c. 1700–1750* (Wiesbaden, 1979); Michelguglielmo Torri, 'In the deep blue sea: Surat and its merchant class during the Dyarchic Era (1759–1800)', *Indian Economic and Social History Review* 19: 3–4 (1982), 267–300; Lakshmi Subramanian, 'Capital and crowd in a declining Asian port city: the Anglo-Bania order and the Surat riots of 1795', *Modern Asian Studies* 19:2 (1985), 205–37; Lakshmi Subramanian, 'Banias and the British: the role of indigenous credit in the process of imperial expansion in western India in the second half of the eighteenth century', *Modern Asian Studies* 21:3 (1987), 473–510; Ghulam A. Nadri, *Eighteenth-Century Gujarat: the Dynamics of its Political Economy, 1750–1800* (Leiden and Boston, 2009).

[122] MSA/Misc/HCR/MRC/34: 507–9.

[123] XCHR/MHR/Correspondence (incoming) (30 October 1781).

working for each other, sons acting on behalf of fathers, wives representing their absent husbands. Beyond the family, there was a clear preference for agents and brokers from within one's own intimate community. This was standard practice among Gujarati Jains, Iraqi Armenians, Bengali Shīʿīs, Cochin Jews, Najafi Sufis, Bombay Parsis and western Europeans. But this preference for intimates must be set against the numerous relationships driven largely by mutual self-interest that transcended ethnic markers of difference.

Intermediaries were in short ubiquitous within the arena; thanks to their particular qualities, there was frequent recourse to them by those active in circulation and exchange. At the same time, the relationship between an intermediary and his principal was rarely straightforward. This is because of the asymmetries inherent to it. Most of these asymmetries turned on the intermediary knowing more about his principal's affairs locally than the principal, who was usually far away. This was compounded by the constraints on the distant principal to act, even if fully aware of the current situation. The arena's participants grappled with this fundamental problem on a daily basis. They resolved it to their practical satisfaction on three levels that reinforced each other. On one level, discussed in the previous chapter, great importance was attached to an individual's reputation, together with widespread acceptance of the procedures, rules and principles for settling potential disputes. On a second level, an intermediary would be given considerable latitude to act as he saw fit in light of his own knowledge of the local conditions. For the principal, to do so was a pragmatic, if inevitable, response to the basic limits within which he operated. For the intermediary, echoing a point made in Chapter 5, this was in keeping with the entrepreneurial mind-set expected of him. In consequence, he had to be attentive to the possibly negative consequences for his principal's interests of unforeseen developments – as well as to the profitable ventures that these might give rise to in the near future. On a third level, to which I return below, care was taken over the terms on which – and the manner in which – the services of a broker or agent were obtained. They could be employed on a permanent basis, for a fixed period of time or for the duration of a single transaction. Intermediaries enjoyed authority that ranged across the spectrum, from merely initiating contact with potential buyers or sellers to full power of attorney. And for these services, they could be paid in the form of a salary, commission, fee or privileges.

A basic practical challenge faced by all those seeking intermediaries was how to identify someone appropriate and then make contact with him. This was relatively easy for an intermediary chosen from within the intimate community; the potential intermediary would already be a familiar figure, his strengths and weaknesses common knowledge. The challenge was much more acute for outsiders for whom any intermediary was essentially a stranger. How such individuals typically met this challenge is treated in Chapter 6 on the political order within the framework of reputation and creditworthiness. As detailed there, a would-be employer could find out about potential intermediaries in a given locality through up-to-date manuals borrowed from associates or available for purchase. Much more commonly, however, this information was picked up as a matter of course by virtue of their involvement in networks in which it was widely dispersed. All that needed to be done was to get in touch. Chapter 6 also details the ways in which this happened, either directly by, say, sending a letter out of the blue or indirectly through, for example, a mutual acquaintance.

Making successful contact between strangers who stood to benefit from one another was perhaps the most difficult step of all in establishing a relationship. So once it had been established, the individuals concerned would take care to prevent it lapsing. This is why we see letters being exchanged regularly whose main purpose was to remind the recipient of the author's existence, and his readiness and willingness to serve. In 1747, Jawhar Darankal wrote to Ṣāliḥ Uzmalī in Calcutta,

> With the arrival of this letter with whoever is heading [towards you], we inform you [that] whatever you want, we will do it for you ... Whatever interest or need reveals [itself to you] on this side, tell us [and] we will undertake it for you upon notification. And do not cut us off from your auspicious news. We request its arrival.[124]

In a more poetic register, similar sentiments were expressed in 1747 to Muḥammad ʿAlī Khān in Bengal:

> This letter is [sent] in the revered service of that kind, true friend. And whatever you have done and do and will do, [God] knows that it is etched in my *dil*. And no matter that has been written, verily, no other work is being done for any other gentleman which is greater than that effort [we make] for you. This work comes from you ... And for each kind of plan that afterwards you will also embark upon, it will be the fount of skill and the perfection of valour and success. But seemingly the instructions we have from you are so modest that I am unable to express [myself] in words and writing.[125]

Heuristically, intermediaries may be subdivided into brokers and agents. But in so doing, it should be borne in mind that this distinction was rarely strict: an individual could be engaged as a broker for several clients and, at the same time, act as a local agent for others. The typical

[124] BL/Lansdowne/1046, doc. 75. [125] BL/Lansdowne/1046, doc. 16.

circumstances of a broker and agent did, however, differ in important respects. Brokers were on the whole permanent or long-term residents of the settlement where they had acquired their valued expertise.[126] They belonged to particular families or communities, such as the Gujarati *baniyās* in eighteenth-century Masqat,[127] which had the official blessing of the local government. They were often employed simultaneously by several individuals and, though their relationships might persist for many years, their commissions usually remained limited to specific kinds of transactions. When in the 1770s about a dozen of Bombay's leading merchants and ship-owners – some indigenous to western India, some British – were questioned about the manner in which brokers were commissioned, they agreed that, by custom, a principal would give orders to his broker orally and in camera.[128] While this did not preclude the presence of 'sundry creditable and respectable merchants',[129] it remained a secretive affair. Indeed, to do otherwise, as one of them put it, would be 'rather incredible and totally contrary to the practice of merchants, who would surely never give a commission to a broker in a publick manner in the presence and hearing of others which might be the means of frustrating the intentions of the merchant'.[130]

On being commissioned, there was a strong presumption that the employer was personally liable for the execution of any agreement negotiated by his broker.[131] This lay at the core of many disputes in Bombay and Surat in the middle of the eighteenth century. They revolved around whether or not the broker had carried out his employer's instructions to the letter. It accounts too for the pains taken over the terms of a commission and, above all, the degree of authority delegated to the broker. Any ambiguity or misunderstanding over these could sow the seeds for a future dispute. In the event of a dispute, the employer frequently refused to honour his broker's agreement or to pay compensation. This was Muḥammad Ṣūfī's position. In 1779, his broker of more than a decade's standing, Hemraz Gopaldas, entered into an agreement on his behalf to purchase cotton from a Bombay-based merchant. Pressed by the latter to take the goods off his hands, Muḥammad Ṣūfī declared the deal void because, so he claimed, his broker had not done what he had been commissioned to do. On the eve of the English East India Company's auction of its cotton, Hemraz Gopaldas had been summoned and told to

[126] Cf. the discussion of brokers and middlemen in Goitein, *A Mediterranean Society*, I, 160–1.

[127] Calvin H. Allen, 'Indian merchant community of Masqat', *Bulletin of the School of Oriental and African Studies* 44:1 (1981), 39–53.

[128] MSA/Misc/HCR/MRC/45: 1412–21. [129] MSA/Misc/HCR/MRC/45: 1402.

[130] MSA/Misc/HCR/MRC/45: 1410. [131] MSA/Misc/HCR/MRC/45: 1412–21.

find out whether there was anyone else willing to sell 200 bales of ahmoody cotton at 95 rupees per candy on two month's credit. Muḥammad Ṣūfī stated clearly that he would accept any deal negotiated by Hemraz as long as he received notification of it by nine o'clock on the day of the Company's auction or, at the very latest, before ten o'clock, when the sale was due to begin. Otherwise, he would go ahead and purchase the cotton from the Company. He deposed later that he did not receive the stipulated notification from his broker by ten o'clock, and so he bid for 200 bales of cotton and was successful in acquiring them. Only after the event was he informed that Hemraz had negotiated a deal on his behalf. But as this happened between ten and eleven o'clock, Hemraz had thereby exceeded the terms of his commission, and so Muḥammad Ṣūfī did not consider himself bound by the deal.[132]

For any service that a broker could provide, it was normally possible to find an agent who could do it just as well. The main difference between them lay in the greater latitude afforded to agents in the use of their personal initiative. Furthermore, agents generally remained in their principal's employment for longer periods, and they tended to be more mobile.[133] The value of an agent is clear-cut in circumstances like those in which Felix de Conçeicão found himself in 1784. He was overwhelmed by an unexpected flurry of business that prevented him from being able to deal personally with his far-off associates in Goa. So as not to break his standing obligations to them, he granted power of attorney to an agent to handle affairs on his behalf.[134] In other commonplace scenarios, agents were appointed to manage the principal's ongoing interests at a settlement where he did not reside himself, or to set up ties in a place where he was planning to establish a presence.

We may gain insights into how relationships between a principal and his agent were typically patterned through studying the way in which power of attorney was granted and what it actually entailed. Consider the practicalities surrounding the passage from Bengal to Najaf of a sum of money for charitable purposes. One such instance is recounted in the prologue. As noted there, the donation, which was much anticipated and needed, finally reached Basra in 1747. On learning of its arrival, the members of the Sufi brotherhood in Najaf, who were its intended recipients, straightaway made the necessary arrangements to have it, along

132 MSA/Misc/HCR/MRC/45: 1401–4.

133 Cf. the discussion of agents and the 'representative of the merchants' in Goitein, *A Mediterranean Society*, I, 183–92. Also see the discussion of brokers and agents in chapter 13 of Robert Bertram Serjeant's *Customary and Shari'ah Law in Arabian Society* (Aldershot, 1991).

134 XCHR/MHR/Correspondence (incoming) (2 December 1784).

with several other items from Bengal, collected in Basra and then couriered to Najaf.

Central to these arrangements was a *vikālatnāmah* (or *vikālatnāmchah*). This was drawn up and issued in Najaf on 30 August 1747 by Shāh Kawthar, who appears to have been the brotherhood's main representative. By means of this document, Sayyid ʿĪsā was formally appointed Shāh Kawthar's 'lawful agent and deputy' (*vakīl va nāʾib-i manāb-i sharʿī*). The purpose of the appointment was detailed in simple, clear terms. Sayyid ʿĪsā was to

> take and collect one thousand sikka rupees sent by the high-ranked *khān* Muḥammad ʿAlī Khān belonging to this side, together with the two bundles of Gujarati paper and two of Patna paper, and forty pieces of cotton goods, and one-and-a-half Machilipatnam bowls of apple-flavoured tobacco, and four Indian hookah pipes sent by the high-presences Mīr Muḥammad ʿAlī Majhalibandarī and Mīr Muḥammad Kāẓim.[135]

Having received these items himself from the 'Christian headman of the merchants', Minas de Eliaz, who had been entrusted with their passage from Bengal to Basra, he was ordered to send them on to Najaf. They were to be accompanied by 'a secure licence (*dastūr*) or another kind [of document] that you know of in the name of the shareholders'.[136]

This choice testifies to a general characteristic of the arena noted above. Given the endemic uncertainties, a principal had to concede to his agent a significant degree of freedom to make his own decisions on the basis of his own knowledge and assessment of the prevailing situation. By the same token, an agent was expected to take the initiative – to behave in effect as an entrepreneur – for the betterment of his principal's interests. But even in a scenario of complete trust and total independence, there were certain basic matters that remained the principal's responsibility and to the extent practicable could not be left up to chance. Perhaps most basic of all was the matter of the physical location of the would-be agent. Any power of attorney drawn up and issued would have been moot if there was no one to receive it, let alone act on it. One way of pre-empting this eventuality was by injecting redundancy into the practice. So Shāh Kawthar took account of the potential absence of Sayyid ʿĪsā by nominating a second individual as a fall-back:

> If ... the *sayyid ṣāḥib* ... has left for Baghdad and is not present in Basra ... Ḥājī ʿAbd al-Hādī will [act] on behalf of Shāh Kawthar by the orders written in the text of the *vakīl va ṣāḥib-i ikhtiyār* [document] so that, if *allāh* wishes, [the task] will be accomplished in the aforesaid manner. And he will collect the sent items which

135 BL/Lansdowne/1046, doc. 43. 136 Ibid.

were brought by Khvājah Minas . . . and with the before-mentioned licence cause them to arrive here.[137]

Having specified the agent, stated what was required of him and indicated the parameters within which he was free to act, the power of attorney was dated, witnessed and sealed – in this case by an ʿAbd Allāh. In the *vikālatnāmah* itself, there is no indication of the sovereign or his regime. But an accompanying letter suggests that agents could be held accountable for their principal's behaviour through formal institutions. As argued in previous chapters, the option of recourse to mechanisms like these was crucial in contexts where trust between parties was largely impersonal. So pressing was their need for money in Najaf, the Sufis very grudgingly agreed to the shockingly poor rate at which Minas had converted the donated rupees into tomans, one of the area's main currencies.[138] But they were certainly not going to take this lying down. The Najaf Sufis were determined to gain redress for the amount they had forgone. That they could hope to do so was by virtue of a legal option being available to them, which they exercised without further ado. In a letter written to an associate in Bengal, he was instructed, 'Certainly, certainly, certainly, having summoned [Minas's] agent to court (*kachahrī*), you will punish him and collect the remaining sum of money in any way you know.'[139]

Sovereign intervention and, indeed, the willingness of ordinary individuals to deal with agents was predicated not just on the existence of formal documents like a *vikālatnāmah*. It also required them to be 'authentic'[140] and composed in a 'trustworthy, sound, legal' fashion.[141] Furthermore, the grant of a power of attorney on its own was seldom enough for the principal's orders to be executed without a hitch. It was invariably reinforced and supplemented by other mechanisms, especially other kinds of documentation. In the case of Shāh Kawthar, these other mechanisms included letters that sought to inform, assure and exhort Minas, who was to hand over to his agent in Basra the items from Bengal, as well as receipts attested and sealed in the proper manner.[142] Shāh Kawthar stated, 'I had written, sealed [and] sent to . . . Sayyid ʿĪsā, whom I had made my agent, the receipts specifying the money. I also made the agent write on their reverse side and place his seal on them [confirming] that we have received the money.'[143] The mechanisms referred to in this letter may be treated as elements of a more general practice of documentation and recordkeeping within the arena, which I discuss in the section below on settling deferred transactions.

[137] Ibid. [138] BL/Lansdowne/1046, doc. 31. [139] BL/Lansdowne/1046, doc. 27.
[140] BL/Lansdowne/1046, doc. 51. [141] BL/Lansdowne/1046, doc. 43.
[142] BL/Lansdowne/1046, docs. 21, 27, 31, 51. [143] BL/Lansdowne/1046, doc. 31.

That Shāh Kawthar's *vikālatnāmah* was typical of documents granting power of attorney within the arena may be shown by juxtaposing it to those found in settlements in western India under Portuguese control. Towards the end of the eighteenth century, relations between principals and agents were formalised in Goa and its subordinate territories by means of a 'public document of general and sufficient proxy with powers and agency'.[144] In 1791 in Daman, the Gujarati Dharamchand Tarachand had just such a document drawn up in favour of Dulab Hemchand, which was then signed before witnesses in the office of the local notary. Its terms stated that the authority vested in the agent was valid in Daman and wherever else he had to travel for the purposes of executing his principal's orders. Dulab Hemchand was to be Dharamchand Tarachand's representative in his business affairs. Specifically, he undertook to receive his principal's debts, goods, money and bullion; stand in for him in any litigation, whether as plaintiff or defendant; issue 'public receipts' (*quitaçoens publicas*) and sign documents in his name; and strive to obtain the greatest possible benefit for him and his heirs. All that the principal reserved for himself were 'summons to appear for old or new disputes' (*citação da causa nova ou velha*).[145]

Though the document issued in Dharamchand Tarachand's name was far more general in scope than Shāh Kawthar's, the two share an underlying template that seems to have been widespread in the period. After stating the name of the principal and his agent, there followed an account of the latter's responsibilities and the purpose for which he had been delegated authority to act on his principal's behalf. Any limits on his authority beyond the customary duties and expectations familiar to the arena's people would be detailed. Otherwise, the presumption was that the agent was free – indeed, beholden – to take decisions on his own initiative. This could even extend to nominating others as agents for his principal through conferring on them in turn the power of attorney. In 1790, before his departure for Bombay, José Nicolão Mutel, the Goa agent for Luis da Costa and João da Costa of Bengal, had a document drawn up and duly stamped by a notary. By this document, he delegated the right to act on behalf of the da Costas jointly to João Nepomuceno Picardo and to the brothers Veṅkateśa and Nārāyaṇa Kāmat.[146]

All the documents noted thus far granting power of attorney, or commenting on the relationship between principals and agents, invoked the

[144] For instances of this and subsequent technical terms discussed in the paragraph, see XCHR/MHR/Legal Records (23 November 1786, 14 February 1787); XCHR/MHR/Other Documents (15 September 1791).
[145] XCHR/MHR/Other Documents (15 September 1791). [146] Ibid.

authority of the ruler in some fashion. This could take the form of a court or the office of a notary. However, similar to the resolution of disputes examined in the previous chapter, the great majority of such relationships must have been institutionalised and enacted without any sovereign intervention whatsoever. This would have been true above all for those imbued with personal trust of the type found among intimate kindred, confessional brethren and close friends. Insights into these are scattered among the papers of Minas de Eliaz, whom we have already met in this chapter. While these papers are silent on the precise workings of everyday dealings between principals and their agents, they do elucidate the manner in which agents were appointed between members of the same ethnic community.

In the late 1740s, Minas travelled on the *Santa Catharina* on its commercial voyage from Bengal to Basra. He was central to several aspects of this venture. In consultation with the captain and officers of the ship, he had responsibility for its management and itinerary. He sailed as a merchant trading for his own account. He was the agent for a number of individuals residing in Isfahan, Basra, Surat and Bengal. They were mainly Armenians with strong ties to New Julfa in Iran; some of those living in Surat were closely related to him.[147] However, his primary task in this venture was to be the supercargo for an Armenian 'company' in which he himself was a partner. This company had hired the *Santa Catharina* and supplied most of its freight for the voyage to Basra. Minas's total remuneration was made up of three elements: a percentage commission from the sale of the goods consigned to him by his principals, any profits resulting from the sale of goods that he was freighting on his own account, and a fee from his company 'for his liberty or privilege and provisions', which amounted to 'one thousand dinares . . . out of which he is to buy his victuals and cloaths'.[148] During the voyage, he was aided by his brother-in-law, Johannes de Nazar, who went as his clerk,[149] and Johannes de Gregory, a fellow Armenian trader, agent and partner in the company.[150]

Minas's papers suggest that the mode of his appointment as agent, be it for the company or for specific individuals, followed the same pattern. For each commission, he was delivered a letter endorsed by the principal or principals. This letter specified the items being placed in his charge. It also gave instructions regarding their disposal and stated the degree of authority vested in him. Though the length of the description of the consigned items varied according to their number and nature, his orders

[147] NA/HCA/42/25 (St Catharina): 156–60. [148] NA/HCA/42/25 (St Catharina): 77.
[149] NA/HCA/42/25 (St Catharina): 122.
[150] Johannes de Gregory is listed as one of the seven share-holders in the company that hired and freighted the *Santa Catharina*. NA/HCA/42/25 (St Catharina): 8–9.

and delegated powers were expressed concisely, even pithily. As supercargo, Minas was entrusted with the cargo in which his company had invested its capital. He was formally required 'to dispose of the same to the benefit of the ship in the best manner as he should think fit'. He had the 'power to give to and take receipts from the Captain and to go in the said ship to Bassora, where he may buy or sell whatever he should find to our advantage'.[151] The terms of his appointment gave him, in effect, a free hand to do as he wished on his company's behalf. His principals consented to this willingly because Minas was known personally and by repute to honour his obligations. This is why he ended up having 'under his charge not only the Company's interest but also [that] of many other people'.[152]

When news leaked out in 1746 that Minas would be sailing to Basra as supercargo, other Armenians in Bengal were quick to seek him out in order to offer him commissions. The simplest accepted by Minas were orders to deliver the goods consigned to him to named recipients in or around Basra. Others instructed him to receive a sum of money at Basra from, say, a debtor or his local agent, and then to deliver the sum personally to a specified individual, or to ensure its secure dispatch by specialised courier or caravan.[153] More commonly, Minas was asked to sell the goods in his care in Basra at the current price and then invest the proceeds in locally available goods of his own choosing to be freighted back to Bengal, all for the account of his principal. For his efforts, he earned a commission of about 3 per cent on the sale price, the precise value being negotiated separately with each principal. Joaquim Wulles was typical in this regard. In a letter that he sent Minas from Calcutta, he noted that:

> He had embarked in his ship one bale of silk on account of Mr. Satur de Jogiamal. He begs of him to endeavour to sell it at the current price at Bassorah and after having sold the same to pay himself for his commission and from the proceed thereof to buy gold or any other sort of goods as he shall judge the fittest and to lade the same on board of the said ship to be delivered to him or to Mr Satur de Jogiamal.[154]

Alongside such well-honed commissions, Minas also undertook others that necessitated special attention on his part. One that stands apart from the norm was an order 'to deliver the letter . . . in the French language to Mr Dumont[,] Governor of the [French] Company [in Basra,] in whose custody did remain some goods on his account'. In the event that Dumont had 'sent them already, it was well, but if he has not sent

[151] NA/HCA/42/25 (St Catharina): 2–3. [152] NA/HCA/42/25 (St Catharina): 124.
[153] NA/HCA/42/25 (St Catharina): 70. [154] NA/HCA/42/25 (St Catharina): 71.

them', Minas was asked 'to receive and bring the same on board of his ship'.[155]

The art of negotiation

As seen in the first section of this chapter, establishing and managing relations with intermediaries was essential for corresponding over large distances and, more generally, for communication within the arena. Several of the examples given in the second section point to another key role played by intermediaries. That was in negotiations where it was not possible – or desirable – for the principal to be involved in person. For both principals and intermediaries, negotiations constituted a widely dispersed practice in their own right, a practice marked by a certain artistry. It is this practice to which I now turn.[156]

Predicated on the convergence of a buyer's and seller's desire, and capacity to, transact, the negotiation that ensued could be direct or indirect, continuous or staggered in time, and occur in one or several different locations. While the governing authorities in India and the Islamic heartlands occasionally supported facilities to aid negotiations, individuals, and their agents and brokers, tended to make their own arrangements. Among the most basic matters that needed arranging were the venue for the negotiation and its scheduling. A range of venues were commonly available. The most accessible of these, which also tend to be the best documented, were the court of the local ruler, auction rooms, bazaars and caravanserais. Others are more obscure to us. In principle, these could be anywhere that the negotiators deemed suitable for their discussions, such as a warehouse or a ship's audience chamber. Of course, the venue was seldom an innocent or neutral choice. Its advantages for one side over the other would usually manifest themselves in subtle ways. But they need not always be so subtle. As the experiences of Sīkrān Hīrjī's agents (and kinsmen) in Mocha in the early 1770s testify,[157] a venue could be chosen for the express purpose of intimidation.

These considerations notwithstanding, the evidence suggests that negotiators were normally relaxed about where their discussions took place. In the course of 1773, the Armenian Petrus Mellick and Michael

155 Ibid.

156 My account of this practice is ethnographic in tenor. It resonates with the account of negotiations presented in John Middleton, 'Merchants: an essay in historical ethnography', *Journal of the Royal Anthropological Institute* 9:3 (2003), 509–26. It is also worth comparing with the discussion of 'personal dealings', 'public sales' and 'transaction procedures' in Goitein, *A Mediterranean Society*, I, 192–7.

157 MSA/Misc/HCR/MRC/27; IOR/P/341/33.

Riley, a British 'surgeon' in the service of the English East India Company who also traded for his own account, had several conversations about various goods – mainly lac and tin – that the latter was thinking of buying. Their first conversation took place in the private rooms of the chief of the Company's factory in Basra. Mellick and Riley discussed price, quantity and quality, but:

> Here the conversation ended, and they separated. Some days after ... [Petrus Mellick] met the Doctor in the street, and there asked him whether he would buy the goods they had before talked about, or not. The Doctor said he would, on the conditions he had before offered. They then discoursed touching the black tin ... They then discoursed regarding the lack ... They then separated again without concluding upon any thing. A few hours after ... [Petrus Mellick] met the Doctor at dinner at Mr Abrahams. He then asked him whether he would raise his price any more for the tin and lump lack. The Doctor said he would not ... [Petrus Mellick] then told him he should have the goods for the prices he had offered ... The bargain was struck.[158]

In a similar fashion, negotiations were characterised by a range of temporalities. For many spot transactions, exemplified by auctions, the deal was struck there and then, being sealed without need for any further deliberation. Such speed was far less common in negotiations concerning transactions not due to reach term for some time to come. This was often the case for insurance policies and freight contracts. Their negotiations could require several discrete rounds of discussions. The pause between rounds gave each party an opportunity to make further inquiries, say, to verify for themselves the claims of the other party. In instances where the principals were present, the exchange of views would be simultaneous and ongoing. If, however, the negotiation was being conducted on their behalf by brokers or agents, or by means of correspondence, the process was frequently a staggered affair; ratification by the absent principal was usually required at its most critical stages, particularly in situations where full authority had not been delegated. Finally, the temporality of negotiations had to take account of local circumstances. Prominent among these were festivals and holidays observed by the resident communities. Other less spectacular traditions framing daily life too could influence a negotiation's progress. In 1773, Kirparam Bhairam, a Gujarati *baniyā*, explained that it would not be possible for him to pick up tomorrow the counterpart to an agreement just negotiated by his employer because the day was 'an unlucky one'.[159]

In practical terms, the simplest negotiations – and in all likelihood the most widespread – were undertaken in person by the principals

[158] MSA/Misc/HCR/MRC/35: 1122–3. [159] MSA/Misc/HCR/MRC/34: 507–9.

themselves. Among the most valuable sources that we have for elucidating such unexceptional, yet constitutive, practices are descriptions left by sympathetic and knowledgeable contemporaries. They were occasionally participants themselves; more usually, they were travellers with a penchant for observing. The discussion below is based on three such descriptions from the eighteenth century. In the first, Paulinus, a Carmelite monk living in southern India, witnessed how '*Anandacetti*, a merchant at *Mattincera*', went about his business:

[He] always kept by him, for sale[,] *Teka* wood to the value of five lacks of rupees. The stuffs and different articles of cotton which he had in his warehouses, without reckoning other merchandise, were worth four lacks more. This man purchased and sold, sometimes in a quarter of an hour, a whole ship's cargo valued at five millions of rupees. Such instances are not uncommon in India. The merchants show to each other catalogues of their goods; select the principal articles by which they think they can acquire profit; mark and erase, sell, exchange and purchase, according as they find it for their advantage; and in this manner gain often in a single hour incredible sums.[160]

The salient features of this passage find echoes in the observations by Abraham-Hyacinthe Anquetil-Duperron made during his stay in Surat in the 1750s where:

It is known that these deals [for the sale and purchase of goods], which often involve several millions, are conducted [between merchants] with the greatest calm and in complete good faith . . . The merchant states the price without lengthy preliminaries. The purchaser responds by putting his hand inside that of the other under a shawl or some other cover. He indicates by the number of bent or extended fingers how much below the asking price he is prepared to pay and sometimes the deal is concluded without any word being said. In order to confirm the deal, they hold hands a second time, and it is concluded by a gift presented to the purchaser by the seller in proportion to the transaction and the status of the contracting parties. It has never been the case that an agreement made in this manner has not been kept.[161]

Carsten Niebuhr noted similar techniques being used in the course of his journey across Arabia in the 1760s. This was not unexpected because, prior to his departure, he had learnt from 'some account' that 'the Orientals have a special method of concluding a deal in the presence of several people without any of them knowing the stipulated price'. He was troubled by this practice since having 'recourse to this device . . . allows the broker or agent to deceive his principal, even in his presence'. In order

160 Paulinus A. S. Bartholomaeo, *A Voyage to the East Indies* . . . (London, 1780), 165–6.
161 Abraham-Hyacinthe Anquetil-Duperron, *Voyage en Inde 1754–1762: relation de voyage en préliminaire a la traduction du Zend-Avesta* (Paris, 1997), 360.

to probe the veracity of his source, he allowed a purchase to be made on his behalf 'using such a practice'. And this is what he saw:

> The two parties make it known, on the one side what he desires, on the other what he is willing to pay, by touching each other's fingers or the joints of the hand, which signify 100, 50, 10, etc. One does not make a mystery of this device which, if it were a secret, it would not be of great utility. But, due to [the presence of] the assistants, one covers the hand with the end of one's cape.[162]

The most impressive feature of these observations is that, whatever the sums involved, negotiations in wholesale settings appear to have been very well organised. They were normally conducted 'with the greatest calm' and sealed swiftly, 'often in a single hour', 'sometimes in a quarter of an hour'. Part of their effectiveness derives from the simplicity and robustness of the techniques deployed. It seems that such negotiations generally took place orally or through gestures in the form of erasable marks on catalogues of goods for sale or 'tactile' codes. These techniques, which are elaborated as forms of language in Chapter 5, were functional, the focus being on conveying intent and details about type, price and quantity. Documents appear to have played a marginal role at best, and there is little evidence for the involvement of anyone other than the negotiators themselves: draft agreements were not drawn up and revised; there was no need for the good offices of an umpire; witnesses are conspicuous by their absence. These negotiators appear to have inhabited a domain in which sovereign or official scrutiny was unnecessary. Indeed, scrutiny of this kind was very probably shunned. The lack of any obvious, institutionalised centre meant that these techniques must have been arrived at through triage and piecemeal evolution over many years, motivated and guided by the goal of improving prospects for material gain. As discussed in the previous chapter, their reliability and authority was, in the final reckoning, assured by the active policing of others in the arena. Though the statement that 'it has never been the case that an agreement made in this manner has not been kept' is certainly too good to be true, nevertheless it contains more than a kernel of truth. At the very least, this kind of statement expresses yet one more reason for negotiators to approach these techniques in 'good faith'.

Whether as agent, broker or principal, much the same panoply of stratagems was exploited to gain the upper hand in negotiations, or to constrain the prior advantages enjoyed by the other party. In situations where one party felt unable to take the other at its word, there were a number of options that could be exercised in order to minimise the risks of

[162] Niebuhr, *Description de l'Arabie*, I, 145.

a deal turning sour. Often purchasers – and even vendors – insisted on a sample of the goods being inspected before finalising any deal. In the course of negotiating the sale of a quantity of lac and tin in Basra in 1773, Petrus Mellick told the prospective buyer, Michael Riley, 'that before settling any price with him, he must go and look at the goods'.[163] This could be done in person. But for Riley that proved unnecessary 'as he was satisfied from the report he had from people that had seen the goods'.[164] Many buyers who did not have Riley's faith or access to the required information usually wanted to examine the goods themselves prior to any agreement. This is why Boulade, a Frenchmen based in Basra, kept close to hand a sample to show to prospective buyers of the pistachio nuts he was hoping to sell in 1747.[165]

It was considered perfectly reasonable during negotiations to seek a second opinion about the other's claims. This occurred, for example, in 1770 during a fraught exchange that took place on board a ship anchored in Mocha's harbour between Thomas Mathewson, a British merchant-official, and a pair of Gujarati *baniyās*. In mid-discussion, the ship's purser, David Bristow, was called into the cabin and asked whether or not the bill of exchange that the *baniyās* had just presented to Mathewson was good.[166] A negotiation could even be suspended to accommodate such demands. The discussions between Robert Taylor and Hemraz Gopaldas in Bombay were halted in 1779 while Taylor sounded out an associate over whether he should accept the terms being offered for Hemraz's cotton or wait until the English East India Company's auction was held later the same day. He dispatched his clerk Ganpat Vitoji to find his associate and bring back the response as soon as possible. This he did with alacrity. Within a few minutes, he was back with the deal-making advice: it would be better to accept Hemraz's offer rather than run the gauntlet of the auction.[167]

Recourse to such techniques was a natural response to the prevalence of minimal disclosure. In Bombay, such reticence was recognised as standard procedure. Negotiations were 'transacted with secresy and so cautious was the broker in this respect that he would not disclose the purchaser's name until the bargain was concluded'.[168] When Hemraz Gopaldas was asked by Robert Taylor 'who the merchant was who had commissioned him to purchase the cotton':

> [Hemraz,] agreeable to the custom observed by brokers not to discover the name of their employer untill the bargain is struck, refused to tell Mr Taylor the name of

[163] MSA/Misc/HCR/MRC/035: 1122. [164] MSA/Misc/HCR/MRC/035: 1123.
[165] NA/HCA/30/682 (13 October 1747). [166] MSA/Misc/HCR/MRC/27: 63.
[167] MSA/Misc/HCR/MRC/45: 1392. [168] MSA/Misc/HCR/MRC/45: 1410.

> the merchant who had commissioned him until Mr Taylor would engage to sell the cotton at the price offered. When Mr Taylor agreed to dispose of the 100 candies of Ahmood cotton at 95 rupees per candy and one months credit to commence from the day of purchase, ... Hemraz Gopaldas declared that he was commissioned to purchase the 100 candies of cotton by Mahomed Sophi [Muḥammad Ṣūfī] and that Mahomed Sophi was the purchaser of the said cotton.[169]

Reticence and secrecy were only at one remove from half-truths, or even outright deception. For sure, negotiators could not always resist the temptation to be less than honest. A common technique was to initiate discussions under the presumption that they were exclusive to the parties involved, when in reality the vendor was engaged in discussions with other prospective buyers at the very same time. Inevitably, agreements reached under these auspices were at risk of being unilaterally anulled. This was the bitter experience of the Parsis Manakji Dorabji and Tarabhai Borah. In 1781, they applied to Shankarseth, whom they believed to be William Dickson's broker, for the purchase of cargo of piece-goods recently brought to Bombay by Dickson. After discussions with Dickson at his home, with Shankarseth in attendance, the Parsis went away thinking that they had clinched a deal to purchase the cargo on two months' credit. But on presenting themselves at Dickson's warehouse the following morning in order to pick up the piece-goods, Dickson refused to hand them over. He explained that Nasarvanji Manakji, 'whom he called his broker', had sold the goods the previous day to someone else. He pleaded ignorance of the fact that Nasarvanji had been seeking buyers at the very same time they themselves had been discussing the matter. Manakji Dorabji and Tarabhai Borah were outraged by this unexpected turn of events. As they put it, such behaviour was 'contrary to the custom and good faith of merchants', and was sure to damage their 'credit and character'.[170]

There was, of course, a correlation between the relative status of the parties and the range of possible stratagems available to them in the course of a negotiation. The more elevated an individual's position, the greater his freedom to adopt the tactic best suited to achieving the desired outcome. It was not uncommon to demand, or purchase, the patronage of local officials as additional leverage in negotiations. This was observed in Surat in 1770. Exploiting his close ties to both Daniel Draper, an influential figure in Surat's government, and Thomas Hodges, the governor of Bombay, Maulana Fakhr al-Dīn managed to engross much of

[169] MSA/Misc/HCR/MRC/45: 1398–9. [170] MSA/Misc/HCR/MRC/52: 173–90.

the freight traffic between Surat and the Red Sea area.[171] In return for a sizeable payment, the British officials twice assembled local merchants at the English East India Company's factory in Surat and pressed them to transport their goods on the Maulana's ships. The Maulana would go on to enjoy bumper profits that season.[172] In extreme cases, disparities in status within the local polity allowed for the use of physical intimidation or even outright force. Though not a daily occurrence, it was common enough to be seen as one of the perils of doing business in the arena.[173]

Ceremony and ritual were endemic to all phases of a negotiation. But it was at its conclusion that these features were most evident. Clasping hands was among the simplest of gestures signifying an agreement. On the terms being settled for the purchase in Bombay in 1781 of a consignment of piece-goods, Shankarseth Babuseth joined 'the hands of... [the principals and] struck them with his hand in token of its being a firm bargain'. In his experience, this was 'the method commonly practised by the merchants of this place and is considered as the confirmation of a bargain'.[174]

Often, however, the symbolism that accompanied the successful conclusion of a negotiation was more elaborate, involving perhaps an exchange of gifts, the offer of refreshments or a divine blessing. This drama might be enacted in a purposefully theatrical setting. A theatre, of course, requires an audience and actors, and, to persist with the analogy, it was the boisterous witnesses who thronged the stalls and the slips. In this theatrical finale to the negotiation, the principals and their intermediaries were scripted the leading roles. The cast, especially for the larger transactions, could even include roles for the local glitterati, for the notaries, judges, headmen and other representatives of the ruling elites. And with the arrival of the witnesses, the negotiation that had hitherto been a closed, even secretive, affair was transformed into a spectacle. Anquetil-Duperron was privy to just such a spectacle while living in Surat in 1758. As he 'entered the room of the English factory at ten o'clock in the morning', he observed:

> It was full of people sitting cross-legged on mats. They were placed according to their rank, which is to say according to their wealth. We saw there Hindus, Parsis,

[171] Further details on the relationship between Surat and the Red Sea area are given in Das Gupta, *Indian Merchants and the Decline of Surat* and Ashin Das Gupta and Michael N. Pearson (eds.), *India and the Indian Ocean 1500–1800* (New Delhi, 1987).

[172] MSA/Misc/HCR/MRC/31: 155–6.

[173] For an unusually well-documented case in Mocha in 1770s, see the account of the dispute between Sikrān Hirjī *et al.* and Thomas Mathewson in MSA/Misc/HCR/MRC/27 and IOR/P/341/33.

[174] MSA/Misc/HCR/MRC/52: 174.

Armenians, Muslims, Sidis, Mughals and Arabs. The last, who are the most respected, had chairs placed to the right and left of the seats that were waiting for us. This assembly, marked by a throng of different colours and attire, was generally, in the case of the Muslims, engaged in smoking hookah and, for the rest, chewing betel (with the exception of the Parsis). When the session started, Jagrenat [Jagannath Laldas], the broker of the English [East India Company], announced the sale and presented the list of goods. Even several specimens were shown for form's sake. Each of the merchants once more stated under a cloth to Mr Spence [a Company official] the amount they had purchased. The gifts were then distributed; they consisted of shawls, pieces of muslin and packets of betel. The hookah coals were once again lit, followed by a sprinkling of rose water, and refreshments, that is to say small cups of coffee served boiling and without sugar, were given several times to the Arabs. After this, everyone departed.[175]

This passage tantalises our senses with the pageantry of the moment. The striking resemblance to levees presided over by the Mughal emperor in Delhi or by his great provincial *manṣabdārs* was intentional; the ceremony borrowed heavily from Indo-Persian courtly practices of the era, consciously styled after the *dargāh*, with the charismatic ruler at its centre.[176] By capturing some of the mystique and sanctity associated with the *dargāh*, the choreographers hoped to weave the same kind of bonds, bonds that would tie the participants in the assembly ever more firmly to one another. Theirs was no ordinary show. By tapping hallowed orthodoxy and exploiting its prestige, they sought to harness the forces thus unleashed to impose fidelity on all parties to the agreement.

Rituals and ceremony, whether or not played out in the kind of lavish setting recounted by Anquetil-Duperron, had consequences that transcended the world of the here-and-now. The drama that unfolded at the end of a negotiation was a powerful reminder that the agreement expressed a moral and ethical duty which had been registered by God and their cosmos's other divine figures. The symbolism evoked the ontological dangers associated with failure to keep one's word. This reinforced the symbolism's more prosaic, albeit more tangible, consequences. In being transformed from a personal matter to a formal undertaking, the agreement was rendered visible to the polity at large and became subject to monitoring and enforcement within the arena. From now on, one's reputation was seen as entwined with the execution of the transaction as framed by the contract. As reputation was among the most coveted and

[175] Anquetil-Duperron, *Voyage en Inde 1754–1762*, 360.

[176] On courtly ritual and ceremony in the region, see in particular John F. Richards (ed.), *Kingship and Authority in South Asia* (Delhi, 1998), 327–48; Stewart Gordon (ed.), *Robes of Honour: Khil'at in Pre-Colonial and Colonial India* (New Delhi, 2003); Albrecht Fuess and Jan-Peter Hartung (eds.), *Court Cultures in the Muslim World: Seventh to Nineteenth Centuries* (New York, 2011).

valued of assets that an individual could possess, the implied threat to it usually sufficed to ensure faithfulness. And if it did not, the aggrieved party could seek redress in forums that specialised in resolving disputes.

Settling deferred transactions

Negotiating an agreement was predicated on effective mechanisms for remitting proceeds from the ensuing transaction and settling outstanding debts. Without such mechanisms, many everyday transactions within the arena would simply not have been entertained, especially those that bridged far-off places and did not come to term for a season or more. The focus of this last section is on the techniques that were commonly deployed for settling such deferred transactions from a distance. These constituted a practice that rested on two foundations: a stable unit of account recognised throughout the arena, and the capacity and willingness of its participants to extend credit to one another.

A consideration of personal and business correspondence from the middle of the eighteenth century reveals that the main techniques by which deferred transactions were settled are as follows: the remittance of value in the form of consumable or non-consumable goods; adjustments to the current account; and recourse to bills of exchange or other kinds of commercial paper. With the partial exception of cowrie shells,[177] commodity money seems to have had a relatively minor presence within the arena.

Goods deemed suitable for payment generally needed to be convertible into coins that were current at the settlement for which they were destined. The specifics, however, varied according to the type of good. If it were a consumable or a gem, there had to be local demand for it; only then could it be exchanged for cash or mintable bullion.[178] If it were instead a precious metal, it could be melted down at the mint and refashioned in an appropriate currency, or it could be sold as a commodity. Minas de Eliaz, the supercargo and agent on board the *Santa Catharina*, had the latter idea in mind as he prepared to leave Basra in early 1748 for his return voyage to Bengal. All the available space in his ship was taken up by cargo that had been purchased at Basra. Measured in terms of value, by far the most significant item was the silver filling the chests kept in the hold. Most of this was in the form of

[177] Cowrie shells were commonly used for trade along the African coast and in the Arabian Sea area. See HAG/Persian Documents, doc. 27 and Jan Hogendorn and Marion Johnson, *Shell Money of the Slave Trade* (Cambridge, 1986).

[178] For an example of a payment in Bengal in the late 1740s by a Shīʿī merchant that took the form of goods dispatched from Basra, see BL/Lansdowne/1046, doc. 11.

zolotas, a coin often seen in the period in Ottoman territories. A much smaller number of chests contained gold in the form of ducats. Minas's plan was to freight the silver to Pondicherry or to Madras on behalf of his principals. After being converted at the mint into rupees, the silver was to be shipped to Bengal, where it was hoped a profit of at least 18 per cent would be made.[179]

Precious metals came in a host of shapes and sizes. As discussed in Chapter 1, some of them circulated as gold or silver ingots of known purity and composition. By specifying the weight, its monetary value could be readily determined in any of the region's widely used currencies. Precious metals also circulated as coins, of which there were a myriad of types in the region at the time. These coins were metallic alloys of theoretically fixed composition, with standardised proportions of gold, silver, copper and iron.[180] In the correspondence, they are defined by their vernacular names and the places with which they were generally associated. So we read about Arcot rupees, 'current Baghdad zolotas', sikka rupees and 'Basra *nādirī* tomans'.[181] These coins, however, functioned as money in only one of its several senses, as a store of wealth. It was rare for them to function as a medium of exchange because they were frequently clipped or had been worn down naturally over time by repeated handling. In view of such treatment, coins were not fungible as coins per se. It would be more accurate to describe them as bullion. Their

[179] HCA/42/25 (St Catharina): 125. There are many other examples of Minas being commissioned to freight chests of silver. See 197, 199, 224, 225, 229–30, 239, 244, 246–7, 249, 252–3, 260, 272, 308–9.

[180] Valuable work has been done on the interlinked subjects of precious metals, coins, currencies and money. Especially worth noting with regard to Islamicate Eurasia in our period are Irfan Habib, 'Monetary system and prices', in Tapan Raychaudhuri and Irfan Habib (eds.), *Cambridge Economic History of India, vol. I: c. 1200–c. 1750* (Cambridge, 1982), 360–81; Shireen Moosvi, 'The silver influx, money-supply, prices and revenue-extraction in Mughal India', *Journal of the Economic and Social History of the Orient* 30:1 (1987), 47–94; John F. Richards (ed.), *The Imperial Monetary System of Mughal India* (New Delhi, 1987); Frank Perlin, 'World economic integration before industrialisation and the Euro-Asian monetary continuum', in Eddy van Cauwenberghe (ed.), *Money, Coins, and Commerce: Essays in the Monetary History of Asia and Europe* (Leuven, 1991), 239–374; Najaf Haider, 'Precious metal flows and currency circulation in the Mughal empire', *Journal of the Economic and Social History of the Orient* 39:3 (1996), 298–364; Michel Tuchscherer, 'Quelques réflexions sur les monnaies et la circulation monétaire en Égypte et en mer Rouge au XVIe et au début du XVIIe siècle', *Annales islamologiques* 33 (1999), 263–81; Rudolph P. Matthee, 'Between Venice and Surat: he trade in gold in late Safavid Iran', *Modern Asian Studies* 34:1 (2000), 223–55; Şevket Pamuk, *A Monetary History of the Ottoman Empire* (Cambridge, 2000); Şevket Pamuk, 'Interaction between the monetary regimes of Istanbul, Cairo and Tunis, 1700–1875', in Nelly Hanna (ed.), *Money, Land and Trade: an economic history of the Mediterranean* (London, 2002), 177–205.

[181] Examples of these and other types of coins are scattered throughout BL/Lansdowne/1046.

value lay not in their shape and size, or in their symbolic representation of a ruler's authority. Rather, it lay in their metal composition. Knowledge of coins whose composition was consistent for each instance of that type was widely dispersed within the arena, be it orally or through handwritten lists and tables.[182] That is why creditors who were to be paid in such coins were not satisfied by their names alone. They wanted to be informed as well of their total number and weight, or their equivalent value in units of an accepted standard of gold or silver.

This last point is illustrated by a Shīʿī agent who in 1748 shipped to his principal in Bengal the proceeds from the sale of some goods in Basra. The proceeds were in the form of ashrafis. They were accompanied by letters to the agent's associates in Bengal. He specified in these letters the name of the coin (*ashrafī-yi dū-būtī*, 'ashrafi with two idols'), the precise number of coins being dispatched (128) and their total weight (*vazn*) in Shirazi *mithqāl*s. He also specified their value in three different ways: in 'Basra rates' (*nirkh-i baṣra*), in 'white Basra gold' (*zar-i safīd-i ṣarf-i baṣra*) and in general units of account (tomans and dinars).[183] Specifying coins along multiple dimensions appears to have been the norm. Given this kind of information, the recipient of the ashrafis would have been able to calculate all the more easily their value in whatever currency he desired.

Though commodities were frequently used as a means of payment within the arena, they came attached with certain characteristic difficulties. Some of the most challenging stemmed from the fact that prices in distant places were seldom predictable, especially months or a year in advance. The uncertainties this fostered were only increased by the risk of losses through robbery, piracy or shipwreck, or through delays and alterations to the itinerary because of armed conflict or inclement weather.

The story of the *Santa Catharina* again offers a good example. It was late in reaching Basra, as a result of which it missed the winds that, if all had gone to plan, would have carried it back to Bengal the same season. Individuals residing locally sought to profit from this unforeseen delay. Johannes de Parcelius wrote on 20 July 1747 that the 'said interval of time will redound to their own advantage for they will reap some benefit by changing the zolotas in rupees on the [Coromandel] Coast'.[184] This early optimism, however, was short-lived; towards the end of the year, news

[182] See IOL/Mss Eur/F110/11 for an example of such handwritten lists and tables. Printed manuals containing this kind of information were also available in the region but, for reasons outlined in Chapter 6, they had a very limited readership, essentially being confined to Europeans and European trading factories.
[183] BL/Lansdowne/1046, docs. 14, 17, 45.
[184] NA/HCA/42/25 (St Catharina): 242–3; also see 246.

started filtering into Basra of intensified naval hostilities between the French and British. The people of the arena now had to factor into their calculations the possibility of blockages, seizures and further delays. The *Santa Catharina* would have to run the gauntlet of all these risks on its return voyage and, moreover, the news would affect in unpredictable ways the prices at the ports where the ship was scheduled to drop anchor. In these circumstances, those with a stake in the *Santa Catharina* were forced to lower their expectations. They instructed the supercargo, or their agents travelling on board, to use their best judgement within the broadest parameters. Having wished Minas and his clerk a safe and profitable voyage, Mexitar de Tarus begged 'of them but especially of Mr Minas' that:

> He[, Mexitar,] having laden on board ... four chests with silver ... on account of Jogia Shain de Giabre gives power to the said messieurs ... to the end that they in any city where they should put on that [Coromandel] Coast, where they should change their own zelotas, to change also those of the four chests ... and to deliver the same at their arrival at Bengal to the said Jogia Shahin de Giabre.[185]

This example highlights the mix of uncertainties and risks that raised the cost of using commodities for payment. And that is to say nothing about the charges incurred in transporting them, whether by ship or by caravan. Such complications were absent in the other two techniques available within the arena for settling deferred transactions.

It was a widespread practice among associates separated by large distances and long silences to maintain current accounts for one another.[186] Indeed, this cleaved to a more general practice by means of which the salient details of individual transactions were systematically written down on sheaves of paper, or less often palm-leaves. Its importance was such that correspondents would repeatedly instruct, or remind, one another to 'record' specified pieces of information.[187] The utility of this was clear; it obviated the need to memorise all the details. As long as they were preserved in the accounts, they could be referred to as required. Of course, in order to operate in this manner, the accounts needed to be close to hand. But that was not always possible. In writing to his principal

[185] NA/HCA/42/25 (St Catharina): 220.

[186] There is little historical scholarship on accounting that is directly relevant to the concerns of this book. Of what there is available, I have found the following of value: H. Kazem Zadeh, 'Chiffres siyak et la comptabilite persane', *Revue de monde musulman* 30 (1915), 1–51; Basil S. Yamey, 'Scientific bookkeeping and the rise of capitalism', *Economic History Review* 1:2–3 (1949), 99–113; Holden Furber, 'East India Company's financial records', *Indian Archives* 7:2 (1953), 100–14; Goitein, *A Mediterranean Society*, I, 200–9; Basil S. Yamey, 'Notes on double entry bookkeeping and economic progress', *Economic History Review* 4 (1975), 717–23.

[187] BL/Lansdowne/1046, docs. 6, 65, 66.

in 1747 about the requested chalk, ʿInāyat Allāh noted, 'Perhaps thirty rupees of your claim has remained [unfulfilled], the totality of which was sixty rupees.' However, 'as the record of accounts (*daftar*) was not here, I did not know what is the [precise] amount. It may be more or less [than thirty]'.[188]

Accounts are denoted by several different terms in the documents that I have examined – *ṭūmār, majallah, siyāhah, daftar, ḥisāb*. It is difficult, however, to establish whether these terms are essentially synonymous, or whether they refer to distinct kinds of accounts. What we can say is that, on the whole, they covered a fixed period of time and normally contained details on names of goods purchased or sold, quantities of each good in specified units, price per unit, total price, expenses (e.g., brokerage, porter charges), bills of exchange issued or redeemed (stating name of beneficiary and value), and the calculation of the balance (i.e., revenue minus expenses) on a given date.[189] The prices and values were usually defined in one of the regional accounting units – tomans or sikka rupees were popular choices – perhaps accompanied by their equivalent in a local currency or precious metal standard. In modern parlance, this type of account is akin to a profit and loss statement in which the revenue and expenses of a business are recorded over a fixed period. Such accounts are useful for showing whether the business made or lost money over this period, and by how much. Businesses today also produce balance sheets in which their assets and liabilities are stated. There is no evidence of anything akin to a balance sheet in the documents produced by and for the arena's people.

The current accounts that associates within Islamicate Eurasia maintained for one another were in general divided into two parts, one for credits, the other for debits. In this arrangement, settling individual transactions was then a simple matter of making an entry containing the relevant details – date, value, item – in the appropriate part. The books were balanced either at the end of the financial cycle – the duration of which was determined by custom or through prior agreement – or on an ad hoc basis with the consent of those involved. The latter was commonplace in situations where a relationship was expected to last for only a single venture. Payments between intimates were frequently made by adjustments to the current accounts. This practice also extended to strangers. So we see recourse to this mode of payment by a Shīʿī merchant in Cochin and a Hindu *mahājan* in Hugli;[190] a Hindu *dallāl* in Calcutta and a Shīʿī merchant in Basra;[191] Arabs in Damascus and

[188] BL/Lansdowne/1046, doc. 17.
[189] BL/Lansdowne/1046, docs. 6, 19.
[190] BL/Lansdowne/1046, doc. 11.
[191] BL/Lansdowne/1046, docs. 65, 66.

Basra;[192] and Armenian kindred in Basra and Cochin.[193] Ultimately, the success of this technique depended on the willingness of both sides to extend credit to, and accept deposits from, one another until the end of the established cycle or pre-arranged period. In effect, they were acting as each other's personal bankers.[194] For reasons detailed in Chapters 4 and 6, this would not have been possible without the prior existence of personal trust or, failing that, the presence of mechanisms facilitating impersonal trust.

The third established means of payment depended on commercial paper. This was known by an array of names, among the most common being *barāt*, *hundi* and *ḥawāla*.[195] Despite many differences in their details, all such paper may be viewed as variants on personalised debt. This is because the debt was attached to the individuals mentioned, and could not be freely used to make purchases or redeem loans. For commercial paper to function effectively as a means of payment, one needed to find a local *ṣarrāf* – literally, a money-changer, though his livelihood would seldom be confined to this activity alone – who maintained a relationship with another *ṣarrāf* at the place for which the money was destined. The procedure then was as follows. An individual would give the local *ṣarrāf* the sum of money, or its commodity equivalent, to be transferred. In return, the payer received a bill drawn up on a *ṣarrāf* at the destination in favour of his expectant associate for the appropriate sum. The value of the bill would normally be stated in one of the arena's most widespread units of account, often a standardised rupee, together with a note of the date on which it could be redeemed. It would then be dispatched to the associate who would present it to the *ṣarrāf* at its destination. If all was in order, he would be given the face value of the bill in one of the local currencies on the agreed date.

This mode of payment relied on an effective system of bookkeeping and, more generally, recordkeeping and other forms of documentation. The skills and techniques associated with recordkeeping and documentation themselves constituted a practice that was generally dispersed within the arena. While the topic merits a full and systematic treatment, which has yet to be undertaken, a few remarks in the interim may be of value;

192 ANOM/FC/E/137 (Dourdon). 193 BL/Lansdowne/1046, doc. 67.

194 Cf. the discussion of payment, credit, debts and loans discussed in Goitein, *A Mediterranean Society*, I, 197–200, 250–62.

195 NA/HCA/42/25 (St Catharina): 71–2, 236–7. On commercial paper, see Goitein, *A Mediterranean Society*, I, 240–50; Irfan Habib, 'System of bills of exchange (*hundis*) in the Mughal Empire', in Satish Chandra (ed.), *Essays in Medieval Indian Economic History* (New Delhi, 1987), 207–21; Muḥammad Aḥmad Sirāj, *al-Awrāq al-tijarāya fī al-sharā'a al-Islāmīya* (Cairo, 1988); Marina Martin, 'Hundi/hawala: the problem of definition', *Modern Asian Studies* 43:4 (2008), 909–37.

they are certainly pertinent to this and earlier chapters.[196] There is little doubt that recordkeeping and documentation were essential for activities vested in circulation and exchange. To use the language of contract theory, they enabled verification, signalling, correction, monitoring and enforcement. In so doing, they reinforced and complemented relationships, enlarged the possibilities for communication, underpinned the centrality of reputation and creditworthiness, and helped in the process of resolving disputes.

The specific types of recordkeeping and documentation that figured most prominently in the arena can be defined in terms of their physical situation. There were those that always remained in the possession of an individual or the association which framed his livelihood, very often his family. Some, especially letters received, drafts of letters dispatched, copies of orders issued, inventories and current accounts, were for daily use in-house, mainly for reference. Others, for example, licences, passports, wills, letters of recommendation, powers of attorney, grants of privileges or official appointments, were carefully preserved, to be exhibited as and when appropriate, usually to strangers. And then there were those composed in order to be delivered. The delivery could take place with nothing being given in return, for example, a report on the present state of affairs or a witnessed and signed confirmation. Conversely, something of material value would be given in exchange for, say, a receipt, quittance or bill of lading.

Returning to the issue of settling deferred transactions by means of commercial paper, the form of recordkeeping that counted above all was accounts. They were maintained between the *ṣarrāfs* in a way similar to that described above: payments were noted through adjustments in their current accounts for one another. As for the salient forms of documentation, much of their credibility derived from them being crafted in the proper fashion. Great attention was thus paid to the quality of the paper, the wording of the text and its writing style, and the seals and signatures which accompanied it. Any deviation from the approved templates, no

[196] Despite their isolated nature, there do exist invaluable studies. See, for example, Goitein, *A Mediterranean Society*, I, 169–79, 250; Jeanette Wakin, *The Function of Documents in Islamic Law: the Chapters on Sales from Ṭahāwī's Kitāb al-shurūṭ al kabīr* (Albany, NY, 1972); Wael B. Hallaq, 'Model *shurūṭ* works and the dialectic of doctrine and practice', *Islamic Law and Society* 2:2 (1995), 109–34; Jonathan Bloom, *Paper before Print: the History and Impact of Paper in the Islamic World* (New Haven, 2001), 135–41; Boğaç A. Ergene, *Local Court, Provincial Society and Justice in the Ottoman Empire: Legal Practice and Dispute Resolution in Çankırı and Kastamonu (1652–1744)* (Leiden and Boston, 2003), 125–41; Boğaç A. Ergene, 'Evidence in Ottoman courts: oral and written documentation in early-modern courts of Islamic law', *Journal of the American Oriental Society* 124:3 (2004), 471–91.

matter how slight, could be grounds for refusal to honour the document when presented for payment.

It is thus not surprising that the arena's people were sensitive about such matters. This sensitivity is clearly expressed in the reasons given in 1747 by a Shīʿī agent in Basra to his principal for a bill of exchange not being accepted. He wrote:

> After the quittance and the power of attorney for the amount of five tomans and five thousand dinars, which is equivalent to a hundred rupees, that Shaykh ʿAbd al-Nabī, the successor of the late Shaykh Mufīd, had sent from Shiraz, was not honoured (*muʿatabar*) because neither I nor any of the people of Shiraz recognised the handwriting (*khaṭṭ*) and the seal (*muhr*) and the witnesses (*shuhūd*). I thus asked for a surety from your agent. Since he did not give a surety, the money will therefore remain blocked until you send another reputable quittance. Afterwards having given the money, I will send the following season its receipt.[197]

But all was not necessarily lost if the contents of the bill lacked sufficient detail or had been drawn up in an unorthodox fashion. That same year, Jawhar Darankal wrote from Basra to Ṣāliḥ Uzmalī, living at the time in Calcutta. He complained that Ṣāliḥ Uzmalī had neglected to specify either in his letter or in the bill itself (*ḥawāla*) whether the amount to be received from Khvājah Gentilhomme was to be in 'whole' (*ṣaḥīḥ*) or 'pierced' (*manqūb*) gold *funduqī*s. But Jawhar Darankal did not wait around to receive a corrected bill. He took steps on his own initiative to mitigate for the imperfections of the one already in his hands. This was ultimately possible because he could leverage his reputation on behalf of his principal. 'After a thousand difficulties', which involved calling upon the good offices of an arbitrator (*fayṣal*), he was able to collect from the drawee 'half the *funduqī* as whole and half as pierced'.[198]

The corollary of the requirement that a bill be drawn up and handled in the proper fashion was that, once issued, it was likely to be honoured, no matter what the circumstances that had produced it. This amounted in effect to a decoupling of authorial intent from the action embodied in the document, helping to shield such transactions from arbitrariness or deceit. At a minimum, the authority vested in a legitimate bill enlarged its scope as a device for transferring money between far-off places and between strangers. These attributes of commercial paper are brought to the fore in a fractious dispute over the validity of a bill of exchange that was played out between Mocha and Bombay in the 1770s.

At the heart of this dispute lay a bill with a face value of 20,000 dollars. It had been drawn up in Mocha in 1770 by the Gujaratis

[197] BL/Lansdowne/1046, doc. 14. [198] BL/Lansdowne/1046, doc. 75.

Hansaraj Vanockji and Ratanji Madhuji on their associate Rupji Dhanji of Bombay in favour of a British merchant-official, Thomas Mathewson.[199] But Rupji refused to honour the bill when Mathewson presented it to him later that year. Mathewson then sought redress from Bombay's government, naming Sīkrān Hīrjī as the bill's guarantor and thus ultimately liable for its payment. In their account of events, the Gujaratis claimed that they had issued the document under duress. Intriguing for us is their stated rationale for caving in to the pressure put on them by Mathewson. They did so because they believed the bill would *not* be accepted. To be sure of this, and of course acting behind Mathewson's back, they had written to Rupji 'requesting him not to pay any money on that piece of paper, as it is not a bill nor was ever intended as such, but was merely wrote to get clear of Mr Mathewson'.[200] But when advised by the purser on board Mathewson's ship that 'a bill was the same as money' and that 'they should be very cautious how they drew bills that would not be paid',[201] they took fright. They informed Sīkrān, then in Porbandar in Gujarat, of their plight. He was urged to use his influence in Bombay to ensure that Rupji did not pay the bill and that their house was not held liable for it.

On learning of this affair, Sīkrān travelled to Bombay and made the Gujaratis' case in person before the town's governor and council. When questioned about Mathewson's bill, Sīkrān began by claiming that it was invalid. Describing it as a 'paper' or 'note' rather than a bill, he asked rhetorically: 'Doth this paper carry with it any appearance of a Bill of Exchange amongst merchants?'[202] But he chose not to dwell on the question, perhaps because he did not think an answer would win over this particular audience. He turned instead to the matter of who was liable for the bill's non-payment:

> Suppose it should be so admitted [that this is a valid bill]. In what manner doth it effect your Orator? Doth it mention as drawn by his order, or on his [account], or it is drew even on him? Which was that the case he is no ways liable to a pressuation, if it is drawn and admited even as a Bill of Exchange, and is protested.

[199] The bill under dispute contained the following (MSA/Misc/HCR/MRC/027: 54):
'To Rupjee Dhunjee
'That we Hanssaraz and Ruttonjee do hereby say that you will pay unto Mr Mathewson the sum of dollars /20,000/ the signal for which payment is the letter we have wrote you and the time of payment is three monthys this Bhadavah Sood 3 or Nowroz 343 [*c.* August 1770].'

[200] MSA/Misc/HCR/MRC/27: 54. [201] IOR/P/341/33: 561.

[202] MSA/Misc/HCR/MRC/27: 54.

Lett the drawers stand to the consequences, your orator hath nothing to do with it.[203]

Elsewhere, Sīkrān deposed:

Even admiting that piece of paper on which Mr Mathewson founds his claim to be a bill drawn in the usual form of bill of exchange, no Law or Custom of merchants can oblige a fourth person whose name is not any where mentioned in it to be countable for it. On the contrary when a bill is drawn in the fairest manner, and for which the drawer hath received value effect, the person on whom it is drawn he may justly refuse to accept the same and cannot be sued for it.[204]

In laying out this reasoning, however, Sīkrān revealed his concern that the bill, which appears to have been drawn up properly, might well have to be honoured for that very reason. This is why he stressed that only those explicitly named in the bill could be held liable for it, seeking to absolve himself from any responsibility. His assertion that a bill may be 'justly' refused even if 'drawn in the fairest manner' indicates that the primary obligation for ensuring a bill be honoured lay with the one who drew it up. It was thus the drawer's reputation and creditworthiness which was ultimately being tapped – and so at stake – whenever a bill was issued.

Practices as useful and reliable knowledge

This is the longest chapter in the book. It is also the most wide-ranging in terms of the subjects covered, from letter-writing to settling deferred transactions by way of intermediation and the art of negotiation. The thread which ties these subjects together is useful and reliable knowledge.[205] It was this knowledge, mostly experiential, that lay at the centre of the practices that I have sought to reconstruct.

Unlike the cognitive patterns and the orders treated earlier in the book, the practices detailed here, though crucial for the activities of the arena, were not restricted to the arena nor to India and the Islamic heartlands. The same skills and techniques – or at least those analogous to them – were found in other regions of the early modern world. Indeed, a plausible argument can be made that, before the rise of industrial capitalism and the emergence of the modern state, such skills and techniques were

[203] Ibid. [204] MSA/Misc/HCR/MRC/27: 56–7.

[205] This understanding of knowledge has stimulated some interesting work recently. Among the examples that could be given, see in particular Inkster, 'Potentially global; Patrick O'Brien, 'Historical foundations for a global perspective on the emergence of a western European regime for the discovery, development, and diffusion of useful and reliable knowledge', *Journal of Global History* 8:1 (2013), 1–24; Maxine Berg, 'Useful knowledge, "industrial enlightenment", and the place of India', *Journal of Global History* 8:1 (2013), 117–41.

true of all regions of the world marked by a division of labour. This argument is plausible because the basic challenges faced by those active in regional-scale circulation and exchange everywhere had a familial resemblance to one another. At root, these challenges pivoted on the principal–agent problem.[206] What this problem amounted to in everyday terms was finding ways, for a context that could not be monitored in person, of keeping sufficiently informed about that context, and ensuring that the instructions concerning it were carried out sufficiently well. In short, the problem was about information and control.

These considerations were acute for transactions characterised by large distances and long silences. The practices examined in this chapter were suitably attuned for dealing with the challenges associated with transactions of just that kind. Of course, the four that have been examined do not cover all the relevant practices. Documentation and recordkeeping, for example, is one that was manifestly relevant but which has merely been touched upon here. Further work on this and other practices is bound to pay rich dividends. Because of the resonances between the various types of experiential knowledge found in the early modern world, a study of practices lends itself to comparative history on global scales.[207] Moreover, because no one population was beholden to or proprietorial regarding them – on the contrary, by encouraging their dissemination, it was more likely that they would remain fit for purpose in a changing world – a study of practices may reveal broader changes that were already afoot but which for the time being remained obscure to contemporaries.

206 For a good account of this problem, from the viewpoint of economics, see Jean-Jacques Laffont and David Martimort, *The Theory of Incentives: The Principal–Agent Model* (Princeton, 2002).

207 The possibilities are illustrated by the chapter on 'the instruments of exchange' in Fernand Braudel's *Civilization and Capitalism, 15th–18th Century*, vol. II: *The Wheels of Commerce* (New York, 1981), 25–137.

8 Flows and interactions: the arena's connective tissue

Throughout this book, I have tried to show that individuals in isolation were not able to husband, marshal and allocate valued, often scarce, resources. Rather, they managed these resources through, and on behalf of, the associations to which they belonged. These associations are observed in the documents as relatively stable and dense groupings of individuals who were members by virtue of, say, residence, birth, religious affiliation, livelihood or education. In the final reckoning, it is these associations that are the arena's movers and shakers.[1]

The arena was populated by numerous such associations in the eighteenth century. Among the most formative were households, extended families and neighbourhoods.[2] The larger associations that they sustained have been frequently characterised as diasporas, ethnic communities and trading networks. These were manned by historiographical luminaries such as the Gujarati *baniyās*, Julfan Armenians and Baghdadi Jews.[3] Intersecting them were organisations that had developed an expertise in

[1] As ideal-types, the two main types of named and bounded associations are organisations and groups. The key difference between them is that organisations are open (i.e., they have porous boundaries as far as membership is concerned) and groups are closed (i.e., they are endogamous). Bringing networks into the picture, the arena may then be understood as made up of unnamed, bounded and open networks of relationships between individuals who represented one or more organisations or groups.

[2] There is still very little scholarship on the families and households of the region in premodern times. What there is is discussed in the latter half of this chapter. On neighbourhoods, we are better served, often under the rubric of urban history. See, for example, Najwa al-Qattan, 'Litigants and neighbours: the communal topography of Ottoman Damascus', *Comparative Studies in Society and History* 44:3 (2002), 511–33; Nancy Ajung Um, 'Spatial negotiations in a commercial city: the Red Sea port of Mocha, Yemen, during the first half of the eighteenth century', *Journal of the Society of Architectural Historians* 62:2 (2003), 178–93; Anne-Sophie Vivier-Muresan, 'Communitarian neighbourhoods and religious minorities in Iran: a comparative analysis', *Iranian Studies* 40:5 (2007), 593–603.

[3] For an overview, see Frédéric Mauro, 'Merchant communities, 1350–1750', in James D. Tracy (ed.), *The Rise of Merchant Empires: Long-Distance Trade in the Early Modern World, 1350–1750* (Cambridge, 1990), 255–86 and, for an incisive critique of the scholarly literature, see Sanjay Subrahmanyam (ed.), *Merchant Networks in the Early Modern World* (Aldershot, 1996), xv–xvi.

particular sectors to do with circulation and exchange. Family firms, merchant houses and the European East India companies are the most prominent of these in the historical scholarship.[4] Less well known, though certainly no less important, were organisations such as the guild-like *ṣinf*s of the bazaar merchants and artisans of Safavid Iran,[5] the occupational *mahājani*s and *nagarseth*s of Mughal India,[6] and the pattamar couriers of southern India.[7] The ruling elites, where they could, paid close heed to these and similar associations on which much of their income and stability depended. This concern was institutionalised through elements of their bureaucracy – notably, the mint, imperial factories, the custom house, sovereign law courts – situated within the arena.[8] For reasons of legitimacy and self-preservation, the ruling elites also had a stake in individuals and organisations formally dedicated to piety and learning. These, however, operated mostly beyond their purview. Physically rooted in places of higher education and religious instruction, in temples and madrasas, in *khāniqāh*s, *ribāṭ*s and *takīya*s, they were simultaneously of local and regional significance, playing constitutive roles in the transmission of knowledge across India and the Islamic heartlands.[9]

[4] A sense of the literature may be gleaned from Edmund M. Herzig, 'The family firm in the commercial organisation of the Julfa Armenians', in Jean Calmard (ed.), *Etudes safavides* (Paris, 1993), 287–304; Ernestine Carreira, 'Les Kamat et le commerce français en Inde, 1778–1819', *Moyen Orient et Océan Indien* 7 (1990), 157–77; Kirti N. Chaudhuri, *The Trading World of Asia and the English East India Company, 1660–1760* (Cambridge, 1978); George D. Winius and Marcus P. M. Vink, *The Merchant-Warrior Pacified: the VOC (the Dutch East India Company) and its Changing Political Economy in India* (New Delhi, 1991).

[5] Mehdi Keyvani, *Artisans and Guild Life in the Later Safavid Period: Contributions to the Social-Economic History of Persia* (Berlin, 1982).

[6] Dilbagh Singh, 'The role of mahajans in the rural economy in eastern Rajasthan during the 18th century', *Social Scientist* 2:10 (1974), 20–31; Shirin Mehta, 'The mahajans and the business communities of Ahmedabad', in Dwijendra Tripathi, *Business Communities of India* (New Delhi, 1984), 173–84; Dwijendra Tripathi and M. J. Mehta, 'The Nagarseth of Ahmedabad: the history of an urban institution in a Gujarat city', in Satish Chandra (ed.), *Essays in Medieval Indian Economic History* (New Delhi, 1990), 262–75.

[7] Gagan D. S. Sood, 'The informational fabric of eighteenth-century India and the Middle East: couriers, intermediaries and postal communication', *Modern Asian Studies* 43:5 (2009), 1085–116.

[8] Among the general studies on the Islamicate empires, see Linda T. Darling, *Revenue Raising and Legitimacy: Tax Collection and Finance Administration in the Ottoman Empire, 1560–1660* (Leiden, 1996); Willem Floor, *Safavid Government Institutions* (Costa Mesa, CA, 2001); Ishtiaq H. Qureshi, *The Administration of the Mughal Empire* (New Delhi, 1990).

[9] There is a large and growing body of work on these topics. Important contributions include Nikki R. Keddie (ed.), *Scholars, Saints, and Sufis: Muslim Religious Institutions in the Middle East since 1500* (Berkeley, CA, 1972); George Makdisi, *The Rise of Colleges: Institutions of Learning in Islam and the West* (Edinburgh, 1981); Nehemia Levtzion and John O. Voll (eds.), *Eighteenth-Century Renewal and Reform in Islam* (Syracuse, NY, 1987); Jonathan P. Berkey, *Popular Preaching and Religious Authority in the Medieval Islamic Near East* (Seattle, WA, 2001).

From the perspective of resources then, the historical actors were ultimately named and bounded associations of the kind noted above. Individuals are present in so far as they acted as their representatives. It follows that our access to the arena's people is filtered through the associations rooted that framed their livelihoods. Similarly, the subjects treated in the preceding chapters were invoked and articulated not by individuals per se, but by individuals operating through, and on behalf of, their associations rooted in specific contexts. It is true that the cognitive patterns, orders and practices were preserved in everyday behaviour, natural language and other forms of symbolic expression. But because they did not exist in isolation, they cannot be comprehended apart from the associations which in effect brought them into being. The fact that these subjects *have* been treated separately in this book means that, properly speaking, they are analytical constructs. While this approach has merit in giving us a heuristic purchase on core features of the arena, what it cannot do is to give us a visceral, palpable sense of its sinews and lifeblood, a sense, in other words, of what produced and sustained – or undermined – its wholeness. Through this approach, we cannot get at the mundane flows and interactions that enmeshed the arena's constitutive elements in a web of mutually reinforcing ties, which endowed the arena with its characteristic knittedness.

To get at the arena's flows and interactions, we need to consider it from the standpoint of its associations. That is what I seek to do in the present chapter. The discussion up to this point in the book may thus be viewed as background or preparation for what is to be addressed in the coming pages; we have examined the salient parts and are now ready to behold them in their totality. I do so over two sections which are intended to complement one another. Each is anchored in two case studies. In the first section, I examine ties between individuals who were their associations' main representatives within the arena. This takes the form of a detailed account of the evolution of two distinct, but comparable, relationships that were simultaneously embedded in several networks. In the second section, I examine an association – the family household – that was foundational for the arena's existence. This is carried out by giving an account at a particular moment in time of two families that had region-wide interests vested in trade, finance and intermediation.

Relationships in networks

This section centres on two sets of relationships between individuals active in circulation and exchange. As mentioned above, these individuals were not active as free agents, working purely for their own account. Rather, they operated through, and on behalf of, one or more associations as their acknowledged representatives. At the same time, these individuals were embedded in, and drew sustenance from, several networks which furnished the conduits for regional flows and interactions. The main flows and interactions are readily identified.[10] To begin with, a small, but significant, fraction of those who made their livelihood in the arena was mobile. This made travel among the far-flung administrative, commercial and pilgrimage centres of India and the Islamic heartlands a commonplace occurrence. Closely associated with travel was the movement of objects between people and places. If measured in terms of units, volumes, weights and rates, commodities for sale or barter made up almost the entirety of such objects. But if reckoned instead by the admittedly more elusive notion of value, we must also include gifts and other tokens. While travel and the movement of objects cannot be decoupled from their physical materiality, that is not so with communication, the third factor responsible for the arena's connective tissue. As detailed in Chapter 5, much of this was mediated by the written word, usually on paper. But equally important in this period was communication by word of mouth.

While the networks of concern here were formally made up of linkages between the organisations and groups populating the arena, I focus on individuals who were their face for the outside world. This is justified on the grounds that it was through such individuals their associations actually manifest themselves in the historical record. Therefore, I describe the character of the relationships between individuals and their evolution over time, all the while paying special heed to the flows and interactions in which they had a stake. In this way, we can elucidate the morphology of the networks within which these individuals and their associations were situated. The extent to which these goals may be realised depends, of course, on the sources. For my account, I tap a collection of documents that, as far as I am aware, have not previously been examined with such goals in mind.[11]

[10] In thinking about this matter, I have found the following of particular value: Shelomo D. Goitein, *A Mediterranean Society: the Jewish Communities of the Arab World as Portrayed in the Documents of the Cairo Geniza*, vol. I (Berkeley, CA, 1967), 156–8; Philip D. Curtin, *Cross-Cultural Trade in World History* (Cambridge, 1984); Jerry H. Bentley, *Old World Encounters: Cross-cultural Contacts and Exchanges in Pre-Modern Times* (New York, 1993); Francis Robinson, 'Ottomans–Safavids–Mughals: shared knowledge and connective systems', *Journal of Islamic Studies* 8:2 (1997), 151–84; Houari Touati, *Islam et voyage au Moyen Age: histoire et anthropologie d'une pratique lettrée* (Paris, 2000); Kenneth Pomeranz and Steven Topik, *The World that Trade Created: Society, Culture, and the World Economy, 1400 to Present* (3rd edn, Armonk, NY, 2012).

[11] This collection is known as the Mhamai House Records and is preserved in the Xavier Centre of Historical Research, Alto Porvorim, Goa, India. It is described in several papers by Teotonio R. de Souza: 'Mhamai House Records: indigenous sources for "Indo"-

The collection consists of the papers of the Mhamai Kāmats. This was a Hindu family based in Goa who enjoyed local prominence over much of the eighteenth century.[12] The specific documents that I have studied are mainly in Portuguese and contain details on the everyday dealings of the family with a wide range of individuals active in the arena.

In concrete terms, my argument proceeds by describing and analysing two distinct sets of relationships, both involving the Kāmat family, in the second half of the eighteenth century. One set is between the brothers Veṅkateśa and Nārāyaṇa Kāmat, and the brothers Zogu and Shankar Śeṇvī, the latter living in Bombay at the time. The other set is between the same Kāmat brothers and Nasarvanji Manakji, who also resided in Bombay. An examination of these relationships in their own right is of historical interest. Their interest, however, is enhanced by adopting a comparative standpoint that highlights the similarities and differences between them. All those involved were contemporaries living in western India and their livelihoods derived to a significant extent from their participation in the arena of circulation and exchange. Furthermore, they were engaged in many of the same kinds of activities within the same or overlapping networks. What separated them was their genealogy and background. Nasarvanji and the Kāmats were strangers to one another, belonging to distinct ethnic communities and brought up in different places. In contrast, the Kāmats and the Śeṇvīs, while not intimates to begin with, were kinsmen through their common heritage as Gauḍ Sārasvat brahmins.

The Gauḍ Sārasvat brahmins formed a large and dispersed community.[13] Subdivided into numerous *jātis*, *gotras* and extended families, they were

Portuguese historiography', *Indian History Congress* 41 (1980), 435–45; 'Mhamai House Records: indigenous sources for Indo-Portuguese historiography', *Indian Archives* 31:1 (1982), 25–45; 'Mhamai House Records: indigenous sources for Indo-Portuguese historiography', in Luis de Albuquerque and Inacio Guerreiro (eds.), *II seminário internacional de história indo-portuguesa: actas* (Lisbon, 1985), 933–41.

[12] The family's history is elaborated in Teotonio R. de Souza, 'French slave-trading in Portuguese Goa (1773–1791)', in Teotonio R. de Souza (ed.), *Essays in Goan History* (New Delhi, 1989), 119–31; Teotonio R. de Souza, 'Goa–Mahe trade links (late 18th–early 19th centuries): a new source-material', in K. S. Mathew (ed.), *Studies in Maritime History* (Pondicherry, 1990); Carreira, 'Les Kamat et le commerce Français en Inde, 1778–1819'; Celsa Pinto, *Trade and Finance in Portuguese India: a Study of the Portuguese Country Trade, 1770–1840* (New Delhi, 1994), 53–6; Charles J. Borges, 'Native Goan participation in the Estado da Índia and the inter-Asiatic trade', in Artur Teodoro de Matos and Luís Filipe F. Reis Thomaz (eds.), *A Carreira da Índia e as rotas dos estreitos: actas do VIII seminário internacional de história indo-portuguesa* (Braga, Portugal, 1998), 672–83.

[13] For further details about the community, see Reginald E. Enthoven, *Tribes and Castes of Bombay*, vol. I (Bombay, 1920), 249–252; Frank F. Conlon, 'Caste and urbanism in historical perspective: the Saraswat Brahmans', in Richard G. Fox (ed.), *Urban India: Society, Space and Image* (Durham, NC, 1970), 25–38; N. K. Wagle, 'The history and social organization of the Gauda Sāraswata Brāhmanas of the west coast of India', *Journal of Indian History* 48 (1970), 7–25, 295–333; Frank F. Conlon, 'Caste by association: he

spread out across western and southern India in the eighteenth century. Several of their community's families had carved out an expertise in trade, banking, intelligence, accounting and related services. Such activities were major concerns of the Kāmats of Goa and of the Śeṇvīs of Bombay.[14] For much of the latter half of the eighteenth century, the leading members of these families were, respectively, the brothers Veṅkateśa and Nārāyaṇa Kāmat and the brothers Shankar and Zogu Śeṇvī. In both cases, they had gained control of their family's interests following the deaths of their fathers (and only after a struggle in the case of the Kāmats). Likewise, Nasarvanji Manakji was a leading member of his family, the Wadias of Bombay.[15] The Wadias held a prominent place among the Parsis of western India.[16] The basis for this prominence had been secured by Nasarvanji's grandfather when he accepted in 1735 the English East India Company's invitation to resettle in Bombay and take over management of their ship-building activities. Nasarvanji extended his grandfather's legacy by developing the family's stake in trade and shipping. These concerns brought him into regular contact with individuals of varied backgrounds, not least the Kāmats.

Gauḍa Sārasvata Brāhmaṇa unification movement', *Journal of Asian Studies* 33:3 (1974), 351–65; Frank F. Conlon, *A Caste in a Changing World: the Chitrapur Saraswat Brahmans, 1700–1935* (Berkeley, 1977); Michael N. Pearson, 'Banyas and brahmins: their role in the Portuguese Indian economy', in Michael N. Pearson, *Coastal Western India: Studies from the Portuguese records* (New Delhi, 1981), 93–115; Kumar Suresh Singh, P. P. Shirodkar and H. K. Mandal (eds.), *People of India*, vol. XXI*: Goa* (Bombay, 1993), 185–9.

[14] Kāmat and Śeṇvī were *jātīs* within the Gauḍ Sārasvat community. Mhamai was the name given to the family deity of a certain branch of the Kāmat *jātī* living in Goa. The manner in which their names are spelt here differs considerably from their spellings in the eighteenth century. Kāmat was usually written as 'Camotim' or 'Camotty' in the French- and Portuguese-language documents, and Śeṇvī appears as 'Sinai' or 'Sinay'. On the grounds of accuracy and consistency, I opt to write their names in accordance with current transliteration conventions.

[15] On the Wadia family and its role in Bombay's maritime, commercial and public life in the eighteenth and nineteenth centuries, see MSA/Misc/HCR/MRC/52: 174; Dosabhai F. Karaka, *History of the Parsis*, vol. II (London, 1884), 60–76; Ruttonjee Ardeshir Wadia, *Bombay Dockyard and the Wadia Master Builders* (Bombay, 1955).

[16] The history of the Parsi community in India (and maritime Asia more generally) since the eighteenth century is the subject of S. P. Davar, *The History of the Parsi Punchayet of Bombay* (Bombay, 1949); Christine Dobbin, 'The Parsi Panchayat in Bombay City in the Nineteenth Century', *Modern Asian Studies* 4:2 (1970), 149–64; David L. White, 'Parsis as entrepreneurs in eighteenth-century western india: the Rustum Manock family and the Parsi community of Surat and Bombay' (unpublished Ph.D. thesis, University of Virginia, 1979); Asiya Siddiqi, 'The business world of Jamshetjee Jejeebhoy', *Indian Economic and Social History Review* 19:3–4 (1982), 301–24; Amalendu Guha, 'More about the Parsi Sheths: their roots, entrepreneurship and comprador role, 1650–1918', in Tripathi Dwijendra (ed.), *Business Communities of India* (New Delhi, 1984), 109–50; David L. White, 'Parsis in the commercial world of western India, 1700–1750', *Indian Economic and Social History Review* 24:2 (1987), 183–203.

Though Veṅkateśa and Nārāyaṇa Kāmat, on the one hand, and Zogu and Shankar Śeṇvī, on the other,[17] were members of the same Gauḍ Sārasvat community, they belonged to different *jātis* within it. Whatever blood or marriage ties existed between them – and the evidence I have seen has nothing definitive to say on the matter – they were at best distant kindred. Certainly, they had not been reared together in the same household nor had they known each other as children. The documents that enable us to access their relationship mostly detail the ebb and flow of their dealings in the latter half of the eighteenth century. In the main, these documents are the originals of correspondence received by the Kāmat brothers and the drafts of their outgoing correspondence. This correspondence is supplemented by a small number of legal records, and by the current accounts that were kept by the Kāmats for clients, partners and ventures in which both they and the Śeṇvīs had a stake.[18] A notable feature of this material is that it does not contain a single item exchanged directly between the Kāmats and the Śeṇvīs.[19] Save one letter addressed to the Śeṇvīs by a Portuguese merchant, the entirety of the correspondence that offers insights into their relationship is between the Kāmats and their mutual associates. Nevertheless, these and other documents show clearly that the Śeṇvīs were enmeshed in some of the same networks as the Kāmats, at times working together, at times independently.

The nature of this material forces us to approach the relationship between the Śeṇvīs and the Kāmats obliquely, through allusions, passing remarks and instructions. On the whole, the documents tend to discuss their ties in formal terms, with few explicit details on its messy, inner workings. Luckily, there is an exception to this in the Kāmats' correspondence with third parties. We gain insights through the discussion there of transactions and ongoing ventures in which both the Kāmats and Śeṇvīs were involved, through references to personal favours, complaints and disputes that

[17] Shankar Śeṇvī appears more frequently in the documents that I have studied than Zogu Śeṇvī. Interestingly, whenever Zogu's name is mentioned, it is always accompanied by Shankar's name, in the form: 'Zogu and Shankar Śeṇvī'. We are told nothing about Zogu as an individual or his relationship with Shankar. In the absence of evidence to the contrary, I shall assume that they were brothers. For the purposes of my analysis in this section, I treat the two as a single unit that dealt jointly with the Kāmats.

[18] Of the surviving Portuguese-language material, the items that shed light on the relationship between the Kāmats and the Śeṇvīs were composed in the period 1776–91, and include sixty letters received and despatched by the Kāmats, one letter sent to the Śeṇvīs, nine sets of accounts, and four contracts and notarised documents. The majority of these are spread across two periods: 1779–80 and 1785–91. This distribution is the reason why my analysis here centres on the discrete evolution of the relationship between the two periods, highlighting the constants and the changes.

[19] Presumably, any direct correspondence between them is preserved among the papers in Marathi (or Konkani), which was their mother tongue. Unfortunately, I do not know either of these languages and so was unable to make use of this material.

concerned them, and even through the occasional piece of unsolicited advice about the current state of their dealings from an outsider's standpoint. Such insights allows us to build up a picture of how the Kāmats' relationship with the Śeṇvīs was preserved, managed and developed. It also allows us to apprehend how they were perceived within their shared networks.

The earliest document referring to both the Kāmats and the Śeṇvīs dates from January 1779, by which time they had been involved with one another for some years. We are not told about the manner in which they were first put in touch, though it is very likely the introduction was made by a fellow member of their shared community.[20] Come the late 1770s, their relationship was active in several networks, which, though distinct from one another, had many points in common. These networks may be delineated from several perspectives: their principal functions, the general background of their participants, and the physical domain that they spanned. Framed thus, it is apparent that the Kāmats and the Śeṇvīs were heavily engaged in at least three networks.

The first network centred on Pune. This was the administrative and sovereign capital of the Maratha regime, an alliance of petty rulers and notables that dominated much of central and western India in the middle of the eighteenth century.[21] The key players in this network were members of groups that specialised in the provision of scribal, linguistic, commercial, intelligence and banking services. Alongside Gauḍ Sārasvat brahmins like the Kāmats and the Śeṇvīs, Gujarati *baniyās*, Chitpavan brahmins, Parsis and Luso-Indians played significant roles. In the main, they were employed or commissioned by Maratha, French and Portuguese officials, and were tasked above all with raising funds and transferring money, relaying sensitive information, supplying armies and providing facilities to store goods.

Many of the members of this first network participated as well in a second network. This stretched across the western coast of India, with the ports of Daman, Surat, Bombay and Goa among its major hubs. Very much like the first, the primary functions of this network were to enable secure communication, to borrow money and make payments, and to transport goods. A key difference lay in the backgrounds of those who derived greatest advantage from these functions. Though the local sovereign regimes made regular use of the resources offered by this network, the main beneficiaries were transient British, Portuguese and French merchant-officials and private traders seeking to further their own

[20] A promising candidate is Anta Śeṇvī.

[21] For a good overview of the regime, see Stewart Gordon, *The Marathas, 1600–1818* (Cambridge, 1998).

interests. These western Europeans were present, however, not just as clients; they also helped to sustain the network. This is most apparent in the maritime realm, where much of the shipping in this period was owned and managed by Europeans.[22]

That fact underscores the centrality of Europeans in the third network in which the Kāmats and the Śeṇvīs were active. This covered much of the Arabian Sea, the Persian Gulf and Red Sea, and extended into the Bay of Bengal. Most of the flows and interactions that it facilitated were channelled through the area's main ports, namely, Calcutta, Madras, Bombay, Surat, Basra, Masqat, Mocha, Jidda and Ile de France. Unlike the other two networks, this one was predicated on a single form of transport: ocean-going vessels. From early in the eighteenth century, these vessels were predominantly under the control of the European East India companies and European private traders. While no longer important as ship-owners, members of communities that had been involved in this network since at least the seventeenth century, such as Julfan Armenians, Gujarati *baniyā*s and Malabari Jews, continued to participate as freighters, insurers, creditors and brokers.

These, in brief, were the three main networks within which the relationship between the Kāmats and Śeṇvīs was situated. As might be expected, their relationship changed with the passage of years. In the process, the ways in which it contributed to, and drew strength from, its networks also changed. Comparing their ties in the late 1770s with those in the late 1780s, we see that their dealings broadened and deepened, even while the Kāmats' position as the senior party was never challenged. This evolution may be charted in two ways. The first is rhetorically. Assuming that the general manner and tone in which the Kāmats referred to the Śeṇvīs reflected the current state of their relationship, I analyse their correspondence (with mutual associates) to identify patterns in how they addressed the Śeṇvīs and how these patterns changed. The second focuses on performance. Here, the trajectory of their relationship is charted by studying the development of the Śeṇvīs' roles in their dealings with the Kāmats.

With one instance excepted, whenever the Kāmats mentioned the Śeṇvīs by name, it was accompanied by one or more attributes.[23] These were, in their singular form, *senhor* ('mister'), *amigo* ('friend'), *correspondente* ('agent' or 'representative'), *constituinte* ('agent' or 'representative'), *socio* ('partner')

[22] On the European presence in western India in the eighteenth and early nineteenth century, see Ashin Das Gupta, *Malabar in Asian Trade, 1740–1800* (Cambridge, 1967); Pamela Nightingale, *Trade and Empire, 1783–1806* (Cambridge, 1970); Lakshmi Subramanian, *Indigenous Capital and Imperial Expansion: Bombay, Surat and the West Coast* (Delhi, 1996).

[23] The one exception is XCHR/MHR/Correspondence (outgoing) (5 April 1786a).

Table 7. *Frequency distribution of personal attributes used to describe the Śeṇvīs in the Kāmats' correspondence with third parties.*[a]

	year									
	1779	1780	1785	1786	1787	1788	1789	1790	1791	total
[without attributes]	0	0	0	1	0	0	0	0	0	**1**
senhor(es)	1	0	1	3	11	14	3	0	2	**35**
amigo(s)	0	0	0	0	0	3	0	1	1	**5**
correspondente(s)	1	0	0	0	1	1	0	0	0	**3**
constituinte(s)	0	0	0	3	0	1	1	0	0	**5**
socio(s)	0	0	0	0	0	1	0	0	0	**1**
negociante(s)	0	0	0	0	1	2	0	0	0	**3**
number of letters	**2**	**0**	**1**	**7**	**12**	**14**	**4**	**1**	**2**	

Note: [a] The reason for the discrepancy between the total number of letters (43) and the total number of attributes (53) is that the Śeṇvīs were sometimes named more than once in a letter, occasionally with multiple or differing attributes.
Source: XCHR/MHR.

and *negociante* ('merchant'). Table 7 gives the frequency with which these attributes were used over the period covered by the documents. It shows that by far the most popular attribute was *senhor*, a standard mode of addressing a man in Portuguese (and found in thirty-five out of a total of fifty-three instances in which the Śeṇvīs are named). All the others were used much more sparingly: *amigo* (five), *constituinte* (five), *correspondente* (three), *negociante* (three) and *socio* (one). The frequency distribution of these attributes suggests that the relationship became closer and more intricate in the course of the 1780s. The changes in the modes of addressing harmonises with a relationship that was, until about 1780, akin to one between an agent and a principal. In this relationship, the former undertook a narrow and well-defined range of services, which while useful were of marginal significance for the latter. By the late 1780s, however, the situation had been transformed. The Śeṇvīs had been elevated to the status of (junior) partners, confidants and friends, permitted – and, arguably, encouraged – by the Kāmats to exercise their personal judgement for their joint benefit. So in 1779 the Śeṇvīs were designated merely as the Kāmats' *correspondentes*. From 1787, however, the Śeṇvīs were designated by a wider range of terms – as the Kāmats' *constituintes* or *socios*, or even as *negociantes* in their own right.

The growing intimacy and complexity of the ties between the two sides was paralleled by increasing personal regard for one another. From the late 1780s, for example, the Kāmats begin referring to the Śeṇvīs as their *amigos*. Awareness of this did not long remain confined to themselves alone; it also percolated into the stock of dispersed knowledge within their networks. In 1791, one of their associates recognised this state of affairs by describing the Śeṇvīs as the Kāmats' '*onrrado*', their honourable colleague or friend.[24] The shift reflected functional changes in their relationship over this period. During the 1780s, in step with the Kāmats' growing confidence in the Śeṇvīs, the Śeṇvīs became more deeply involved in the Kāmats' dealings with their non-Marathi-speaking associates.

The role of the Śeṇvīs in transactions in which both parties had a stake were generally of three types: services relating to finance, notably credit, minting and remittances; services relating to commodities, especially their purchase, sale, transport and storage; and services relating to information, particularly the provision of commercial intelligence and advice. In principle, these services could have been undertaken by the Śeṇvīs on a commission basis. By the end of the 1770s, however, their relationship had passed that point. This is seen in the fact that they were now commonly designated as the Kāmats' agents (*correspondente, constituinte*). So what happened next?

Table 8 summarises the involvement of the Śeṇvīs in the affairs of the Kāmats. It shows that, for much of their collaboration, the Śeṇvīs operated largely as the Kāmats' agents in Bombay, performing a range of financial services to facilitate their ventures in partnership with others. The Śeṇvīs were typically asked to receive and dispatch bills and specie, and update the Kāmats' current accounts with their Bombay-based clients that the Śeṇvīs maintained on their behalf. But from the early 1780s the Kāmats started making more extensive use of the Śeṇvīs' skills and resources. A legal document from 1782 testifies to the degree of confidence that the Kāmats had in their judgement by this date. Leading up to 1782, the Kāmats were contracted by a Portuguese merchant, Elias Joze Francisco do Valle, to sell his cargo of sugar. If there was insufficient demand for it in Goa, they agreed to ship it to Bombay, whereupon the Śeṇvīs would undertake to find buyers. Any amount that remained unsold in Bombay was to be dispatched to Surat 'to merchants whom the said Shankar Śeṇvī and Co. select in conformity with the wishes of Elias Joze Francisco do Valle'. In the event that 'the said agent in Surat is not a man of probity and good faith', the Kāmats held themselves responsible for 'all possible guarantees'.[25] This venture illustrates that, though the Śeṇvīs continued to function as the Kāmats' agents, they were now entrusted

[24] XCHR/MHR/Correspondence (incoming) (15 March 1791).
[25] XCHR/MHR/Legal Records (13 December 1782).

Table 8. *Frequency distribution of the services performed by the Śeṇvīs for the Kāmats.* [a]

	year													
	1779	1780	1781	1782	1783	1784	1785	1786	1787	1788	1789	1790	1791	total
financial services as:														
agent	3	1	0	0	1	0	1	8	12	15	2	4	4	**50**
partner	0	0	0	0	0	0	0	0	0	1	0	0	0	**1**
commodity services as:														
agent	0	0	0	1	0	0	0	0	2	4	3	1	2	**16**
partner	0	0	0	0	0	0	0	0	0	1	0	0	0	**1**
informational services as:														
agent	0	0	0	1	0	0	0	0	0	0	0	0	1	**2**
partner	0	0	0	0	0	0	0	0	0	1	0	0	0	**1**
number of transactions	**3**	**1**	**0**	**1**	**1**	**0**	**1**	**8**	**14**	**19**	**5**	**5**	**7**	

Note: [a] For some years, the total of the services performed by the Śeṇvīs differs from the number of transactions in which they were involved with the Kāmats. This is unsurprising because of the wide range of services that they could offer the Kāmats.
Source: XCHR/MHR.

with the authority to take key decisions affecting the course and outcome of their joint affairs in light of their own assessment of the situation. They now enjoyed considerable latitude to act as they saw fit.

The Śeṇvīs importance in the Kāmats' ventures appears to have continued its upward trajectory in the latter part of the 1780s. Over these years, the Śeṇvīs were regularly engaged in the transport and storage of goods belonging to the Kāmats or their associates. Furthermore, the judgement of the Śeṇvīs was now trusted in matters of general strategy. It seems their relationship reached a new level in 1788 when the Kāmats and the Śeṇvīs cooperated for the first time as full partners. At the heart of the venture was the *Bom Sucesso*. This ship was hired for a commercial voyage from Goa to Macao, via Bombay. The Śeṇvīs participated in every aspect of this venture: they were central to raising funds, purchasing the cargo, formulating policy and issuing orders.[26] As the ship was being readied for departure, the Kāmats went so far as to express their warm feelings for the

[26] XCHR/MHR/Correspondence (incoming) (20 April, 2 May 1788), XCHR/MHR/Correspondence (outgoing) (8 February–16 November 1788, 18 March–15 May, 9 May 1788).

Śeṇvīs and their debt of gratitude to them. In a letter to Chevalier de Lespinasse, a Frenchman who was to travel on the *Bom Sucesso*, they asked him and his fellow officers to treat Senhor Śeṇvī 'well and with affection ... [for] he is a person to whom we are much obliged. And if you have any apprehension regarding him, forgive him because he is a man who bears no ill-will.'[27]

The story of the Kāmats' developing ties with the Śeṇvīs exemplifies relationships that involved an elusive mix of material and affective motivations. But this need not always be the case. Many ties were forged within the arena in which the main, or even sole, expectation was material gain. Such appears to have been the basis for dealings in the 1780s and early 1790s between Veṅkateśa and Nārāyaṇa Kāmat and the Bombay-based Parsi Nasarvanji Manakji. These are the decades covered by the available documents. Written in Portuguese, they number about eighty in total.[28] They comprise accounts and letters, about half of which were exchanged directly between Nasarvanji and the Kāmats, with the remainder sent by the Kāmats to mutual associates.

Whether viewed in terms of their physical span, the background of their members or their core functions, there is extensive overlap between the two main networks of which both Nasarvanji and the Kāmats were part. These networks were both oriented towards the maritime realm. In one, the central hubs were settlements along or near India's western coast. Many of those active in this belonged to resident communities with an established presence in cross-cultural trade and intermediation, as well as in maritime transport. They included Parsis, Armenians, Gujarati *baniyā*s, Gauḍ Sārasvat brahmins, Malabari Jews and Luso-Indians, alongside European private traders and the merchant-officials of the European East India companies. The second network had a more far-flung physical presence, embracing the Arabian Sea area, but going beyond it too. The types of individuals active in this were the same as in the first, though western Europeans were more dominant because of their effective control of ocean-going vessels. Both networks performed similar

[27] XCHR/MHR/Correspondence (outgoing) (18 March–12 May 1788).

[28] The correpondence exchanged between Nasarvanji and the Kāmats was normally written in Portuguese. On the few occasions that Nasarvanji wrote to the Kāmats in another European language, they requested he keep to Portuguese in future. Only if this were not possible, say, because a translator was unavailable, did they consent to receiving correspondence from him in English. XCHR/MHR/Correspondence (outgoing) (29 January–22 December 1787). This request makes it clear that the two sides were not conversant with one another's mother tongues – Gujarati in the case of Nasarvanji, Marathi or Konkani in the case of the Kāmats – and that the preferred lingua franca was Portuguese, with English as a fall-back.

functions. They facilitated the purchase and sale of goods, provided access to credit and insurance, and enabled the transport of bullion and other merchandise. The evident commonalities between these two networks and those in which the Śeṇvīs and Kāmats were situated are tempered, however, by big differences. The networks shared by Nasarvanji and the Kāmats, centred as they were on flows and interactions mediated by sea routes, seldom extended beyond the hinterland of the ports that constituted their principal hubs. This orientation underlies a second big difference. And that is the fact these networks had little involvement in political intelligence; their primary concerns were mercantile and financial.

The earliest record of collaboration between the Kāmats and Nasarvanji dates from 1784. At this time, all three were in their early to mid-thirties[29] and their relationship was of recent provenance, perhaps less than a year old. It had most probably been established as a result of decisions taken by French and Portuguese officials based in India. Soon after the cessation of hostilities between the British and French in the American War of Independence, Nasarvanji Manakji was officially appointed 'broker to the French nation' in Bombay. The practical consequence of this was that he became the preferred intermediary for French private traders who called at Bombay to buy and sell goods, and to provision their ships. Nasarvanji added to this post the one for the Portuguese in the closing months of 1784.[30] On gaining these posts, he came into contact with Veṅkateśa and Nārāyaṇa Kāmat. This was almost inevitable because the brothers had been official brokers in Goa for the Portuguese and French since the 1760s and 1770s, respectively.[31] Nasarvanji's appointment shaped the future contours of their relationship. Henceforth, their role as official brokers was the chief dynamic in their dealings.

After 1784, Nasarvanji and the Kāmats were engaged in transactions that required them to share information and give advice, and to help their associates secure credit and facilitate the sale and purchase of goods. Their emoluments were made up of fees, interest on money advanced

[29] In 1784, Veṅkateśa Kāmat was thirty-four years old, Nārāyaṇa Kāmat thirty-two and Nasarvanji thirty-one.

[30] In 1784, Nasarvanji was described by the Kāmats as 'corretor desta nascan Portugueza'. XCHR/MHR/Correspondence (outgoing) (22 November–30 December 1784). In a letter from Nasarvanji to the Kāmats a few years later, he refers to the posts that the two parties occupied at the time as 'corretor da nação fidelissimo Portugues e Franceza'. XCHR/MHR/Correspondence (incoming) (26 November 1789).

[31] The Kāmats inherited the office of Portuguese broker on the death of their father, Suba, in 1765. They were appointed brokers to the French in Goa in 1777.

and a portion of the profits. Almost every transaction in which they collaborated involved Europeans, at times in the capacity of principals, at times as agents or partners. Among these Europeans, Portuguese merchant-officials dominated. The French too figured prominently. British private traders and merchant-officials, however, were few and far between, which is perhaps surprising given their major – and growing – role in Indian Ocean trade by the middle of the eighteenth century. It was not uncommon for Nasarvanji and the Kāmats to participate in ventures in which Europeans of differing nationalities pooled their resources to form associations. At the same time, the Kāmats and Nasarvanji excepted, what is notable about these ventures is the near total absence of those belonging to communities indigenous to Islamicate Eurasia.[32] This absence suggests that the relationship between Nasarvanji and the Kāmats operated in a highly specialised niche, one that was essentially restricted to Europeans and the maritime realm.

The dealings between the Kāmats and Nasarvanji never ranged beyond business. So there is no evidence to suggest that their relationship was sweetened by gifts of, say, fresh fruit. As for any personal favours undertaken, they were driven by cold logic in which the expected return was the uppermost consideration. Their roles in this relationship pivoted mainly on financing transactions, remitting money and disseminating information concerning the venture at hand. In performing these tasks, they normally acted as agents for third parties. I have seen only two instances in which one side instructed the other regarding a venture for their own account.[33] The majority of the tasks demanded by their relationship were to receive, forward, accept or draw up bills of exchange, to receive sums of money, and to make payments. Their instructions to each other also dealt with the transport and storage of goods, and their purchase and sale. Occasionally, one party would be asked to help out an associate scheduled to reach their port in the near future.[34] The Kāmats and Nasarvanji passed on messages to third parties and acted as the other's enforcer, particularly for the collection of money that had fallen due.[35] The accomplishment of these tasks was noted in their daybooks and ledgers, many of which were maintained separately for individual associates and

[32] The few exceptions are noted in XCHR/MHR/Correspondence (incoming) (10 March 1787, 4 April, 30 December 1791) and XCHR/MHR/Correspondence (incoming) (undated): 11.

[33] These are noted in XCHR/MHR/Correspondence (incoming) (undated): 11 and XCHR/MHR/Correspondence (incoming) (4 April, 30 December 1791).

[34] XCHR/MHR/Correspondence (outgoing) (29 January–22 December 1787), XCHR/MHR/Correspondence (incoming) (12–16 March 1787, 20 May 1788).

[35] XCHR/MHR/Correspondence (incoming) (12–15 March 1787).

ventures.[36] These accounts were balanced on a regular basis, either at the end of the financial cycle or on the venture's conclusion. The practice injected their networks with flexibility because it gave each side the option of using the accounts maintained by the other with a third party to make and receive payments.[37] The one between the Kāmats and Nasarvanji was then adjusted to reflect this payment. It is worth noting, however, that from the standpoint of the frequency and types of functions each side carried out for the other little changed with the passing years. The character of their relationship, whether evaluated in terms of the intensity or pattern of activities, remained fairly constant throughout the 1780s and into the 1790s.

This lack of development may well have been linked to their strict and narrow focus on business. An analysis of the formulae and idiom used to open and close the letters exchanged between them, and the manner in which they referred to the other in their correspondence with third parties, lends support to this view. It suggests that, whatever other factors may have been at work in their interactions, affection was not one of them. The findings are summarised in Tables 9 and 10.

These tables highlight the point that in general their names were evoked, and their relationship described, in remarkably simple terms. So in about one-quarter of the instances in which Nasarvanji Manakji is mentioned in the Kāmats' letters to mutual associates, his name is unadorned by any title or epithet, even by the near universal *senhor*. This tendency coincided with periods during which they were in sporadic contact or in conflict. In their direct correspondence, conversely, their names never appear without one or more attributes. Most often this is *senhor*.[38] *Amigo* was also occasionally used to describe the other side.[39] The context, however, generally belied the word's literal meaning. In almost every instance in which it was invoked, the letter concerned a matter that was out of the ordinary, be it a request for an unusual favour[40] or an attempt to placate the other party for a perceived

[36] XCHR/MHR/Correspondence (incoming) (12–16 March 1787), XCHR/MHR/Correspondence (outgoing) (8 February–16 November 1788).

[37] XCHR/MHR/Correspondence (outgoing) (14 March 1788).

[38] This title was used in four-fifths of cases of their name being invoked in direct correspondence between the Kāmats and Nasarvanji, and in two-thirds of cases in the Kāmats' correspondence with third parties.

[39] It occurs in the following letters: XCHR/MHR/Correspondence (outgoing) (14 November–15 December 1784, 24 August–29 December 1784, 12 April–12 November 1786, 29 January–22 December 1787), XCHR/MHR/Correspondence (incoming) (4 April, 30 Dceember 1791), XCHR/MHR/Correspondence (incoming) (undated): 11.

[40] XCHR/MHR/Correspondence (outgoing) (12 April–12 October 1786, 29 January–22 December 1787), XCHR/MHR/Correspondence (incoming) (undated): 11.

Table 9. *Frequency distribution of personal attributes used to describe Nasarvanji Manakji in his letters from the Kāmats.*

	year									
	1784	1785	1786	1787	1788	1789	1790	1791	1792+	total
[without attributes]	0	0	0	0	0	0	0	0	0	**0**
senhor(es)	3	0	7	16	6	1	2	2	1	**38**
amigo(s)	0	0	1	1	0	0	0	1	1	**4**
[formulaic prose]	0	0	0	2	2	1	1	1	1	**8**
number of letters	**3**	**0**	**7**	**16**	**6**	**1**	**2**	**2**	**1**	

Source: XCHR/MHR.

Table 10. *Frequency distribution of personal attributes used to describe Nasarvanji Manakji in the letters from the Kāmats to third parties.*

	year									
	1784	1785	1786	1787	1788	1789	1790	1791	1792+	total
[without attributes]	3	0	0	0	1	0	0	3	0	**7**
senhor(es)	4	0	3	5	4	0	0	1	0	**17**
amigo(s)	3	0	0	0	0	0	0	0	0	**3**
number of letters	**8**	**0**	**3**	**5**	**5**	**0**	**0**	**4**	**0**	

Source: XCHR/MHR.

slight.[41] The formulaic opening and closing parts of their letters were normally brief and perfunctory; sometimes they were omitted altogether.[42] Indeed, the correspondence between the two sides is notable for its directness of style, unembroidered with rhetorical niceties. The few cases of an effusive declaration of loyalty or a verbose promise to help in any way possible are invariably accompanied by a petition for a special request[43] or by apologies for, say, having failed to

41 XCHR/MHR/Correspondence (outgoing) (14 November–15 December 1784, 24 August–29 December 1784).

42 This resonates with the epistolary templates underlying personal and business correspondence in Latin-script languages. For a detailed treatment, see the first section of Chapter 7.

43 XCHR/MHR/Correspondence (incoming) (20 May 1788), XCHR/MHR/Correspondence (outgoing) (29 January–22 December 1787, 2 August–16 November 1788), XCHR/MHR/Correspondence (incoming) (26 October 1789), XCHR/MHR/Correspondence (incoming) (undated): 11.

execute an order or being remiss in keeping up a regular correspondence.[44]

That relations between the Kāmats and Nasarvanji Manakji were hard-headed and driven almost entirely by material concerns is put across forcefully in two letters which discuss their roles as official brokers for the Portuguese and French. In 1784, soon after Nasarvanji's appointment as the Portuguese 'corretor', the Kāmats wrote to offer him their congratulations.[45] Their relationship had been troubled of late because of a disagreement over how to divide up the losses in a venture in which both sides had been creditors.[46] Nasarvanji's appointment presented an opportunity to put this disagreement behind them. The Kāmats weighed up the cost of bearing a greater portion of the losses versus the prospect of additional income were Nasarvanji to funnel a greater volume of business towards them in the coming years. The realisation of this prospect required them, however, to maintain a modicum of cordiality in their dealings with him. In light of this, they opted for a compromise: they approached Feliciano António Nogueira, a close associate, to help them resolve their differences.[47] His mediation proved successful (on which more below).

The next explicit reference to the role of the Kāmats and Nasarvanji as official brokers occurs five years later, in October 1789. Nasarvanji asked the Kāmats to protect him from slanderous aspersions then being cast against his character by a Portuguese merchant. But why the Kāmats? Because, as he put it, we are 'friends and we are brokers of the most faithful Portuguese and French nations, one supporting the other'.[48] Of the two arguments made here, references to their friendship may be dismissed out of hand: the two sides had not been in contact for the preceding six months and there was nothing in their dealings over the previous few years to suggest any kind of personal rapport. The second argument, however, does have some merit. The Kāmats and Nasarvanji occupied analogous positions in their home settlements as far as the affairs of the French and Portuguese were concerned. This had become the central plank of their relationship. Considerations of self-interest thereby dictated that they ought to do whatever possible to uphold one another's reputation within the arena. It was thanks to such

44 XCHR/MHR/Correspondence (outgoing) (29 January–22 December 1787, 8 February–16 November 1788), XCHR/MHR/Correspondence (incoming) (undated): 11.
45 XCHR/MHR/Correspondence (outgoing) (22 November–30 December 1784).
46 XCHR/MHR/Correspondence (outgoing) (24 August 1784).
47 XCHR/MHR/Correspondence (outgoing) (24 August–29 December 1784).
48 XCHR/MHR/Correspondence (incoming) (26 October 1789).

considerations, certainly not affection or a desire for the greater good, that the Kāmats came to his aid.

Perhaps the most compelling evidence in support of the claim that the relationship between the Kāmats and Nasarvanji Manakji was inherently fragile or unstable is the frequent lament about long gaps in their correspondence. This was a recurrent feature of the ties between them. On at least four occasions between 1784 and 1791, letters begin with complaints, gentle rebukes or apologies for the excessive length of time that had elapsed since the other party's last missive.[49] In 1784, the Kāmats swallowed their pride and took the initiative so as to patch up their current differences, as a result of which their dealings of late had ground to a halt. 'We have decided to sue for peace in the present dispute, and by this, in [our] heart, we set great store,' they informed Nasarvanji. 'Now we desire for you to join us in a happy correspondence so that we may fulfil with pleasure our duties.'[50] Together with Nogueira's intervention, this démarche appears to have done the trick and their correspondence was resumed – at least for the time being. A few years on, after another bout of inactivity, the Kāmats told Nasarvanji that they felt 'a little disconsolate' at not having received letters from him for such a long time.[51] In October 1789, following yet another extended period of silence, it was Nasarvanji's turn to be conciliatory. Since 16 May, he wrote, 'I have not had any [letter] from you. [But] not even I have had the occasion [to write] that I supposed. Now, as this occasion presents itself, I cannot fail in my obligation [to you].'[52] Nasarvanji expressed his feelings most openly about these seemingly endemic disruptions in their correspondence when he noted in the 1790s that not having received news from the Kāmats is 'equal to me having little of [their] estimation'.[53] The regularity with which their correspondence was suspended shows that there was, at a minimum, a lack of interest by one or both sides in maintaining robust ties. That the relationship persisted in some fashion was because of the demands of their European associates.

Another means of gaining insights into the basic contours of the ties between the Kāmats and Nasarvanji is through their dealings with third parties. The most significant of these third parties in the 1780s was the aforementioned Feliciano António Nogueira, a Portuguese private trader

[49] The shortest gap was about six months. XCHR/MHR/Correspondence (outgoing) (29 January–22 December 1787), XCHR/MHR/Correspondence (incoming) (26 October 1789), XCHR/MHR/Correspondence (incoming) (undated): 11.

[50] MHR/Correspondence (outgoing) (22 November–30 December 1784)

[51] XCHR/MHR/Correspondence (outgoing) (29 January–22 December 1787).

[52] XCHR/MHR/Correspondence (incoming) (26 October 1789).

[53] XCHR/MHR/Correspondence (incoming) (undated): 11.

and until 1787 the director of the Estado da Índia's factory at Surat. His relations with both parties were complex and mercurial. He engaged with them on both a personal level and an official level, the boundaries between the two often being blurred. Furthermore, he interacted with them sometimes jointly, at other times with one side independently of the other. Well aware of Nogueira's proximity to Nasarvanji and of his position in the upper echelons of the Estado da Índia, the Kāmats asked him in October 1784 to go to Bombay and, with their full support, to resolve their ongoing dispute with Nasarvanji.[54] This dispute centred on the proportion of the losses each side was to bear in a venture in which both had had an interest and which had failed to turn out as expected. When Nogueira was called in, the relationship between the Kāmats and Nasarvanji was at a nadir. They were no longer in direct contact. But they could not afford to allow this situation to persist; their official positions required them to work together on behalf of their clients. The Kāmats hoped that Nogueira, who was well known to them through their many dealings, could help bridge the differences. After his arrival in Bombay, Nogueira spoke to Nasarvanji and explained the Kāmats' point of view. Soon thereafter, letters between the two sides started flowing once again.

If the Kāmats and Nasarvanji had an intimate community in common, they would have been able to depend on various close kindred or friends – individuals for whom they had personal regard and to whom they were obligated – to iron out problems arising in their relationship. Indeed, it is unlikely a complete breach would ever have occurred in such circumstances. The difficulty would have been recognised at a much earlier stage and it would have been tamed long before it got out of hand. But the actual nature of their dealings, and of the networks of which they were part, did not permit this. Their recourse to Nogueira shows that their dealings were mostly impersonal, dominated by their material interests and by their utilitarian loyalty to their clients. These considerations ensured that they continued to work together, whatever their true sentiments for one another. However, that was not without consequences for their relationship. As a result of the lack of personal trust between them, they adopted a cautious and distant posture towards each other. It is thus unsurprising that their interactions were irregular, marked by alternating periods of intense activity and silence.

In the latter half of the eighteenth century, the Kāmats had dealings both with Nasarvanji Manakji, mainly in his capacity as the official broker to the Portuguese and the French in Bombay, and with Zogu and Shankar

[54] XCHR/MHR/Correspondence (outgoing) (24 October–29 December 1784).

Śeṇvī, who first appear as their local agents in Bombay. There was considerable overlap between the networks in which their relationships were situated, especially between those centred on western India and the Arabian Sea area. The documents suggest that this very overlap was a source of conflict for those involved: as either of the Kāmats' Bombay-based correspondents were in principle able to execute most of their instructions equally well, the Kāmats continually had to balance their communal loyalties and obligations towards the Śeṇvīs against their formal commitments to Nasarvanji and their European clients. Their mutual associates would have been well aware of this tension. Francisco Gomes Loureira, for instance, hinted at this state of affairs when he told the Kāmats that he had not received from them any orders to make a certain payment nor, he added, from Shankar Śeṇvī or from Nasarvanji Manakji. He made a point of mentioning both.[55] Of course, Nasarvanji was aware of the potential conflict of interest this situation could give rise to, especially since he openly recognised the Śeṇvīs as the Kāmats' agents in Bombay.[56] This conflict, however, did not become debilitating because of the Kāmats' overall policy towards the networks in which European merchant-officials and private traders had the greatest stake. Because of the offices that they held, the Kāmats tended in the 1780s and 1790s to make use of the services offered by Nasarvanji in Bombay. At the same time, they sought to involve the Śeṇvīs in as many of their transactions as possible, and increasingly so from the mid-1780s on.[57]

Juxtaposing these two relationships also throws into sharp relief several intriguing differences. Perhaps the most glaring is that the ties between the Śeṇvīs and the Kāmats deepened and broadened over time, whereas those between the Kāmats and Nasarvanji remained on the whole static and short-termist. One possible rationalisation for this difference is that dealings between the Kāmats and Nasarvanji were determined almost entirely by material self-interest and the specific expectations which went with their positions as official brokers to the French and Portuguese 'nations' at Goa and Bombay. The documents reveal no convincing evidence of there ever having been meaningful friendship or even respect between the two sides. The main props of their relationship were a desire to generate income and their formal duties towards their European principals, agents and clients. Both were required for their relationships to prosper. However, without ties of sentiment, and the personal trust that

55 XCHR/MHR/Correspondence (incoming) (29 October, 25 November 1788), XCHR/MHR/Correspondence (outgoing) (30 September–16 November 1788).
56 XCHR/MHR/Correspondence (incoming) (20 May 1788).
57 XCHR/MHR/Correspondence (outgoing) (8 February–16 November 1788, 1 August 1788a).

accompanied them, this situation was basically unstable. Their relationship was delicately balanced. That it persisted for as long as it did is a testament to the mechanisms dispersed throughout the arena. These made impersonal trust between them possible through effective monitoring from afar and the resolution of potential disputes to their mutual satisfaction. But take away one of the main props and the relationship would founder. And this is what often happened. Contrast that with the Kāmats' relationship with the Śeṇvīs, which, despite its peaks and troughs, continued to be resilient and vibrant, branching into new areas as it grew with time. Much of the difference is most plausibly accounted for by their shared communal background and the fount of personal trust vested in it.

Individuals in family households

The focus of the previous section is on dealings between individuals embedded in shared networks. It examines the nature and functioning of two relationships, and the course that they followed over several decades in the eighteenth century. The point has already been made that those involved did not work for themselves alone. Rather, they acted through, and on behalf of, well-defined organisations or groups. Certainly the most widespread and the most important of these associations was the family household. It provided the setting for Chapter 3 where the analysis suggests that the family household was the pivot around which turned the everyday feelings, thoughts and actions of the region's inhabitants. It was the smallest social unit that required the acceptance or willing engagement of more than one person, and which endured across the generations (even as it was reinvented). Be they scribes or linguists, teachers or clerics, brokers or merchants, it was the family household that shaped their livelihoods. And it was within the family environment that individuals active in the arena were educated, trained and formed, furnishing the crucible which forged their bearing in the region's polities.[58]

Despite the manifest significance of the family to so many aspects of the past, we know surprisingly little about the actual character and function of families in any part or period of India and the Islamic heartlands before the nineteenth century.[59] If we aspire towards a grounded understanding of daily life in this region before colonisation, the family in all of its guises

[58] Albeit for a very different premodern context, Shelomo D. Goitein makes a similar argument regarding the family in his *A Mediterranean Society*, I, 180–3.

[59] The exceptions for our period include Haim Gerber, 'Anthropology and family history: the Ottoman and Turkish families', *Journal of Family History* 14:4 (1989), 409–21; Judith

must be given its due by scholars. The present section is about the family in one of its many guises, the family household. My focus here is intended to complement that of the first half of this chapter. More generally, the account given here of ordinary families found within the arena seeks to highlight a major lacuna in our historical knowledge and, at the same time, contribute something towards filling it.

The account that follows is built on, and framed by, three basic concepts: the family, the household and kinship.[60] Intuitively, these concepts are closely related to one another. It is widely accepted today that the family, no matter how it is defined, expresses a great deal of diversity and complexity. So if the notion is to have any utility, its definition cannot be normative or universalising. This is reflected in the cognitive patterns marshalled by the arena's participants. As discussed in the chapter on those patterns, the vernacular language in their personal correspondence reveals no term – like *usra, khānvādah* or *parivār* – that referred solely and unambiguously to a 'family'. This does not mean, however, the family was absent. What we see instead is the family and, more specifically, the family household referred to by a variety of nominal phrases like 'the people [or inhabitants] of the house' (*ahl al-bayt*). In this formulation, a general collective is qualified by the attribute deemed most salient to the group in question. It suggests that the family existed for contemporaries as an identifiable entity, even though it was articulated in more than one way. The language marshalled for this purpose was thus imbued with a flexibility that allowed for differences found among real families, while maintaining a shared core. My approach in this section is characterised by the same spirit.

The analysis of family life presented here begins from a minimalist position. This entails specification of the necessary attributes that marked

E. Tucker, 'Ties that bound: women and family in eighteenth- and nineteenth-century Nablus', in Nikki R. Keddie and Beth Baron (eds.), *Women in Middle Eastern History: Shifting Boundaries in Sex and Gender* (New Haven, CT, 1991), 233–53; Nelly Hanna, *Making Big Money in 1600: the Life and Times of Isma'il Abu Taqiyya, Egyptian Merchant* (Syracuse, NY, 1998); Sumit Guha, 'Household size and household structure in western India, *c.*1700–1950: beginning an exploration', *Indian Economic and Social History Review* 35:1 (1998), 23–33; Margaret L. Meriwether, *The Kin who Count: Family and Society in Ottoman Aleppo, 1770–1840* (Austin, TX, 1999); Beshara Doumani (ed.), *Family History in the Middle East: Household, Property, and Gender* (Albany, NY, 2003); Dilbagh Singh, 'Regulating the domestic: notes on the pre-colonial state and the family', *Studies in History* 19:1 (2003), 69–86; Indrani Chatterjee (ed.), *Unfamiliar Relations: Family and History in South Asia* (New Brunswick, NJ, 2004). See below for the modern published scholarship of specific relevance to the case studies presented in this section.

60 The ways in which these concepts have been deployed in historical scholarship is usefully summarised, and critiqued, in Naomi Tadmor, 'The concept of the household-family in eighteenth-century England', *Past and Present* 151 (1996), 111–40 and Tadmor, *Family and Friends in Eighteenth-Century England: Household, Kinship and Patronage* (Cambridge, 2001).

out particular individuals as members of a given family household. I take as the starting point the existence of a significant and enduring bond between a parent and a child. Working outwards from this, the entity of interest is conceptualised as the smallest subset of kindred or intimate relationships centred on a single household capable of biological and social reproduction within its ambient polity.[61] In this conception, the entity is most accurately labelled the 'family household'. For the sake of convenience, however, I use 'family' as a shorthand. So wherever 'family' is seen unqualified in the remainder of this chapter, it should be read as 'family household'.

While kindred are central to any family, I do not restrict membership to them alone. Undoubtedly, the great majority of families were populated and dominated by those between whom ties were defined by either consanguine descent or affinal ritual, marriage and adoption being the most common examples of the latter. It is nevertheless important to leave open the possibility of other kinds of ties being constitutive for families. This is why affective intimacy forms part of my minimal definition (which in certain situations is a more useful marker for identifying a family's outer bounds than kinship). It is also worth noting that families coexisted with, and were intersected by, other groups and organisations, particularly ethnic and religious communities, and that this broader nexus was involved in giving families historical meaning. There is no denying that a family's internal reality was primarily determined by the duties, expectations and privileges attached to its individual members, and by the sentiments embodied in their relationships. At the same time, the family as a named, bounded and closed association was policed and reinforced by outsiders who, at the very least, had the power to confer – or withhold – recognition.

Given this minimal definition, then, what is the best method for recovering the family in a given milieu, time and place? The one that I have adopted is dictated, on the one hand, by the state of the relevant scholarly literature and, on the other, by the extant and available sources. For Islamicate Eurasia in the eighteenth century, the scholarship on the subject of families is patchy and of little practical help. As for the sources, they are rarely forthcoming about the daily realities of family life for those beyond the circles of the conspicuous elites. The documents that have made this book possible are, however, an exception to the rule. Many of these documents are personal letters. Through them, we are able to

[61] By household, I mean residence in a shared locality – which could be, though need not be, a single building or contiguous plot – that was the permanent home of the family's leading female member, invariably a wife or a mother.

describe and analyse two families in the middle of the eighteenth century – one Shīʿī and based in Bengal, the other Armenian and based in southern Iraq – whose interests extended across much of the region. The nature of their correspondence is rich in detail though limited in scope. Because of this, I proceed in a two-pronged fashion. I study the kinship terminology used by its authors so as to apprehend the structuring of their families and their overall form.[62] I also pay attention to the sentiments that the family members avowed for one another, juxtaposing wherever possible their sentiments against their actual behaviour.[63] This approach generates valuable insights into the contours and dynamics of two real families whose livelihoods depended on activities characterised by large distances and long silences. By keeping in view the flows and interactions in which they participated, we thereby sharpen our understanding of the arena's connective tissue.

In 1748, as Sayyid Muṣṭafā's ship was crossing the Arabian Sea on its way to Iraq, the winds changed direction and he was forced to turn back. While waiting out the monsoon in ports along India's Malabar coast, this pious, homesick Shīʿī had ample time to reflect on the problems that were sure to arise from this unexpected detour.[64] Of course, Sayyid Muṣṭafā knew that such vicissitudes were among the inescapable hazards of his age; they simply had to be endured and made the best of. Knowing this,

[62] There has long been an interest in kinship terminology (and ties) among scholars, especially anthropologists, working on India. See, for example, Thomas R. Trautman, *Dravidian Kinship* (Cambridge, 1981); Sylvia Vatuk, 'Forms of address in the north Indian family', in Ákos Östör, Lina Fruzzetti and Steve Barnett (eds.), *Concepts of Person: Kinship, Caste, and Marriage in India* (Cambridge, MA, 1982), 56–98; Farhat Hasan, *State and Locality in Mughal India: Power Relations in Western India, c. 1572–1730* (Cambridge, 2004), 71–90; Sylvia Vatuk, 'Muslim kinship in the Dravidian heartland', in Cynthia Talbot (ed.), *Knowing India: Colonial and Modern Constructions of the Past* (New Delhi, 2011), 108–34. For a discussion of the analytical value of kinship terminology as a method, and further citations of the historical scholarship that uses it, see Robert Wheaton, 'Observations on the development of kinship history, 1942–1985', *Journal of Family History* 12:1–3 (1987), 285–301.

[63] Though there has yet to be meaningful research into the history of sentiments in India or the Islamic heartlands in premodern times, the subject is of growing interest among historians more generally. For an account of its development and prospects, see Nicole Eustace, Eugenia Lean, Julie Livingston, Jan Plamper, William Reddy and Barbara Rosenwein, 'AHR conversation: the historical study of emotions', *American Historical Review* 117:5 (2012), 1487–531.

[64] Sayyid Muṣṭafā and his family belonged to one of the Shīʿī communities of Bengal. On the Shīʿīs of Bengal and, more generally, India before modern times, see Saiyid Athar Abbas Rizvi, *A Socio-Intellectual History of the Isna ʿAshari Shiʿis in India*, 2 vols. (Canberra, 1986); Juan R. I. Cole, *Roots of North Indian Shīʿism in Iran and Iraq: Religion and State in Awadh, 1722–1859* (Berkeley, CA, 1988); Richard M. Eaton, *The Rise of Islam and the Bengal Frontier, 1204–1760* (Berkeley, CA, 1993); Juan R. I. Cole, 'Popular Shīʿism', in Richard M. Eaton, *India's Islamic Traditions, 711–1750* (New Delhi, 2003), 311–41.

however, did little to raise his spirits. His journey, which was at once a commercial venture, a pilgrimage to the shrine city of Karbala and a quest for a family tree, would now be much prolonged, delaying by nearly half a year his return home to Bengal – and to his beloved son.[65]

Fortunately for us, Sayyid Muṣṭafā wrote over this period of enforced stasis several letters in Persian to his intimates in Bengal.[66] In them, he was open about his thoughts and feelings. He described his current predicament and future plans. He issued orders and offered suggestions so as to mitigate – and even profit from – the unforeseen changes to his itinerary. But he did not stop there. In giving full vent to his frustration, he left his correspondents in no doubt that his physical separation from those closest to him at home was a constant preoccupation. And it was with them that he dwelt on the very fundamentals of being, on duty, fate, sociability, death and God. These letters furnish the basis for my account of Sayyid Muṣṭafā's family. The account is pieced together from the ways in which he related to and talked about those at home who were nearest and dearest to him. With the notable exception of his son, however, the letters do not permit us to reconstruct the distinctive roles and statuses of individual members of the family, nor of Sayyid Muṣṭafā's sentiments for them as individuals. They do, however, allow us to reconstruct the family's overall size and shape, and sketch out its internal structuring. (See Figure 11.)

In contemplating his family at home, the person who loomed largest for Sayyid Muṣṭafā – and by a considerable margin – was his son, Sayyid Murtaḍā. The son's significance was both emotional and practical. The patrifilial relationship has been discussed from a number of perspectives in Chapters 2, 3 and 4. To minimise repetition, it is only touched upon here, the stress instead being on the relationship in the context of the family as a whole. The correspondence makes it clear that Sayyid Muṣṭafā harboured deep affection for his son. This is seen most clearly in the steadfastness and tenderness with which he expressed his feelings for him. His feelings were greatly heightened by their separation from one another. Sayyid Muṣṭafā missed his son terribly. The way in which he tried to cope

[65] This was a journey that many others had made before Sayyid Muṣṭafā. The early modern linkages between India and Iran (and parts of Iraq) are discussed in Sanjay Subrahmanyam, 'Persians, pilgrims and Portuguese: the travails of Masulipatnam shipping in the western Indian Ocean, 1590–1665', *Modern Asian Studies* 22:3 (1988) 503–30; Sanjay Subrahmanyam, 'Iranians abroad: intra-Asian elite migration and early modern state formation', *Journal of Asian Studies* 51:2 (1992), 340–64; Elizabeth Lambourn, 'Of jewels and horses: the career and patronage of an Iranian merchant under Shah Jahan', *Iranian Studies* 36:2 (2003), 213–58.

[66] Based on a comparison of their materiality, handwriting, writing style and content, Sayyid Muṣṭafā is very likely to have been the author of documents numbered 39, 40, 49, 50, 54, 55, 56, 58 and 60 in BL/Lansdowne/1046. It is also probable that he was responsible for documents numbered 37 and 38.

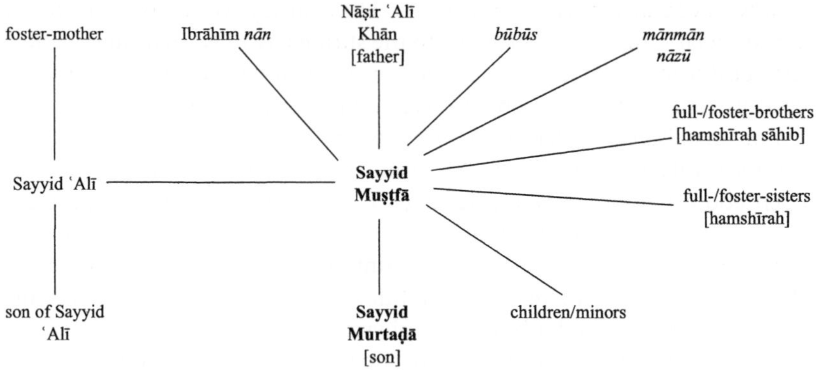

Figure 11. The structure of Sayyid Muṣṭafā's family.
Source: BL/Lansdowne/1046.

with his yearning for him was by preserving and nurturing his image in his mind,[67] by reminding them both that powers spiritual and temporal were sure to reunite them in due course,[68] and by seizing on every opportunity to write to him.[69] The father's affection for his son also revealed itself in his abiding concern for his well-being.[70] This concern was reinforced by a profound sense of paternal duty. He desired for Sayyid Murtaḍā an honourable and successful life at home and within their community. But he was unwilling to leave this to chance. That is presumably why so much of his correspondence is given over to instructions and advice on what is the correct work ethic[71] and on how his son ought to behave with his juniors,[72] elders[73] and others more generally.[74] All this indicates that Sayyid Muṣṭafā was heavily involved in his son's formation in the broadest sense, in his training,[75] in his personal character,[76] and in his knowledge of life, piety and the cosmos.[77] In turn, the son was expected to remember his father in his prayers,[78] to keep him informed of his latest news,[79] to love, respect and obey him.[80]

Taking the correspondence as a whole, Sayyid Murtaḍā was in his father's eyes a young man on the threshold of maturity. He was given duties appropriate for male adults. At the same time, his elders, above all

[67] BL/Lansdowne/1046, docs. 49, 56. [68] BL/Lansdowne/1046, doc. 49. [69] Ibid.
[70] BL/Lansdowne/1046, doc. 58. [71] BL/Lansdowne/1046, doc. 49.
[72] BL/Lansdowne/1046, doc. 56. [73] BL/Lansdowne/1046, docs. 49, 58.
[74] BL/Lansdowne/1046, docs. 49, 56, 58, 60. [75] BL/Lansdowne/1046, doc. 60.
[76] BL/Lansdowne/1046, doc. 49. [77] BL/Lansdowne/1046, docs. 49, 56, 58.
[78] BL/Lansdowne/1046, doc. 60. [79] BL/Lansdowne/1046, doc. 49.
[80] BL/Lansdowne/1046, docs. 49, 58.

his father, kept him on a short leash. This enables us to place some bounds on his age in the late 1740s. Sayyid Murtaḍā is likely to have been marriageable and, if already married, any children he may have had would have been infants. By the same token, his father was most probably in his thirties. Their relationship was marked, furthermore, by a stark hierarchy in which their respective statuses and roles are clearly defined. These were well known within the family and to their intimates. And that was not just because of their closeness to them; it was also their business to keep themselves informed since their collective well-being was yoked to the health of the relationship between a father and his mature sons. Perhaps the most noteworthy fact to emerge from Sayyid Muṣṭafā's letters is that no other member of the family was under so much scrutiny as his son, by the father for sure, and by others too. From this point of view, Sayyid Murtaḍā occupied a category that was entirely his own.

In shifting our gaze to the rest of the family, we discover that few of its members are ever specified by their given names. Rather, Sayyid Muṣṭafā addressed them through nicknames, sobriquets and idiomatic expressions. By their very nature, these are open to interpretation; they do not permit us to say much about the character of the addressees' ties to Sayyid Muṣṭafā, or to each other, beyond their generational position within the family. But even that is of value.

The youngest in Sayyid Muṣṭafā's family were described pithily as 'the children' (*aṭfāl*).[81] This could have been a reference to just his own children and grandchildren or, as is more probable, to all the minors who formed part of his household.[82] If the latter is the case, it would have embraced both his direct and collateral descendants. Though it was in relation to his son that Sayyid Muṣṭafā most often invoked the epithet *nūrchashm-i man* ('the light-of-the-eye'),[83] by no means was it restricted to him alone. On one occasion, we find *nūrchashm* written in the plural within the phrase *hamah-yi nūrchashmān*, 'all of the lights-of-my-eye'.[84] In literary Persian, *nūrchashm* designates someone with whom one has a close emotional bond, say, a beloved child or a dear friend.[85] In Sayyid Muṣṭafā's letters, the word's most likely sense included both his biological children and grandchildren, and those of his brothers and sisters who continued to live together in a joint household or nearby within the same

[81] BL/Lansdowne/1046, docs. 49, 50, 56.
[82] It is possible that *aṭfāl* also included the female members of the household.
[83] BL/Lansdowne/1046, docs. 39, 49, 56, 58, 60. [84] BL/Lansdowne/1046, doc. 60.
[85] See the entry for 'nūrchashm' in ʿAlī Akbar Dihkhudā, *Lughatnāmah*, 14 vols. (Tehran, 1993–4).

locality.[86] *Bābā-yi man* ('my bābā')[87] was used by him in practically the same sense as *nūrchashm* to address his son or junior members of the family.

In referring to those of his own generation, Sayyid Muṣṭafā drew upon terms which, if taken literally, meant that they that had all been suckled by the same woman or women. This would have been restricted in practice to his mother and aunts. But there is an alternative view if the terms are taken figuratively. In this alternative, the terms were intended rather to acknowledge the shared experience of having been reared together as children. Whether literal or figurative, the fact is that none of these individuals is named by Sayyid Muṣṭafā. They are instead described as his *hamshīrah*[88] and *hamshīrah ṣāḥibān*,[89] his full and foster sisters and brothers, respectively.[90] As for his elders, Sayyid Muṣṭafā made a point of mentioning his late father[91] and Sayyid ʿAlī's foster-mother (*dāyah*).[92] His other maternal and paternal uncles and aunts were denoted by familial diminutives such as *mānmān nāzū* and *būbū*.[93] Ibrāhīm Nān, who seems to have been his maternal grandfather, is the only member of his grandfather's generation to be mentioned explicitly by name.[94]

With the presence of 'the children', a mature son, brothers and sisters, uncles and aunts, and a grandparent, Sayyid Muṣṭafā's household in

[86] In the language of kinship studies, at the level of his children's generation, Sayyid Muṣṭafā switched between the Eskimo (or lineal) or Hawaiian kinship systems, subject to the qualification that the gender is unspecified.

[87] BL/Lansdowne/1046, doc. 48. [88] BL/Lansdowne/1046, doc. 58.

[89] BL/Lansdowne/1046, doc. 60.

[90] In premodern Persian, *hamshīrah* can refer to a full or foster brother or sister. In modern usage, however, its meaning is restricted to the latter. Furthermore, for his own generation, the way in which Sayyid Muṣṭafā referred to his relatives coheres with the Hawaiian kinship system.

[91] BL/Lansdowne/1046, doc. 56. [92] BL/Lansdowne/1046, doc. 60.

[93] BL/Lansdowne/1046, docs. 56, 58, 60. Elsewhere, he writes *būbū dilgūshād* (BL/Lansdowne/1046, doc. 56) and *būbū gulchaman* (BL/Lansdowne/1046, doc. 60). From these nicknames alone, it is not possible to specify the gender of these individuals nor their precise relationship to Sayyid Muṣṭafā. It is only from the contexts in which they are invoked that it may be inferred they were kindred belonging to the generation of his father. If this inference is correct, the terminology would be an instance of the Eskimo kinship system. It is conceivable that the terms used by Sayyid Muṣṭafā, rather than being nicknames, were variants on those that had currency within his community in Bengal and referred to particular ties within the family. His terminology would then be better interpreted as an instance of the Dravidian kinship system at the level of his parents' generation. However, I have yet to find evidence to support this latter interpretation.

[94] BL/Lansdowne/1046, doc. 49. In several of the Indo-Aryan languages dominating northern and central India, a *nānā* refers to the maternal grandfather and *nānī* the maternal grandmother. Given that Sayyid Muṣṭafā's family was resident in Bengal, it is likely they had absorbed into their vernacular Persian terminology from other languages which denoted specific relationships among kindred. This is the main justification for treating Ibrāhīm Nān as Sayyid Muṣṭafā's maternal grandfather.

Bengal spanned at least four generations. If the meaning of *aṭfāl* encompassed grandchildren too, then his family spanned five generations. I have attempted to depict this in Figure 11. It is notable that, with the exception of *nān* and *vālid*, none of the kin terms used by Sayyid Muṣṭafā distinguished his consanguine from his affine relatives. Also, they were not correlated to genealogical distance from him. This is in keeping with the interpretation that, for addressing purposes (and by extension for denoting respect), Sayyid Muṣṭafā gave roughly equal weighting to family members of a given generation – and presumably gender – whether they were related to him through marriage or descent. Persisting with this line of argument, it is possible that, in practice, his relationships within his household were determined more by his kindred's generational position (and age) than their lineage membership or genealogical separation from him. If so, this would run counter to the received idea of Muslim families as strongly patrilineal.

Sayyid Muṣṭafā's correspondence is peppered with messages for his many relatives and other intimates. These tend to be variants on a small number of pithy templates. Usually towards the end of a letter, he would ask the recipient to pass on to particular family members his 'blessing and greeting and a kiss-on-the-eye'.[95] Sometimes he included assurances of his 'devotion'[96] to them and his 'desire that all is well'.[97] In a few instances, he wrote more personalised messages. He wanted Ibrāhīm Nān, for example, to know that 'I remember your words and you'.[98] His messages also contain requests for small, tender favours. 'Kiss the face of the son of Sayyid ʿAlī on my behalf,' he asked on one occasion; '*khudā* is the witness that his countenance is oftentimes in my mind.'[99] While it was with his son that Sayyid Muṣṭafā lowered his guard sufficiently to reveal his innermost feelings and thoughts, he would also unburden himself to others at home. This would frequently be through palpable metaphors and allusions. To an intimate, whose name we are not given, he wrote:

> I have been present in your service just as Abyssinian slaves are in devotion . . . It is hoped that you do not banish this black-faced slave at prayer time from the corner of your mind since it is only through your blessings will I obtain my spiritual and temporal desires. And having been favoured by your personal blessings, there will come your fragrance. Having allowed it on my face, I will inhale your aspects which will [then] pass into [my] *dil*. And I am always praying for you [to which] *khudā* and his messenger are witnesses.[100]

[95] BL/Lansdowne/1046, doc. 60.
[96] BL/Lansdowne/1046, docs. 56, 58.
[97] BL/Lansdowne/1046, doc. 56.
[98] BL/Lansdowne/1046, doc. 49.
[99] BL/Lansdowne/1046, doc. 40.
[100] BL/Lansdowne/1046, doc. 50.

That all his intimates back home – not just his son – were ever-present in Sayyid Muṣṭafā's thoughts is a common refrain. And while Sayyid Muṣṭafā had an unquenchable thirst for information about his correspondents individually, he also insisted that they keep him abreast of any news about the rest of the family and household. In a telling passage, he instructed his son:

> It is necessary that in your letter there are details about the reality of your constitution and work, and about the circumstances of the children, especially in which way their temperament is [developing] and may [all] this be in your remarks. That is to say, you must write to me in full detail what has happened in the period [since my departure both] inside and outside the house (*khānah*) concerning [both] the young and the old, so that I may be consoled . . . Do not neglect [to tell me] about the condition of the children.[101]

This passage is of special interest to us. Through it, we gain a tangible sense of those whom Sayyid Muṣṭafā considered his intimates at home. It suggests, moreover, that his family in Bengal lived in, or constituted, a *khānah*. But we cannot go beyond this to say whether he intended by *khānah* a single physical residence or a group of residences occupied by the joint family in the same locality, or whether he intended the idea of a family in abstraction.

Collating the insights scattered throughout his correspondence, it appears that Sayyid Muṣṭafā's family household had up to two dozen intimates related to him through marriage and biological descent, on both his maternal and paternal sides. Within this group, Sayyid Muṣṭafā occupied a position of authority. This derived from his role as one of the chief breadwinners and from the fact he was a middle-aged man in full control of his physical and mental faculties who was experienced in the ways of the world. From Sayyid Muṣṭafā's perspective, his ties to his son had primacy over all others. This bond formed the family's central axis around which everything else revolved. Sayyid Muṣṭafā's letters make it evident that this bond was strong and deep, imbued with tenderness, and candid in tenor. But the father's gushing prose and his habitual concern for the son's behaviour, both in his dealings with him as his father as well as with others in his family, betray anxiety and uncertainty in relation to his son.[102]

[101] BL/Lansdowne/1046, doc. 49.

[102] In anthropological parlance, Sayyid Muṣṭafā lived in a collaterally extended family. Though Shīʿī families are patrilineal by sharia, Sayyid Muṣṭafā's actual kinship terminology, the importance he accorded to generational status and the feelings he avowed for his intimates suggests that, in practice, his family is better described as lying somewhere between non-unilineal (bilateral or cognatic) and moderately patrilineal.

In being forced to wait out the monsoon in western India, Sayyid Muṣṭafā was not the only one to experience misfortune in 1748. Living close to Basra, Māralīnā was short of money and feeling abandoned. It had been a long, long time since she had last set eyes on her husband. To make matters worse, she had recently bid farewell to her eldest son, off to India to join his father there. Like many wives and mothers of her Armenian community, she belonged to a family of itinerant merchants, agents and brokers.[103] The menfolk were expected to spend much of their lives abroad, often for years at a stretch. But before the onset of old age, they were expected to bring their peregrinations to a halt and remain close to home. Māralīnā was indignant that her husband was refusing to give her what she knew to be her due, leaving her at the mercy of others.

The correspondence in Arabic sent by her and other members of her family in southern Iraq to her far-off husband and son bear witness to this.[104] They also brim with details about the family's situation at home, and give the latest on the doings of their brethren scattered throughout the region, from Istanbul in the west to Calcutta in the east. The letters contain news and rumour, advice and instructions, requests for favours, and frank admissions of their worries, joys and foibles. We gain, as a

[103] There is a fairly large body of work on the Armenian diaspora communities of the early modern world. The contributions that overlap with the concerns of this book include George Bournatian, 'The Armenian community of Isfahan in the seventeenth century', *Armenian Review*, 24 (1971), 27–45 and 25 (1972), 33–50; Vartan Gregorian, 'Minorities of Isfahan: the Armenian community of Isfahan, 1587–1722', *Iranian Studies* 7:3–4 (1974), 652–80; Michel Aghassian and Kéram Kévonian, 'Le commerce arménien dans l'Océan Indien aux 17e et 18e siècles', in Denys Lombard and Jean Aubin (eds.), *Marchands et hommes d'affaires asiatiques dans l'Océan Indien et la Mer de Chine 13–20 siècles* (Paris, 1988), 155–81; Edmund M. Herzig, 'Armenian merchants of New Julfa, Isfahan: a study in premodern Asian trade' (unpublished D. Phil. thesis, Oxford University, 1992); Edmund M. Herzig, 'The family firm in the commercial organisation of the Julfa Armenians', in Jean Calmard (ed.), *Etudes Safavides* (Paris, 1993), 287–304; Michel Aghassian and Kéram Kévonian, 'The Armenian merchant network: overall autonomy and local integration', in Sushil Chaudhury and Michel Morineau (eds.), *Merchants, Companies and Trade: Europe and Asia in the Early Modern Era* (Cambridge, 1999), 74–94; Ina Baghdiantz McCabe, *Shah's Silk for Europe's Silver: the Eurasian Trade of the Julfa Armenians in Safavid Iran and India (1530–1750)* (Atlanta, GA, 2002); Vahan Baibourtian, *International Trade and the Armenian Merchants in the Seventeenth Century* (New Delhi, 2004); Sebouh D. Aslanian, *From the Indian Ocean to the Mediterranean: the Global Trade Networks of Armenian Merchants from New Julfa* (Berkeley, CA, 2010).

[104] These letters are numbered 67, 68, 69, 70, 71 and 78 in BL/Lansdowne/1046. They are addressed either to Shukr Allāh or ʿAbd Allāh b. Ḥassūn, and their authors were Māralīnā, three of her kindred (Niʿmat Allāh b. Mikhāyīl Jurūh, Ḥanna b. ʿAbd al-Dāʾim and ʿAbd al-ʿAṭī b. Yūsuf Ḥumṣī) and Jarjī, an employee or slave of Shukr Allāh. It should be noted that it is highly unlikely that Māralīnā, being female, wrote her letters herself. Instead, they were probably dictated to a male intimate, possibly a working scribe, who then wrote them up in neat. For more details, and evidence to support this claim, see the discussion on literacy in Chapter 6.

result, insights into the lives of the family members both inside and outside the home. We discover how they related to their temporal surroundings and to their cosmos, to this world, death and the world to come. We learn about an ordinary family handling the daily tasks that arose from being engaged in circulation and exchange in the middle of the eighteenth century.

Māralīnā's family was a tangled web. Marriages between close kindred meant that members were severally related to one another across generations. We are fortunate that the multiple viewpoints offered by their surviving correspondence permit us to apprehend the family's internal structuring, despite its complexity, in greater detail than is possible for Sayyid Muṣṭafā's family. Because of this very complexity, however, it might be useful to delineate Māralīnā's family as a whole before considering its specifics. The evidence shows that the family comprised both affine and consanguine kindred, and spanned at least four generations. At one end, there was Māralīnā's recently born granddaughter;[105] at the other end, there were her uncles and aunts.[106] Her extended family may be pictured as a constellation of at least three patrilineal clusters linked by one or more marriages. As depicted in Figure 12, these marriages were between Māralīnā's daughter and Yūsuf Ḥumṣī's son ʿAbd al-ʿAṭī; between Māralīnā's son Shukr Allāh and Niʿmat Allāh b. Mikhāyīl Jurūh's sister Kātrīnā Khātūn; and between another of Niʿmat Allāh b. Mikhāyīl Jurūh's sisters and Māralīnā's brother-in-law Ḥannā b. ʿAbd al-Dāʾim. Leaving minors aside, this family had at least thirty members.

As with Sayyid Murtaḍā, mature sons in Māralīnā's family were treasured and their relationships with their fathers constituted the family's principal axis. This reality did not, however, foreclose the possibility of other highly consequential relationships. Those found in Māralīnā's family included ties between a mother and her son, a son and his parents, a husband and wife, a woman and her son's brother-in-law, and between brother-cousins. These have already been examined in chapters 3 and 4. So it will suffice to summarise here the individual ties that constituted Māralīnā's family, which in turn will allow us to focus on the family as a whole rather than on its component elements.

Māralīnā was acutely conscious of the fact that the future prospects for her immediate family depended on a close and effective working relationship between her husband and son. What this meant in practice were love, generosity and forgiveness on the father's part, and the acceptance by her son Shukr Allāh of his lowly status before his father.[107] That Shukr Allāh

[105] BL/Lansdowne/1046, doc. 71. [106] BL/Lansdowne/1046, docs. 69, 70.
[107] BL/Lansdowne/1046, doc. 69.

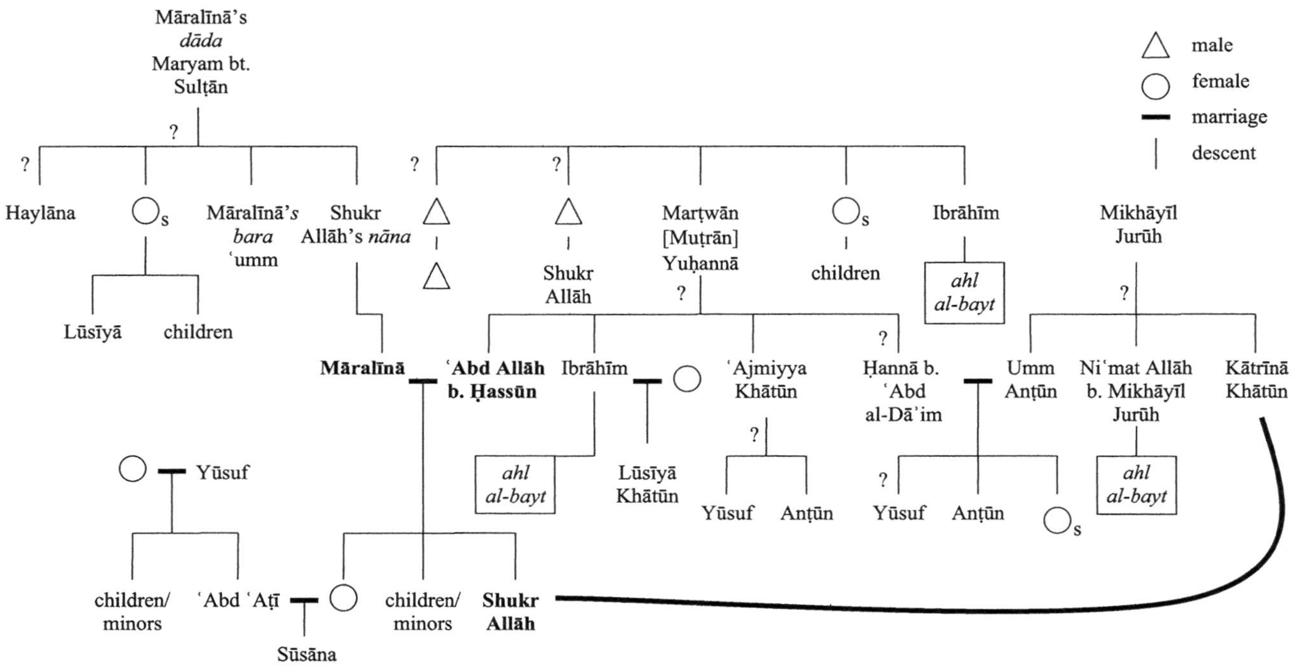

Figure 12. The structure of Māralīnā and 'Abd Allāh's family.
Source: BL/Lansdowne/1046.

was now a mature man, attested to by his recent marriage,[108] did not fundamentally alter the situation. Intimates at home insisted that he could not do without the support and counsel of his father, who as his teacher and guide had to be obeyed and respected.[109] Māralīnā's correspondence with her son and her husband also shows that she cared deeply for her son, was anxious for his safety, wanted the best for him and could not be reconciled to his separation from her.[110] Such concerns were echoed in her practical dealings on behalf of him. Whenever possible, she strove to carry out any instructions he sent her regarding their livelihood in the arena.

This points to a role played by women with potentially wide ramifications. Māralīnā's status was that of a dependant and her physical movements were essentially confined to the locality of her home, which is where her primary duties lay. Nevertheless, she was actively involved in the livelihood of her closest kinsmen. The letters demonstrate that, when her husband and son were abroad, she was expected to safeguard items left in her care, keep note of current expenses, confirm the completion of important tasks and fulfil any orders they might send her as part of their ongoing transactions. These could be to receive or deliver specified goods, to issue or take payments, or to supervise purchases or sales for the family's account. She was not, however, encouraged to use her own initiative. This was reserved for her daughter-in-law's brother Niʿmat Allāh, who was at the time living nearby, and for an employee (*khidmatkār, ajīr*) by the name of Jarjī.[111]

Māralīnā's situation illustrates the ways in which women could be of crucial significance for a family engaged in activities bridging India and the Islamic heartlands, especially if their menfolk were travelling or working in distant lands. The responsibilities with which the women were entrusted made a virtue of their proximity to home. In effect, they operated as warehouse-keepers and accountants, receiving goods and money, and distributing them according to need. Alongside this, they managed a kind of sorting office, directing letters between itinerant correspondents. From a broader perspective, women such as Māralīnā helped the family maintain a coherent archive and preserve its institutional memory. But there is more. Māralīnā also petitioned on behalf of her son, not always with his knowledge, so as to ease his life and to bring him success.[112] This was, of course, ultimately to her benefit. As a mature son, Shukr Allāh was expected in turn to look after his mother in ways not

[108] BL/Lansdowne/1046, docs. 69, 70. [109] BL/Lansdowne/1046, doc. 71.
[110] BL/Lansdowne/1046, docs. 67, 69, 70.
[111] BL/Lansdowne/1046, docs. 67, 69, 70, 78. [112] BL/Lansdowne/1046, doc. 69.

dissimilar to the obligations of his father towards her.[113] That is why sons who were old enough and capable of carrying out their filial duties – and yet failed to do so – left themselves open to unbridled condemnation by their kindred and other intimates.[114]

There was a great deal that a mother and father had in common in their relationships with their son. This is most obvious in their affection for him and willingness to help whenever possible, in their concerns for his well-being and future success, and, if currently abroad, in their desperation for any recent news about him.[115] With regard to other aspects of their son's life, however, it is the differences in the roles of a mother and a father that stand out. These differences were paralleled in a wife's relationship with her husband. By the late 1740s, Māralīnā's husband, ʿAbd Allāh b. Ḥassūn, had been away from home for several years. In her letters to him and her son, Māralīnā reiterated her desire for ʿAbd Allāh's physical companionship and her desperation for the material support which his presence would guarantee.[116] But he showed no sign of giving way.

Māralīnā had been avowing such thoughts and feelings for some time now even though she was well aware that long and regular separations from their menfolk were the lot of wives, mothers and sisters whose families earned their keep through the arena. Tension was thus as common as unity of purpose. She was torn between her love, worry and need for her son and husband, and the knowledge that they had to spend much of their lives abroad for their family's well-being. Māralīnā embodied these countervailing interests. This is what makes the strident tone which she deployed in her letter to her husband so fascinating; it gives us a sense of the limits that were seldom transgressed within families of her kind.

Māralīnā's formal status in relation to ʿAbd Allāh was very low within the family. She acknowledged this fact in a variety of ways, not least through her deferential modes of addressing her husband and her confession of her total dependence on him.[117] That inferiority, however, coexisted with, and was tempered, by a keen awareness of the legitimate and inalienable entitlements owed by him to her and her immediate family.[118] She was not afraid of asserting these forcefully and it was on their basis that she was prepared to hold her husband to account. But in the late 1740s, Māralīnā's bitterness, sarcasm and anger at her husband's behaviour suggest that she was not hopeful of a change for the better. So is it any surprise that she began looking for someone else in order to save

[113] BL/Lansdowne/1046, doc. 71. [114] BL/Lansdowne/1046, doc. 77.
[115] BL/Lansdowne/1046, doc. 68. [116] BL/Lansdowne/1046, doc. 69.
[117] BL/Lansdowne/1046, docs. 69, 77. [118] BL/Lansdowne/1046, doc. 71.

her? As she reported in her correspondence, that saviour was Niʿmat Allāh, a close kinsman of her husband. Her description of his generosity towards her in her moment of need, and her obvious gratitude and affection for him, serves to highlight all the more what she perceived as ʿAbd Allāh's gross negligence towards her and his family at home. She wanted him to be left in no doubt that, though far from ideal, what was his place by right, expectation, wish and duty was now occupied by a man who was not her husband.[119]

The foregoing discussion of the sentiments, obligations and perquisites embedded in ties central to Māralīnā's family may be complemented by an analysis of the terms frequently used to refer to those same ties. These terms are most often seen in the series of greetings and salutations with which personal letters tended to close. They were relayed by their authors to specific intimates, or clusters of intimates, at the letter's destination, or they were relayed by the authors on behalf of intimates residing where the letter was written. These short messages open a window on to how different segments and branches of Māralīnā's family were constituted, and how they related to one another. This kinship terminology is supplemented by references to different kinds of ties in the addressing modes adopted by correspondents, and in the titles and epithet invoked by authors regarding particular individuals.

Those who wished to convey their respects were invariably designated by the author through their relationship to him or to the letter's recipient. For example, Māralīnā told her son that 'my paternal aunts send you many greetings'.[120] Whether or not individually specified, it was as common to trace the lineage of intimates through the father as through the mother. So Māralīnā mentions: 'my governess Maryam, the daughter of Sulṭān', 'the daughter of your paternal uncle, Lūsiya Khātūn', 'the children of your paternal aunt, Yūsuf and Anṭūn', 'the children of my maternal aunt'.[121] These communicated the pertinent biographical information, which need not always – and often did not – include given names. Intimates could be identified just as well through their relationship to a named child, along the lines of 'the mother of Anṭūn'[122] or 'the father of Naṣr Allāh'.[123]

Be it in the preamble, the main subject or the closing of a letter, the manner in which Māralīnā denoted intimates enabled its recipient to place them within their family structure. As a result, at least two differing conceptions of the family and kinship can be inferred. In one, the language used gives the generational position, lineage membership and

[119] BL/Lansdowne/1046, docs. 67, 69. [120] BL/Lansdowne/1046, doc. 70. [121] Ibid.
[122] Ibid. [123] BL/Lansdowne/1046, doc. 12.

genealogical distance of the individual, both with respect to the letter's recipient and to its author. The information provided is sufficiently fine-grained to separate parallel relatives and cross-relatives, patrilineal and matrilineal descent, and affines and consanguines. In the other conception, by contrast, the language used is so encompassing as to mask genders and generations.

For Māralīnā's parents' generation, the terms invoked were typically 'father' (*wālid, abū*), 'father's brother' (*ʿamm*), 'father's sister' (*ʿamma*), 'mother' (*wālida, umm*), 'mother's brother' (*khāl*), 'mother's sister' (*khāla*). This enabled, for instance, a paternal uncle (*ʿamm*) to be readily distinguished from a maternal uncle (*khāl*) or father (*wālid*). The terms used to specify relatives at the level of Māralīnā's own generation were 'brother' (*akh*), 'sister' (*ukht*), 'full brother' (*shaqīq*) and 'full sister' (*shaqīqa*). These could be combined to trace out a relationship in greater detail, as shown in the examples above. They also referred to individual kin types. The exception to this rule was *akh* (and possibly *ukht*). Its application extended from a full brother (*shaqīq*) to a brother of a brother-in-law[124] to yet other, more distant intimates. The only limit on its reach was that the intimate be conceived as belonging to the same generation.[125] Minors were often grouped together under the collective 'children' (*awlād*). The only individualised terms used to specify members of that generation are 'son' (*ibn*) and 'daughter' (*bint*). These were usually qualified to the extent required for intimates to be defined unambiguously. And then there was a separate category of terms for affines, whose meanings in isolation could be rather broad. Those found in the correspondence include *ʿarūsa*[126] and *ḥurma*[127] (wife), *ṣihr* (sister's father-in-law[128] or daughter's father-in-law[129]), and *aḥmāʾ* (father-in-law).[130] Though on marriage Māralīnā adopted as her own her husband's consanguine relations, this did not require her to disassociate herself from her maiden family. So in her letter to her husband, Māralīnā felt able to talk freely about '*our* paternal aunts and their children', '*our* paternal uncle, the darling Ibrāhīm' and 'the son of *our* paternal uncle'.[131]

As already noted, individuals in Māralīnā's family were multiply related to one another in a number of generational dispositions. Relations between kindred could, at least in theory, be designated in several different ways. That one was usually preferred for particular ties and in given contexts offers us additional insights into the internal structuring of the family, especially concerning the relative significance of lineage,

[124] BL/Lansdowne/1046, doc. 67.
[125] BL/Lansdowne/1046, doc. 68.
[126] BL/Lansdowne/1046, doc. 70.
[127] BL/Lansdowne/1046, doc. 69.
[128] BL/Lansdowne/1046, doc. 70.
[129] BL/Lansdowne/1046, doc. 69.
[130] BL/Lansdowne/1046, doc. 70.
[131] BL/Lansdowne/1046, doc. 69.

generational position and genealogical distance. Take the case of Niʿmat Allāh. He was tied to Shukr Allāh via two marriages spanning two generations: one of his sisters was married to Shukr Allāh himself and another of his sisters was married to Shukr Allāh's paternal uncle. Niʿmat Allāh was, as a result, Shukr Allāh's brother-in-law and at the same time his affine uncle. Though Shukr Allāh's relationship to him could be described in a literal vein as 'the son of your [Shukr Allāh's] father-in-law' (*ibn aḥmāʾik*),[132] Niʿmat Allāh himself always referred to and addressed Shukr Allāh as his 'brother' (*akh*).[133] It is notable that a same-generational term was preferred even though formally Niʿmat Allāh occupied a more elevated status in their extended family. Niʿmat Allāh was doubly related to Anṭūn as well, again over two different generations: one of Niʿmat Allāh's sister was Anṭūn's mother, another of his sisters was married to Anṭūn's paternal uncle's son. Their relationship was described as being between brothers by Anṭūn's father.[134] In a letter to Shukr Allāh, however, Niʿmat Allāh referred to Anṭūn as 'the son of my sister' (*ibn ukhtī*).[135] Here we see, in contrast to his relationship with Shukr Allāh, genealogy being preferred to generation in denoting their respective ties.

Alongside words and expressions that concerned individuals, the letters contain a variety of collective terms that group members of the family in different configurations. This lexicon is of special interest because it helps us mark out the inner and outer boundaries of Māralīnā's family as Māralīnā herself understood it. Correspondents typically passed on brief and formulaic messages from 'children',[136] 'brothers'[137] and 'sisters'[138] who were identified by name or by their relationship to the letter's author or recipient. In contrast, the terms 'house' (*bayt*) and 'the people of the house' (*ahl al-bayt*)[139] denoted a nuclear family, invariably consisting of a married man, his wife and their unmarried children. *Ahl* on its own seems to have had a looser meaning, referring to a person's intimate group at home.[140] But we cannot say whether the larger framing was the household into which the person in question had been born or *all* kindred related to him through biological descent.

Both these meanings of *ahl* are possible in Niʿmat Allāh's letter to Shukr Allāh in which he informed him that, even though Māralīnā was in desperate need of money, no one from her *ahl* proved willing to help her out financially.[141] He contrasted the irresponsible conduct of Māralīnā's

[132] BL/Lansdowne/1046, doc. 70. [133] BL/Lansdowne/1046, doc. 67.
[134] BL/Lansdowne/1046, doc. 68. [135] BL/Lansdowne/1046, doc. 67.
[136] BL/Lansdowne/1046, docs. 69, 70. [137] BL/Lansdowne/1046, doc. 71. [138] Ibid.
[139] BL/Lansdowne/1046, docs. 69, 70, 71. [140] BL/Lansdowne/1046, docs. 67, 68, 71.
[141] BL/Lansdowne/1046, doc. 67.

ahl with his own willingness to provide for her. As Niʿmat Allāh was Māralīnā's kinsman through marriage, and as it was generally known that the menfolk of her immediate family were abroad at the time, by *ahl* he was almost certainly referring to Māralīnā's maiden family. Though it is not possible to be definitive given the available evidence, it is likely that *ahl* meant specifically her biological father and his immediate descendants. Moreover, Niʿmat Allāh's tacit condemnation of Māralīnā's *ahl* indicates that, in the absence of her husband and mature sons, coming to the aid of a married woman in distress was primarily the duty of her consanguine relatives.

Other terms used to designate clusters of individuals were 'relatives' (*aqribāʾ, aqārib*)[142] and the 'ethnic group' (*ṭāʾifa*).[143] There was also recourse to the 'old and young' (*kibār wa-ṣighār*),[144] and 'those who have love [for you]' (*muḥibbūn*).[145] These referred to people at home who had close ties to the correspondents, without it being stated whether or not they were kindred. The context, however, suggests that these terms were a convenient shorthand, gesturing to those familial intimates who had not been named individually. As with Sayyid Muṣṭafā's family, it is not obvious whether home for these intimates was physically centred on a single building or plot, or distributed across buildings in the same locality.[146]

Considering the totality of insights offered by the kinship terminology marshalled by Māralīnā and her close kindred, we may situate her family somewhere between the smallest (*awlād, ikhwān, shaqāʾiq*) and the largest (*kibār wa-ṣighār, muḥibbūn*) of the collectives noted. All its members had intimate ties to one another that were largely, but not necessarily, between kindred. The ties embodied a varying assortment of obligations, rights and expectations. Māralīnā's family embraced kindred from both the mother's and the father's side, though the latter tended to dominate. More generally, the family was multi-generational and home was found where the womenfolk, especially the wives and mothers, resided. It subsumed more than one *ahl*, but was never more than a tiny subset of the local ethnic community.[147]

[142] BL/Lansdowne/1046, docs. 68, 71. [143] BL/Lansdowne/1046, doc. 68. [144] Ibid.

[145] BL/Lansdowne/1046, doc. 71.

[146] The correspondence reveals that Māralīnā had recently moved into more suitable accommodation. She was sharing the place with the son of her husband's maternal uncle and she was much happier there. BL/Lansdowne/1046, docs. 69, 70, 71.

[147] In anthropological terms, Māralīnā's family may be classified as collaterally extended. The ways in which relations and authority within her family were articulated gave significant weighting to generational position, lineage and genealogical distance. This is seen in the fact that, while manifestly patriarchal, they allowed mature women considerable freedom and power within their home environment. Though her family

The family household was the single most important social entity in the everyday lives of those involved in circulation and exchange. This is an obvious point and yet precious little is known about such families, their internal structuring and their roles within their communities and surrounding polities. The account presented in this section of two real families active in the arena in the middle of the eighteenth century is thus of value on two levels. It is of value for giving us a firmer purchase on a type of association that was elemental in facilitating and shaping regional-scale activities. It is also of value for helping to bridge a significant gap in our knowledge of the socioeconomic fabric of India and the Islamic heartlands at a moment of tremendous changes. The picture that emerges in trying to elucidate the families of Sayyid Muṣṭafā and Māralīnā is admittedly patchy and indistinct. We must therefore proceed cautiously in making generalisations. Nevertheless, the picture is highly suggestive, a potentially fertile source of hypotheses and ideas.

Arguably, the most significant finding of the two case studies presented here is that, notwithstanding major differences in their historical experiences and backgrounds, the families exhibited a remarkable degree of similarity. This may be understood as a consequence of their belonging to the same networks, of the type detailed in the first half of this chapter. These networks were, among other things, conduits for the dispersal of certain kinds of knowledge – to do above all with concepts, images and ways of meeting the world – that encouraged convergence. The similarity may be understood too in a more functionalist vein. The Bengal Shīʿī and Iraqi Armenian families occupied analogous positions in comparable polities and, moreover, were both engaged in activities characterised by large distances and long silences. These facts would have encouraged convergence as well.

So in letters written by its members, the family was acknowledged as being of signal importance for their livelihoods and essential for the integrity of their communities. These families were extended in character. They spanned several generations. They included relatives through both descent and marriage, and also embraced other intimates, perhaps in the guise of fictive kinship. Their families were furthermore strongly patriarchal and hierarchical, with patrilineality favoured, though not exclusively so. Great respect was accorded to husbands and sons, and to elders in general. But it was fathers who had the greatest prestige and authority. The relationship between them and their sons was of crucial importance

in theory may well have been strongly patrilineal in character, in practice, it would be more accurate to describe it as lying somewhere between non-unilineal (bilateral or cognatic) and moderately patrilineal.

for the household, even as fathers expressed disquiet about their sons. While women normally occupied an inferior status relative to their husbands and grown-up sons, this did not preclude them from having substantial material rights and freedom of action, especially within the home environment. Their kinsmen were not permitted to deny them these and, indeed, were obligated to protect them. Ties between kindred could be very close, notably between a father and son, husband and wife, and mother and son. There was a general presumption that, in the event of a clash, an individual's autonomy and personal desires had to yield to the collective interests of their family household and intimate community. And finally, though kinsmen were often abroad for long periods of time, home always remained with the wife and the mother.

Conclusion

If this book has any claim to novelty, it stems from a resolutely vernacular and regional approach. The genesis of this approach may be traced back to an image of flux, an image of everyday knowledge, objects and people in movement, of their various circulations and exchanges. These I have elaborated for India and the Islamic heartlands in the middle of the eighteenth century. By doing so, this book recaptures a vanished and forgotten world, a world at the core of which lay an arena of activities.

Why this arena is of interest can be summed up by an apparent paradox. It existed mostly, if not entirely, beyond the sovereign purview. And yet it was of broader historical significance, closely bound up with important features of the early modern world and of its differentiated transition into modern times. Two such features are the overland routes across Eurasia and the relationship of states to their societies in Eurasia's Islamicate polities. By elaborating circulation and exchange on regional scales, we stand to gain a better understanding of these and their early modern fates.

But we also stand to gain a better understanding of other features that were less structural and more processual. Of these more processual features, there are two in particular that centre on the specific moment – the middle of the eighteenth century – around which this book pivots. Given what immediately preceded and followed it, that moment was notable for its in-between quality: the fragmentation, disappearance and hollowing out of the Ottoman, Safavid and Mughal empires provided its immediate backdrop, while in the foreground there were the beginnings of the consolidation of Europe's modern global empires. In lieu of towering, hegemonic regimes able to cast a shadow over much of the region, the middle of the eighteenth century was marked by a plethora of smaller regimes of several different types, from the revival of the Mamlūk beys in Egypt and the Georgian pashas in Iraq to the Iranian tribal confederacies and the nizamate of Bengal. These successors to the great Islamicate empires were locked in a struggle over scarce resources and riven by a host of internal tensions.

Political upheaval and military conflict were thus widespread and endemic to the region. Even so, and perhaps surprisingly, mundane transactions characterised by large distances and long silences continued to take place on a regular and frequent basis. This is strong evidence in favour of an arena of circulation and exchange that straddled both India and the Islamic heartlands in 1750. The evidence also flags a missing dimension in current histories of the region and of its various polities. That is why recapturing the arena has the potential to open up new vistas on developments that were transformative. The two worth highlighting above all are the 'general crisis' in the region, which reached its highest pitch of intensity in the eighteenth century, and the transition to colonialism under European dominance, which ushered in the Middle East and South Asia.

The features just noted are central to a number of debates and questions that have exercised scholars over recent generations. These debates and questions remain salient for scholars today. I return to them in the latter half of this conclusion, where I discuss the ways in which this book, and further work in its vein, can contribute to them. Meanwhile, they serve to make the point that this book's larger thesis operates on two levels simultaneously: on the level of an arena of circulation and exchange of broad historical significance, and on the level of the arena's relevance to issues of current historiographical concern. If we accept this prima facie, the challenge then is to demonstrate the arena's existence. I have sought to do this by reconstructing its connective tissue.

However, that is not a simple task. Reconstructing the arena's connective tissue is complicated, in particular, by the fact that such entities have traditionally been obscured or neglected in the scholarly literature. This reflects the predominance of certain perspectives. Because of their limitations for the subject of this book, my strategy has involved bypassing these perspectives, without importantly losing sight of them. The most influential are rooted in the imperial state, especially at the centre,[1] and in religion, learning and literature.[2] But these are not the only perspectives

[1] Many of the classic works on the Islamicate empires take this perspective. See, for example, Halil Inalcık, *The Ottoman Empire: the Classical Age, 1300–1600*, trans. Norman Itzkowitz and Colin Imber (London, 1973); Roger M. Savory, *Iran under the Safavids* (Cambridge, 1980); M. Athar Ali, *The Mughal Nobility under Aurangzeb* (Aligarh, 1966).

[2] Recent and significant contributions include Sholeh A. Quinn, *Historical Writing during the Reign of Shah ʿAbbas: Ideology, Imitation and Legitimacy in Safavid Chronicles* (Salt Lake City, UT, 2000); Muzaffar Alam, *The Languages of Political Islam in India, 1200–1800* (Chicago, 2004); Dina Le Gall, *A Culture of Sufism: Naqshbandīs in the Ottoman World, 1450–1700* (Albany, NY, 2005).

that I have negotiated from afar. Others include those that confine themselves to a given polity, going under the rubric of what used to be called 'state and society',[3] and those whose horizons potentially encompass the whole world.[4] Though this book does not cleave directly to the scholarship that expresses these perspectives, it does have a complementary relationship to it.

In contrast, the relationship of this book is much more direct to scholarship that expresses two additional perspectives. The one with an older pedigree is fundamentally about merchants and rulers. In this, primacy is given to the intersection between the spheres of politics and trade, usually within the context of their ambient political economy.[5] The second is of more recent provenance. Popularly labelled 'global history', it stresses parallels and linkages within what was avowedly a polycentric early modern world.[6] In my choice of subject, as well as for my approach to it, the present book is beholden to both these perspectives.

Directly or indirectly, the success of this book in contributing to the inherited scholarly literature depends on the quality and scope of its findings. At the base of these findings lie the rich, intimate, penetrating details about daily life of the individuals responsible for the empirical sources animating this book. These details allow us to reconstruct key structures of the world that they inhabited, traversed and knew. Apprehended as perceived realities and the behavioural patterns associated with them, these structures (described in chapters 1–7) were widely

3 This is typified by H. A. R. Gibb and Harold Bowen, *Islamic Society and the West: a Study of the Impact of Western Civilization on Moslem Culture in the Near East* (London, 1950–7); Ann K. S. Lambton, *Landlord and Peasant in Persia: a Study of Land Tenure and Land Revenue Administration* (rev. edn, London, 1969); Irfan Habib, *The Agrarian System of Mughal India, 1556–1707* (3rd edn, London, 2012).

4 Three of the most celebrated works are William H. McNeill, *The Rise of the West: a History of the Human Community* (Chicago, 1963); Immanuel M. Wallerstein, *The Modern World-System*, 4 vols. (New York, 1974–2011): Fernand Braudel, *Civilization and Capitalism, 15th–18th Century*, 3 vols., trans. Siân Reynolds (London, 1981).

5 Exemplary in this regard are Michael N. Pearson, *Merchants and Rulers in Gujarat: the Response to the Portuguese in the Sixteenth Century* (Berkeley, CA, 1976); André Raymond, *Artisans et commerçants au Caire au XVIIIe siècle*, 2 vols. (2nd edn, Damascus, 1999); Rudolph P. Matthee, *The Politics of Trade in Safavid Iran: Silk for Silver 1600–1730* (Cambridge, 1999); Ashin Das Gupta, *Malabar in Asian Trade, 1740–1800* (Cambridge, 1967); James D. Tracy (ed.), *The Political Economy of Merchant Empires: State Power and World Trade, 1350–1750* (Cambridge, 1991).

6 This covers a broad range of approaches and subjects that have yet to crystallise as a well-defined field. A sense of this breadth and the field's elusiveness may be gleaned from Sanjay Subrahmanyam, 'Connected histories: notes towards a reconfiguration of early modern Eurasia', *Modern Asian Studies* 31:3 (1997), 735–62; Maxine Berg, 'In pursuit of luxury: global history and British consumer goods in the eighteenth century', *Past and Present* 182 (2004), 85–142; John-Paul A. Ghobrial, 'The secret life of Elias of Babylon and the uses of global microhistory', *Past and Present* 222 (2014), 51–93.

dispersed within their world, at once constraining and enabling their everyday lives. By situating (in Chapter 8) these structures in the flux – the flows and interactions – that gave them vitality, this world reveals itself as an arena of circulation and exchange that spanned much of India and the Islamic heartlands in the middle of the eighteenth century.

The details presented in the book's substantive chapters support two general findings. The first is that the arena *cannot* simply be collapsed into, or interpreted solely in terms of, trade or culture, *nor* is it appropriate to view the individuals populating it merely as members of close-knit ethnic communities, diasporic or otherwise. Of course, there is no denying that regional trade in cash crops, luxuries, bullion, manufactures and bulk goods was a major concern within the arena. But in relative and absolute terms that trade was paltry compared with trade within any one of the region's polities.[7] That, however, is a narrow take on the matter. As regional trade was inextricably entwined with other activities such as pilgrimage, news-gathering and study, it cannot be properly comprehended in isolation from them. So by seeing it enmeshed within a larger arena of circulation and exchange, we are able to discern this trade's broader significance for the region's sovereigns and their regimes. There is also no denying that the notion of culture can provide an insightful window on to the past. On its own, however, it does not readily allow for the interweaving of thought, feeling and action, as a result of which culture's relationship to social reality is often uncertain. Accounts that stress culture to the exclusion of all else thus have an elusive quality about them.[8] I have tried to pre-empt that outcome by adopting an approach that may be glossed as socioeconomic and sociocultural. Lastly, there is no denying the considerable influence exerted within the arena by ethnic communities, especially the more prominent diasporas.[9] But

[7] The relevance of foreign trade to the Indian polity is discussed in Tirthankar Roy, *An Economic History of Early Modern India* (London and New York, 2013), 74–9.

[8] Perhaps more worrying is the risk of anachronism inherent in the concept because of its very genealogy. An attempt is made to elucidate this in Andrew Sartori, 'The resonance of "culture": framing a problem in global concept-history', *Comparative Studies in Society and History* 47:4 (2005), 676–99.

[9] On the Jewish, the Armenian and the (many) 'Indian' diasporas, see Jonathan I. Israel, *Diasporas within a Diaspora: Jews, Crypto-Jews and the World Maritime Empires, 1540–1740* (Leiden, 2002); Francesca Trivellato, *The Familiarity of Strangers: the Sephardic Diaspora, Livorno, and Cross-Cultural Trade in the Early Modern Period* (New Haven, CT, 2009); Ina Baghdiantz McCabe, *Shah's Silk for Europe's Silver: the Eurasian Trade of the Julfa Armenians in Safavid Iran and India (1530–1750)* (Atlanta, GA, 2002); Sebouh D. Aslanian, *From the Indian Ocean to the Mediterranean: the Global Trade Networks of Armenian Merchants from New Julfa* (Berkeley, CA, 2010); Stephen F. Dale, *Indian Merchants and Eurasian Trade, 1600–1750* (Cambridge, 1994); Claude Markovits, *The Global World of Indian Merchants, 1750–1947: Traders of Sind from Bukhara to Panama*

other kinds of associations and relationships too had a presence that was no less formative, and these were frequently not between kindred or between those from the same ethnic background (and in the event they were, it is not always appropriate to interpret them in terms of kinship or ethnicity).

The foregoing point gestures to the book's second general finding. I categorise those who were most actively involved in the arena as sub-elites. This is because, despite being literate and worldly as a collective, they did not have de jure access to sovereign authority and so tended to be inconspicuous. The specifics of their religious, ethnic or linguistic heritage did not alter this basic reality. Their position within their polities was shaped much more by the fact that their livelihoods revolved around transactions which were regional in scope, crossing a multitude of boundaries as a matter of course. Though the word 'class' is seldom used in the book – I use 'people' in its stead – my argument is that these individuals essentially belonged to a shared class. Now, I am certainly not the first to place individuals of this kind at the centre of my concerns or to view them as a class. But I differ in one crucial respect from how other scholars have examined them. And that is by purposefully choosing *not* to position them in relation to sovereign power. As a result, it is easier to see those active in circulation and exchange as something more than a service class (whose raison d'être was to receive commissions from the ruling elites). While I freely concede that servicing the ruling elites was significant for many of their livelihoods, conceptually unshackling class from sovereignty opens up fresh interpretative possibilities. Not least, it allows us to recover these individuals, and the arena that they manned, on their own terms; it allows us to recover how they actually related to other aspects of their region's polities, many of which did not fall under the sovereign purview.[10]

These two general findings are of immediate value for our understanding of India and the Islamic heartlands in the middle of the eighteenth century. But the book is also of value for our broader understanding of the region's past. This is through its contribution to an agenda centred on the paradigm of Islamicate Eurasia. Though a great deal of work needs to be done before the goals of that agenda come within reach, the necessary work could be facilitated by the vernacular and regional approach of this

(Cambridge, 2000); Scott C. Levi, *Indian Diaspora in Central Asia and its Trade, 1550–1900* (Leiden, 2002); Samira Sheikh, *Forging a Region: Sultans, Traders, and Pilgrims in Gujarat, 1200–1500* (Delhi, 2010).

10 Sanjay Subrahmanyam gives a brief, punchy and incisive overview of the scholarly literature on merchants in the early modern world in his introduction to Sanjay Subrahmanyam (ed.), *Merchant Networks in the Early Modern World* (Aldershot, 1996). Of particular relevance to the present discussion is his critique of the class, community and network (diaspora) notions that permeate this literature.

book. I hope this book has shown that its approach is well suited to recovering empirical details which in turn motivate useful findings, both general (discussed in this chapter) and specific (discussed in preceding chapters). I also hope it has shown that the approach lends itself to reconstructing the lineaments of a hitherto obscured, neglected world of meaningful historical significance.

These then are the intellectual possibilities which this book's approach renders attainable in practice. Furthermore, this book is another step towards recapturing the connective tissue of Islamicate Eurasia's arena of circulation and exchange, and situating it within its regional setting. As already noted, much more work needs to be done to achieve that end. Some of this work needs to be in the vein of what I have attempted here; gaps wait to be filled, the weaknesses shored up. That, however, requires the discovery and analysis of more sources like those contained in the postbag at the core of this book, sources written by and for those who resided permanently in the region. But this is easier said than done if only because such sources are rare and usually difficult to access. Nevertheless, given our current ignorance, the pay-off will amply justify the effort expended in locating them and subjecting them to careful study. The arena also needs to be placed in time. As things stand, what I offer in this book is merely a snapshot. The temporal axis is absent. Only by elucidating the evolution of the arena, both as a whole and in terms of it constituent structures, can we fully comprehend its historical nature and role. And then there is need for research that goes beyond the parameters of this book. Transactions that occurred on specifically regional scales have yet to be juxtaposed with those on other scales, particularly the smaller scales of the region's individual polities, and the larger trans-regional or global scales. Consumption and production too have yet to be brought into the frame, and juxtaposed with circulation and exchange.

In the final reckoning, work of this kind matters because of its potential utility to scholars in adjacent fields. That may be best appreciated through a consideration of the bigger historiographical debates and questions with which it is necessarily in conversation. Four of these were touched upon at the start of this conclusion. It is with them that I bring this book to a close.

The first issue deals with the fate of the routes spanning continental Eurasia in the early modern era. The one fully developed thesis to tackle this explicitly dates from the 1970s.[11] It argues that the routes

[11] This thesis is detailed in Niels Steensgaard, *The Asian Trade Revolution of the Seventeenth Century: the East India Companies and the Decline of the Caravan Trade* (Chicago, 1974). It should be read in conjunction with M. A. P. Meilink-Roelofsz, 'The structures of trade in Asia in the sixteenth and seventeenth centuries. Niels Steensgaard's "Carracks, Caravans and Companies": A critical appraisal', *Mare Luso-Indicum* 4 (1980), 1–43.

connecting Inner Asia and India to the Mediterranean basin and Europe were sapped of their vitality early in the seventeenth century. The prime culprit for this, so the thesis goes, was the innovations ushered in by the Dutch and English East India companies from the turn of the century; their activities redirected Eurasia's overland trade and ancillary services to the Indian Ocean rim and the overseas route to western Europe via the Cape of Good Hope. Subsequent research, however, has thrown doubt on this chronology and the factors thought to underpin it.[12] In part, the revisionist findings stem from research into relatively neglected areas of the region; in part, they stem from a more critical stance on the purported distinctions between maritime and continental routes. As a result, there is a growing awareness that the routes between, say, Agra and Istanbul, or Cairo and Bukhara, far from withering away, remained in regular, frequent and intensive use well into the eighteenth century. The broader significance of this research could be greatly sharpened by anchoring it in a larger context – which is just what Islamicate Eurasia's arena of circulation and exchange is in a position to do. This arena is a natural choice because of its emphasis, on the one hand, on regional flows and interactions, and, on the other, on common structures that were mainly socioeconomic and sociocultural in nature.

[12] Notable contributions since the appearance of Steensgaard's thesis include Stephen F. Dale, 'Indo-Russian trade in the eighteenth century', in Sugata Bose (ed.), *South Asia and World Capitalism* (Delhi, 1990), 140–56; Sanjay Subrahmanyam, *The Political Economy of Commerce: Southern India, 1500–1650* (Cambridge, 1990); Morris Rossabi, 'The "decline" of the Central Asian caravan trade', in James D. Tracy (ed.), *The Rise of Merchant Empires: Long-Distance Trade in the Early Modern World, 1350–1750* (Cambridge, 1990), 351–70; Muzaffar Alam, 'Trade, state policy and regional change: aspects of Mughal–Uzbek commercial relations, *c.*1550–1750', *Journal of the Economic and Social History of the Orient* 37:3 (1994), 202–27; Jos J. L. Gommans, 'The horse trade in eighteenth-century South Asia', *Journal of the Economic and Social History of the Orient* 37:3 (1994), 228–50; Dale, *Indian Merchants and Eurasian Trade*; Robert D. McChesney, '"Barrier of heterodoxy"? Rethinking the ties between Iran and Central Asia in the seventeenth century', in Charles Melville (ed.), *Safavid Persia: the History and Politics of an Islamic Society* (London, 1996), 231–67; Audrey Burton, *The Bukharans: A Dynastic, Diplomatic and Commercial History, 1550–1702* (Richmond, Surrey, 1997); Scott C. Levi, 'India, Russia and the eighteenth-century transformation of the Central Asian caravan trade', *Journal of the Economic and Social History of the Orient* 42:4 (1999), 519–48; Niels Steensgaard, 'The route through Quandahar: he significance of the overland trade route from India to the West in the seventeenth century', in Sushil Chaudhuri and Michel Morineau (eds.), *Merchants, Companies and Trade: Europe and Asia in the Early Modern Era* (Cambridge, 1999), 55–73; Gilles Veinstein, 'Commercial relations between India and the Ottoman empire (late fifteenth to the late eighteenth centuries): a few notes and hypotheses', in Sushil Chaudhuri and Michel Morineau (eds.), *Merchants, Companies and Trade: Europe and Asia in the Early Modern Era* (Cambridge, 1999), 95–115; Matthee, *The Politics of Trade in Safavid Iran*; Scott C. Levi (ed.), *India and Central Asia: Commerce and Culture, 1500–1800* (New Delhi, 2007).

The arena also encourages a different perspective, through a reconceptualisation, on the character of the state and its function in the history of India and the Islamic heartlands before the nineteenth century. This second issue is manifestly relevant to the longstanding debates which hinge on the state, especially those to do with the distinction between premodern states and their modern heirs, the relationship of different types of states to their societies, and the role of states in the process of modernisation.[13] Transposing the logic of this book, the sovereign regimes to which the region played host may be treated within the framework of a distinct, coherent arena of their own – say, that of conspicuous sovereignty.[14] This would occupy the same analytical footing as the arena of circulation and exchange. Having elaborated them separately, the task would then be to show how these arenas intersected with one another, highlighting their mutual dependence through perhaps a study of the exceptional individuals and associations who bridged them, and at the same time were at home in both. Such an approach would have several immediate benefits: the agnosticism implicit in the formulation means that the nature of the state is not prejudged; it acts as a firm check on the tendency, still going strong, to examine past polities through the filter of the state and its conspicuous elites; it facilitates the construction of grand narratives that, at least in the context of the history of the Islamic world, do not place undue emphasis on privilege to religion and politics; and it promises a more robust basis for comparing and contrasting sovereign regimes in different parts of the early modern world.

Recapturing the flows and interactions that systemically linked together different parts of the region raises the prospect of contributing to a third issue of enduring interest. This is by addressing the missing dimension in current accounts of the 'general crisis' said to have afflicted much of India and the Islamic heartlands from the seventeenth century onwards.[15] Because of the absence of this dimension, these accounts are

[13] Current thinking on the state and state systems in the period has recently been surveyed in Peer H. H. Vries, 'Governing growth: a comparative analysis of the role of the state in the rise of the West', *Journal of World History* 13:1 (2002), 67–138. It should be noted that the paper's chief focus is on western Europe. For a more global perspective, see Michael N. Pearson, 'Merchants and states', in James D. Tracy (ed.), *The Political Economy of Merchant Empires: State Power and World Trade, 1350–1750* (Cambridge, 1991), 41–116.

[14] One possibly fruitful way of envisaging this is as an arena of temporal power and authority expressed symbolically and through governance.

[15] An influential synthesis of the standard views on this is found in the first two chapters of Christopher A. Bayly, *Imperial Meridian: the British Empire and the World, 1780–1830* (London, 1989). On the general crisis more generally, see Niels Steensgaard, 'The seventeenth-century crisis and the unity of Eurasian history', *Modern Asian Studies* 24:4 (1990), 683–97; Geoffrey Parker, *Global Crisis: War, Climate Change and Catastrophe in the Seventeenth Century* (New Haven, CT, 2013).

unable to demonstrate convincingly that the crisis, which culminated with the emergence of a kaleidoscope of successor regimes by the middle of the eighteenth century, was caused by factors primarily internal to the region. The existing synthesis discusses regional parallels and commonalities in relation to, say, economic growth, provincial elites, revenue farming and tribal restiveness, and pays heed to the processes operating on trans-regional or global scales that were sustained by exports and imports. But centre stage is occupied by developments occurring within the region's individual polities, most of which involved the ruling elites. What we do not see are the exchanges and circulations that took place on specifically regional scales. At best, these are mentioned in passing. Their active presence in the evolution of the region's general crisis is certainly not given its due. By giving it its due, we can facilitate a step change in our understanding of key elements of the evolution of this crisis. Take, for example, the urban settlements in the provinces and frontier areas, and the sub-elites who dominated the provision of financial, administrative and mercantile services. These settlements and sub-elites, which usually enjoyed a great deal of autonomy, did not depend solely on the imperial capital or metropolitan centre for their well-being. While they were undoubtedly rooted in a given regime and locality, they were also vested in an arena of activities that transcended any one polity. It follows that inserting the arena into the existing synthesis will alter our view of their role in the crisis, and force us to revisit the grand processes of urbanisation, commercialisation, monetisation and marketisation that figure so prominently in the received accounts.

Moreover, the general crisis was not merely about the political economy. The decentralisation of power that forms its central thread could not have occurred without a rearticulation of loyalty and a reconsideration of how the world ought to be ordered. Given the remarkable coincidence between the decline in the power of the Islamicate empires and the rise of their successor regimes, the circulation and exchange of information and ideas on regional scales must have been of crucial significance. Without the presence of an overarching arena of activities, it is difficult to rationalise the rapid, sustained and widespread dispersal of knowledge about developments elsewhere in the region, and of new or alternative world-views, particularly those advocated by the contemporaneous movements for Islamic revival or reform.[16] This dispersal was enmeshed with

[16] The subject may be entered through Nehemia Levtzion and John O. Voll (eds.), *Eighteenth-Century Renewal and Reform in Islam* (Syracuse, NY, 1987); Ira M. Lapidus, 'Islamic revivals and modernity: the contemporary movements and historical paradigms', *Journal of the Economic and Social History of the Orient* 40:4 (1997), 444–56; Fazlur Rahman, *Revival and Reform in Islam: a Study of Islamic Fundamentalism* (Oxford, 2000).

education and scholarship, with pilgrimage to shrine cities and with acts of social piety, especially charitable donations from afar. All of these were important concerns within the arena. Bringing the arena into the existing synthesis will thus greatly strengthen the case for a truly regional general crisis.

A fourth issue in favour of further work on Islamicate Eurasia pivots on our present understanding of the region in the period before European dominance. The empirical detail yielded by examining it through the lens of an arena of circulation and exchange brings into focus many aspects of everyday life previously hidden from view. More generally, it sheds light on a coherent and largely self-regulating arena of activities that was essential for maintaining the overall integrity of the region's polities. This has a direct bearing on any evaluation of the varying impact of European colonisation, a topic responsible for one of the liveliest and most contentious debates of recent decades. The question at its core is: did Europe's presence in the region from the latter part of the eighteenth century herald continuity, organic change or a fundamental breach with earlier periods?

For a proper answer, two avenues of research need to be pursued. One is to juxtapose given features in the period immediately prior to sustained European involvement with ideally the same or, failing that, congruent features once that involvement had become institutionalised. The other is to reconstruct the specific mechanisms by means of which the transition to colonialism actually occurred. Scholarly practice, however, has tended to demur from this; judgements on the implications of European dominance have too often been based on axioms, models or theories that project back into the past findings from, at the earliest, the latter part of the eighteenth century, when the consolidation of European control was already under way. This will not do. To move the debate forward, what is required is further empirical work under the auspices of an explicit and plausible analytical framework for the era preceding the start of this consolidation.[17] The substantive chapters of this book are a realisation of one such framework. Additional work in this vein will then permit us to carry out systematic comparisons of specific moments on either side of the

[17] This is in keeping with the agenda that Sheldon Pollock has been advocating with great insistence and passion over the past decade. His argument is that, in order to apprehend the nature and scope of what occurred in the nineteenth century, we need to carry out far more research on early modern and precolonial Asia. For a recent restatement of this argument, see his introduction in Sheldon I. Pollock (ed.), *Forms of Knowledge in Early Modern Asia: Explorations in the Intellectual History of India and Tibet, 1500–1800* (Durham, NC, 2011).

historical juncture that is currently thought to bridge the premodernity and modernity of the region's polities. It will also permit us to gain a much better purchase on how the transformations that began to gather pace from the beginning of the nineteenth century really took place.

Such are the tasks confronting us if we wish to comprehend the unravelling of an Islamicate Eurasia, and its eventual partitioning into the Middle East and South Asia. Such are the challenges facing us if we wish to grasp the significance of older parallels and linkages withering away, as newer ones were forged in the era of Europe's modern global empires. If we are prepared to undertake these tasks and meet these challenges, the goal of a longstanding quest may at last come within sight: to discover what actually happened as the inhabitants of India and the Islamic heartlands shifted their gaze to other horizons in a world being refashioned around them.

Glossary

Note: Words and expressions were commonly shared across multiple languages in the eighteenth century. Many of the historical terms glossed below were thus found in two or more of the region's languages in the period. These included, but were not limited to, Arabic, Hindi, Ottoman Turkish and Persian.

agent	One of the two main types of intermediaries in the arena of circulation and exchange (the other being a broker). Agents tended to be employed by their principals for extended periods of time, and were afforded considerable latitude to act on their behalf. They could also be very mobile.
ahl	People, followers; inhabitants; kin, relatives. In our period, the expression *ahl al-bayt* covered the spectrum from the nuclear family to all those belonging to a given household.
akçe	Small silver Ottoman coin and unit of account. Following major reforms begun at the end of the seventeenth century, its value was fixed at a third of a para.
allāh	Term for God in several of the region's religious traditions.
arena (of activities)	Distinct, coherent, self-regulating, regional-scale entity that spanned much of India and the Islamic heartlands in the eighteenth century. Several such entities existed before modern times. This book is focused specifically on the arena of activities responsible for the circulation and exchange of valued items, particularly goods, tokens, ideas and information.

ashrafi (*ashrafī*) Series of gold coins modelled on the Venetian or Florentine ducat. They circulated in Egypt, Anatolia, the Levant and Iran from the sixteenth century, and provided the dominant standard for gold coins in Iran in the seventeenth and eighteenth centuries.

association Ideal-type encompassing groups, organisations and networks. The two main types of named and bounded associations are groups and organisations, the former being closed (e.g., endogamous ethnic communities), the latter open (e.g., trading companies, Sufi brotherhoods). Networks, in contrast, are unnamed, bounded and open associations.

***baniyā* (*bania*, *vania*)** An individual, typically from northern or western India, whose livelihood derived from trade, banking or commerce. In the eighteenth century, *baniyā*s were often linked to communities based in Gujarat and Sind that had an established presence in buying and selling goods and services.

broker One of the two main types of intermediaries in the arena of circulation and exchange (the other being an agent). Brokers tended to be permanent or long-term residents of the settlement where they had acquired their valued expertise.

conspicuous elites Individuals and groups who were visible within their polities by virtue of their status and positions of authority in the realms of high politics, warfare, government bureaucracy, art, the belles-lettres and/or formal learning. These elites differed from the great bulk of the population which was, in status and authority terms, inconspicuous.

customs Modes of behaviour understood by contemporaries as legitimate and timeless. They constituted a major source of law for resolving disputes in the region's communal and occupational forums.

dallāl — Broker, commission merchant; an individual who brings together a buyer and seller.

dil — Heart; abdomen; stomach; mind, understanding; courage, valour; vital centre or middle (of a sentient being).

dinar (*dīnār*) — Gold or silver coin. In the eighteenth century, it functioned primarily as a unit of account, with the value of one toman fixed at 10,000 silver dinars.

family household — The smallest subset of kindred or intimate relationships based in a definable household that was capable of biological and social reproduction within its ambient polity.

hundi — Commercial paper used as a means of payment and for transferring money. *Hundi*s were in effect a form of personalised debt, often equated by Christian Europeans to a bill of exchange.

intimates (intimate collective) — An inherently subjective notion referring to those who were multiply tied to one another and who had a deep attachment to the same locality and a sense of personal responsibility for the well-being of the collective as a whole. It stands in contrast to the notion of a stranger (q.v.).

Iskandar — The name by which Alexander the Great was known in the region. He was a familiar figure through stories preserved and recounted in popular epics such as *Iskandarnāmah* and *Shāhnāmah*.

Islamicate — Qualifying term that acknowledges the significance of Islam and of Muslims, while leaving open the possibility of non-Muslim individuals, organisations and groups being of comparable significance (e.g., Islamicate Eurasia, Islamicate empires).

jān — Breath of life, vitality, life; soul, spirit, mind; energy, power, force; darling, beloved.

khudā — Term for God in several of the region's religious traditions.

Khvājah (*khwājā*) — Gentleman, man of distinction. In the eighteenth century, the term was normally reserved for non-Muslim merchants.

kuruş (*qurūsh*) — Heavy silver Ottoman coin. It was introduced around the turn of the eighteenth century with a value fixed at 40 paras or 120 akçes. In the languages of Christian Europe, it was called piastre.

mahājan Individual belonging to guild-like organisations (*mahājanī*s) in northern India, each associated with a particular occupation. *Mahājan*s were especially prominent in small-scale moneylending.

mithqāl Standard weight. It was originally fixed at about 4.25 grams. In later periods, however, its weight ranged from less than 4 grams to more than 5 grams.

padshah (*pādishāh*) Title given to Muslim rulers, particularly emperors.

para (*pāra*) Silver Ottoman coin and unit of account. In the new monetary scale established in the early eighteenth century, its value was fixed at 3 akçes or a fortieth of a kuruş.

rabb Term for God in several of the region's religious traditions.

rupee Silver Indian coin and unit of account. It was first issued in the sixteenth century, and quickly established itself as a standard in India and elsewhere in the region. Rupees described as sikka referred to those that had been recently minted and were not yet liable to discount because of depreciation.

sharia (*sharīʿa*) Totality of a divinely revealed or prophetic religion; rules and regulations governing the lives of the adherents of such a religion.

stranger Opposite of intimate (q.v.). Strangers were those with whom one interacted as a matter of course in daily life but who were situated outside one's intimate community.

sultan (*sulṭān*) Title of ruler whose absolute independence was generally recognised; having supreme temporal authority.

ṭāʾifa People; clan, tribe; extended family, intimate community; confessional group, local branch of Sufi brotherhood; ethnic community; corporation, occupational group; nation.

toman (*tūmān*) Unit of account. This formed the basis of the currency system in Iran (and surrounding areas) from the Safavid period onwards. The value of a toman was fixed at 10,000 silver dinars.

trust Analytically, there were two kinds of trust between individuals: personal and impersonal. Central to personal trust was the role of affect or sentimental attachments, and an intuitive sense of an individual's nature. It was typically found among intimate kindred, confessional brethren and close friends. Between strangers (q.v.), however, there was only impersonal trust. This was predicated on external factors, above all, an effective transport and communications infrastructure; practices for supervising, managing, verifying and signalling behaviour from afar; and organisations capable of arriving at, and implementing, decisions. It was also predicated on reputation being a highly valued asset and on the existence of forums for resolving disputes.

zolota (*zulṭa*) Heavy silver Polish coin. This circulated extensively in Ottoman territories during the seventeenth and eighteenth centuries. In the eighteenth century, it was valued at three-quarters of a kuruş, 30 para or 90 akçes.

Bibliography

Unpublished sources

Archives nationales d'outre-mer, Aix-en-Provence, France (ANOM)

Fonds ancien ou de la Compagnie des Indes (CdI)
Fonds ministériels, Premier empire colonial (FC)

Bibliothèque nationale de France, Paris, France (BnF)

Collections du département des manuscrits, Division occidentale (MssOcc)
Nouvelles acquisitions françaises (NAF)

British Library, London, UK (BL)

IOL/Mss Eur
IOR/G, P
Lansdowne/1046

Historical Archives of Goa, Panjim, Goa, India (HAG)

Persian Documents

Maharashtra State Archives, Mumbai, India (MSA)

High Court Records (HCR)
Mayor's and Recorder's Court Records (MRC)

National Archives, Kew, UK (NA)

Admiralty Records (ADM)
High Court of Admiralty and Colonial Vice-Admiralty Courts (HCA)

Tamil Nadu State Archives, Chennai, India (TNSA)

Persian Records
Mayor's Court Records

Xavier Centre for Historical Research, Alto Povorim, Goa, India (XCHR)

Mhamai House Records (MHR)

Published sources

Anquetil-Duperron, Abraham-Hyacinthe, *Voyage en Inde 1754–1762: relation de voyage en préliminaire à la traduction du Zend-Avesta*, ed. Jean Deloche, Manonmani Filliozat and Pierre-Sylvain Filliozat (Paris, 1997).
Bartholomaeo, Paulinus A. S., *A Voyage to the East Indies* ... (London, 1780).
Blancard, Pierre, *Manuel du commerce des Indes Orientales et de la Chine* (Paris, 1806).
Hanway, Jonas, *Historical Account of the British Trade over the Caspian Sea* ... (London, 1753).
Lane, Edward W., *Account of the Manners and Customs of the Modern Egyptians* ... (London, 1860).
Lockyer, Charles, *Account of the Trade in India* ... (London, 1711).
Niebuhr, Carsten, *Description de l'Arabie, d'après les observations et recherches faites dans le pays même* ... (Paris, 1779).
Travels through Arabia and Other Countries in the East, trans. Robert Heron, 2 vols. (Edinburgh, 1792).
Sonnerat, Pierre, *Voyage aux Indes Orientales et à la Chine* ... (Paris, 1782).

Published studies

Abdullah, Thabit A. J., *Merchants, Mamluks, and Murder: the Political Economy of Trade in Eighteenth-Century Basra* (Albany, NY, 2001).
Abrams, Philip, *Historical Sociology* (Ithaca, NY, 1982).
Abu-Husayn, Abdul-Rahim, *Provincial Leaderships in Syria, 1575–1650* (Beirut, 1985).
Abu-Lughod, Janet L., *Before European Hegemony: the World System AD 1250–1350* (Oxford, 1989).
Agarwal, Usha, 'An account of the postal system in India from 1650 to 1750', *Bengal Past and Present* 85 (1966), 40–57.
'Historical account of the roads from Kabul to Calcutta during the seventeenth and eighteenth centuries', *Quarterly Review of Historical Studies* 9:3 (1969–70), 147–60.
'Roads from Surat to Agra in the seventeenth and eighteenth centuries', *Quarterly Review of Historical Studies* 5:3 (1965–6), 148–55.

Aghassian, Michel and Kéram Kévonian, 'The Armenian merchant network: overall autonomy and local integration', in Sushil Chaudhury and Michel Morineau (eds.), *Merchants, Companies and Trade: Europe and Asia in the Early Modern Era* (Cambridge, 1999), 74–94.

'Le commerce arménien dans l'Océan Indien aux 17e et 18e siècles', in Denys Lombard and Jean Aubin (eds.), *Marchands et hommes d'affaires asiatiques dans l'Océan Indien et la Mer de Chine 13–20 siècles* (Paris, 1988), 155–81.

Agmon, Iris and Ido Shahar, 'Theme issue: shifting perspectives in the study of Shariʿa courts: methodologies and paradigms', *Islamic Law and Society* 15:1 (2008), 1–19.

Ahmad, Muhammad Basheer, *Judicial System of the Mughal Empire* (2nd edn, Karachi, 1978).

Alam, Muzaffar, *The Crisis of Empire in Mughal North India: Awadh and the Punjab, 1707–48* (Delhi, 1986).

'The culture and politics of Persian in precolonial Hindustan', in Sheldon I. Pollock (ed.), *Literary Cultures in History: Reconstructions from South Asia* (Berkeley, CA, 2003), 131–98.

The Languages of Political Islam in India, 1200–1800 (Chicago, 2004).

'Pursuit of Persian: language in Mughal politics', *Modern Asian Studies* 32:2 (1998), 317–49.

'*Shariʿa* and governance in the Indo-Islamic context', in David Gilmartin and Bruce B. Lawrence (eds.), *Beyond Turk and Hindu: Rethinking Religious Identities in Islamicate South Asia* (Gainesville, FL, 2000), 216–45.

'Trade, state policy and regional change: aspects of Mughal–Uzbek commercial relations, *c.*1550–1750', *Journal of the Economic and Social History of the Orient* 37:3 (1994), 202–27.

Alam, Muzaffar and Sanjay Subrahmanyam, 'Exploring the hinterland: trade and politics in the Arcot Nizamate (1700–1732)', in Rudrangshu Mukherjee and Lakshmi Subramanian (eds.), *Politics and Trade in the Indian Ocean World: Esssays in Honor of Ashin Das Gupta* (Delhi, 1998), 113–64.

Indo-Persian Travels in the Age of Discoveries, 1400–1800 (Cambridge, 2007).

'Making of a munshi', *Comparative Studies of South Asia, Africa and the Middle East* 24:2 (2004), 61–72.

'Witnesses and agents of empire: eighteenth-century historiography and the world of the Mughal *munshī*', *Journal of the Economic and Social History of the Orient* 53: 1–2 (2010), 393–423.

Alam, Muzaffar, Françoise Delvoye and Marc Gaborieu (eds.), *The Making of Indo-Persian Culture: Indian and French Studies* (New Delhi, 2000).

Alavi, Seema, *Islam and Healing: Loss and Recovery of an Indo-Muslim Medical Tradition, 1600–1900* (Ranikhet, 2007).

'Medical culture in transition: Mughal gentleman physician and the native doctor in early colonial India', *Modern Asian Studies* 42:5 (2008), 853–97.

Albert, Pierre, *Correspondre: Jadis et naguère* (Paris, 1997).

Algar, Hamid, 'Shiʿism and Iran in the eighteenth century', in Thomas Naff and Roger Owen (eds.), *Studies in Eighteenth Century Islamic History* (London, 1971), 288–302.

Allen, Calvin H., 'Indian merchant community of Masqat', *Bulletin of the School of Oriental and African Studies* 44:1 (1981), 39–53.

ʿAmrī, Ḥusayn ʿAbd Allāh, *Miʾat ʿām min tārikh al-Yaman al-ḥadīth, 1161–1264 h./1748–1784 m.* (Damascus: Dār al-fikr, 1984).

The Yemen in the 18th and 19th Centuries: a Political and Intellectual History (London, 1985).

Arasaratnam, Sinnappah, 'Recent trends in the historiography of the Indian Ocean, 1500 to 1800', *Journal of World History* 1:2 (1990), 225–48.

Ariès, Phillipe, *L'enfant et la vie familiale sous l'Ancien Régime* (Paris, 1960).

Arnason, Johann P., S. N. Eisenstadt and Bjorn Wittrock (eds.), *Axial Civilizations and World History* (Leiden, 2005).

Asad, Talal, 'Reading a modern classic: W. C. Smith's *The Meaning and End of Religion*', *History of Religions* 40:3 (2001), 205–22.

Aslanian, Sebouh D., *From the Indian Ocean to the Mediterranean: the Global Trade Networks of Armenian Merchants from New Julfa* (Berkeley, CA, 2010).

Astuti, Rita, 'Are we all natural dualists? A cognitive developmental approach', *Journal of the Royal Anthropological Institute* 7:3 (2001), 429–47.

Athar Ali, M., *The Mughal Nobility under Aurangzeb* (Aligarh, 1966).

Atiyeh, George N. (ed.), *The Book in the Islamic World: the Written Word and Communication in the Middle East* (Albany, NY, 1995).

Axworthy, Michael, *The Sword of Persia: Nader Shah, from Tribal Warrior to Conquering Despot* (London, 2006).

al-ʿAẓma, ʿAzīz, *Muḥammad ibn ʿAbd al-Wahhāb* (Beirut: Riyād al-Rayyis lil-kutub wa-al-nashr, 2000).

al-Azmeh, Aziz, *Muslim Kingship: Power and the Sacred in Muslim, Christian and Pagan Polities* (London, 1997).

Babaie, Sussan, Kathryn Babayan, Ina Baghdiantz-McCabe and Massumeh Farhad, *Slaves of the Shah: New Elites of Safavid Iran* (London, 2004).

Babayan, Kathryn and Afsaneh Najmabadi (eds.), *Islamicate Sexualities: Translations across Temporal Geographies of Desire* (Cambridge, MA, 2008).

Baer, Marc, Ussama Makdisi and Andrew Shryock, 'Tolerance and conversion in the Ottoman empire: a conversation', *Comparative Studies in Society and History* 51:4 (2009), 927–40.

Baghdiantz McCabe, Ina, *Shah's Silk for Europe's Silver: the Eurasian Trade of the Julfa Armenians in Safavid Iran and India (1530–1750)* (Atlanta, GA, 2002).

Baghdiantz McCabe, Ina, Gelina Harlaftis and Ionna Pepelasis Minoglou (eds.), *Diaspora Entrepreneurial Networks: Four Centuries of History* (Oxford, 2005).

Baibourtian, Vahan, *International Trade and the Armenian Merchants in the Seventeenth Century* (New Delhi, 2004).

Baker, Colin F., 'Judaeo-Arabic material in the Cambridge Genizah Collections', *Bulletin of the School of Oriental and African Studies* 58 (1995), 45–54.

Baker, D., 'Arab paper making', *The Paper Conservator* 15 (1991), 28–35.

Baldwin, James, 'Petitioning the sultan in Ottoman Egypt', *Bulletin of the School of Oriental and African Studies* 12:3 (2012), 499–524.

Barbir, Karl K., *Ottoman Rule in Damascus, 1708–1758* (Princeton, NJ, 1980).

Barkey, Karen, *Empire of Difference: the Ottomans in Comparative Perspective* (Cambridge, 2008).

Barnett, Richard B., *North India between Empires: Awadh, the Mughals and the British, 1720–1801* (Berkeley, CA, 1980).
Barth, Fredrik (ed.), *Ethnic Groups and Boundaries: the Social Organization of Culture Difference* (Boston, 1969).
Barton, David and Nigel Hall (eds.), *Letter Writing as a Social Practice* (Philadelphia, 2000).
Bashir, Shahzad, *Sufi Bodies: Religion and Society in Medieval Islam* (New York, 2011).
Bausani, Alessandro, *Persia Religiosa* (Milan, 1959).
Bayburdyan, Vahan A., *International Trade and the Armenian Merchants in the Seventeenth Century* (New Delhi, 2004).
Bayly, Christopher A., *The Birth of the Modern World, 1780–1914: Global Connections and Comparisons* (Oxford, 2004).
Empire and Information: Intelligence Gathering and Social Communication in India, 1780–1870 (Cambridge, 1996).
Imperial Meridian: the British Empire and the World, 1780–1830 (London, 1989).
'Knowing the country: empire and information', *Modern Asian Studies* 27:1 (1993), 3–43.
Bearman, Peter, Robert Faris and James Moody, 'Blocking the future: new solutions for old problems in historical social science', *Social Science History* 32:4 (1999), 501–33.
Bentley, Jerry H., *Old World Encounters: Cross-Cultural Contacts and Exchanges in Pre-Modern Times* (New York, 1993).
Benton, Lauren, *Law and Colonial Cultures: Legal Regimes in World History, 1400–1900* (Cambridge, 2002).
Berg, Maxine, 'In pursuit of luxury: global history and British consumer goods in the eighteenth century', *Past and Present* 182 (2004), 85–142.
'Useful knowledge, "industrial enlightenment", and the place of India', *Journal of Global History* 8:1 (2013), 117–41.
Berkey, Jonathan P., *Popular Preaching and Religious Authority in the Medieval Islamic Near East* (Seattle, WA, 2001).
Blair, Sheila and Jonathan Bloom, *The Art and Architecture of Islam, 1250–1800* (New Haven, CT, 1994).
Blau, Joshua, *A Handbook of Early Middle Arabic* (Jerusalem, 2002).
Bleuchot, Hervé, *Les institutions traditionelles dans le monde arabe* (Paris, 1996).
Bloom, Jonathan, *Paper before Print: the History and Impact of Paper in the Islamic World* (New Haven, 2001).
Bodman, Herbert, *Political Factions in Aleppo, 1760–1826* (Chapel Hill, NC, 1963).
Bonine, Michael E., Abbas Amanat and Michael E. Gasper (eds.), *Is there a Middle East? The Evolution of a Geopolitical Concept* (Stanford, CA, 2012).
Bonner, Michael D., 'The naming of the frontier: ʿAwāṣim, thughūr, and the Arab geographers', *Bulletin of the School of Oriental and African Studies* 57:1 (1994), 17–24.
Borges, Charles J., 'Native Goan participation in the Estado da Índia and the inter-Asiatic trade', in Artur Teodoro de Matos and Luís Filipe F. Reis Thomaz (eds.), *A Carreira da Índia e as rotas dos estreitos: actas do VIII*

seminário internacional de história indo-portuguesa (Braga, Portugal, 1998), 672–83.
Bournatian, George, 'The Armenian community of Isfahan in the seventeenth century', *Armenian Review*, 24 (1971), 27–45 and 25 (1972), 33–50.
Boyer, Pascal, *Religion Explained: the Evolutionary Origins of Religious Thought* (New York, 2001).
Braddick, Michael J. (ed.), *The Politics of Gesture: Historical Perspectives* (Oxford, 2009).
Braudel, Fernand, *Civilization and Capitalism, 15th–18th Century*, trans. Siân Reynolds, 3 vols. (London, 1981).
Brauer, Ralph W., *Boundaries and Frontiers in Medieval Muslim Geography* (Philadelphia, 1995).
Brown, Donald E., *Human Universals* (New York, 1991).
Brunschvig, Robert, 'Le système de la preuve en droit musulman', *Etudes d'Islamologie* 2 (1976), 201–19.
Burke III, Edmund, 'Marshall G. S. Hodgson and the hemispheric interregional approach to world history', *Journal of World History* 6:2 (1995), 237–50.
Burton, Audrey, *The Bukharans: a Dynastic, Diplomatic and Commercial History, 1550–1702* (Richmond, Surrey, 1997).
Busch, Allison, *Poetry of Kings: the Classical Hindi Literature of Mughal India* (New York, 2011).
Calmard, Jean (ed.), *Etudes safavides* (Paris, 1993).
Campbell, John K., *Honour, Family and Patronage: a Study of Institutions and Moral Values in a Greek Mountain Community* (Oxford, 1964).
Cantwell Smith, Wilfred, *The Meaning and End of Religion: a New Approach to the Religious Traditions of Mankind* (New York, 1963).
On Understanding Islam: Selected Studies (The Hague, 1981).
Carreira, Ernestine, 'Les Kamat et le commerce français en Inde, 1778–1819', *Moyen Orient et Océan Indien* 7 (1990), 157–77.
Casale, Giancarlo, 'The ethnic composition of Ottoman ship crews and the "Rumi challenge" to Portuguese identity', *Medieval Encounters* 13 (2007), 122–44.
Chakravarti, Ranabir, 'Nakhudas and nauvittikas: ship-owning merchants in the west coast of India (*c.* AD 1000–1500)', *Journal of the Economic and Social History of the Orient* 43:1 (2000), 34–64.
Chandra, Satish (ed.), *Essays in Medieval Indian Economic History* (New Delhi, 1990).
Chartier, Roger, Alain Boureau and Cécile Dauphin, *Correspondence: Models of Letter-Writing from the Middle Ages to the Nineteenth Century*, trans. Christopher Woodall (Cambridge, 1997).
Chatterjee, Indrani (ed.), *Unfamiliar Relations: Family and History in South Asia* (New Brunswick, NJ, 2004).
Chatterjee, Indrani and Richard M. Eaton (eds.), *Slavery and South Asian History* (Bloomington, IN, 2006).
Chatterjee, Kumkum, *Merchants, Politics and Society in Early Modern India: Bihar, 1733–1820* (Leiden, 1996).
'Scribal elites in Sultanate and Mughal Bengal', *Indian Economic and Social History Review* 47:4 (2010), 445–72.

Chaudhuri, Kirti N., *Asia before Europe: Economy and Civilisation of the Indian Ocean from the Rise of Islam to 1750* (Cambridge, 1990).

'Reflections on the organizing principle of premodern trade', in James D. Tracy (ed.), *The Political Economy of Merchant Empires: State Power and World Trade, 1350–1750* (Cambridge, 1991), 421–42.

The Trading World of Asia and the English East India Company, 1660–1760 (Cambridge, 1978).

Chaudhury, Sushil, *From Prosperity to Decline: Eighteenth Century Bengal* (New Delhi, 1995).

Chaudhury, Sushil and Michel Morineau (eds.), *Merchants, Companies and Trade: Europe and Asia in the Early Modern Era* (Cambridge, 1999).

A Chronicle of the Carmelites in Persia and the Papal Mission of the XVIIth and XVIIIth Centuries, 2 vols. (London, 1939).

Cifoletti, Guido, *La lingua franca mediterranea* (Padua, 1989).

Çizakça, Murat, *Comparative Evolution of Business Partnerships: the Islamic World and Europe, with Specific Reference to the Ottoman Archives* (Leiden, 1996).

Clammer, John, Sylvie Poirier and Eric Schwimmer, 'Introduction: the relevance of ontologies in anthropology – reflections on a new anthropological field', in John Clammer, Sylvie Poirier and Eric Schwimmer (eds.), *Figured Worlds: Ontological Obstacles in Intercultural Relations* (Toronto, 2004), 3–22.

Clarence-Smith, William G., *Islam and the Abolition of Slavery* (Oxford, 2006).

Cohen, Marcel, *La grande invention de l'écriture et son évolution* (Paris, 1958).

Cohn, Bernard S., 'Political systems in eighteenth century India: the Banaras region', *Journal of the American Oriental Society* 82:3 (1962), 312–20.

Cole, Juan R. I., 'Popular Shīʿism', in Richard M. Eaton, *India's Islamic Traditions, 711–1750* (New Delhi, 2003), 311–41.

Roots of North Indian Shīʿism in Iran and Iraq: Religion and State in Awadh, 1722–1859 (Berkeley, CA, 1988).

Coleman, James S., *Foundations of Social Theory* (Cambridge, MA, 1990).

Conlon, Frank F., 'Caste by association: the Gauḍa Sārasvata Brāhmaṇa unification movement', *Journal of Asian Studies* 33:3 (1974), 351–65.

A Caste in a Changing World: the Chitrapur Saraswat Brahmans, 1700–1935 (Berkeley, 1977).

'Caste and urbanism in historical perspective: the Saraswat Brahmans', in Richard G. Fox (ed.), *Urban India: Society, Space and Image* (Durham, NC, 1970), 25–38.

Cook, Michael A. (ed.), *Studies in the Economic History of the Middle East from the Rise of Islam to the Present Day* (Oxford, 1970).

Crone, Patricia, *God's Rule: Government and Islam* (New York, 2004).

Pre-Industrial Societies (Oxford, 1989).

Cuno, Kenneth M., *The Pasha's Peasants: Land, Society and Economy in Lower Egypt, 1740–1858* (Cambridge, 1992).

Curtin, Philip D., *Cross-Cultural Trade in World History* (Cambridge, 1984).

Dakhlia, Jocelyne, *Lingua franca: histoire d'une langue métisse en Méditerranée* (Arles, 2009).

Dale, Stephen F., *Indian Merchants and Eurasian Trade, 1600–1750* (Cambridge, 1994).

'Indo-Russian trade in the eighteenth century', in Sugata Bose (ed.), *South Asia and World Capitalism* (Delhi, 1990), 140–56.

The Muslim Empires of the Ottomans, Safavids, and Mughals (Cambridge, 2010).

Darling, Linda T., *Revenue Raising and Legitimacy: Tax Collection and Finance Administration in the Ottoman Empire, 1560–1660* (Leiden, 1996).

Darwin, John, *After Tamerlane: the Global History of Empire since 1405* (London, 2007).

Das Gupta, Ashin, *Indian Merchants and the Decline of Surat, c. 1700–1750* (Wiesbaden, 1979).

Malabar in Asian Trade, 1740–1800 (Cambridge, 1967).

Das Gupta, Ashin and Michael N. Pearson (eds.), *India and the Indian Ocean 1500–1800* (New Delhi, 1987).

Davar, S. P., *The History of the Parsi Punchayet of Bombay* (Bombay, 1949).

Davis, Donald R., jr, 'Intermediate realms of law: corporate groups and rulers in medieval India', *Journal of the Economic and Social History of the Orient* 48:1 (2005), 92–117.

Deloche, Jean, *Transport and Communications in India prior to Steam Locomotion*, vol. I: *Land Transport*, vol. II: *Water Transport* (New Delhi, 1993–4).

Derrett, John D. M., *Religion, Law and the State in India* (London, 1968).

Descola, Philippe, 'Beyond nature and culture', *Proceedings of the British Academy* 139 (2006), 137–55.

Dharwadker, Vinay, 'The historical formation of Indian-English literature', in Sheldon Pollock (ed.), *Literary Cultures in History: Reconstructions from South Asia* (Berkeley, CA, 2003), 199–267.

Dhavan, Purnima, *When Sparrows Became Hawks: the Making of the Sikh Warrior Tradition, 1699–1799* (New York, 2011).

Dihkhudā, ʿAlī Akbar, *Lughatnāmah*, 14 vols. (Tehran, 1993–4).

Diringer, David, *Writing* (London, 1982).

Dobbin, Christine, 'The Parsi Panchayat in Bombay City in the nineteenth century', *Modern Asian Studies* 4:2 (1970), 149–64.

Doumani, Beshara (ed.), *Family History in the Middle East: Household, Property, and Gender* (Albany, NY, 2003).

Dursteler, Eric R., 'Speaking tongues: language and communication in the early modern Mediterranean', *Past and Present* 217 (2012), 47–77.

Eaton, Richard M., *The Rise of Islam and the Bengal Frontier, 1204–1760* (Berkeley, CA, 1993).

Eisenstadt, Shmuel N., *Political Systems of Empires* (New York, 1963).

Elkjaer, Joergen R., 'The entrepreneur in economic theory: an example of the development and influence of a concept', *History of Economic Ideas* 13:6 (1991), 805–15.

Ellickson, Robert C., *Order without Law: How Neighbors Settle Disputes* (Cambridge, MA, 1991).

Endress, Gerhard, *An Introduction to Islam*, trans. Carole Hillenbrand (New York, 1988).

Enthoven, Reginald E., *Tribes and Castes of Bombay* (Bombay, 1920).

Ergene, Boğaç A., 'Evidence in Ottoman courts: oral and written documentation in early-modern courts of Islamic law', *Journal of the American Oriental Society* 124:3 (2004), 471–91.

Local Court, Provincial Society and Justice in the Ottoman Empire: Legal Practice and Dispute Resolution in Çankırı and Kastamonu (1652–1744) (Leiden and Boston, 2003).

'On Ottoman justice: interpretations in conflict (1600–1800)', *Islamic Law and Society* 8:1 (2001), 52–87.

'Social identity and patterns of interaction in the sharia court of Kastamonu (1740–44)', *Islamic Law and Society* 15:1 (2008), 20–54.

Ernst, Carl W. and Richard C. Martin (eds.), *Rethinking Islamic Studies: From Orientalism to Cosmopolitanism* (Columbia, SC, 2010).

Esposito, John L. (ed.), *The Oxford History of Islam* (Oxford, 2000).

Eustace, Nicole, Eugenia Lean, Julie Livingston, Jan Plamper, William Reddy and Barbara Rosenwein, 'AHR conversation: the historical study of emotions', *American Historical Review* 117:5 (2012), 1487–531.

Evans, Peter, Dietrich Rueschemeyer and Theda Skocpol (eds.), *Bringing the State Back In* (Cambridge, 1985)

Ewald, Janet J., 'Crossers of the sea: slaves, freedmen, and other migrants in the northwestern Indian Ocean, *c.* 1750–1914', *American Historical Review* 105:1 (2000), 69–91.

Faḍāʾilī [Fażāʾilī], Ḥabīb Allāh, *Aṭlas-i khaṭṭ: Taḥqīq-i dar khaṭūṭ-i Islāmī* (Tehran, 1350/1971–2).

Taʿlīm-i khaṭṭ (Tehran, 1356/1977–8).

Farooqi, Naim R., 'Moguls, Ottomans and pilgrims: protecting the routes to Mecca in the sixteenth and seventeenth centuries', *International History Review* 10:2 (1988), 198–220.

Farooque, Abul Khair Muhammad, *Roads and Communications in Mughal India* (Delhi: Idarah-i Adabiyat-i Delli, 1977).

Faroqhi, Suraiya, 'Camels, wagons, and the Ottoman state in the sixteenth and seventeenth centuries', *International Journal of Middle East Studies* 14:4 (1982), 523–39.

The Ottoman Empire and the World Around It (London, 2004).

Pilgrims and Sultans: the Hajj under the Ottomans, 1517–1683 (London, 1994).

Faroqhi, Suraiya (ed.), *Animals and People in the Ottoman Empire* (Istanbul, 2010).

Faruqi, Shamsur Rahman, *Early Urdu Literary Culture and History* (New Delhi, 2001).

The Flower-Lit Road: Essays in Urdu Literary Theory and Criticism (Allahabad, 2005).

'Stranger in the city: the poetics of Sabk-i Hindi', *Annual of Urdu Studies* 19 (2004), 1–93.

Fattah, Hala, *Politics of Regional Trade in Iraq, Arabia and the Gulf, 1745–1900* (Albany, NY, 1997).

Felek, Özgen and Alexander D. Knysh (eds.), *Dreams and Visions in Islamic Societies* (Albany, NY, 2012).

Fisher, Michael H., *A Clash of Culture: Awadh, the British, and the Mughals* (New Delhi, 1987).

'The office of Akhbar Nawis: the transition from Mughal to British forms', *Modern Asian Studies* 27:1 (1993), 45–82.

Fleischer, Cornell H., 'Between the lines: realities of scribal life in the sixteenth century', in Colin Heywood and Colin Imber (eds.), *Studies in Ottoman History in Honour of Professor V. L. Ménage* (Istanbul, 1994), 45–61.

Fletcher, Joseph F., 'Integrative history: parallels and interconnections in the early modern period, 1500–1800', *Journal of Turkish Studies* 9 (1985), 37–57.

Floor, Willem, *Safavid Government Institutions* (Costa Mesa, CA, 2001).

'The secular judicial system in Safavid Persia', *Studia Iranica* 29:1 (2000) 9–60.

Flynn, Dennis O. and Arturo Giráldez. 'Introduction: monetary substances in global perspective', in Dennis O. Flynn and Arturo Giráldez (eds.), *Metals and Monies in an Emerging Global Economy* (Aldershot, 1997), xv–xl.

Frevert, Ute, Christian Bailey, Pascal Eitler, Benno Gammerl, Bettina Hitzer, Margrit Pernau, Monique Scheer, Anne Schmidt and Nina Verheyen, *Emotional Lexicons: Continuity and Change in the Vocabulary of Feeling* (Oxford, 2014).

Fuess, Albrecht and Jan-Peter Hartung (eds.), *Court Cultures in the Muslim World: Seventh to Nineteenth Centuries* (New York, 2011).

Furber, Holden, 'East India Company's financial records', *Indian Archives* 7:2 (1953), 100–14.

'Overland route to India in the 17th and 18th centuries' in *Journal of Indian History* 29:2 (1951), 105–34.

Furūgh Iṣfahānī, Muḥammad Mahdī, *Furūghistān: Dānishnāmah-yi fann-i istifa va siyāq*, ed. Irāj Afshār (Tehran, 1999).

Gaborieau, Marc, *et al.* (eds.), *The Encyclopaedia of Islam* (3rd edn, Leiden, 2007–)

Gacek, Adam, *Arabic Manuscripts: a Vademecum for Readers* (Leiden, 2009).

Garcin, Jean-Claude, *et al.*, *États, sociétés et cultures du monde musulman médiéval: Xe–XVe siècle*, 3 vols. (Paris, 1995).

Gaur, Albertine, *Writing Materials of the East* (London, 1979).

Gelb, Ignace J., *A Study of Writing* (rev. edn, Chicago, 1963).

Gellner, Ernest, *Plough, Sword and Book: the Structure of Human History* (Chicago, 1988).

Gerber, Haim, 'Anthropology and family history: the Ottoman and Turkish families', *Journal of Family History* 14:4 (1989), 409–21.

Islamic Law and Culture 1600–1840 (Leiden, 1999).

State, Society, and Law in Islam: Ottoman Law in Comparative Perspective (Albany, NY, 1994).

Ghobrial, John-Paul A., 'The secret life of Elias of Babylon and the uses of global microhistory', *Past and Present* 222 (2014), 51–93.

Ghosh, Amitav, *In an Antique Land* (London, 1992).

Gibb, H. A. R. and Harold Bowen, *Islamic Society and the West: a Study of the Impact of Western Civilization on Moslem Culture in the Near East* (London, 1950–7 [in two parts]).

Gibb, H. A. R., *et al.* (eds.), *The Encyclopaedia of Islam* (2nd edn, Leiden, 1960–2004).

Gilʿadi, Avner, *Children of Islam: Concepts of Childhood in Medieval Muslim Society* (London, 1992).

Gilbar, Gad G., 'Muslim *tujjār* of the Middle East and their commercial networks in the long nineteenth century', *Studia Islamica* 100/1 (2005), 183–202.

Gilmartin, David and Bruce B. Lawrence (eds.), *Beyond Turk and Hindu: Rethinking Religious Identities in Islamicate South Asia* (Gainesville, FL, 2000)

Ginzburg, Carlo, *Il formaggio e i vermi: Il cosmo di un mugnaio del '500* (Turin, 1976).

Goffman, Erving, *Interaction Rituals: Essays on Face-to-Face Behaviour* (New York, 1967).

The Presentation of Self in Everyday Life (New York, 1959).

Goitein, Shelomo D., 'The documents of the Cairo Geniza as a source for Mediterranean social history', *Journal of the American Oriental Society* 80:2 (1960), 91–100.

A Mediterranean Society: the Jewish Communities of the Arab World as Portrayed in the Documents of the Cairo Geniza, 6 vols. (Berkeley, 1967–93).

'Mediterranean trade in the eleventh century: some facts and problems', in Michael A. Cook (ed.), *Studies in the Economic History of the Middle East from the Rise of Islam to the Present Day* (Oxford, 1970), 51–62.

Goitein, Shelomo D. and Mordechai A. Friedman, *India Traders of the Middle Ages: Documents from the Cairo Geniza 'India Book'* (Leiden, 2008).

Goldberg, Jessica L., 'Choosing and enforcing business relationships in the eleventh-century Mediterranean: reassessing the "Maghribī traders"', *Past and Present* 216 (2012), 3–40.

Gole, Susan, *Indian Maps and Plans: From Earliest Times to the Advent of European Surveys* (New Delhi, 1989).

Gommans, Jos J. L., 'Empires and emporia: the orient in world historical space and time', *Journal of the Economic and Social History of the Orient* 53: 1–2 (2010), 3–18.

'The horse trade in eighteenth-century South Asia', *Journal of the Economic and Social History of the Orient* 37:3 (1994), 228–50.

The Rise of the Indo-Afghan Empire, c. 1710–1780 (Leiden, 1995).

Goody, Jack, *The Logic of Writing and the Organization of Society* (Cambridge, 1986).

Gordon, Stewart, 'Legitimacy and loyalty in some successor states of the eighteenth century', in John F. Richards (ed.), *Kingship and Authority in South Asia* (Delhi, 1998), 327–348.

The Marathas, 1600–1818 (Cambridge, 1998).

Marathas, Marauders and State Formation in Eighteenth-Century India (Delhi, 1994).

'Robes of honour: a "transactional" kingly ceremony', *Indian Economic and Social History Review* 33:3 (1996), 225–42.

Gordon, Stewart (ed.), *Robes of Honour: Khil'at in Pre-Colonial and Colonial India* (New Delhi, 2003).

Green, Nile, 'Blessed men and tribal politics: notes on political culture in the Indo-Afghan world', *Journal of the Economic and Social History of the Orient* 49:3 (2006), 344–60.

Greene, Molly, *Christians and Muslims in the Early Modern Mediterranean* (Princeton, NJ, 2000).

Gregorian, Vartan, 'Minorities of Isfahan: the Armenian community of Isfahan, 1587–1722', *Iranian Studies* 7: 3–4 (1974), 652–80.

Greif, Avner, 'Cultural beliefs and the organization of society: a historical and theoretical reflection on collectivist and individualist societies', *Journal of Political Economy* 102:5 (1994), 912–50.

Grewal, J. S., *The Sikhs of the Punjab* (Cambridge, 1990).

Guha, Amalendu, 'More about the Parsi Sheths: their roots, entrepreneurship and comprador role, 1650–1918', in Dwijendra Tripathi (ed.), *Business Communities of India* (New Delhi, 1984), 109–50.

Guha, Sumit, 'Household size and household structure in western India, *c.* 1700–1950: beginning an exploration', *Indian Economic and Social History Review* 35:1 (1998), 23–33.

Gully, Adrian, *The Culture of Letter-Writing in Pre-Modern Islamic Society* (Edinburgh, 2008).

Guy, John, *Palm-leaf and Paper: Illustrated Manuscripts of India and Southeast Asia* (Melbourne, 1982).

Habib, Irfan, *The Agrarian System of Mughal India, 1556–1707* (3rd edn, London, 2012).

'Merchant communities in precolonial India', in James D. Tracy (ed.), *The Rise of Merchant Empires: Long-Distance Trade in the Early Modern World, 1350–1750* (Cambridge, 1990), 371–99.

'Monetary system and prices', in Tapan Raychaudhuri and Irfan Habib (eds.), *Cambridge Economic History of India,* vol. I: *c. 1200–c. 1750* (Cambridge, 1982), 360–81.

'Postal communications in Mughal India', *Proceedings of the Indian Historical Congress,* 46th session (Delhi, 1986), 236–52.

'System of bills of exchange (*hundis*) in the Mughal empire', in Satish Chandra (ed.), *Essays in Medieval Indian Economic History* (New Delhi, 1987), 207–21.

Haider, Najaf, 'Precious metal flows and currency circulation in the Mughal empire', *Journal of the Economic and Social History of the Orient* 39:3 (1996), 298–364.

Hall, Bruce S., 'How slaves used Islam: the letters of enslaved Muslim commercial agents in the nineteenth-century Niger Bend and Central Sahara', *Journal of African History* 52:3 (2011), 279–97.

Hallaq, Wael B., 'Model *shurūṭ* works and the dialectic of doctrine and practice', *Islamic Law and Society* 2:2 (1995), 109–34.

Hanafi, Shah Mahmoud, *Connecting Histories in Afghanistan: Market Relations and State Formation on a Colonial Frontier* (Stanford, CA, 2008).

Hanaway, William L. and Brian Spooner, *Reading Nasta'liq: Persian and Urdu Hands from 1500 to the Present* (Costa Mesa, CA, 1995).

Hanna, Nelly, *In Praise of Books: a Cultural History of Cairo's Middle Class, Sixteenth to the Eighteenth Century* (Syracuse, NY, 2003).

'Literacy and the "great divide" in the Islamic world, 1300–1800', *Journal of Global Hisotry* 2:2 (2007), 175–93.

Making Big Money in 1600: the Life and Times of Isma'il Abu Taqiyya, Egyptian Merchant (Syracuse, NY, 1998).

Hanna, Nelly, (ed.), *Money, Land and Trade: an Economic History of the Mediterranean* (London, 2002).

Harley, John B. and David Woodward (eds.), *The History of Cartography*, vol. II, bk 1: *Cartography in the Traditional Islamic and South Asian Societies* (Chicago, 1992).

Harvey, David, *Spaces of Global Capitalism: a Theory of Uneven Geographical Development* (London, 2006).

Hasan, Farhat, *State and Locality in Mughal India: Power Relations in Western India, c. 1572–1730* (Cambridge, 2004).

Hathaway, Jane, *The Politics of Households in Ottoman Egypt: the Rise of the Qazdaglis* (Cambridge, 1997).

A Tale of Two Factions: Myth, Memory and Identity in Ottoman Egypt and Yemen (Albany, NY, 2003).

Headland, Thomas N., Kenneth L. Pike and Marvin Harris (eds.), *Emics and Etics: the Insider/Outsider Debate* (Newbury Park, CA, 1990).

Henare, Amiria, Martin Holbraad and Sari Wastell, 'Introduction: thinking through things', in Amiria Henare, Martin Holbraad and Sari Wastell (eds.), *Thinking through Things: Theorising Artefacts Ethnographically* (London, 2007), 1–31.

Herzig, Edmund M., 'The family firm in the commercial organisation of the Julfa Armenians', in Jean Calmard (ed.), *Etudes safavides* (Paris, 1993), 287–304.

Heywood, Colin, *Writing Ottoman History: Documents and Interpretations* (Aldershot, Hampshire, 2002).

Hirschler, Konrad, *The Written Word in the Medieval Arabic Lands: a Social and Cultural History of Reading Practices* (New York and Edinburgh, 2012).

Hodgson, Marshall G. S., *Rethinking World History: Essays on Europe, Islam, and World History* (Cambridge, 1993).

Venture of Islam: Conscience and History in a World Civilization, 3 vols. (Chicago, 1974).

Hogendorn, Jan and Marion Johnson, *Shell Money of the Slave Trade* (Cambridge, 1986).

Hohfeld, Wesley N., 'Some fundamental legal conceptions as applied in judicial reasoning', *Yale Law Journal* 23:1 (1913), 16–59.

Hooker, M. Barry, *Legal Pluralism: an Introduction to Colonial and Neo-Colonial Laws* (Oxford, 1975).

Hopkins, Anthony G., 'The historiography of globalization and the globalization of regionalism', *Journal of the Economic and Social History of the Orient* 53:1 (2010), 19–36.

Hoskins, Halford L., *British Routes to India* (New York, 1928).

Hourani, Albert H., *A History of the Arab Peoples* (London, 1991).

Howlett, Peter and Mary S. Morgan (eds.), *How Well do Facts Travel? The Dissemination of Reliable Knowledge* (Cambridge, 2011).

Hunter, Dard, *Papermaking: the History and Technique of an Ancient Craft* (2nd edn, New York, 1947).

Husain, Iqbal, *The Ruhela Chieftaincies: the Rise and Fall of Ruhela Power in India in the Eighteenth Century* (Delhi, 1994).

Inalcık, Halil, *The Ottoman Empire: the Classical Age, 1300–1600*, trans. Norman Itzkowitz and Colin Imber (London, 1973).

Inalcık, Halil and Donald Quataert (eds.), *An Economic and Social History of the Ottoman Empire, 1300–1914* (Cambridge, 1994).

Inkster, Ian, 'Potentially global: "useful and reliable knowledge" and material progress in Europe, 1474–1914', *International History Review* 28:2 (2006), 237–86.

Irvine, William, *Later Mughals*, vol. I: *1707–1720,* vol. II: *1719–1739* (Calcutta, 1922).

Islam, Riazul, *Calendar of Documents on Indo-Persian Relations (1500–1750)* (Tehran, 1979).

Israel, Jonathan I., *Diasporas within a Diaspora: Jews, Crypto-Jews and the World Maritime Empires, 1540–1740* (Leiden, 2002).

Jennings, Ronald C., 'Kadi, court, and legal procedure in 17th-century Ottoman Kayseri', *Studia Islamica* 48 (1978), 133–72.

'Zimmis (non-Muslims) in early seventeenth century Ottoman judicial records: the sharia court of Anatolian Kayseri', *Journal of the Economic and Social History of the Orient* 21:1–3 (1978), 225–93.

Johansen, Baber, 'Formes de langage et fonctions publiques: stéréotypes, témoins et offices dans la preuve par l'écrit en droit musulman', *Arabica* 44 (1997), 333–76.

Joshi, Chitra, 'Dak roads, dak runners, and the reordering of communication networks', *International Review of Social History* 57:2 (2012), 169–89.

Kafadar, Cemal, 'A death in Venice (1575): Anatolian Muslim merchants trading in the Serenissima', *Journal of Turkish Studies* 10 (1986), 191–218.

Kahane, Henry, Renée Kahane and Andreas Tietze, *Lingua Franca in the Levant: Turkish Nautical Terms of Italian and Greek Origin* (Urbana, IL, 1958).

Karaka, Dosabhai F., *History of the Parsis* (London, 1884).

Karateke, Hakan T. and Maurus Reinkowski (eds.), *Legitimizing the Order: the Ottoman Rhetoric of State Power* (Leiden, 2005).

Kazem Zadeh, H., 'Chiffres siyâk et la comptabilité persane', *Revue de monde musulman* 30 (1915), 1–51.

Keddie, Nikki R. (ed.), *Scholars, Saints, and Sufis: Muslim Religious Institutions in the Middle East since 1500* (Berkeley, CA, 1972).

Keddie, Nikki R. and Beth Baron (eds.), *Women in Middle Eastern History: Shifting Boundaries in Sex and Gender* (New Haven, CT, 1991).

Keyvani, Mehdi, *Artisans and Guild Life in the Later Safavid Period: Contributions to the Social-Economic History of Persia* (Berlin, 1982).

Khalid Masud, Muhammad, Brinkley Messick and David S. Powers (eds.), *Islamic Legal Interpretation: Muftis and their Fatwas* (Cambridge, MA, 1996).

Khalid Masud, Muhammad, Rudolph Peters and David S. Powers (eds.), *Dispensing Justice in Islam: Qadis and their Judgements* (Leiden, 2005).

Khalilieh, Hassan S., *Islamic Maritime Law: an Introduction* (Leiden, 1998).

Khanbaghi, Aptin, *The Fire, the Star and the Cross: Minority Religions in Medieval and Early Modern Iran* (London, 2006).

Khoury, Dina R., 'Administrative practice between law (Shari'a) and state law (Kanun) on the eastern frontiers of the Ottoman empire', *Journal of Early Modern History* 5:4 (2001), 305–30.

State and Provincial Society in the Ottoman Empire: Mosul, 1540–1834 (Cambridge, 1997).

Knapp, Karlfried and Christiane Meierkord (eds.), *Lingua Franca Communication* (Frankfurt am Main, 2000).

Kopytoff, Igor (ed.), *The African Frontier: the Reproduction of African Traditional Societies* (Bloomington, IN, 1987).

Koselleck, Reinhart, *Futures Past: On the Semantics of Historical Time*, trans. Keith Tribe (New York, 2004)

Krätli, Graziano and Ghislaine Lydon (eds.), *The Trans-Saharan Book Trade: Manuscript Culture, Arabic Literacy, and Intellectual History in Muslim Africa* (Leiden, 2011).

Laffont, Jean-Jacques and David Martimort, *The Theory of Incentives: the Principal–Agent Model* (Princeton, 2002).

Lambourn, Elizabeth, 'Of jewels and horses: the career and patronage of an Iranian merchant under Shah Jahan', *Iranian Studies* 36:2 (2003), 213–58.

Lambton, Ann K. S., *Landlord and Peasant in Persia: a Sudy of Land Tenure and Land Revenue Administration* (rev. edn, London, 1969).

'Pīshkash: present or tribute?', *Bulletin of the School of Oriental and African Studies* 57:1 (1994), 145–58.

Lapidus, Ira M., *A History of Islamic Societies* (2nd edn, Cambridge, 2002).

'Islamic revivals and modernity: the contemporary movements and historical paradigms', *Journal of the Economic and Social History of the Orient* 40:4 (1997), 444–56.

Larson, Pier M., *Ocean of Letters: Language and Creolization in an Indian Ocean Diaspora* (Cambridge, 2009).

Latour, Bruno, *Nous n'avons jamais été modernes: essai d'anthropologie symétrique* (Paris, 1991).

Lattimore, Owen, *Studies in Frontier History: Collected Papers 1928–1958* (London, 1962).

Le Gall, Dina, *A Culture of Sufism: Naqshbandīs in the Ottoman World, 1450–1700* (Albany, NY, 2005).

Le Roy Ladurie, Emmanuel, *Montaillou: village occitan de 1294 à 1324* (Paris, 1975).

Lelyveld, David, 'Colonial knowledge and the fate of Hindustani', *Comparative Studies in Society and History* 35 (1993), 665–82.

Leonard, Karen, 'The Hyderabad political system and its participants', *Journal of Asian Studies* 30:3 (1971), 569–82.

Levi, Scott C., 'Hindus beyond the Hindu Kush: Indians in the Central Asian slave trade', *Journal of the Royal Asiatic Society of Great Britain and Ireland* (third series) 12:3 (2002), 277–88.

'India, Russia and the eighteenth-century transformation of the Central Asian caravan trade', *Journal of the Economic and Social History of the Orient* 42:4 (1999), 519–48.

Indian Diaspora in Central Asia and its Trade, 1550–1900 (Leiden, 2002).

Levi, Scott C., (ed.), *India and Central Asia: Commerce and Culture, 1500–1800* (New Delhi, 2007).
Levtzion, Nehemia and John O. Voll (eds.), *Eighteenth-Century Renewal and Reform in Islam* (Syracuse, NY, 1987).
Lewicka, Paulina B., 'Restaurants, inns and taverns that never were: some reflections on public consumption in medieval Cairo', *Journal of the Economic and Social History of the Orient* 48:1 (2005), 40–91.
Lewis, Bernard, *The Middle East: 2000 Years of History from the Rise of Christianity to the Present Day* (London, 1995).
Lewis, Martin W. and Kären E. Wigen, *Myth of Continents: a Critique of Metageography* (Berkeley, CA, 1997).
Libson, Gideon, 'On the development of custom as a source of law in Islamic law', *Islamic Law and Society* 4:2 (1997), 131–55.
Lieberman, Victor, *Strange Parallels: Southeast Asia in Global Context, c. 800–1830*, vol. I: *Integration on the Mainland* (Cambridge, 2003), vol. II: *Mainland Mirrors: Europe, Japan, China, South Asia, and the Islands* (Cambridge, 2009).
Lockhart, Laurence, *The Fall of the Safavid Dynasty and the Afghan Occupation of Persia* (Cambridge, 1958).
Lombard, Denys and Jean Aubin (eds.), *Marchands et hommes d'affaires asiatiques dans l'Océan Indien et la Mer de Chine 13–20 siècles* (Paris, 1988).
Lorenzen, David N., 'Hindu sects and Hindu religion: precolonial and colonial concepts', in Cynthia Talbot (ed.), *Knowing India: Colonial and Modern Constructions of the Past* (New Delhi: Yoda Press, 2011), 251–78.
'Who invented Hinduism?', *Comparative Studies in Society and History* 41:4 (1999), 630–59.
Losensky, Paul E., *Welcoming Fighānī: Imitation and Poetic Individuality in the Safavid-Mughal Ghazal* (Costa Mesa, CA, 1998).
Lubin, Timothy, Donald R. Davis jr and Jayanth K. Krishnan (eds.), *Hinduism and Law: an Introduction* (New York, 2010).
Ludden, David, 'Presidential address: maps in the mind and the mobility of Asia', *Journal of Asian Studies* 62:4 (2003), 1057–78.
Luhmann, Niklas, *Essays on Self-Reference* (New York, 1990).
Lydon, Ghislaine E., 'Contracting caravans: partnership and profit in nineteenth- and early twentieth-century trans-Saharan trade', *Journal of Global History* 3:1 (2008), 89–113.
On Trans-Saharan Trails: Islamic Law, Trade Networks, and Cross-Cultural Exchange in Nineteenth-Century Western Africa (New York, 2009).
'A paper economy of faith without faith in paper: a reflection on Islamic institutional history', *Journal of Economic Behaviour and Organization* 71 (2009), 647–59.
'Slavery, exchange and Islamic law: a glimpse from the archives of Mali and Mauritania', *African Economic History* 33 (2005), 117–48.
McChesney, Robert D., '"Barrier of heterodoxy"? Rethinking the ties between Iran and Central Asia in the seventeenth century', in Charles Melville (ed.), *Safavid Persia: the History and Politics of an Islamic Society* (London, 1996), 231–67.

'The Central Asian Hajj-pilgrimage in the time of the early modern empires', in Michel M. Mazzaoui (ed.), *Safavid Iran and her Neighbors* (Salt Lake City, UT, 2003), 129–56.

McGowan, Bruce, 'The age of the ayans, 1699–1812', in Halil Inalcık and Donald Quataert (eds.), *An Economic and Social History of the Ottoman Empire, 1300–1914* (Cambridge, 1994), 637–758.

Machado, Pedro, 'A forgotten corner of the western Indian Ocean: Gujarati merchants, Portuguese India and the Mozambique slave trade, *c.*1730–1830', *Slavery and Abolition* 24:2 (2003), 17–32.

McLane, John R., *Land and Local Kingship in Eighteenth-Century Bengal* (Cambridge, 1993).

McNeill, William H., *The Rise of the West: a History of the Human Community* (Chicago, 1963).

Macro, Eric, 'South Arabia and the overland route to India', *Proceedings of the Seminar for Arabian Studies* 12 (1982), 49–60.

Maghen, Ze'ev, 'Theme issue: the interaction between Islamic law and non-Muslims', *Islamic Law and Society* 10: 3 (2003), 267–75.

Majumdar, Mohini Lal, *The Postal History of Zemindari Dawk (1707–1906)* (Calcutta: Ṛddhi-India, 1984).

Makdisi, George, *The Rise of Colleges: Institutions of Learning in Islam and the West* (Edinburgh, 1981).

Makdisi, John, 'Legal logic and equity in Islamic law', *American Journal of Comparative Law* 33:1 (1985), 63–92.

Marcus, Abraham, *Middle East on the Eve of Modernity: Aleppo in the Eighteenth Century* (New York, 1989).

Markovits, Claude, *The Global World of Indian Merchants, 1750–1947: Traders of Sind from Bukhara to Panama* (Cambridge, 2000).

Marlow, Louise, *Hierarchy and Egalitarianism in Islamic Thought* (Cambridge, 1997).

Marmon, Shaun E. (ed.), *Slavery in the Islamic Middle East* (Princeton, NJ, 1999).

Martin, Marina, 'Hundi/hawala: the problem of definition', *Modern Asian Studies* 43:4 (2008), 909–37.

Masters, Bruce A., *The Origins of Western Economic Dominance in the Middle East: Mercantilism and the Islamic Economy in Aleppo, 1600–1750* (New York, 1988).

Masum Billah, Mohd., 'Islamic insurance: its origins and development', *Arab Law Quarterly*, 13:4 (1998), 386–422.

Matthee, Rudolph P., 'Between Venice and Surat: the trade in gold in late Safavid Iran', *Modern Asian Studies* 34:1 (2000), 223–55.

Persia in Crisis: Safavid Decline and the Fall of Isfahan (London, 2012).

The Politics of Trade in Safavid Iran: Silk for Silver 1600–1730 (Cambridge, 1999).

The Pursuit of Pleasure: Drugs and Stimulants in Iranian History, 1500–1900 (Princeton, NJ, 2005).

Mauro, Frédéric, 'Merchant communities, 1350–1750', in James D. Tracy (ed.), *The Rise of Merchant Empires: Long-Distance Trade in the Early Modern World, 1350–1750* (Cambridge, 1990), 255–86.

Mauss, Marcel, *The Gift: Form and Reason for Exchange in Archaic Societies*, trans. W. D. Hall (London, 1990).

Mazzaoui, Michel M. (ed.), *Safavid Iran and her Neighbors* (Salt Lake City, UT, 2003).

Mehta, Shirin, 'The mahajans and the business communities of Ahmedabad', in Dwijendra Tripathi (ed.), *Business Communities of India* (New Delhi, 1984), 173–84.

Meilink-Roelofsz, M. A. P., 'The structures of trade in Asia in the sixteenth and seventeenth centuries. Niels Steensgaard's "Carracks, Caravans and Companies": a critical appraisal', *Mare Luso-Indicum* 4 (1980), 1–43.

Meloy, John L., *Imperial Power and Maritime Trade: Mecca and Cairo in the Later Middle Ages* (Chicago, 2010).

Melville, Charles (ed.), *Safavid Persia: the History and Politics of an Islamic Society* (London, 1996).

Meriwether, Margaret L., *The Kin who Count: Family and Society in Ottoman Aleppo, 1770–1840* (Austin, TX, 1999).

Messick, Brinkley, *Calligraphic State: Textual Domination and History in a Muslim Society* (Berkeley, CA, 1993).

'Legal documents and the concept of "restricted literacy" in a traditional society', *International Journal of the Sociology of Language* 42:1 (1983), 41–52.

'The mufti, the text and the world: legal interpretation in Yemen', *Man* 21:1 (1986), 102–19.

Michaud, Jean, 'Editorial – Zomia and beyond', *Journal of Global History* 5:2 (2010), 187–214.

Michel, Nicolas, 'The individual and the collectivity in the agricultural economy of pre-colonial Morocco', in Nelly Hanna (ed.), *Money, Land and Trade: an Economic History of the Mediterranean* (London, 2002), 15–36.

Middleton, John, 'Merchants: an essay in historical ethnography', *Journal of the Royal Anthropological Institute* 9:3 (2003), 509–26.

Mikhail, Alan, 'Unleashing the beast: animals, energy, and the economy of labor in Ottoman Egypt', *American Historical Review* 118:2 (2013), 317–48.

Mohiuddin, Momin, *Chancellery and Persian Epistolography under the Mughals: From Babar to Shah Jahan (1526–1658)* (Calcutta, 1971).

Moosvi, Shireen, 'The silver influx, money-supply, prices and revenue-extraction in Mughal India', *Journal of the Economic and Social History of the Orient* 30:1 (1987), 47–94.

Mukherjee, Rudrangshu and Lakshmi Subramanian (eds.), *Politics and Trade in the Indian Ocean World: Esssays in Honor of Ashin Das Gupta* (Delhi, 1998).

Musallam, Basim, 'The ordering of Muslim societies', in Francis Robinson (ed.), *Cambridge Illustrated History of the Islamic World* (Cambridge, 1996), 164–207.

Mutaf, Abdülmecid, 'Amicable settlement in Ottoman law: Sulh system', *Turcica* 36 (2004), 125–40.

Nadri, Ghulam A., *Eighteenth-Century Gujarat: the Dynamics of its Political Economy, 1750–1800* (Leiden and Boston, 2009).

Naff, Thomas and Roger Owen (eds.), *Studies in Eighteenth Century Islamic History* (London, 1971).

Naregal, Veena, 'Language and power in pre-colonial western India: textual hierarchies, literate audiences and colonial philology', *Indian Economic and Social History Review* 37:3 (2000), 259–94.

Nayeem, M. A., *The Evolution of Postal Communications and Administration in the Deccan (from 1294 AD to the Formation of the Hyderabad State in 1724 AD)* (Hyderabad, 1969).

The Philatelic and Postal History of Hyderabad, 2 vols. (Hyderabad, 1970).

Nieuwenhuis, Tom, *Politics and Society in Early Modern Iraq: Mamluk Pashas, Tribal Shaykhs and Local Rule between 1802 and 1831* (The Hague, 1982).

Nightingale, Pamela, *Trade and Empire, 1783–1806* (Cambridge, 1970).

O'Brien, Patrick, 'Historical foundations for a global perspective on the emergence of a western European regime for the discovery, development, and diffusion of useful and reliable knowledge', *Journal of Global History* 8:1 (2013), 1–24.

O'Hanlon, Rosalind 'Performance in a world of paper: Puranic histories and social communication in early modern India', *Past and Present* 219 (2013), 87–126.

'The social worth of scribes: Brahmins, Kayasthas and the social order in early modern India', *Indian Economic and Social History Review* 47:4 (2010), 563–95.

O'Hanlon, Rosalind and C. Minkowski, 'What makes people who they are? Pandit networks and the problem of livelihoods in early modern western India', *Indian Economic and Social History Review* 45:3 (2008), 381–416.

Östör, Ákos, Lina Fruzzetti and Steve Barnett (eds.), *Concepts of Person: Kinship, Caste, and Marriage in India* (Cambridge, MA, 1982).

Othman, Aida, '"An amicable settlement is best": *Ṣulḥ* and dispute resolution in Islamic law', *Arab Law Quarterly* 21 (2007), 64–90.

Palmer, Edward Henry and F. Pincott, *Oriental Penmanship: Specimens of Persian Handwriting* (London, 1886).

Pamuk, Şevket, 'Interaction between the monetary regimes of Istanbul, Cairo and Tunis, 1700–1875', in Nelly Hanna (ed.), *Money, Land and Trade: an Economic History of the Mediterranean* (London, 2002), 177–205.

A Monetary History of the Ottoman Empire (Cambridge, 2000).

Panzac, Daniel, 'Le contrat d'affrètement maritime en Méditerranée: droit maritime et pratique commerciale entre Islam et Chrétienté (XVIIe–XVIIIe siècles)', *Journal of the Economic and Social History of the Orient* 45:3 (2002), 342–62.

'L'economie-monde Ottomane en question: les clauses monétaires dans les contrats d'affretèment maritime au XVIIIe siècle', *Journal of the Economic and Social History of the Orient* 39:3 (1996), 368–78.

Papas, Alexandre, Thomas Welsford and Thierry Zarcone (eds.), *Central Asian Pilgrims: Hajj Routes and Pious Visits between Central Asia and the Hijaz* (Berlin, 2011).

Parker, Geoffrey, *Global Crisis: War, Climate Change and Catastrophe in the Seventeenth Century* (New Haven, CT, 2013).

Parks, David and Ruth Barnes (eds.), *Ships and the Development of Maritime Technology in the Indian Ocean* (London, 2002).

Pearson, Michael N., 'Banyas and Brahmins: their role in the Portuguese Indian economy', in Michael N. Pearson, *Coastal Western India: Studies from the Portuguese Records* (New Delhi, 1981), 93–115.

Merchants and Rulers in Gujarat: the Response to the Portuguese in the Sixteenth Century (Berkeley, CA, 1976).

'Merchants and states', in James D. Tracy (ed.), *The Political Economy of Merchant Empires: State Power and World Trade, 1350–1750* (Cambridge, 1991), 41–116.

Pilgrimage to Mecca: the Indian Experience, 1500–1800 (Princeton, NJ, 1996).

Peirce, Leslie P., *Morality Tales: Law and Gender in the Ottoman Court of Aintab* (Berkeley, Los Angeles and London, 2003).

Perlin, Frank, *Invisible City: Monetary, Administrative and Popular Infrastructures in Asia and Europe, 1500–1900* (Aldershot, 1993).

'Of white whale and countrymen in the eighteenth-century Maratha Deccan: extended class relations, rights and the problem of rural autonomy under the old regime', *Journal of Peasant Studies* 5:2 (1978), 172–237.

'World economic integration before industrialisation and the Euro-Asian monetary continuum', in Eddy van Cauwenberghe (ed.), *Money, Coins, and Commerce: Essays in the Monetary History of Asia and Europe* (Leuven, 1991), 239–374.

Perry, John R., 'Forced migration in Iran in the seventeenth and eighteenth centuries', *Iranian Studies* 8:4 (1975), 199–215.

Karim Khan Zand: a History of Iran, 1747–1779 (Chicago, 1979).

Phukan, Shantanu, '"Through throats where many rivers meet": the ecology of Hindi in the world of Persian', *Indian Economic and Social History Review* 38:1 (2001), 33–58.

Pinto, Celsa, *Trade and Finance in Portuguese India: a Study of the Portuguese Country Trade, 1770–1840* (New Delhi, 1994).

Polastron, Lucien, *Le papier: 2000 ans d'histoire et de savoir-faire* (Paris, 1999).

Polier, Antoine-Louis-Henri, *A European Experience of the Mughal Orient: the I'jaz-i arsalani (Persian letters 1773–1779) of Antoine-Louis-Henri Polier*, trans. and intro. Muzaffar Alam and Seema Alavi (New Delhi, 2001).

Pollock, Sheldon I., 'Cosmopolitan and vernacular in history', *Public Culture* 12:3 (2000), 591–625.

'The cosmopolitan vernacular', *Journal of Asian Studies* 57:1 (1998), 6–37.

'Literary culture and manuscript culture in precolonial India', in Simon Eliot, Andrew Nash and Ian Willison (eds.), *Literary Cultures and the Material Book* (London, 2006), 77–94.

Pollock, Sheldon I., (ed.), *Forms of Knowledge in Early Modern Asia: Explorations in the Intellectual History of India and Tibet, 1500–1800* (Durham, NC, 2011).

(ed.), *Literary Cultures in History: Reconstructions from South Asia* (Berkeley, CA, 2003).

Pomeranz, Kenneth, *Great Divergence: Europe, China and the Making of the Modern World Economy* (Princeton, NJ, 2000).

Pomeranz, Kenneth and Steven Topik, *The World that Trade Created: Society, Culture, and the World Economy, 1400 to Present* (3rd edn, Armonk, NY, 2012).

Popovic, Alexandre, *Un ordre de derviches en terre d'Europe* (Lausanne, 1993).
Porter, Yves, *Peinture et arts du livre: essai sur la littérature technique indo-persane* (Paris, 1992).
Prasad Tripathi, Ram, 'The Turko-Mongol theory of kingship', in Muzaffar Alam and Sanjay Subrahmanyam (eds.), *Mughal State 1526–1750* (New Delhi, 1998), 115–25.
al-Qalqashandī, Aḥmad b. ʿAlī (1355–1418), *Ṣubḥ al-aʿshā fī ṣṣināʿat al-inshāʾ* (ms., 7 vols., completed 1412; ed. Muḥammad ʿAbd al-Rasūl Ibrāhīm, 14 vols., Cairo, 1331–8/1913–20).
al-Qattan, Najwa, 'Dhimmis in the Muslim court: legal autonomy and religious discrimination', *International Journal of Middle East Studies* 31:3 (1999), 429–44.
'Litigants and neighbours: the communal topography of Ottoman Damascus', *Comparative Studies in Society and History* 44:3 (2002), 511–33.
Quataert, Donald, *The Ottoman Empire, 1700–1922* (2nd edn, Cambridge, 2005).
Quinn, Sholeh A., *Historical Writing during the Reign of Shah 'Abbas: Ideology, Imitation and Legitimacy in Safavid Chronicles* (Salt Lake City, UT, 2000).
Qureshi, Ishtiaq H., *The Administration of the Mughal Empire* (New Delhi, 1990).
Rafeq, Abdul-Karim, 'Making a living or making a fortune in Ottoman Syria', in Nelly Hanna (ed.), *Money, Land and Trade: an Economic History of the Mediterranean* (London, 2002), 101–23.
The Province of Damascus 1723–1783 (Beirut, 1966).
Rahman, Fazlur, *Revival and Reform in Islam: a Study of Islamic Fundamentalism* (Oxford, 2000).
Rahman, Tariq, *From Hindi to Urdu: a Social and Political History* (Karachi, 2011).
Rai, Alok, *Hindi Nationalism* (London, 2001).
Raymond, André, *Artisans et commerçants au Caire au XVIIIe siècle*, 2 vols. (2nd edn, Damascus, 1999).
Reid, Megan H., *Law and Piety in Medieval Islam* (Cambridge, 2013)
Richards, John F., 'The formulation of imperial authority under Akbar and Jahangir', in John F. Richards (ed.), *Kingship and Authority in South Asia* (Delhi, 1998 [1978]), 285–326.
'Warriors and the state in early modern India', *Journal of the Economic and Social History of the Orient* 47:3 (2004), 390–400.
Richards, John F. (ed.), *The Imperial Monetary System of Mughal India* (New Delhi, 1987).
(ed.), *Kingship and Authority in South Asia* (Delhi, 1998 [1978]).
Richards, John F. and Velchuru Narayana Rao, 'Banditry in Mughal India: historical and folk perceptions', *Indian Economic and Social History Review* 17:1 (1980), 95–120.
Rieu, Charles, *Catalogue of the Persian Manuscripts in the British Museum*, 3 vols. and suppl. vol. (London, 1879–95).
Rispler-Chaim, Vardit, 'Insurance and semi-insurance transactions in Islamic history until the 19th century', *Journal of the Economic and Social History of the Orient* 34:3 (1991), 142–58.
Risso, Patricia, 'Cross-cultural perceptions of piracy: maritime violence in the western Indian Ocean and Persian Gulf region during a long eighteenth century', *Journal of World History* 12:2 (2001), 293–319.

Rizvi, Saiyid Athar Abbas, *A Socio-Intellectual History of the Isna 'Ashari Shi'is in India*, 2 vols. (Canberra, 1986).
Robinson, Francis, 'Ottomans–Safavids–Mughals: shared knowledge and connective systems', *Journal of Islamic Studies* 8:2 (1997), 151–84.
'Technology and religious change: Islam and the impact of print', *Modern Asian Studies* 27:1 (1993), 229–51.
Robinson, Francis, (ed.), *Cambridge Illustrated History of the Islamic World* (Cambridge, 1996).
Rosenthal, Franz, 'Child psychology in Islam', *Islamic Culture* 26 (1952), 1–22.
Gambling in Islam (Leiden, 1970).
'The stranger in medieval Islam', *Arabica* 44 (1997), 35–75.
'Sweeter than Hope': Complaint and Hope in Medieval Islam (Leiden, 1983).
Rossabi, Morris, 'The "decline" of the Central Asian caravan trade', in James D. Tracy (ed.), *The Rise of Merchant Empires: Long-Distance Trade in the Early Modern World, 1350–1750* (Cambridge, 1990), 351–70.
Roy, Tirthankar, *An Economic History of Early Modern India* (London and New York, 2013).
'Where is Bengal? Situating an Indian region in the early modern world economy', *Past and Present* 213 (2011), 115–46.
Safwat, Nabil F., *The Art of the Pen: Calligraphy of the 14th to 20th Centuries*, with a contribution by Mohamed Zakariya (Oxford, 1996).
Sahai, Nandita Prasad, *The Politics of Patronage and Protest: the State, Society, and Artisans in Early Modern Rajasthan* (New York, 2006).
Sampson, Geoffrey, *Writing Systems* (Stanford, CA, 1985).
Sarkar, Jadunath, *The Fall of the Mughal Empire*, 4 vols. (Calcutta, 1932–50).
Sartori, Andrew, 'The resonance of "culture": framing a problem in global concept-history', *Comparative Studies in Society and History* 47:4 (2005), 676–99.
Sartori, Paolo, 'The evolution of third-party mediation in Sharīʿa courts in 19th- and early 20th-century Central Asia', *Journal of the Economic and Social History of the Orient* 54:3 (2011), 311–52.
Sartori, Paolo and Ido Shahar, 'Legal pluralism in Muslim-majority colonies: mapping the terrain', *Journal of the Economic and Social History of the Orient* 55:4–5 (2012), 637–63.
Savory, Roger M., *Iran under the Safavids* (Cambridge, 1980).
Schacht, Joseph, *Introduction to Islamic Law* (Oxford, 1964).
Schilcher, Linda, *Families in Politics: Damascene Factions and Estates of the Eighteenth and Nineteenth Centuries* (Stuttgart, 1985).
Schimmel, Annemarie, *Mystical Dimensions of Islam* (Chapel Hill, NC, 1975).
Schmidtke, Sabine, 'Homoeroticism and homosexuality in Islam: a review article', *Bulletin of the School of Oriental and African Studies* 62:2 (1999), 260–6.
Sen, Amartya K., 'Rational fools: a critique of the behavioural foundations of economic theory', *Philosophy and Public Affairs* 6:4 (1977), 317–44.
Serjeant, Robert B., *Customary and Shariʿah Law in Arabian Society* (Aldershot, 1991).
Farmers and Fishermen in Arabia: Studies on Customary Law and Practice (Aldershot, 1995).

'Maritime customary law off the Arabian coasts', in Michel Mollat (ed.), *Sociétés et compagnies de commerce en Orient et dans l'Océan indien: actes du huitième colloque international d'histoire maritime (Beyrouth, 5–10 septembre 1966)* (Paris, 1970), 195–207.

Studies in Arabian History and Civilisation (London, 1981).

Society and Trade in South Arabia (Aldershot, 1996).

Sewell, William H., *Logics of History: Social Theory and Social Transformation* (Chicago, 2005).

Shabana, Ayman, *Custom in Islamic Law and Legal Theory: the Development of the Concepts of* 'urf *and* 'ādah *in the Islamic Legal Tradition* (New York, 2010).

Shackle, Christopher and Rupert Snell (eds.), *Hindi and Urdu since 1800: a Common Reader* (London, 1990).

Shaham, Ron, *The Expert Witness in Islamic Courts: Medicine and Crafts in the Service of the Law* (Chicago, 2010).

Shaham, Ron, (ed.), *Law, Custom, and Statute in the Muslim World: Studies in Honor of Aharon Layish* (Leiden, 2006).

Shahar, Ido, 'Legal pluralism and the study of Shari'a courts', *Islamic Law and Society* 15 (2008), 112–41.

Shahshahānī, 'Abd al-Vahhāb b. Muḥammad 'Amīn Ḥusaynī, *Baḥr al-javāhir fī 'ilm al-dafātir va sarrishtah-yi siyāq-i ḥisāb* (Tehran, 1271/1854; Isfahan, *c*. 1880).

al-Shaykh Khaz'al, Ḥusayn Khalaf, *Tārīkh al-Jazīra al-'Arabīya fī 'aṣṣr al-Shaykh Muḥammad 'Abd al-Wahhāb* (Beirut: Maṭba'a dār al-kutub, 1972).

Sheikh, Samira, *Forging a Region: Sultans, Traders, and Pilgrims in Gujarat, 1200–1500* (Delhi, 2010).

Shulman, David and Guy G. Stroumsa (eds.), *Dream Cultures: Explorations in the Comparative History of Dreaming* (Oxford, 1999).

Siddiqi, Asiya, 'The business world of Jamshetjee Jejeebhoy', *Indian Economic and Social History Review* 19:3–4 (1982), 301–24.

Siddiqi, Muhammad Zameeruddin, 'The intelligence services under the Mughals', in *Medieval India: a Miscellany*, vol. II (London, 1972), 53–60.

Silverstein, Adam J., *Postal Systems in the Pre-Modern Islamic World* (Cambridge, 2007).

Singh, Dilbagh, 'Regulating the domestic: notes on the pre-colonial state and the family', *Studies in History* 19:1 (2003), 69–86.

'The role of mahajans in the rural economy in eastern Rajasthan during the 18th century', *Social Scientist* 2:10 (1974), 20–31.

The State, Landlords and Peasants: Eastern Rajasthan in the 18th Century (Delhi, 1990).

Singh, Kumar Suresh, P. P. Shirodkar and H. K. Mandal (eds.), *People of India*, vol. XXI: *Goa* (Bombay, 1993).

Sirāj, Muḥammad Aḥmad, *al-Awrāq al-tijarāya fī al-sharā'a al-Islāmīya* (Cairo, 1988).

Siroux, Maxime, 'Les caravanserais routiers safavids', *Iranian Studies* 7:1–2 (1974), 348–75.

Sood, Gagan D. S., 'Circulation and exchange in Islamicate Eurasia: a regional approach to the early modern world', *Past and Present* 212 (2011), 113–62

'"Correspondence is equal to half a meeting": the composition and comprehension of letters in eighteenth-century Islamic Eurasia', *Journal of the Economic and Social History of the Orient* 50:2–3 (2007), 172–214

'The informational fabric of eighteenth-century India and the Middle East: couriers, intermediaries and postal communication', *Modern Asian Studies* 43:5 (2009), 1085–16

'Sovereign justice in precolonial maritime Asia: the case of the Mayor's Court of Bombay, 1726–1798', *Itinerario* 37:2 (2013), 46–72.

de Souza, Teotonio R., 'French slave-trading in Portuguese Goa (1773–1791)', in Teotonio R. de Souza (ed.), *Essays in Goan History* (New Delhi, 1989), 119–31.

'Goa–Mahe trade links (late 18th–early 19th centuries): a new source-material', in K. S. Mathew (ed.), *Studies in Maritime History* (Pondicherry, 1990).

'Mhamai House Records: indigenous sources for "Indo"-Portuguese historiography', *Indian History Congress* 41 (1980), 435–45.

'Mhamai House Records: indigenous sources for Indo-Portuguese historiography', *Indian Archives* 31:1 (1982), 25–45.

'Mhamai House Records: indigenous sources for Indo-Portuguese historiography', in Luis de Albuquerque and Inacio Guerreiro (eds.), *II seminário internacional de história indo-portuguesa: actas* (Lisbon, 1985), 933–41.

Steensgaard, Niels, *The Asian Trade Revolution of the Seventeenth Century: the East India Companies and the Decline of the Caravan Trade* (Chicago, 1974).

'The route through Quandahar: the significance of the overland trade route from India to the West in the seventeenth century', in Sushil Chaudhuri and Michel Morineau (eds.), *Merchants, Companies and Trade: Europe and Asia in the Early Modern Era* (Cambridge, 1999), 55–73.

'The seventeenth-century crisis and the unity of Eurasian history', *Modern Asian Studies* 24:4 (1990), 683–97

Stirling, Paul, *Turkish Village* (London, 1965).

Subrahmanyam, Sanjay, 'Connected histories: notes towards a reconfiguration of early modern Eurasia', *Modern Asian Studies* 31:3 (1997), 735–62.

'Iranians abroad: intra-Asian elite migration and early modern state formation', *Journal of Asian Studies* 51:2 (1992), 340–64.

'Persians, pilgrims and Portuguese: the travails of Masulipatnam shipping in the western Indian Ocean, 1590–1665', *Modern Asian Studies* 22:3 (1988), 503–30.

The Political Economy of Commerce: Southern India, 1500–1650 (Cambridge, 1990).

Subrahmanyam, Sanjay (ed.), *Merchant Networks in the Early Modern World* (Aldershot, 1996).

Subramanian, Lakshmi, 'Banias and the British: the role of indigenous credit in the process of imperial expansion in western India in the second half of the eighteenth century', *Modern Asian Studies* 21:3 (1987), 473–510.

'Capital and crowd in a declining Asian port city: the Anglo-Bania order and the Surat riots of 1795', *Modern Asian Studies* 19:2 (1985), 205–37.

Indigenous Capital and Imperial Expansion: Bombay, Surat and the West Coast (Delhi, 1996).

'A trial in transition: courts, merchants and identities in western India, circa 1800', *Indian Economic and Social History Review* 41:3 (2004), 269–92.

al-Suwaydī, ʿAbd al-Raḥmān ibn ʿAbd Allāh, *Tārikh ḥawādith Baghdād wa-al-Baṣṣra min 1186 ilā 1192 h./1772–1778 m.* (Baghdad: Wizārat al-thaqāfa wa-al-fanūn, 1978).

Tadmor, Naomi, 'The concept of the household-family in eighteenth-century England', *Past and Present* 151 (1996), 111–40.

Family and Friends in Eighteenth-Century England: Household, Kinship and Patronage (Cambridge, 2001).

Talbot, Cynthia (ed.), *Knowing India: Colonial and Modern Constructions of the Past* (New Delhi, 2011).

Tamdoğan, Işık, '*Sulh* and the 18th-century Ottoman courts of Uskudar and Adana', *Islamic Law and Society* 15 (2008), 55–83.

Taqizadeh, S. H., 'Various eras and calendars used in the countries of Islam', *Bulletin of the School of Oriental and African Studies* 9:4 (1939), 903–22 and 10:1 (1939), 107–32.

Teygeler, R. (ed.), *Preservation of Archives in Tropical Climates: an Annotated Bibliography* (Paris, 2001).

Thompson, Edward P., *Customs in Common* (New York, 1991).

Tilly, Charles, *Trust and Rule* (Cambridge, 2005).

'War making and state making as organized crime', in Peter Evans, Dietrich Rueschemeyer and Theda Skocpol (eds.), *Bringing the State Back In* (Cambridge, 1985), 169–91.

Torri, Michelguglielmo, 'In the deep blue sea: Surat and its merchant class during the Dyarchic Era (1759–1800)', *Indian Economic and Social History Review* 19:3–4 (1982), 267–300.

Touati, Houari, *L'armoire à sagesse: bibliothèques et collections en Islam* (Paris, 2003).

Islam et voyage au Moyen Age: histoire et anthropologie d'une pratique lettrée (Paris, 2000).

Toynbee, Arnold J., *A Study of History*, 12 vols. (London, 1934–61).

Tracy, James D. (ed.), *The Political Economy of Merchant Empires: State Power and World Trade, 1350–1750* (Cambridge, 1991).

(ed.), *The Rise of Merchant Empires: Long-Distance Trade in the Early Modern World, 1350–1750* (Cambridge, 1990).

Trautman, Thomas R., *Dravidian Kinship* (Cambridge, 1981).

Tripathi, Dwijendra, *Oxford History of Indian Business* (New Delhi, 2004).

Tripathi, Dwijendra and M. J. Mehta, 'The Nagarseth of Ahmedabad: the history of an urban institution in a Gujarat city', in Satish Chandra (ed.), *Essays in Medieval Indian Economic History* (New Delhi, 1990), 262–75.

Trivellato, Francesca, *The Familiarity of Strangers: the Sephardic Diaspora, Livorno, and Cross-Cultural Trade in the Early Modern Period* (New Haven, CT, 2009).

Tuchscherer, Michel, 'Quelques réflexions sur les monnaies et la circulation monétaire en Égypte et en mer Rouge au XVIe et au début du XVIIe siècle', *Annales islamologiques* 33 (1999), 263–81.

Tucker, Ernest S., *Nadir Shah's Quest for Legitimacy in Post-Safavid Iran* (Gainesville, FL, 2006).

Tucker, Judith E., 'Ties that bound: women and family in eighteenth- and nineteenth-century Nablus', in Nikki R. Keddie and Beth Baron (eds.), *Women in Middle Eastern History: Shifting Boundaries in Sex and Gender* (New Haven, CT, 1991), 233–53.

Tyan, Émile, *Histoire de l'organisation judiciaire en pays d'Islam*, 2 vols. (2nd edn, Leiden, 1960).

Udovitch, Abraham L., 'The "law merchant" of the medieval Islamic world', in G. E. von Grunebaum (ed.), *Logic in Classical Islamic Culture* (Wiesbaden, 1970), 113–30.

Partnership and Profit in Medieval Islam (Princeton, NJ, 1970).

Um, Nancy Ajung, 'Spatial negotiations in a commercial city: the Red Sea port of Mocha, Yemen, during the first half of the eighteenth century', *Journal of the Society of Architectural Historians* 62:2 (2003), 178–93.

Uzunçarşılı, İsmail Hakkı, *Mekke-i mükerreme emirleri* (Ankara: Türk Tarih Kurumu Basımevi, 1972).

Vatuk, Sylvia, 'Forms of address in the north Indian family', in Ákos Östör, Lina Fruzzetti and Steve Barnett (eds.), *Concepts of Person: Kinship, Caste, and Marriage in India* (Cambridge, MA, 1982), 56–98.

'Muslim kinship in the Dravidian heartland', in Cynthia Talbot (ed.), *Knowing India: Colonial and Modern Constructions of the Past* (New Delhi, 2011), 108–34.

Veinstein, Gilles, 'Commercial relations between India and the Ottoman empire (late fifteenth to the late eighteenth centuries): a few notes and hypotheses', in Sushil Chaudhuri and Michel Morineau (eds.), *Merchants, Companies and Trade: Europe and Asia in the Early Modern Era* (Cambridge, 1999), 95–115.

'Marchands ottomans en Pologne-Lituanie et en Moscovie sous le règne de Soliman de Magnifique', *Cahiers du monde russe* 35:4 (1994), 713–38.

'L'oralité dans les documents d'archives ottomans: paroles rapportés ou imaginées?', *Revue du monde musulman et de la Méditerranée* 75–76 [special issue on *Oral et écrit dans le monde turco-ottoman*] (1995), 133–42.

Vink, Marcus P. M., 'Indian Ocean studies and the "new thalassology"', *Journal of Global History* 2:1 (2007), 41–62.

Vivier-Muresan, Anne-Sophie, 'Communitarian neighbourhoods and religious minorities in Iran: a comparative analysis', *Iranian Studies* 40:5 (2007), 593–603.

Voll, John O., 'Islam as a special world-system', *Journal of World History* 5:2 (1994), 213–26.

Vries, Peer H. H., 'Governing growth: a comparative analysis of the role of the state in the rise of the West', *Journal of World History* 13:1 (2002), 67–138.

Wadia, Ruttonjee Ardeshir, *Bombay Dockyard and the Wadia Master Builders* (Bombay, 1955).

Wagle, N. K., 'The history and social organization of the Gauda Sāraswata Brāhmanas of the west coast of India', *Journal of Indian History* 48 (1970), 7–25, 295–333.

Wakin, Jeanette, *The Function of Documents in Islamic Law: the Chapters on Sales from Ṭahāwī's Kitāb al-shurūṭ al kabīr* (Albany, NY, 1972).

Wallerstein, Immanuel M., *The Modern World-System*, 4 vols. (New York, 1974–2011).

Walz, Terence and Kenneth M. Cuno (eds.), *Race and Slavery in the Middle East: Histories of Trans-Saharan Africans in Nineteenth-Century Egypt, Sudan, and the Ottoman Mediterranean* (Cairo and New York, 2010).

Wansbrough, John E., *Lingua Franca in the Mediterranean* (Richmond, Surrey, 1996).

Wheaton, Robert, 'Observations on the development of kinship history, 1942–1985', *Journal of Family History* 12:1–3 (1987), 285–301.

White, David L., 'Parsis in the commercial world of western India, 1700–1750', *Indian Economic and Social History Review* 24:2 (1987), 183–203.

White, Harrison C., *Identity and Control: a Structural Theory of Social Action* (2nd edn, Princeton, NJ, 2008).

Wickham, Chris, 'Gossip and resistance among the medieval peasantry', *Past and Present* 160 (1998), 3–24.

Wills, John E., 'Maritime Asia, 1500–1800: the interactive emergence of European domination', *American Historical Review* 98:1 (1993), 83–105.

Winichakul, Thongchai, *Siam Mapped: a History of the Geo-Body of a Nation* (Honolulu, HI, 1994).

Winius, George D. and Marcus P. M. Vink, *The Merchant-Warrior Pacified: the VOC (the Dutch East India Company) and its Changing Political Economy in India* (New Delhi, 1991).

Wink, André, 'From the Mediterranean to the Indian Ocean: medieval history in geographic perspective', *Comparative Studies in Society and History* 44:3 (2002), 416–45.

Land and Sovereignty in India: Agrarian Society and Politics under the Eighteenth Century Maratha Swarajya (London, 1986).

Winter, Michael, *Egyptian Society under Ottoman Rule, 1517–1798* (London, 1992).

Wong, Roy Bin, 'Entre monde et nation: les régions braudéliennes en Asie', *Annales* 56:1 (2001), 5–41.

Yamey, Basil S., 'Notes on double entry bookkeeping and economic progress', *Economic History Review* 4 (1975), 717–23.

'Scientific bookkeeping and the rise of capitalism', *Economic History Review* 1: 2–3 (1949), 99–113.

Young, M. J. L., J. D. Latham and R. B. Serjeant (eds.), *Religion, Learning and Science in the 'Abbasid Period* (Cambridge, 1990).

Yun-Casalilla, Bartolomé and Patrick K. O'Brien (eds.), *The Rise of Fiscal States: a Global History, 1500–1914* (Cambridge, 2012).

Zarcone, Thierry, Ekrem Isin and Arthur Buehler (eds.), 'The Qadiriyya Order', *Journal of History of Sufism*, special issue 1–2 (2000).

Zilli, Ishtiyaq Ahmad, 'Development of *Inshā* literature till the end of Akbar's reign', in Muzaffar Alam, Françoise Delvoye and Marc Gaborieu (eds.), *The Making of Indo-Persian Culture: Indian and French Studies* (New Delhi, 2000), 309–50.

Unpublished studies

Herzig, Edmund M., 'Armenian merchants of New Julfa, Isfahan: a study in premodern Asian trade' (D.Phil. thesis, Oxford University, 1992).
Ṣāliḥ, Muḥammad, *Siyāq-namah* (*Dastūr al-siyāq*).
White, David L., 'Parsis as entrepreneurs in eighteenth-century western India: the Rustum Manock family and the Parsi community of Surat and Bombay' (Ph.D. thesis, University of Virginia, 1979).

Index